TEACHING
THE PRESERVATION

Editorial direction
FRANZ GRAF

Scientific and editorial coordination
FRANZ GRAF, THIERRY BUACHE, YVAN DELEMONTEY, THIERRY MANASSEH,
GIULIA MARINO

Editing team
YVAN DELEMONTEY WITH TAMARA PELÈGE

Graphic design
JENNIFER CESA, L-ARTICHAUT

Page layout
ANNE KUMMLI, RECTO VERSO

Translation into English of text by Franz Graf, "The Teaching of the TSAM
Laboratory"
RICHARD SADLEIR

Translation into English of all other texts except that of Frank Escher & Ravi
GuneWardena (originally in English)
JANICE GAUGENOT, JO NICOUD-GARDEN

Transcription of the conversation between Anne Lacaton and Frédéric Druot
THIERRY MANASSEH

Transcription of the interview with Martina Vos
CORALIE BERCHTOLD

Cover photographs
Master's project model by Thierry Manasseh for the conservation, conversion,
and extension of the Claude & Duval factory in Saint Dié (architect
Le Corbusier), 2014
Work site for the Sports Center on Rue du Stand, Geneva (architect Paul
Waltenspühl)
Axonometric drawing (view from below) of the auditorium at the Centre
interrégional de perfectionnement (CIP) in Tramelan (architects Heidi & Peter
Wenger), 2020

The authors and publisher would like to thank the École polytechnique fédérale de Lausanne for their financial support in the publication of this book.
This Notebook is published with the financial support of the Institut d'architecture de l'ENAC-EPFL.

EPFL PRESS is an imprint owned by the Presses polytechniques
et universitaires romandes, a Swiss academic publishing company
whose main purpose is to publish the teaching and research works
of the École polytechnique fédérale de Lausanne (EPFL).
PPUR, EPFL-Rolex Learning Center, CM Station 10, CH-1015 Lausanne,
info@epflpress.org

www.epflpress.org

ISBN 978-2-88915-505-7
© 2023, First edition in french (2022), EPFL Press
Printed in Czech Republic
All rights reserved.
Reproduction, in whole or part, in any form or by any means,
is prohibited except with the written permission of the publisher.

TEACHING THE PRESERVATION

FRANZ GRAF

6 **PREFACE**
FRANZ GRAF

8 **TEACHING AT THE LABORATORY OF TECHNIQUES AND PRESERVATION OF MODERN ARCHITECTURE**
FRANZ GRAF

THE THEORETICAL COURSES

16 **DESIGNING IN THE BUILT ENVIRONMENT: THE THEORETICAL TOOLS OF THE PROJECT**
GIULIA MARINO

THE STUDIO, OR TEACHING THE PRESERVATION PROJECT

52 **THE STUDIO, OR TEACHING THE PRESERVATION PROJECT**
FRANZ GRAF
YVAN DELEMONTEY

178 **TO UNDERSTAND IS TO IMAGINE**
GILLES RAGOT

180 **ENGINEERING**
JEAN-PIERRE CÊTRE

182 **IMPLIED VALUES**
RENATO SALVI

PROJECT DESIGN IN THE PRESERVATION ORIENTATION

184 **DIVERSITY AND CONVERGENCES: PROJECT TEACHING IN THE "PRESERVATION" ORIENTATION**
THIERRY MANASSEH

192 **MONUMENTS AND TRACES: PROJECTING MEMORY**
ERICH HUBMANN
ANDREAS VASS

202 **THOUGHTS ON PERSISTENCE AND INVENTION**
DANIEL BOSSHARD
MERITXELL VAQUER

214 TEACHING FRAGMENTS
DENIS ELIET
LAURENT LEHMANN

226 PRESERVATION OF MODERN SCHOOLS: TWO EXAMPLES
JOÃO PEDRO FALCÃO DE CAMPOS
JOÃO SANTA RITA

238 CONSTRUCTION AND CONTINUITY: BUILDING THE TWENTIETH CENTURY IN LOS ANGELES
FRANK ESCHER
RAVI GUNEWARDENA

248 WHAT AND WHO IS ALREADY THERE ?
OPEN CONVERSATION WITH ANNE LACATON AND FRÉDÉRIC DRUOT

266 HOUSING AND THE SACRED
JOSÉ IGNACIO LINAZASORO

276 WORKING ON HERITAGE SITES IN ALPINE SPACES
RAMUN CAPAUL
GORDIAN BLUMENTHAL

286 CULTIVATING THE LANDSCAPE
INTERVIEW WITH MARTINA VOSER

THE MASTER'S PRESERVATION PROJECT

298 MASTER'S PRESERVATION PROJECT
FRANZ GRAF
THIERRY BUACHE

400 BY WAY OF AN EPILOGUE. HOW PRESERVATION CONTRIBUTES TO A CULTURE OF SOCIOECOLOGICAL TRANSITION: ELEVEN SHORT CONSIDERATIONS FOR TODAY
FRANZ GRAF
GIULIA MARINO

406 Speech given by Joseph Abram at the presentation of the insignia of arts and letters to Franz Graf, at the 5th région-architecture grand-est conference, on november 29, 2019, at the Reims congress center

408 List of guest lecturers
at the TSAM laboratory

410 Image credits

FRANZ GRAF

PREFACE

Following on from the volumes *La sauvegarde des grandes oeuvres de l'ingénierie du XXe siècle* and *Les multiples vies de l'appartement-atelier Le Corbusier*, this third TSAM volume assembles and presents the content from the teaching courses we created and have been developing at the EPFL for some fifteen years. The aim is to give increased visibility to preservation as a discipline that without a doubt constitutes one of the main branches in the emerging field of the socioecological transition, which is based on the idea of heritage (quality architecture in a broad sense) as a cultural and economic asset. The aim is also to show how the educational potential of preservation can be harnessed, bringing together as it does many social and scientific disciplines, the history of architecture and architects, materiality and its constructed expression, the theory of architecture and design, and the examination—both abstract and concrete—of what surrounds us in every sense, from the littlest spoon to the entire territory. In short, what a small minority of intelligent and responsible architects has always concerned itself with, that is, a silent and sometimes fragile architecture. These are the qualities that should enable preservation to reform and reconstruct a new design process for architecture, which will in turn lead to a new kind of practice. Teaching, research, and practice are mutually enriched within a polytechnic school where this synergy is in its rightful place and where all are convinced that it would be absurd to oppose—and separate—the materiality of architecture and the technical-scientific question, the immateriality of project design and the issue of culture.

I would like to begin by thanking all those who have contributed to these lessons in so many ways and with such extraordinary commitment: Giulia Marino for the theoretical classes that have continued to develop over time and Yvan Delemontey, Giulia Marino, Christian Bischoff, Michael Wyss, Stephan Ruthishauser, Théo Bellmann, and Thierry Buache for the theory and project studios. My heartfelt thanks go to the entire body of teaching staff for their management of master's projects, as well as to the architects and researchers from multiple backgrounds, too numerous to list here, who have made vital and not inconsequential contributions to our teaching method, as well as Jean-Pierre Côtre, Gilles Ragot, and Renato Salvi, who over time have become indispensable. I would also like to thank the students who attend the classes and studios with great assiduousness, who continue to believe in the relevance of the subject matter, and who allow us to develop and perfect it, as well as all the owners of the buildings and sites visited and analyzed, and the foundations that manage the work of their creators—namely the Fondation Le Corbusier, Max Bill Foundation, and the Heidi & Peter Wenger Foundation—for their goodwill and availability. We hope that the work produced by our students has furthered the process of reflection on the future of their legacy. And finally, I am most grateful to the Presses Polytechniques et Universitaires Romandes for their unflagging support for the *TSAM Notebooks*.

FRANZ GRAF

TEACHING AT THE LABORATORY OF TECHNIQUES AND PRESERVATION OF MODERN ARCHITECTURE (TSAM) AT THE ÉCOLE POLYTECHNIQUE FÉDÉRALE DE LAUSANNE

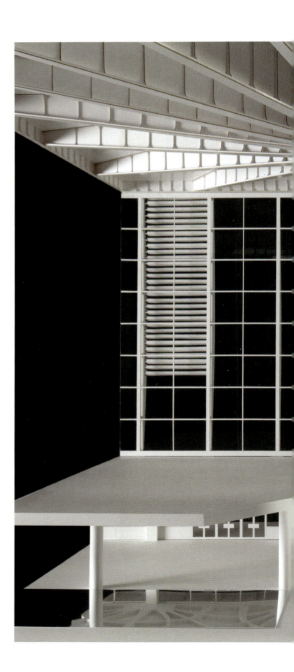

Projects dealing with existing architectural works are a major challenge for the development of the city in the twenty-first century and for the quality of the environment of its users. Preservation projects and projects intervening in the existing environment are part of an established cultural discipline that expands our contemporary architectural practices.[1] Constructing in the built environment is by no means a new occurrence. But what makes it a contemporary attitude is the type of theoretical and practical questions it raises about the architectural object at every scale, as well as its focus on the materiality of the building, which drives the project. The Laboratory of Techniques and Preservation of Modern Architecture (TSAM),[2] founded in 2007, produces and develops knowledge of techniques and the preservation of modern and contemporary architecture. This knowledge is multidisciplinary and requires the critical appraisal of architectural history and material techniques and their implementation, as well as economic and environmental data. It also involves the exercise of specific project strategies (maintenance, preservation, restoration, rehabilitation, restructuring, reuse, and extension) combining theoretical knowledge and technical know-how. TSAM's main objectives are teaching, research, and the development of services related to its skills. This book will be mainly about teaching.

The "preservation" orientation, under my direction at the EPFL since 2012, gives structure to the acquiring of this scientific expertise, through both studio teaching and lecture courses at the bachelor's and master's level, as well as through master's projects and PhD work.

Seventy percent of the activities of architecture firms in Switzerland take place in the existing built environment. The course **"Designing in the Built Environment: Tools and Methods,"** led by Giulia Marino, seeks to give students the necessary theoretical and practical tools to

1 Franz Graf, *Histoire matérielle du bâti et projet de sauvegarde – Devenir de l'architecture moderne et contemporaine* (Lausanne: PPUR, 2014).
2 https://www.epfl.ch/labs/tsam/.

3 https://www.epfl.ch/labs/tsam/page-28043-fr-html/%20le-patrimoine-monumental-du-xxe-siecle/.
4 https://www.epfl.ch/labs/tsam/page-28043-fr-html/patrimoine-et-energie-la-grande-echelle-1945-75/.

5 https://www.epfl.ch/labs/tsam/page-28043-fr-html/the-buildings-of-the-international-organisations-in-geneva-an-outstanding-heritage/.

6 Marino, Giulia, *"Some Like It Hot!* Le confort physiologique et ses dispositifs dans l'architecture du XXe siècle histoire et devenir d'un enjeu majeur" (PhD dissertation, EPFL, 2016). This work was awarded the EPFL thesis prize in 2016.

undertake a project on built heritage in the existing environment but also on works considered to be cultural monuments. This course is offered in the last semester of the bachelor's degree and should therefore be considered a core training unit in the teaching of architecture.

Indeed, designing in the existing built environment is a very broad discipline that calls for multiple and hybrid forms of knowledge, scientific rigor, and imaginative foresight. The cultures of history and technology intertwine and are layered in a creative process that relies on an investigation of the architectural object and continues throughout the entire design process. This intellectual journey is based on the meticulous gathering of knowledge of the built work, its observation and physical analysis, and by the intersecting and synthesizing of the most diverse skills, both theoretical and operational. The principal objective of the course is to understand this complex process. First of all, it is necessary to explain the cultural reasons and the fields of application of the preservation and restoration project, supplemented by some theoretical and legislative concepts, as well as by an introduction to current inventory tools and a prior definition of the heritage value of buildings. This historical-critical introduction continues with a study of the methodological issues of the preservation project, from the first phase of knowledge and analysis to the development of the most appropriate project strategy and its management and implementation.

The essential tools of the project in the existing built environment are approached systematically. An understanding of the constructional specifics of the built heritage and their evolution—structure, materials, implementation methods, etc.—is the unifying thread of the teaching approach. On the basis of this thorough material survey, the main themes of the project in the existing environment are subject to a targeted review. This review makes a broad diagnosis of the state of preservation (including on the level of structural disorders), the various intervention techniques (conservation, repair, consolidation, etc.) and the crucial question of upgrading buildings, as well as their adaptation in terms of use, safety, comfort, etc.

Due to the multidisciplinary nature of the preservation project, there are many synergies with other subject courses—building physics, survey and figurative techniques, structure and materials, etc. As such, specific contributions by lecturers from the EPFL with specific skills in physical-chemical phenomena and the behavior of buildings are organized.

The master's course on **"Theories and Techniques of the Preservation Project,"** led by Franz Graf and Giulia Marino, serves a twofold purpose. The first is to trace the development of the construction systems that marked the architecture of the twentieth century, by addressing key concepts such as new materials, transformations of the modern building site by the introduction of industrialized processes, or devices for the artificial control of comfort. A historical and material analysis of the built environment in the twentieth century, with its constructional particularities, requires us to develop specially devised preservation strategies, combined with a specific know-how drawing on established theoretical skills.

The second objective of the course is the adoption of project tools that take into account the challenges of modern heritage. By studying events that have proved particularly formative for the discipline, the course deals with the theoretical and practical foundations of the project in the existing built environment—from iconic cultural monuments to the most ordinary architecture—as well as with techniques for the restoration and conservation of buildings.

Concepts from the history of the theories of preservation that were developed in the nineteenth and twentieth centuries are addressed throughout the semester, not only to explore the foundations of the discipline, but also to encourage students to adopt a critical and coherent attitude to the project in the existing built environment.

The content of the course is wholly based on research conducted in the TSAM laboratory by Franz Graf and Giulia Marino, including research on the restoration of the monumental heritage of the twentieth century,[3] on the large-scale conflict between heritage and the question of energy efficiency from 1945–75,[4] or on the buildings of international organizations in Geneva.[5]

The master's course **"Comfort by Design in Twentieth-Century Architecture,"** led by Giulia Marino, seeks to restore the centrality of utilities networks, identifying both the cultural reasons and the material issues in the "design of comfort" within "architectural design." The course brings together the disciplines of construction, history, and preservation, and its content comes from the lecturer's notable thesis work.[6] The notion of physiological-hygrothermal comfort, as well as lighting and acoustic well-being, is to be noted among the major imperatives of the architectural production of the twentieth century, and it is still incredibly timely.

The course covers innovative materials and techniques, but also unprecedented industrial systems and processes: although the twentieth century's "constructional revolution" is widely recognized in the history of architecture, equipment designed to ensure comfort, which is fully a part of this revolution, is still often overlooked, if not simply ignored. And yet . . . Skillfully colored sheathes that participate in the expression of "brutalist" interiors . . . Hot water pipes incorporated into the thickness of the floor supporting open-plan layouts . . . Heaters and radiators that are transfigured into partitions or that disappear into the interstices of the envelopes . . . Concealed, incorporated, or later exposed, even literally displayed, these heating, ventilation, and air conditioning networks, which are paradoxically bulky yet often invisible, deserve new consideration as truly structuring elements, not—and quite wrongly—as mere fitted or accessory components.

The hypotheses of the pioneers—from James Marston Fitch to Reyner Banham—remain extremely relevant. Grasping the implications of "climate design" within "architectural design," through a transversal reading located at the crossroads of the perceptible and the material, opens up extremely significant interpretational approaches to modern and contemporary architecture. Structured around a few founding themes of this major step forward—from the industrialization of building to the notions of lightness and transparency—this panorama also makes it possible to identify the cultural reasons for "climate design" and artificial control of the inside environment, a practice that recurs throughout the twentieth century and very directly influences both architectural design and its material implementation, these two factors being inseparable.

The new paradigms of energy saving demonstrate the timeliness of the notion of material well-being in its new meaning of "total comfort." They are treated in relation to the crucial question of the adaptation of the existing building to current standards by targeted interventions to the technical installations.

Opening Photo Model of a fragment of the Palazzo del Lavoro in Turin, by the preservation project studio in 2012, 1:33 scale

With respect to the teaching of the three sections of the Faculty of the Natural, Architectural, and Constructed Environment (ENAC) of the EPFL, namely Architecture, Civil Engineering,

7 Franz Graf and Yvan Delemontey, eds., *Understanding and Conserving Industrialised and Prefabricated Architecture* (Lausanne: PPUR, 2012).
Franz Graf and Giulia Marino, eds., *Building Environment and Interior Comfort in 20th-Century Architecture:*

Understanding Issues and Developing Conservation Strategies (Lausanne: PPUR, 2016).
Franz Graf and Yvan Delemontey, eds., *La sauvegarde des grandes œuvres de l'ingénierie du XXe siècle*, Cahier du TSAM 1 (Lausanne: PPUR, 2016).
Franz Graf and Giulia Marino,

La buvette d'Evian. Maurice Novarina, Jean Prouvé, Serge Ketoff, 1955–2018 (Gollion: Infolio, 2018).
Franz Graf and Yvan Delemontey, eds., *Restaurer les objets techniques. Actualité de l'œuvre de Jean Prouvé, 1945–2019*, Cahier du TSAM 3, (Lausanne: PPUR, forthcoming).

8 See Docomomo-TSAM conferences 2016–2018, www.docomomo.ch.

and Environmental Sciences, the course **"Strategies and Techniques for the Reuse of Twentieth-Century Architecture,"** led by Franz Graf and Giulia Marino, deals with specific themes and know-how, entailing an interdisciplinary approach that touches on the different areas that characterize the faculty. The aim of this course is to develop these themes with reference to the specifics of each field, the environmental impact of a reconversion project, and the structural diagnosis of a building, including the definition of its heritage value. Each student develops a problem related to his or her academic skills and scientific interests, chosen from a list drawn up by the lecturers or proposed by the student. The research topics—with reference to the specifics of twentieth-century buildings—may concern, for example, the pathologies of a building material or its use and the measures for its repair/preservation (reinforced concrete, light alloys, plastics, etc.), the detection of toxic materials in a building (asbestos, PCB, radon, etc.) and the procedures for sanitizing and managing waste on the construction site, or architectural analysis—constructional and spatial—of an object with a view to defining the possibilities of reconversion, etc.

The laboratory organizes **international study days** that link its research activity and its application to teaching for students at the TSAM as well as for EPFL students. These have included "Industrialized and Prefabricated Architecture: Knowledge and Preservation" in June 2011, "Comfort Devices in Twentieth-Century Architecture: Knowledge and Preservation Strategies" in September 2012, "The Restoration of Major Engineering Works of the Twentieth Century" in May 2013, and "Restoring Technical Structures: The Work of Jean Prouvé" in September 2018. These have all been the subject of important publications in this field.[7]

With the same purpose and in collaboration with Docomomo Switzerland, the laboratory offers **lecture series**, such as "Project, History and Construction: New Perspectives on Recent Heritage,"[8] with outstanding guest architects, historians, theorists, and practitioners, such as Ana Tostoes, Françoise Lacaton and Frédéric Druot, Martin Boesch, François Botton, Laurent Stalder, Paul Chemetov, Frank Escher and Ravi GuneWardena, Gilles Ragot, Eduardo Prieto, Richard Klein, Jurg Conzett, Joseph Abram, Marusa Zorec, Martina Voser, France Vanlaethem, Giulia Marino, Uta Pottgeisser, and Patrick Thurston.

The studio on **"Theory and Criticism of the Project"** in the third year teaches the preservation of modern and contemporary architecture. It is led by Franz Graf, and the teaching team is made up of Yvan Delemontey and Thierry Buache. Giulia Marino, Stefan Rutishauser, Christian Bischoff, Michael Wyss, and Theo Bellmann have also taken part. This specific discipline calls for a series of rational and technical investigations that both produce knowledge about the object of study and define potential uses and methods of intervention. Inseparable from the project design, the fullest possible documentation of the work is established by using historical research and graphic and photographic surveys, from its constructional process and materiality to its sensory and sensuous aspects. Its heritage value is determined by situating the structure in its historical, architectural, and urban context, as part of the body of work of the actors who designed and built it, and as an economic and social resource. The analysis of its functional and distribution capabilities, and of its constitution and physical characteristics dictates its potential for use, from maintenance to restructuring.

The preservation project is thus defined as a twofold and inseparable project of conservation and innovation. It is both the conservation, maintenance, strengthening, improvement or recovery of the material substance of an existing object, and the new addition, extension, superposition, and juxtaposition resulting from this existing object. It concerns both the doubling of a metal bay and the addition of a new functional body, and it focuses on the awareness of the relations and interfaces produced and their meaning.

In organizational terms, the studio's work is divided into two fundamental phases which correspond to the intermediate and final reviews: "Survey, Diagnosis, and Repair" and "Intervention Project."

The first concerns the survey and diagnosis of the works on site. The first weeks of the semester are devoted to gaining in-depth knowledge of the subject of the studio. It also involves a diagnosis of the buildings. The observations made during the on-site visits and in the verification and finalization phase of the survey are the subject of consultations with the EPFL experts selected by the students, in order to thoroughly diagnose the selected buildings. At the end of this first phase, the program of the intervention project (renovation, rehabilitation, extension, flanking construction, etc.) is unveiled to the students. The work, which until this point has been collective, develops into individual projects. Issues that were raised during the phase of understanding the architectural object need to find a coherent and appropriate response in the preservation project. Organized successively, these two stages are inseparable, with the knowledge accumulated during the survey of the existing environment inevitably nurturing the new design project. Lectures on themes covered in the studios take place throughout the semester and seek to provide students with key theoretical contributions. In the same way, study trips are organized to observe architecture and architects in direct contact with the current issues of intervention in the existing built environment. These phases of the work always prove very beneficial for the students and are, therefore, essential to their training.

The aim of the studios is to convey to students the theoretical and practical elements of the development of this project discipline, of this "knowledge in action." The building or complex being studied and the subject of the project is part of the city and the region's post-war context, and it is a high-quality, recognized heritage that may be monumental or "ordinary." In this way the studio projects have dealt with industrial objects to be regenerated, such as the Aïre wastewater treatment plant in Geneva by Georges Brera in the 2007–2008 academic year; Olivetti's Ivrea power station by Eduardo Vittoria in 2008–2009; the headquarters of the Geneva Public Roads Department in Vernets by François Maurice in 2009–2010; university and research centers such as CERN in Geneva by Rudolf and Peter Steiger in 2010–2011; the campus of the École Polytechnique Fédérale in Lausanne in 2011–20012, the Swiss Federal Agricultural Research Station in Changins in 2019–2020, the Postgarage in Brig in 2021, and the CIP Centre interrégional de perfectionnement in Tramelan by Heidi and Peter Wenger in 2020–2021; and abandoned masterpieces such as the Palazzo del Lavoro in Turin by Pier-Luigi Nervi in 2012–2013 or the Franziskushaus convent at Dulliken by Otto Glaus in 2018–2019. From 2012 to 2018, in collaboration with the Fondation Le Corbusier, the studio focused its attention on his work, with projects looking at the Quartiers modernes Frugès in Pessac, the Pavillon Suisse and Maison Brésil in the Cité Universitaire de Paris, the Cabanon in Roquebrune Cap-Martin, the Claude & Duval factory, the Unités d'habitation (Marseille, Rezé, Briey-en-Forêt, Berlin, Firminy), the Chapelle Notre-Dame du Haut in Ronchamp, and the Maison de l'Homme in Zurich. This has made it possible to create an unprecedented body of knowledge about the materiality of the architect's work and its restitution in the form of models and analytical axonometric projections, to participate through project design in questions that arise about all these great works, and to closely follow the restoration and work in progress.

At the master's level, the studios in the **Preservation Orientation** deal with the subject and the problem to be studied using the methodological foundations of the discipline: a significant choice in relation to the physical and material state of the object, its potential in the development of the project, a knowledge of it through the survey, in-depth historical investigation, analysis of an imminent problem or implementation of a preventive action, and development of possible intervention strategies while retaining the spatial, material, distributional, and even poetic qualities of the object. It is expected that, unlike the third-year workshop, the architectural object—and the issues surrounding it—could be on a different scale, dealing with the landscape, industrial or railway wastelands, urban or rural mountain complexes, etc. It may also be open to another historical period than the second half of the twentieth century and/or develop the innovative project in a more independent way based on considerations of current production and the use of buildings as a resource. Thus, guest lecturers Andreas Vass and Erich Hubmann in 2012–13 proposed a studio on the reuse of the unintentional monuments of the anti-aircraft towers from the Second World War built around Vienna's city center, and the following year Daniel Bossard and Merixell Vaquer developed a project comparing utopia and the reality of the built landscape, defining the city and in particular the Zurich periphery as a desperate attempt to achieve total urbanization somewhere between a Romantic form of rurality and endless suburbs. In 2014–15, the theme of Denis Eliet and Laurent Lehmann's studio was the rehabilitation and reclamation of all the Grandes Terres built by Marcel Lods and Jean-Jacques Honegger between 1951 and 1961, while João Pedro Falcão de Campos took as his topic the rehabilitation and extension of schools at Teixeira de Pascoais in Lisbon built by Ruy d'Athouguia in 1952–56 and of one of those in Lancy built by Paul Waltenspuhl in the postwar period. The teaching of preservation in the master's courses continued in 2016–17 under the direction of Frank Escher and Ravi GuneWardena, centered on California architecture of the 1950s, including John Lautner's Chemisphere House, the Charles and Ray Eames House, and the Bubeshko Apartments by Rudolph Maria Schindler, while in 2017–18, Anne Lacaton and Frédéric Druot dealt with the rapidly developing built fabric around the Renens train station to demonstrate that "use, reuse, and transformation are today important elements of invention and the creative process in architecture and urban planning." In the first semester of 2018–19, the Linazasoro studio perfectly conducted a highly conclusive teaching experiment on the reclamation of the Poblado de Fuencarral in Madrid (1956–60), confronting without pathos, but with all the means proper to the discipline, the decay of our diffuse urban environment. In the second semester the studio looked at the recovery of a major post-war project by Hans Döllgast on the Alte Pinakothek and St. Bonifaz church in Munich. This was treated radically by the project, which made it possible to understand its complexity and refinement, offering a new reading of various projects and stratifications and new materials to the few architects still interested in such an unrecognized work. In the 2019–20 academic year, two architects from the Grisons, Ramun Capaul and Gordian Blumenthal, focused on the village of Lumbrein to understand the evolution of an alpine village and its architecture, as well as its potential for reasoned development. Martina Voser was called upon from 2020 to 2022 to develop a design project in the existing Swiss landscape—Beznau, Mitholz, or Collombey-Muraz—highlighting the similarity of approaches between the large scale and that of the object, the attention to the gaze, the survey, and the reasoned transformation demanded by the preservation of resources and forms of the territory.

In this way, year after year, the contributions of the most experienced European and Californian architects and teachers in the field enrich what we can now consider as a large-scale think tank on preservation through the design project and its interpretations.

The TSAM laboratory also supervises the diploma work, named the "Master's Project" at the EPFL (a total of 80 such projects since its establishment). Developed over two semesters, the first examining a theoretical statement and the second developing a project, they fit strictly into the issues of preservation in the broad sense of exploring the themes and places of change. As an example, one of them proposed the restoration of the now-derelict sculptural Brazilian Nestlé kindergarten designed by Michel Magnin in the Vallée de la Jeunesse in Lausanne for Expo 64. Another developed a plan for the densification and transformation of the Marta Brunet district on the outskirts of Santiago, Chile, both of which have received the highest possible marks for the quality of the work done.

The TSAM also supervises thesis work, including "The Vestiges of Operation Million in the Work of Georges Candilis" in 2019, "Modern Schools in Angola, 1961–1975: Design with Climate and Heritage" in co-supervision with the IST-Lisbon in 2020, and "The Preservation of Buildings with Suspended Structures and Light Façades: An Innovative Methodology of Modern Heritage (1960–1980)" in 2021.

To conclude, we will say that more than a decade ago the TSAM addressed the question of teaching the preservation of modern and contemporary buildings as a new discipline, specifically and radically different from that of new architecture, both in terms of theoretical courses and the contemporary architecture project. It has established a methodology and a practice based on its research that embrace the whole of polytechnic or university education, whether basic or advanced. Finally, the TSAM affirms the richness and the educational power of preservation and its project, and, beyond the subjective feelings and formalistic emotions, bases them on an objective and multidisciplinary argumentation combining fine observation of materiality, essential theoretical knowledge, and thoughtful creativity.

GIULIA MARINO

DESIGNING IN THE BUILT ENVIRONMENT: THE THEORETICAL TOOLS OF THE PROJECT

When developing this program, it was obvious that the teaching of the preservation project had to be coordinated with the theoretical courses. At all levels of the syllabus, the challenges of intervening in the existing built environment, the theoretical foundations, the methodological instruments, and the operational measures to be undertaken needed to be addressed in a coherent and structured fashion. It was also necessary to view the potential instructive value of the research work carried out in the laboratory as an opportunity to encourage both open and rigorous thought by our future architects.

The class entitled "Theories and Techniques of the Preservation Project" was created from these two goals. Its pedagogical content provides the framework for the master's program of the same name and is designed to reinforce the relationship between the project and its theoretical tools. The subtitle of the class, "Architecture as Resource," was chosen to reflect the multiplicity of the themes addressed. Similarly, the use of the polysemic term "resource" reveals the richness and the diversity of the corpus: in addition to restoring well-known architectural works widely considered to be monuments and thus of value, we also address built environments that are more recent (sometimes very recent) and often considered seemingly ordinary. Such restorations are very topical—for better or for worse—because of the challenges involved in bringing the buildings up to date.

Understanding the values of the built environment, taking a position in the project

The expectations for the master's-level class "Theories and Techniques of the Preservation Project" rely on the fundamental act of every project concerning preservation, that is, an assessment of the heritage value of the built work and the identification of its authenticity and multiple intrinsic worth—historical, architectural, technical, social. This approach originates from a clear observation (also the common thread of the TSAM Laboratory's activities): a project without a memory is an incomplete project. History must be considered as a methodological support as well as a true tool. But it is necessary to go beyond simply anecdotally placing the built work in its original context. It is more a question of clearly establishing the patrimonial value using an assessment that is in no way subjective but that, on the contrary, meets precise and broadly agreed-upon scientific criteria. The particularities of the built work are revealed following a process where it is compared to a corpus of assimilable works. And those particularities—the originality, representativeness, or even when taken to extremes, the uniqueness or its "irrelevance"—dictate the intervention strategies to be undertaken. In other words, the most appropriate project strategy (one that is in line with the values of the building), emerges from the importance and the qualities of the constructed work, no matter whether that strategy aims to respectfully preserve a monument or radically transform an ordinary building. Using the same logic, the detailed analysis of its materiality becomes indispensable for defining intervention measures. And that analysis will help to identify, of course, deficiencies and malfunctions, but also the project's specific potential. This assessment of heritage value, constructed from its material history, is the basis for any intervention on existing buildings and must be carried out before undertaking the project. It guides the planner in his or her choices.

1

2

3

Opening photo Le Lignon housing estate, Addor & Julliard, Louis Payot, architects, Geneva, 1963–1971
1 Mont-Blanc Centre and Le Plaza cinema, Marc J. Saugey, architect, Geneva, 1951–1954
2 Federal Customs Administration Headquarters, Hans & Gret Reinhard, Werner Stücheli, architects, Bern, 1944–1953
3 Biel Congress House, Max Schlup, architect, Biel, 1956–1966
4 The Grand'Mare housing complex (a GEAI industrialized construction technique), Marcel Lods, Paul Depondt, and Henri Beauclair, architects, Rouen, 1968–1969
5 Siedlung Müllerwis (IGECO prefabricated system), Jakob Schilling (general plan drawing), Hans Litz, architects, Ernst Göhner, constructor, Greifensee, 1968–1971

19 DESIGNING IN THE BUILT ENVIRONMENT: THE THEORETICAL TOOLS OF THE PROJECT

1 Carlo Ginzburg, "Signes, traces, pistes. Racines d'un paradigme de l'indice," *Le Débat*, no. 6 (1980): 3–44.

    This is the approach presented to students, who, having acquired the necessary methodological tools over the course of the semester, undertake an in-depth heritage assessment, starting from a given framework and structured according to internationally established good practice. Relying on a thorough investigation of numerous documents, supplemented by a direct investigation of the built work, they follow the "traces, signs, and paths"[1] that allow them to understand its values. They retrace the history of the building, from its creation and construction, through its current state, in order to then reposition it within a context that has become all the broader given the value attributed to it. They will thus be able to give an informed opinion of the reasons for the options chosen during interventions that have already been carried out on this building, noting their coherence (or lack thereof), or even their merits, according to architectural disciplines. In other words, it is a question of experimenting with the process of "backwards" preservation, that is, not by putting one's own project into place but by observing with a critical eye the contemporary interventions that have already been carried out. The graphical representation of a substantial part of the building, on a 1:20 scale, will here be a tool for analyzing and synthesizing, as the established "black/yellow/red" code unambiguously reveals the permanence of the material and, with it, the authenticity of the building, the most vital criterion of any preservation project.

6 Bagno pubblico di Bellinzona, Aurelio Galfetti, Flora Ruchat, and Ivo Trümpy, architects, 1968–1970

7 Architect Aurelio Galfetti speaking about the design and construction of the Bagno pubblico di Bellinzona during a visit with students Philip Bürgi, Viorela Bogato, Alice Fakhri, and Juliette Jancu as part of the thesis preparation for the Theories and Techniques of the Preservation Project class in 2016–2017

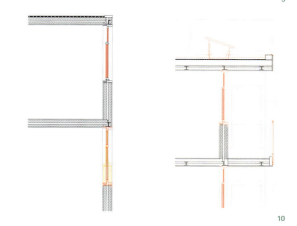

8–9–10 Haus Colnaghi, Paul Artaria, and Hans Schmidt, architects, Riehen / Basel, 1928–1930, original state and current state; 1:20 cross-section from survey drawing of the transformations carried out over the years
11–12–13 International Horology Museum, Georges-J. Haefeli, Pierre Zoelly, architects, La Chaux-de-Fonds, 1972–1974, view of work site and exterior view in 2021; 1:20 survey drawing of the existing state and proposition for restoration and energy performance improvement

14

15

14–15 Clarté building, Le Corbusier & Pierre Jeanneret, architects, Geneva, 1930–1932, original state and current state
16 Jacques-Louis de Chambrier, architect in charge of the restoration of the Clarté building, meeting with students during the Theories and Techniques of the Preservation Project class

16

TEACHING THE PRESERVATION 22

17

18

17–18 Cercle de l'Ermitage, Alberto Sartoris, architect, Epesses, 1935, original state and current state
19 Architect Jean-Christophe Dunant speaking about the challenges of restoring the interiors of the Cercle de l'Ermitage, work by Alberto Sartoris, rediscovered in 2010

19

20

21

22

20 Le Corbusier Primary School, Ugo Brunoni, architect, Geneva, 1980–1989
21 Cantonal Gymnasium and Nyon Business School, Vincent Mangeat, Pierre Wahlen, MW Architects, 1984–1988
22 SFERAX Factory, Bétrix & Consolascio, architects, Cortaillod, 1978–1981
23–24 Lullier Horticultural School, Alfred Damay, Michel Frey, architects, Walter Brugger, landscape architect, Geneva, 1968–1974

2 The students select their study subject from a given list of works. This list has been established over the years according to different criteria, either by typology or function—housing complexes (2012–2013 and 2013–2014), schools (2015–2016), council administrative buildings (2014–2015), etc.—, or in such a way as to show the diversity of twentieth-century buildings and the gradual expansion of the subject field. Establishing a coherent body of works for the list encourages exchange among the students, who work in pairs or small groups.

3 In terms of remarkable public spaces, we can cite the work carried out on the parks and gardens of Lausanne: the Vallée de la Jeunesse or the Bourdonnette park, as well as the Montoie and Bois-de-Vaux cemeteries. Several public swimming pools, sometimes designed in collaboration with well-known landscape architects, have been the subject of in-depth investigative work. This is true, for example, of the Max Frisch swimming pool in Zurich (1949), Maurice Novarina's swimming center in Evian (1966), and also the beautiful swimming pool in Nyon (Jean Serex, architect, 1971).

4 Whether it is Robert Maillart's Vessy bridge (1936) or the Chillon viaduct (Roland Hofer, engineer, 1969), the works proposed (out of the possible choices of structural works of art) elicit essential questions about recognition and preservation.

As for the series of sites proposed for the heritage assessment, we wanted to be part of the process of the gradual (and laudable) broadening of the idea of heritage, which is already in progress.[2] We study, of course, some iconic buildings from the Modern movement and the restorations that were followed over time by other successive projects, revealing the evolution in approaches to monument restoration. But students are also asked to comment on the value of the "types of buildings" that are not yet formally recognized as heritage—twentieth century gardens, including landscaping in housing complexes or cemeteries,[3] or works of art and engineering.[4] Very recent sites are also selected, and their evaluation can and must now be carried out with a necessary but restrained distance, using appropriate scientific tools. This is the case, for example, of so-called "postmodern" architecture: despite the renewed interest of historians, this trend is usually discredited by architects as well as by heritage protection authorities who obviously struggle to find the academic references and tools adapted to its preservation.

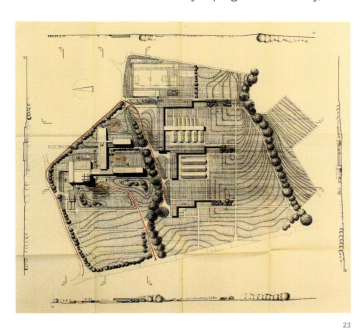

23

One understands then that the objective is to hone the students' perception of modern and contemporary heritage and the practice of its conservation. And what a pleasure it is to see these future architects go beyond current sensibilities (upheld by numerous clichés), appreciating little known (not to say controversial) works from the 1980s, restored to their rightful place within a corpus of heritage works of the highest level. What a pleasure, too, to know that they can provide a precise and reasoned analysis of a 1970s garden, recognizing it as a true "architectural landscape" to be treated according to deontological preservation project good practices, or that they can understand the relevance of "preventive conservation" strategies applied to technical structures such as bridges or dams, in itself an exemplary approach that should be transposed immediately to architectural preservation, which is too rarely the case.

24

25

26

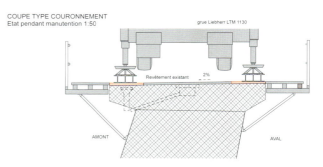

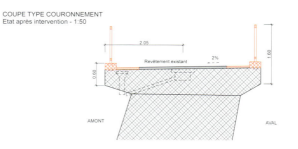

25-26-27 Hongrin dam, Henri Gicot, engineer, Compagnie d'études de travaux public CETP, Château d'Oex, 1963–1971, view of the central abutment and current state; maintenance and repair project
28 Robin Hood Garden, Alison & Peter Smithson, architects, London, 1968–1972
29 Nuovo Corviale, Mario Fiorentino, architect, Rome, 1975–1982
30 Trellick Tower, Ernö Goldfinger, London, 1968–1972
31 The Grand'Mare housing complex, Marcel Lods, Paul Depondt, Henri Beauclair, architects, Rouen, 1968–1969

27

TEACHING THE PRESERVATION   26

28

29

30

31

27   DESIGNING IN THE BUILT ENVIRONMENT: THE THEORETICAL TOOLS OF THE PROJECT

5 We would like to thank Mélanie Delaune Perrin, researcher for the TSAM Laboratory, for her tireless contributions since 2009.
6 See Franz Graf, Giulia Marino, *Le multiples vies de l'appartement-atelier, Le Corbusier*, Les Cahiers du TSAM, no. 2 (Lausanne: Presses polytechniques et universitaires romandes, 2016).
7 See Franz Graf, Giulia Marino, *La buvette d'Évian. M. Novarina, J. Prouvé, S. Ketoff, 1955–2018* (Gollion: Infolio, 2018).
8 See Franz Graf, Giulia Marino, *La cité du Lignon 1963–1971. Étude architecturale et stratégies d'intervention* (Gollion: Infolio, 2012).
9 See Giulia Marino, *"Some Like It Hot!" Les dispositifs du confort artificiel dans l'architecture du XXe siècle* (Geneva: Métispresses, forthcoming).

Research and teaching, the need for coordination

As mentioned, the link between the research work carried out in the TSAM Laboratory and its teaching is a very close one, and this coordination is indispensable in the process of learning about preservation.[5] The experience derived from academic and applied research is made available to students, organized by themes within a course structure whose aim is to look at preservation issues through the use of key examples. Within the framework of the "Theories and Techniques of the Preservation Project," the abundant history of Le Corbusier's apartment-studio,[6] a true permanent work site, a hot spot of spatial, plastic, and constructive experimentation, thus becomes the opportunity to approach the idea of the building as a "palimpsest," with the ethical questions that it raises at the time of its restoration. The material history of a perfectly calibrated technical work such as the Buvette in Évian by Jean Prouvé, Maurice Novarina, and Serge Ketoff,[7] meticulously traced from archival sources and from an in-depth analysis of the current state of the building, suggests a coherent approach to the restoration project. Such an approach, which is based on those technical qualities, then formulates appropriate conservation measures. We can cite too, as a formative moment in the students' training, the visit to Le Lignon housing complex in Geneva, whose restoration relied on the long-term endeavors of applied academic research from the laboratory.[8] The success of this restoration proves that conservation strategies for the existing built environment can be perfectly suited to the contemporary challenges of energy transition.

These theoretical teaching elements are based, to a large extent, on the scientific interests of the laboratory, and in turn they allow the research work to be situated within a broader context. This interwoven relationship has proven itself over the years. And it is, in fact, from one of the laboratory's lines of research[9] that the master's-level class "Comfort by Design in Twentieth-Century Architecture" was created.

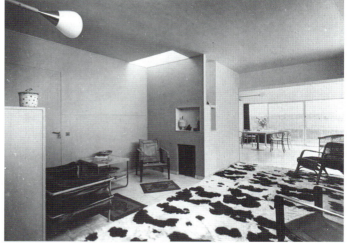

32

33

TEACHING THE PRESERVATION   28

32 Apartment-studio in Rue Nungesser-et-Coli, Le Corbusier, Paris, 1934, view of living room in 1934 and 2014
34–35 Buvette at Évian, Maurice Novarina, architect, Jean Prouvé, constructor, Serge Ketoff, engineer, 1953–1957, general view of work site and current state
36–37 Le Lignon housing estate, Addor & Julliard, Louis Payot, architects, Geneva, 1963–1971, view of work site in 1964 and general view in 2011

34

35

36

37

29 DESIGNING IN THE BUILT ENVIRONMENT: THE THEORETICAL TOOLS OF THE PROJECT

38

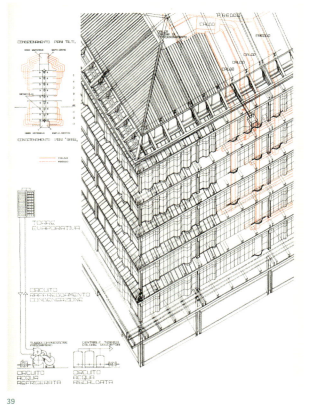

39

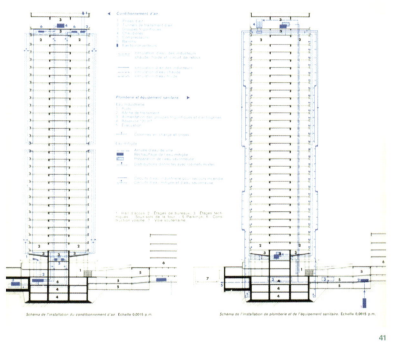

38–39 La Rinascente, commercial building, Franco Albini and Franca Helg, architects, Rome, 1957–1962, recent view and fluid distribution diagram
40–41 Nobel Tower, Jean De Mailly, Jacques Depussé, architects, Jean Prouvé (façades), La Défense, Paris, 1961–1967, view of façade installation site and distribution diagram of the air conditioning systems

"Climate design" or even the artificial control of the inside room temperature thanks to comfort equipment—heat, mechanical ventilation, air conditioning, etc.—is openly recognized as a *node* of Western culture by the convergence of the most diverse sectors among several disciplines. While the twentieth century "constructive revolution"—new materials and techniques, but also new systems and processes—is widely recognized by the history of architecture, the history of technical equipment (an integral part of that broader history) remains often neglected (or simply ignored) as a theme, despite some significant but unrepeated investigations.

In retracing the broad lines of the history and evolution of comfort devices in relation to their close link to the built environment, this course aims to recognize the *centrality of networks* in the architectural project, by restoring, through a historical view situated at the intersection of sensorial and material, the range of technical innovations in the field of comfort equipment. The students are thus asked to explore, for a specific architectural work that has attracted their curiosity and interest, the exact implications of "comfort design" within "architecture design," including in terms of its preservation. Much as when they choose a building, they are allowed complete freedom in their experiments with finding a coherent approach to the themes they treat and in choosing the best work structure for formalizing their research. This is part of the exercise, and it brings about a wealth of ideas.

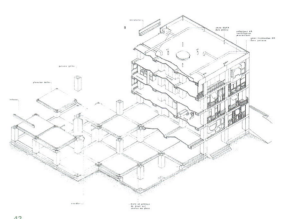

42

43

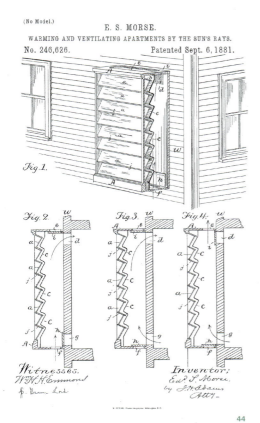

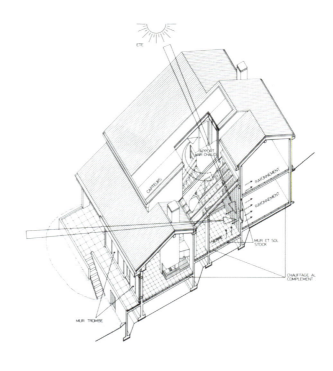

42-43 Les Marelles complex, Georges Maurios, architect, Boussy-Saint-Antoine, 1971–1973, diagram of fluid integration in the elements of the supporting structure and recent view

44-45-46 Adaptations of the "Trombe wall" principle based on E. Morse's patent (1881): the prototype of the solar home in Renens updated by the GRES of the EPFL (Solar Energy Research Group) in 1981 and a contemporary reinterpretation in the administrative building at Zamora by Alberto Campo Baeza, architect (2012)

33 DESIGNING IN THE BUILT ENVIRONMENT: THE THEORETICAL TOOLS OF THE PROJECT

10 The bibliography provided to the class brings together founding texts by authors ranging from James Marston Fitch to Reyner Banham. Ad hoc references are also suggested throughout the semester in the form of more in-depth studies, depending on the subjects chosen by the students.
11 Questions related to a building's use in terms of its energy performance are of more and more interest to new generations of students, who are clearly sensitive to environmental concerns.

Some adopt the model of the monograph, applied to the history of these architectural icons of the twentieth century—from Frank Lloyd Wright's Guggenheim Museum in New York (1959) to the Smithsons' School at Hunstanton (1954)—a rather traditional path, but one that requires a real "detective's investigation" and assembling of clues to make up for a flagrant lack of information in the literature.[10] Others, taking the completely opposite approach, adopt a strategy based on a close reading of the building, aiming to capture its special quality and examine how technology has expressed this spatially. Take, for example, the thermal baths in Vals (1996), explored first by the feeling of heat in the body, by feeling the humidity on the skin, by registering the rhythm of breathing, by listening to the regular sound of a drop of water, in the glare of a sunbeam entering the pool, skillfully directed. It is only afterwards that we descend into the bowels of the building, where the technical equipment and miraculous machines are kept, an invisible but vital element in the experience of Peter Zumthor's architecture.

Retracing the design process of the prefabricated elements and components of Gigi Ghò and Aldo Favini for Kodak (1974) by the integration of aerotherms, documenting the intelligence of an urban heating system installed during the reconstruction of the city of Le Havre by Auguste Perret, or addressing the current state of the art in the refurbishment of a "high-tech" building like the headquarters of Lloyds of London (1985), where architecture is dependent on the expression of networks; these examples represent the many challenges and discoveries that the students must be able to transcribe into their own architectural projects.[11]

47

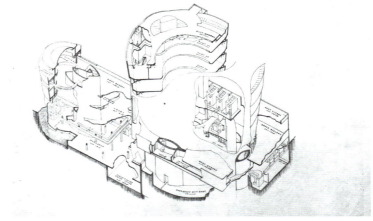

48

47–48 Guggenheim Museum, Frank Lloyd Wright, architect, New York, 1953–1959, recent view and diagram of heating and air conditioning systems
49–50–51–52 Kodak factory, Gigi Ghò architect, Aldo Favini, engineer, Marcianise, 1970–1975, general view and axonometric drawing of the supporting structure that hosts the network; below: sunshades on the facade

49

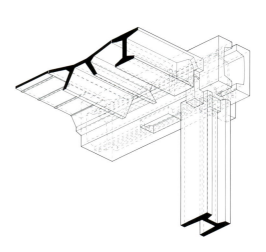

50

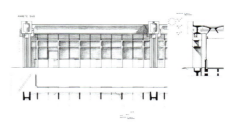

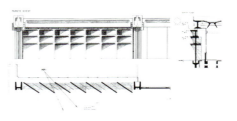

51 52

35 DESIGNING IN THE BUILT ENVIRONMENT: THE THEORETICAL TOOLS OF THE PROJECT

53 to 59 and 59–60 Public lecture series organized by Docomomo Switzerland and the TSAM Laboratory beginning in 2016

TEACHING THE PRESERVATION   36

12 Note that in 2017, the introduction of this course into the compulsory curriculum was at the direct request of the students, as they were increasingly aware of the need for a specific course on this subject, which until then had been missing from theoretical teachings in the architecture department at the EPFL.

Observing project practices in the service of teaching

Since its creation, the TSAM Laboratory has remained committed to its role of observing the architectural practices involved in the preservation of twentieth-century heritage. This has enabled the major trends of the past years to be identified—without straying into doctrine—and has made them part of the lively debate that has been ongoing since the late eighteenth century. Not only does this broadening of the notion of a "cultural asset"—a process that began in the 1970s—focus more attention on recent heritage sites, but this new respect for the material substance of the built heritage indicates a gradual but substantial change in attitude in the preservation project itself, one that is to be welcomed. These considerations are directed above all at projects that take place in existing environments, which, in Switzerland and elsewhere, feature prominently in the activities of architecture firms, a phenomenon that will most certainly increase in years to come.

The TSAM's role as an observer feeds into theory-based teaching, where "practicing architects" are regularly invited to talk about their projects and built works. In order to improve students' knowledge but also enhance their analytical ability, these guest contributions form the basis of the course "Designing in the Built Environment: Tools and Methods" in the third year of the bachelor's degree,[12] which is focused on the fundamentals of projects in existing sites from any period. Alongside sections on the history and theories of the restoration of heritage monuments, current international charters, and tools for recognizing and making an inventory of built assets, a series of lectures reflecting the interplay between the history of architecture and the practices involved in current building projects is given by international speakers: architects, engineers, and historians. Not only are these contributions an integral part of the training of future architects, but their aim is also to widen the professional debate that only too often is lacking. We decided to make these lectures public, thanks to the close

59   60

13 See the lecture series "Projet, histoire, construction. Nouveaux regards sur le patrimoine récent," Docomomo Switzerland and TSAM-EPFL, 2016–2022, under the direction of Franz Graf and Giulia Marino. For the full program, see www.docomomo.ch.

14 The guest lecturers invited as part of the "preservation" orientation are often asked to give lectures for a wider audience, beyond that of the EPFL's architecture department.

relationship that has been established with Docomomo, an international think tank dedicated to the conservation of built heritage from the twentieth century, whose Swiss branch has been housed at the TSAM Laboratory since 2015.[13]

Drawing on such an extended and multifaceted network, these contributions paint the picture of a continuously evolving discipline. The many and varied range of subjects covered is testament to this: from the early protagonists in the field of conservation (in the more contemporary sense of the word) the most diverse strategies can be found, such as architect Hans Döllgast in Munich in the early post-war years to the current issues at play in the restoration of seminal monuments—including Le Corbusier's Unité d'habitation in Marseilles by architect François Botton and Eileen Gray's Villa E1027 (1929) by architect Claudia Devaux—and including the intelligent transformations of more ordinary built heritage undertaken by design studios Lacaton & Vassal and Frédéric Druot. Within this context, the Zurich offices of Boesch Architekten and Diener & Diener give us a convincing demonstration, both sensitive and pragmatic, with their restoration-transformation of the Zurich Convention Center building complex and the Tonhalle concert hall, a major work by Haefeli-Moser-Steiger (1939), who themselves had worked on the existing built environment. Paul Chemetov, a key figure in contemporary French architecture, revisits an iconic work by the Atelier de Montrouge, the EDF housing towers in Ivry-sur-Seine (1969), which, following its listing in the French inventory of historical monuments, was restored accordingly. From Los Angeles architects Frank Escher and Ravi GuneWardena, with their work over the past ten years on the acclaimed Case Study Houses in California, to the Capaul & Blumenthal studio,[14] who intercede delicately in the built environment by appropriating and extending the characteristics of alpine architecture, a wonderfully diverse range of constructions have been worked on using multiple approaches, drawing from a deep understanding of the existing built environment. Patrick Thurston teaches us the art of interpreting traditional techniques in his project on the vernacular buildings designed for the 1939 Swiss National Exhibition in Zurich, where a new *Ersatz*, both functional

61

61 Elisabeth and Martin Boesch (Boesch Architekten, Zurich), extension, repair, and renovation of the Kurththeater Baden, 2007 and 2018–2020 (Lisbeth Sachs, Otto Dorer, architects, 1951–1952)
62 Remo Halter Casagrande (Halter Casagrande Partner AG, Lucerne), Thomas Lussi (Lussi + Partner AG, Lucerne), restoration and transformation of the Lucerne Public Library, 2019 (Otto Dreyer, architect, 1951)
63 Transjurane A16, tunnel RC6, Renato Salvi architect, 1998-2016
64 Fischerstube and Fischerhütte, Patrick Thurston (Architekturbüro Patrick Thurston, Bern), Zurich, 2021
65 Maruša Zorec (Arrea Architecture Ljubljana), restoration and extension of Plečnik House, Ljubljana. 2015 (Jože Plečnik architect 1921–1957)
66 EDF housing towers, Atelier de Montrouge, Ivry-sur-Seine, 1967–1969; concrete repair work site

39 DESIGNING IN THE BUILT ENVIRONMENT: THE THEORETICAL TOOLS OF THE PROJECT

and pleasant, was built. Renato Salvi, Aloïs Diethelm, Remo Halter Casagrande, and Thomas Lussi in Switzerland, Maruša Zorec in Slovenia, and Massimo Narduzzo in Italy, as well as many others, all look back at the practices they have used in preservation projects, in an account that is both personal and intriguing, portraying difficulties and discoveries, and carried along by the undeniably creative approach displayed by all these interventions in existing buildings. We could mention, for example, the Basel studio of Beer-Merz, with its careful restoration of the Christ Scientist Church by Otto R. Salvisberg (1936), along with engineering firm Résonance, who brought the building in line with earthquake standards while preserving its character and substance. Engineers are also called upon in those projects aiming to reproduce the multiple priorities of the preservation project, in other words, its rich diversity. Jürg Conzett provides us with a masterful contribution on the *Weiterbauen* strategy applied to structural works of art, while Aurelio Muttoni ingeniously recounts the rules and gaps in the values of the built environment through the "art of structures." But we also asked architect-historians to investigate the operational approach employed in the historical narrative, either based on important case studies (including Richard Klein on the former Maison de la Culture in Chalon-sur-Saône [D. Petit, 1959–1971] and Joseph Abram on the current state of Livio Vacchini's architecture school in Nancy [1996]) or based on the career paths of architects who have left a profound mark on the creations of last century (including Fritz Haller in a reading by Laurent Stalder, and Gaston Eysselynck, brilliantly portrayed by Belgian architect Marc Dubois).

The various movements within the field of preservation of twentieth-century architecture have thus been addressed head on, both with regard to how heritage monuments have

67 Cartiera Burgo, Pier Luigi Nervi, Gino Covre engineers, Mantua, 1964, restoration Massimo Narduzzo and Studio CREA.RE, 2021
68 Jürg Conzett (Conzett Bronzini Partner, Chur), restoration of the Tavanasa bridge (Walter Versell engineer, 1928)
69 Maison Eysselinck, Gaston Eysselinck architect, Gand, 1930–1931
70 Maison Ronde, Serge Binotto, Mirepoix, 1969

67

68

69

70

15 See Ana Tostões's contribution in the journal *Tracés* focusing on the work of the TSAM Laboratory: Ana Tostões, Zara Ferreira, Joana Gouveia Alves, "Docomomo. Mutations d'une organisation globale," in Franz Graf, Giulia Marino (eds.), Tracés, no. 5–6, 142ᵉ année, 11 March 2016, dossier *TSAM : sauvegarde de l'architecture du 20ᵉ siècle*, 26–27.
16 Serge Binotto (1939–2021) passed away suddenly in August 2021. We would like to take this opportunity to pay tribute to him.

been represented—Véronique Boone recounted the strategies employed by Le Corbusier to stage, as it were, his own works—and to their recognition at an institutional level, an intellectual as much as diplomatic process that led, for example, to the project for the "Architectural Work of Le Corbusier" being listed as a UNESCO World Heritage Site, described by historian Gilles Ragot, who produced the technical file. The issues involved in the management of large-scale heritage sites have also been covered: the current state of the Montreal Olympic Park (R. Taillibert, 1976) teaches us that beyond problems of maintenance and the later adaptation of buildings, where there is a strong need to be inventive, the issue is primarily one of political will and commitment. Within the context of these varied theoretical contributions, it has also been a question of portraying the complex process of recognizing and preserving the built environment in the face of the new contemporary challenges involved in adaptive reuse, by widening the field of action, both geographical and typological—a crucial point raised by Ana Tostões and Uta Pottgiesser, who have in turn been presidents of Docomomo International.[15] Milanese photographers Stefano Perego and Roberto Conte gave us a fine demonstration of this through their curious and careful look at the current state of post-Soviet architecture, far beyond its character as a building designed simply to impress. And finally, the contribution by Serge Binotto, former associate of Jean Prouvé and a wonderful builder, whose account of the building of his Maison Ronde in Mirepoix (1969) is a true architectural lesson and a highly instructive moment—not only for our students.[16]

Understanding the work site, an educational approach

When we invite guest lecturers, we make it very clear on the invitation that they should in no way avoid "technical" questions, but rather seek to give those questions the noble and profound meaning implied by the term itself. These architects do indeed go over the different stages in the preservation project, from the history of the building to the context that drives the project, right through to the process leading to the choice of necessary measurements. The implementation of operational strategies is a key issue. As an opportunity to clarify and

71 Villa "Le Lac," Le Corbusier, Corseaux, 1926: visit to the restoration site with the students from the "Theories and Techniques of the Preservation Project" class in 2013, led by the project team (Nicolas Delachaux, Glatz & Delachaux Architects, Nyon; Jean-Yves Le Baron, L'atelier du paysage, Lausanne; Eric-J. Favre-Bulle, Atelier Saint-Dismas, Lully), and Bénédicte Gandini, architect from the Fondation Le Corbusier, and Patrick Moser, curator at the Villa "Le Lac"
72 The "Educate and Create" pavilion from Expo 64 (today the Théâtre de Vidy), Max Bill, architect, Lausanne, 1964
73 Visit to the restoration site at the Théâtre de Vidy, led by François Jolliet, architect and founder of Bureau Pont12, in charge of the restoration and extension project
74 Aula des Cèdres, Jean Tschumi, architect, Lausanne, 1962
75 Visit to the Aula des Cèdres by Jean Tschumi, led by Yvan Koleček (Koleček Architectural Studio, Lausanne), architect in charge of restoration

71

refine technical solutions in order to preserve the existing material is the only authentic trace and the only one capable of expressing the architectural qualities of the built work, preparing for execution is an important part of the story. In some cases, it is even the mainstay. The work that takes place on existing buildings is thus treated as a stage that is unquestionably meaningful, even rife with meaning, including within a mindset of producing new knowledge of the built environment through an in-depth investigation. And this vital stage, drawing upon the

72

73

74

75

43 DESIGNING IN THE BUILT ENVIRONMENT: THE THEORETICAL TOOLS OF THE PROJECT

17 This contribution is the opportunity to extend a sincere word of thanks to the participants who over the years and with such generosity have agreed to share their experience and knowledge with us and our students.

18 The expression is borrowed from the title of the multidisciplinary conference held in 2012 under the auspices of the Commission technique de la cathédrale de Lausanne, on the question of the preservation of its stone façade facing.

observation of built works, must be examined and analyzed in order for it to be fully grasped; it must be regarded as an important moment in the training of future architects.

In keeping with this logic, we would like to highlight the importance of off-site teaching (among other teaching approaches put in place), including study trips to monuments that have a history that is as complex as it is fascinating, one that takes on new meaning over the centuries. As with the courses on "Theories and Techniques of the Preservation Project" for master's students, the basic principles covered in "Designing in the Built Environment" alternate between formal classes and a series of visits to outstanding restoration work sites in the region, led by the architects in charge of the project. The most recent—the visits to the Aula des Cèdres (1962), one of Jean Tschumi's major works, recently restored by architect Ivan Koleček, and to the site of the transformation and extension of the last remaining building from the Expo 64, Max Bill's Théâtre de Vidy, by François Jolliet of Pont12 Architectes—have provided the opportunity to address both theoretical and technical issues, which—and this becomes quite obvious—take on more meaning *in situ*. Accounts by project planners and site managers explaining programming constraints embody and express the complexity of these preservation projects, which must be grasped with tools (above all intellectual) and built *ad hoc*, a process with which the laboratory had wished to be involved right from the beginning.

In the students' third year of study, the educational benefits of visiting monuments of national significance with complex stratigraphy, such as the Saint-Maire castle or the Notre-Dame cathedral in Lausanne, under the direction of the architects responsible for their preservation, are incontestable.[17] This moment of understanding and exchange clarifies and reinforces the teaching of the history and theory of architecture, whether it concerns the deontology of "reversibility" advocated by the international charters of restoration since the 1960s, or Viollet-le-Duc's highly personal definition of "restoration," an approach he was able to faithfully transcribe during a round of restoration works in the 1870s at the cathedral in Lausanne. Architect Christophe Amsler, who a century later in 1989 picked up the torch for the preservation of monuments, reminded us of the importance (and sometimes the fallibility) of the notion of "material authenticity," where molasse—a clay and sedimentary rock that through its mineralogical composition is soft and friable—sorely tests the "deontology of rock."[18] All this calls

76

77

TEACHING THE PRESERVATION   44

76 Saint-Maire castle, Lausanne
77 Visit to the Saint-Maire castle for students in the "Designing in the Built Environment" class, led by Nicolas Delachaux and Christophe Amsler, architects in charge of restoration
77–79 Visit to the work site for the restoration of the south façade of the Lausanne cathedral for students in the "Designing in the Built Environment" class, led by Christophe Amsler, architect in charge of restoration
80 Elevation perspective of the south façade of the Lausanne cathedral, Henri Assinare 1878–1879

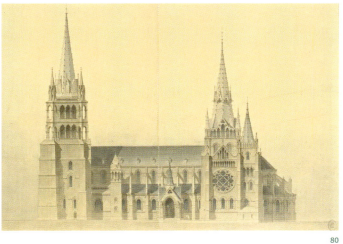

45   DESIGNING IN THE BUILT ENVIRONMENT: THE THEORETICAL TOOLS OF THE PROJECT

to mind the Ship of Theseus, that is, the eternal debate about *identity* and *substance* at the heart of the preservation project, its history and its theories. "Nothing can be understood or resolved without time," Amsler said recently to his students, from high up on the scaffolding on the façades of the cathedral.

An operational process, a multidisciplinary approach

We have made mention of the laboratory's applied academic research devoted to the large-scale heritage sites of the second half of the twentieth century, which are in the spotlight today. But how to respond to the issues involved in the energy transition, while reconciling aspects presented *a priori* (and wrongly so) as antinomic, such as the preservation of heritage sites, the improvement in energy performance, and economic constraints, in an architectural production that lifts the notion of "lightness" into a veritable manifesto? How to go about improving resistance to earthquakes without completely upsetting the intrinsic logic of an architecture for which the generalization of the ad hoc framework has paved the way for a spatial and plastic concept that was unthinkable before? How to respond to the issues of increasing urban density, while becoming part of the existing built environment in a respectful and sensitive, let's say intelligent, way?

These critical issues were addressed in the context of a project at the School of Architecture, Civil and Environmental Engineering (ENAC), "Strategies and Techniques for the Reuse of Twentieth-Century Architecture," a teaching course that is part of the curriculum of the Faculty of the Natural, Architectural, and Built Environment and therefore aimed at master's students from the three disciplines belonging to the ENAC.

Benefiting from the supervision of a multidisciplinary team of lecturers from various fields, which is created depending on the topic, the aim is to raise awareness among students

81–82 Sports center on Rue du Stand, Paul Waltenspühl, architect, Geneva, 1951–1953
83 Proposal for the restoration and energy retrofit of the sports center on Rue du Stand, as part of the ENAC project "Strategies and Techniques for the Reuse of Twentieth-Century Architecture"

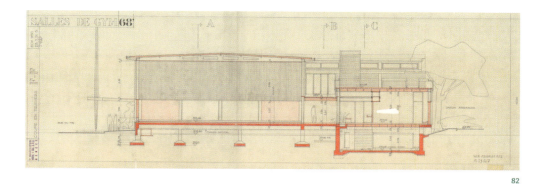

82

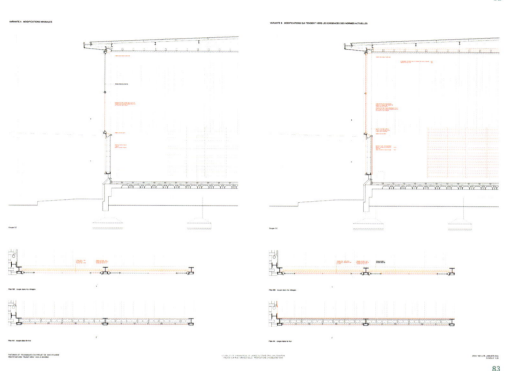

83

of these disciplines as to the possibility of researching a subject that truly interests them. It is also a question of developing a conversation, by building a common language with specialists in other fields, with whom they will inevitably work in their professional life. In these mixed groups of architects and engineers, each person broaches the subject with the tools from his or her own discipline, in an approach combining constructive dialogue and exchange with other actors in the project.

We have been able to observe the benefits from this in the process that eventually led to the vertical extension project of Jean-Marc Lamunière's fine Lancy Towers (1965), a lengthy but successful process of back and forth between the compositional strategies put forward by a young architect, motivated by the need to find the appropriate insertion of his architectural style into the original tectonic framework, and a young engineer, supervised by Professor Aurelio Muttoni, concerned with the structural optimization of the new volume and the effectiveness of the joining devices with the existing framework. The results were impressive. Equally fruitful were the thoughts around the reactivation of a mountain cable car station, in Verbier, a Brutalist work from architect Jean-Paul Darbellay (1973), disfigured after several hasty transformations, despite its remarkable characteristics, or the plan for the preservation and heating improvements for the owners of a community of grouped residences nestled in the Vaudois countryside, which was as remarkable for its pioneering approach in the 1970s in Switzerland as its invisibility during the protection measures implemented by the cantonal authorities, due to its young age.

84

84 Orangerie at La Bourdonnette, Rémy Ramelet, architect, Lausanne, 1956–1961
85–86 Lancy Towers, Jean-Marc Lamunière, architect, Geneva, 1961–1965, original state and vertical extension project, as part of the ENAC project "Strategies and Techniques for the Reuse of Twentieth-Century Architecture"
87–88 La Mottaz neighborhood, Claude Cruchet, architect, Apples, 1968–1974; view of the neighborhood in the 1970s and guidelines for the preservation and energy retrofit project developed for the neighborhood inhabitants as part of the ENAC project "Strategies and Techniques for the Reuse of Twentieth-Century Architecture"

85

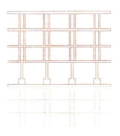

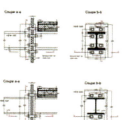

86

87

88

49 DESIGNING IN THE BUILT ENVIRONMENT: THE THEORETICAL TOOLS OF THE PROJECT

19 Giuseppe Galbiati, *La sauvegarde des bâtiments à structure suspendue et façades légères : une méthodologie innovante pour le Retrofitting du Patrimoine moderne (1960–1980)*, PhD thesis under the direction of Franz Graf (EPFL) and Giulia Marino (UCLouvain), in progress. See also pp. 396–399 in this volume.

And finally, let us mention a term paper devoted to the energy rehabilitation of the administrative buildings on the Place Chauderon in Lausanne (AAA, R. Willomet, P. Dumartheray, 1974), a formerly criticized architectural ensemble that is beginning to receive due appreciation, a sign of the change in perspective that has recently taken place regarding the built heritage of the second half of the twentieth century. Beyond the recent drive to recognize the heritage value of this ensemble, the crucial question of its energy rehabilitation remains. What strategy should be adopted for the work required on the prefabricated panels of the façade designed by Jean Prouvé (the aim of which was to improve the building's performance), without altering it, that is, by preserving the material substance of the panels? By applying the multicriteria analysis developed by the laboratory, the students were able to suggest an answer to this vital question. Since then, this case study has been extended to other buildings, which have the same construction characteristics, that is, a suspended structure and lightweight building envelopes, in the context of a doctor's thesis where one of the students from the ENAC project wished to further explore these issues and build on the savoir-faire developed by the laboratory.[19]

Here too, as we do in the bachelor's and master's courses, we can see the pleasure gained from discovery, a discovery above all of recent architecture that has seldom been addressed in history classes and has only rarely been looked at from the viewpoint of its material history. We can also see the pleasure gained from the discovery of an approach to projects dealing with existing buildings that is governed by its own codes—codes that must be learned and mastered but that also open up an inspiring space for personal creation. The students seize onto this eagerly, which is excellent news for the future of the profession.

89

90

TEACHING THE PRESERVATION   50

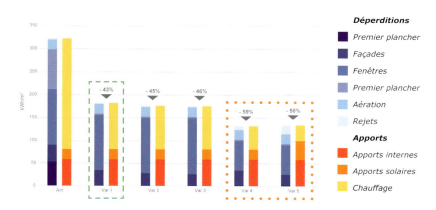
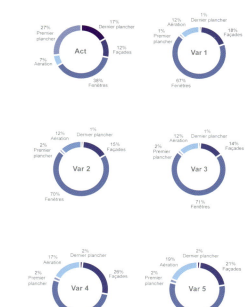

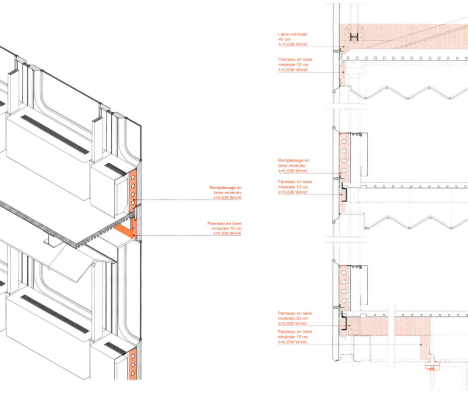

89–90 Administrative buildings on Place Chauderon, AAA (Roland Willomet, Paul Dumartheray, architects), Lausanne, 1974, view of the work site and recent view
91 to 93 Administrative buildings on Place Chauderon, energy retrofit project as part of the ENAC project "Strategies and Techniques for the Reuse of Twentieth-Century Architecture"

51 DESIGNING IN THE BUILT ENVIRONMENT: THE THEORETICAL TOOLS OF THE PROJECT

FRANZ GRAF
YVAN DELEMONTEY

THE STUDIO, OR TEACHING THE PRESERVATION PROJECT

The project studio has been a major component of the EPFL's teaching on preservation from the start.[1] It was put into place in 2007 at the moment the TSAM Laboratory was created, following an earlier crucial pedagogical experience.[2] Over the past fifteen years, it has thus allowed more than five hundred architecture students in their third year of bachelor's study (and very recently master's study too)[3] to discover and appreciate a heritage that despite its contemporaneity is still too little known and too often vilified. It has also allowed them to familiarize themselves with the challenges of preserving twentieth-century heritage and the issues inherent to undertaking projects on existing buildings (indispensable for their future careers), in semester- or year-long courses.[4] As a complement to the theoretical instruction offered by the TSAM related to these questions,[5] the project studio appears to be above all a place for practical experimentation, a privileged space for research and investigation by way of the project.

[1] The following people (in chronological order) have collaborated in teaching this studio since its creation: Giulia Marino (2007–2009), Christian Bischoff (2007–2013), Michael Wyss (2007–2015), Yvan Delemontey (2008–2022), Stephan Rutishauser (2013–2019), Théo Bellmann (2019–2020), and Thierry Buache (2020–2023).
[2] This took place at the EPFL during the winter semester of 2005–2006, when Franz Graf was named guest professor (Christian Bischoff and Giulia Marino, assistants). Concerning the results of this first preservation project studio, see Franz Graf, Christian Bischoff, Giulia Marino, *Un chef-d'œuvre de l'architecture des années 1950 à Genève: les salles de sport de la rue du Stand. Paul Waltenspühl, architecte, 1951–1953* (Lausanne: EPFL, 2008).
[3] In fact, at the time of writing no fewer than 500 students have passed through the project studio, twenty or thirty at a time.
[4] In the beginning, from 2007 to 2012, the project studio was one semester long. From 2012 to 2021, it was transformed into a year-long project, before returning to its current semester-based structure. Starting in 2021, some of the EPFL architectural studios became "vertical," mixing students in their third year with those in their first year of master's study.
[5] See Giulia Marino, "Concevoir dans le construit: les outils théoriques du project," see pp. 16–51 in this volume.

However, the preservation project has its own specificities, objects, and methods. Designed in reverse order to a project for a new building, with its chronological process of genesis going from planning to implementation, the preservation project begins, inversely, with the finished object. For the traditional blank page in front of the project planner, which seems to hold the promise that anything is possible (for better and for worse!), it substitutes the singularity of what exists, the uniqueness of what is already there, this "something rather than nothing" that the planner will have to create, come to know, understand, situate, and interpret. Far from anecdotal, this conceptual inversion contains marvelous educational potential that the preservation project intends to explore. It does this notably through the mobilization of a whole range of multidisciplinary knowledge, involving historical reflection and knowledge of materials, as well as the study of implementation techniques and the analysis of economic or environmental data.

A diversified and coherent corpus

Under these conditions, the studio's choice of buildings to be used as teaching supports is fundamental. Their succession in time constitutes retrospectively a varied but coherent corpus that forms part of our everyday heritage, that of the architecture, town, and territory of the last century. Even though these buildings are mostly from the post-war period, a time of extreme upheaval in our built environment, their temporal affiliation remains broader: from the 1920s animated by the pioneers of the Modern movement to the dawn of the 1990s marked by the decline in postmodernism. Sometimes dictated by circumstances or opportunities, the choice of architectural objects first obeys the studio teaching approach, which requires confrontation with buildings of quality, whether they are known or anonymous, monumental or ordinary, registered as heritage or unknown by the relevant autho-

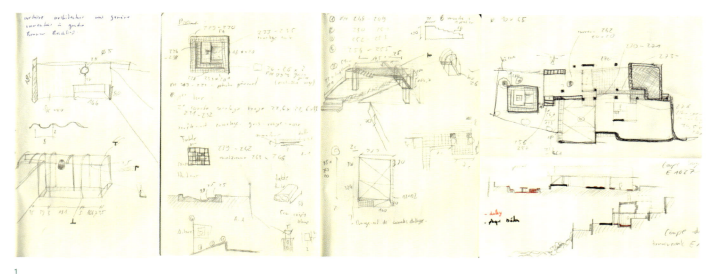

1

6 Many happy connections were thus made with the final Master's Project: this is the case, for example for the Aïre wastewater treatment plant projects (2008–2009), the Vernets Center for the Geneva Public Roads Department (2009–2010), the Flaine winter sports resort (Fall, 2010), the CERN buildings in Meyrin (Spring, 2011), the Claude & Duval factory in Saint-Dié (2013–2014), the Nantes-Rezé Unité d'habitation (2015–2016), the Ronchamp chapel (Fall, 2016), the Franziskushaus in Dulliken (2018–2019), the Swiss Federal Agricultural Research Station (SFRA) in Changins (2019–2020), and the Centre interrégional de perfectionnement (CIP) in Tramelan (2020–2021). See Franz Graf and Thierry Buache, "Le Projet de master en sauvegarde," pp. 298–303 in this volume.

7 This is the case, for example, of two major creations by Valais architects Heidi & Peter Wenger, the SFRA and the CIP, whose heritage value was reevaluated after the students' work.

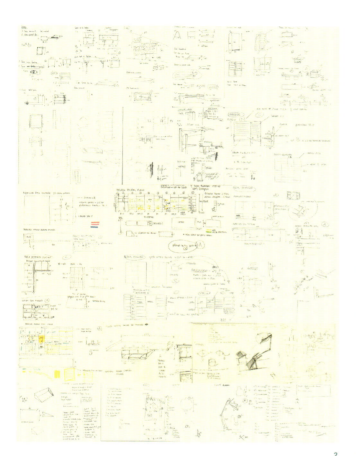

rities. In this last case, the students' work—and sometimes the work of the graduate students who choose as their theme that of the studio[6]—contribute to a work's recognition, an indispensable prelude to its future protection.[7] Thus, our corpus is situated mainly in Switzerland and France, but also in Italy and Germany, drawing as much from big European cities such as Geneva, Turin, Zurich, Paris, or Berlin, as from medium-sized cities (Ivrea, Firminy, Lausanne, Nantes), or more remote locations (Roquebrune-Cap-Martin, Flaine, Ronchamp, Dulliken, Tramelan, Brig, etc.). Furthermore, and this is the advantage of using a longer time span, a large number of key Modernist project types have been covered: individual or collective housing, technical or industrial infrastructures, cultural or touristic facilities, places of teaching and research, sacred architecture, etc. Finally, the most diverse range of architects and constructors have accompanied us, from the most famous, such as Le Corbusier, Eileen Gray, Marcel Breuer, or Pier Luigi Nervi, to the lesser known (at least on an international scale) but immensely talented such as Georges Brera, Eduardo Vittoria, Jacob Zweifel, Otto Glaus, Heidi and Peter Wenger, etc.

The survey as a prerequisite for the project

In preservation, everything begins with the *survey*. Is it possible to imagine a doctor prescribing a treatment to a patient without doing an examination or ordering any tests? Obviously not. It's the same in architecture as it is in medicine, or at least we might be tempted to think so. This is why any project in the existing built environment requires thorough knowledge of the object on which an intervention is planned, and this knowledge is obtained with the survey. We employ the survey in many ways in the studio, because it is at once a survey of general observation, a spatial and geometrical survey, a survey of comfort and use, and a technical and constructive survey. Paired with solid preliminary historical documentation (sketches, implementation plans, photographs of the work site, etc.), the survey work—physical work that requires direct and prolonged contact with and presence in the building—allows for capturing the character of the object studied, identifying within it a constructive logic, and correctly establishing the diagnostic. Is there any better way to "get to know" a building and its architecture? What else but the survey would permit such an intimate and precise understanding of all the facets and dimensions, be they cultural, spatial, material, or constructive? Because drawing is understanding. It means penetrating the object by stepping into the designer's shoes, reconstituting step by step the intellectual process used to design the space, choose a specific material, or resolve a detail. It means getting as close as possible to the conditions that presided over the original design and construction of the work itself.

Opening photo: Studio students and teachers under the pilotis of Le Corbusier's Weissenhof-Siedlung double house in Stuttgart, 2015
1 Survey sketch of Villa E-1027 and its surroundings in Roquebrune-Cap-Martin, 2009
2 Survey sketch of the Wenger house-studio in Brig, 2020

8 The results from this study have been the subject of subsequent publications; see Franz Graf, "Les vies multiples de 'l'Unité d'habitation' (1945–1967–2017). Les temps courts de la reproductibilité du modèle et de l'entropie à l'œuvre," *Matières*, no. 14 (2018): pp. 50–61 and "Innovation of Construction Systems versus Reproducibility of the Architectural Image. Multiple Constructional Processes in the Unité d'habitation (1945–67)," in Ine Wouters, Stephanie Van de Woorde, and Inge Bertels (eds.), *Building Knowledge, Constructing Histories*, proceedings of the Sixth International Congress on Construction History (Brussels, July 9–13, 2018) (Leiden: CRC Press Taylor & Francis Group, 2018), pp. 691–96.

Through this closeness to the object, the survey promotes the constructive dimension of the architecture and its corollary, the *materiality*, a fundamental value that is mostly situated outside the usual categories of the theory and history of architecture. When carried out with rigor, the survey is in reality a formidable tool for the historicity of the discipline, because it makes the constructed object the primary basis for the critical investigation, far from the conventional approaches of the history of art, which are based on the almost exclusive exploitation of archives (graphical pieces, correspondence, reports, estimates, etc.). We experienced this over the many years the studio dedicated itself to the work of Le Corbusier, years during which the survey work allowed us to bring to light many little-known aspects of the "master's" architecture and to formulate a certain number of original hypotheses, in spite of the colossal amount of critical work that has been produced on Le Corbusier's oeuvre. The most pertinent observations were developed during comparative analyses, such as the one that consisted, for example, of comparing the Pavillon suisse and the Maison du Brésil at the Cité internationale universitaire de Paris, two similar building types but built around twenty-five years apart; or even the one, more audacious still, that studied (and thus surveyed) in detail each of the five built Unités d'habitation.[8] Because this is also the exploratory force of a studio, that is, its extraordinary ability to carry out the most ambitious undertakings, as the enthusiasm, collective intelligence, and working capacity of the group prevail over the individual and supposed inexperience of the individuals.

3

3 Final project review with Henri Bresler and Pierre Bonnet, 2011
4 Project models assembled in the studio (project to extend the Maison du Brésil at the Cité internationale universitaire de Paris), 2018
5 Students posing in front of their models of the Le Corbusier Unités d'habitation during final reviews, 2016

57　THE STUDIO, OR TEACHING THE PRESERVATION PROJECT

9 While the reconstruction of architectural objects was essentially carried out in two dimensions for the first few years, the students' ease and familiarity with increasingly powerful computer tools has made it possible in recent years to develop true digital models in three dimensions for all to add to and improve: a sort of BIM before its time! These new capabilities have allowed, for example, the precise creation of a 1:100 scale model of an object as complex and difficult to represent as the Notre-Dame du Haut chapel at Ronchamp.

10 For this purpose, the use of the "black-yellow-red" color code usually used by Swiss architects allows for distinguishing between what is kept (black), what has disappeared (yellow), and what has been added (red). The same color code is then used for the preservation project.

Concretely, the survey takes place on-site with the students divided into groups and supervised by the instructors. It comprises two visits. The goal of the first is to make an initial observation of the studied object and draw up the most complete and precise inventory possible. Once back at the studio, this survey is geometrically reconstructed in three dimensions.[9] The second visit allows the teams to complete any missing information, with the aim of developing and then finalizing the work. This time spent inside the building (from three to five days on average), examining it from every angle in order to discover its finest details, is undoubtedly an important and irreplaceable learning experience for these future architects. Thus, each of them will undoubtedly long remember the days and nights spent at La Tourette observing, over the course of the solar cycle and in all sorts of weather, the metamorphoses of the convent's architecture and spaces, understanding the rhythms dictated by the monastic liturgy of the Dominican brothers still present, and grasping the intimate and profound life of the monastery; in short, making the survey a true architectural "encounter." At the end of this process, the knowledge thus accumulated is redeveloped in the form of axonometric drawings highlighting the different constructive subsystems—load-bearing structures, envelopes, partitions, networks of utilities and equipment—which allow for addressing aspects that are as diverse as thermal and acoustic comfort, natural and artificial light, security and compliance with current standards, changes in use, etc. To all that we can add the question of the site (development of surroundings and relationship to the territory) and the genesis of the object, which must be situated in its historical, architectural, and urban context, in the work of the actors who designed and built it, and as an economic and social resource. Finally, the building is reproduced in the form of differently scaled models and drawings at a scale of 1:50 (plans, sections, elevation), which show the original state as well as the alterations and transformations that have taken place over time.[10]

6

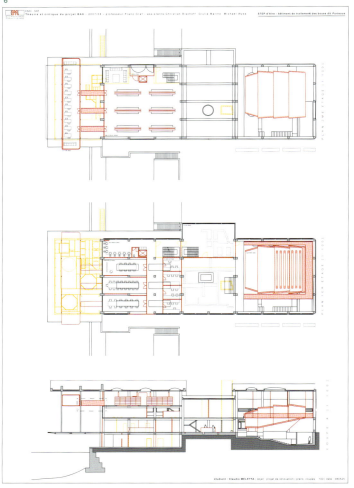

7

TEACHING THE PRESERVATION   58

8

The preservation project as an exploration of the built object

It is only once this first immersive phase is over that the actual *intervention project* begins. These two stages are inseparable, coming one after the other almost naturally, and the questions raised during the survey phase find a coherent and appropriate answer in the design phase. In fact, it is through the analysis of the functional and distribution capacities of the building, its composition and both its physical and immaterial characteristics that its potential for use emerges, no matter the type of intervention, whether simple maintenance or a complete restructuring. To carry out this analysis, there is an extensive range of strategies available to the students—preservation, refurbishment, structural reinforcement, rehabilitation, redevelopment, new addition, heightening, adjacent construction, etc.—and that furthermore can be combined within one project. With regard to the (architectural) programs on offer, although they may be considered academic, they nevertheless always seek to remain grounded in the reality stemming from a needs analysis. This marriage between reality and the as-yet-unbuilt enables us to take the architectural object as far as it can go, while finding a clear balance between what is possible and what is desirable. The deliberate choice to develop projects near or even within Modernist icons, as we have done many times over, is initially and essentially an exploratory method in service to the educational aims of the project and not of some iconoclastic credo.

During the survey phase, work is mostly done in groups, but this gradually develops into individual or pair work. The work progresses through a series of "exercises" that enable

6 Model of the Ronchamp chapel (1:100), created by students in collaboration with the EPFL model studio, 2019
7 Redevelopment project transforming the "Porteous" building at the Aïre wastewater treatment plant into a cultural space, 2008
8 Redevelopment project transforming the depot at the Vernets Center, Geneva Public Roads Department, into an artists' residence and studios, 2010

11 The recent crisis due to the Covid pandemic considerably reduced the options for off-site visits, without, however, calling into question the principle of off-site teaching and site surveys, which forms the teaching basis for the preservation project. The choice that was made in 2020 to focus on sites located only in Switzerland meant that we were not concerned by the inopportune border closures that the pandemic created.

different aspects of the planned building to be addressed in succession: typology, structure, building envelopes, materiality, comfort, etc. Each new topic is connected to the previous one, thus providing a procedure that the students can later employ. Among the various exercises developed by the studio, the "switch" activity, where students exchange and comment on someone else's work, is particularly well-received! Although the act of letting go is initially disconcerting, the experience provides them with a new, uncompromising, and external point of view on their own work, which helps them to improve. Moreover, throughout the semester or academic year, the students benefit from theoretical contributions in the form of lectures on subjects related to the studio themes, as well as "off-site teaching" (visits, study trips) that allows them not only to see and discover architecture but also to meet people who are attuned to contemporary issues of heritage preservation. These moments are always highly productive from a didactic point of view and are therefore indispensable for the students' learning process.[11]

With knowledge of the architectural object gained throughout the survey phase, the students learn to identify and distinguish the "hard," or intangible, parts from the "soft" parts, whose metaphorical plasticity authorizes all sorts of transformations, as long as they are qualitative and justified. In the preservation of architectural works, it is first of all the work itself that dictates the rules, which then considerably limit the possibilities. But is it truly possible to design without constraints? We don't think so. We believe that by applying a degree of resistance to the analysis process (and therefore to the material), the existing structure

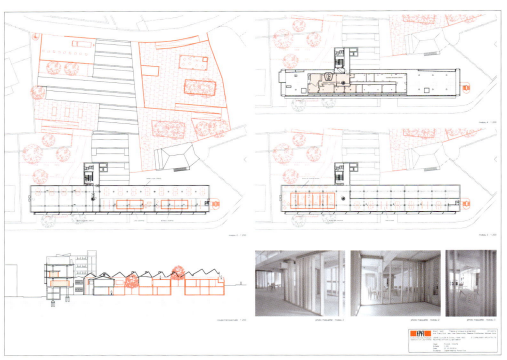

9

12 Looking for architectural images online is a common practice for students in search of inspiration. It is, unfortunately, not an effective method for preservation and often restricts those who use it to a hermetic and self-governing language, with no relation to the existing site.

guides the project designer towards more subtle and appropriate solutions, a far cry from the formal and slightly vain gesticulations of a certain strain of contemporary architecture. By forcing students to confront and embrace it, the existing site encourages them to continue the construction with the same distributive and compositional mindset, rigorously and in a critical and thoughtful manner. Far from reducing or blocking creativity, it stimulates it even further, until unexpected solutions arise that would not have been thought of otherwise. As such, the existing site is a great source of invention, a catalyst that can offer an unexpected variety of design possibilities. Even as professionals, we are always surprised by this and invariably admire the multiple and fresh approaches students come up with, which are always incredibly diverse. This is, in fact, one of the studio's objectives: to demonstrate that it is possible, starting with a known situation and a problem that has been correctly formulated, to obtain a wide range of relevant architectural solutions, each developed with its own intrinsic logic and with the greatest respect for what is already there.

Beyond the personal bias that we each have, the issue of an architectural language is another major and constant preoccupation for those wishing to prolong the life of existing architectural objects. In accordance with the prevailing attitude in the world of heritage preservation, we immediately wish to state our refusal to invent a language that is too personal and that does not have any true connection to the work in question.[12] Once again, the knowledge and appreciation of the qualities of the existing site will dictate the path to follow, without dogmatism or any a priori. In preservation therefore, we will happily call upon imitation or analogy and bring up the issue of copying and the authenticity of the image, or, quite the opposite, to challenge or reverse it, judging its relevance in view of what exists. Once again, there is not one formally correct choice. As the project advances, inspiration occurs, allowing the adoption of intermediary and sometime hybrid approaches stemming from the existence of several modes at once. The design of a preservation project therefore derives its very richness from these many and varied intersections, which are combined with a certain element of restraint. Clearly the project is not there to seek the limelight or use existing sites as a foil. It is instead a question of accentuating the latter while making good use of its qualities in order to better transpose them into the design. The drawn plans document such a stance, which is not at all, or barely, spectacular. And yet, it is a form of humility that is not lacking in ambition. Such is the state of mind and conviction with which we have been teaching the project of preservation for all these years at the EPFL.

9 Conversion project transforming the Claude & Duval factory in Saint-Dié into a design school and annex for the Centre des archives d'architecture du XXᵉ siècle, 2014

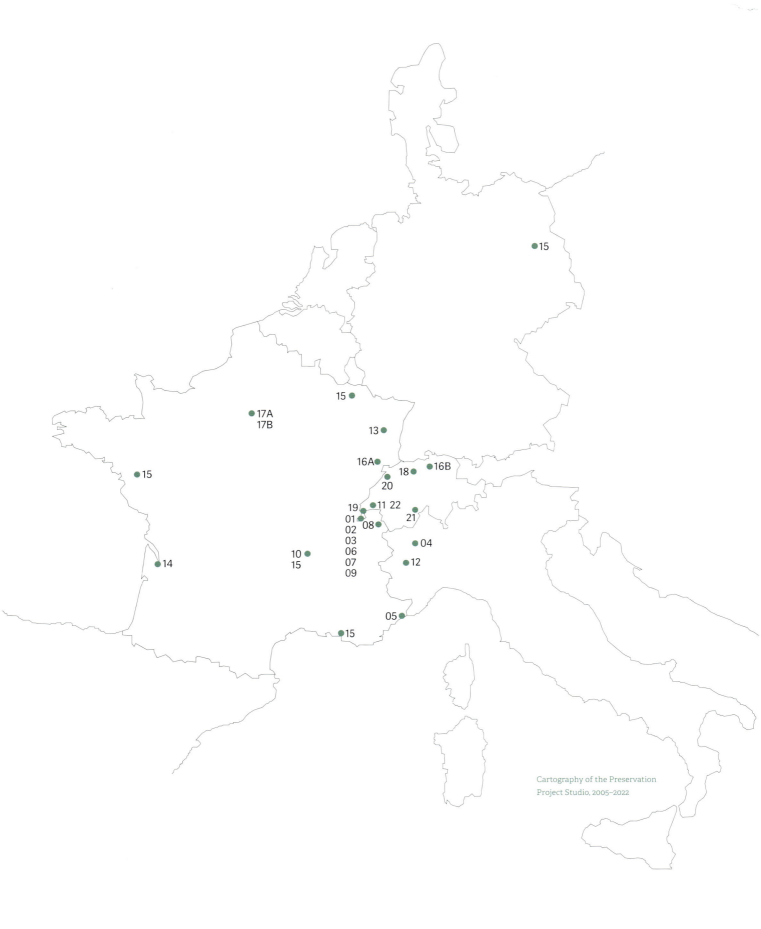

Cartography of the Preservation Project Studio, 2005–2022

TEACHING THE PRESERVATION   62

LIST OF ARCHITECTURAL WORKS AND TOPICS IN THE PROJECT STUDIO

01_Winter 2005
The Rue du Stand sports halls in Geneva
Sports halls, Rue du Stand, Geneva, 1951–1953
Paul Waltenspühl, architect

02_Fall 2007
Recycl'H2O – Past and future of a water treatment plant
Aïre wastewater treatment plant (administrative building), Geneva, 1962–1967
Georges Brera & Peter Böcklin, architects

03_Spring 2008
Recycl'H2O—Past and future of a water treatment plant
Aïre wastewater treatment plant (Porteous building), Geneva, 1962–1967
Georges Brera & Peter Böcklin, architects

04_Fall 2008
Recycl'AU=Q-W—Redevelopment of an industrial structure for the Olivetti company
Thermoelectric power plant, Ivrea, 1956–1959
Eduardo Vittoria, architect

05_Spring 2009
LC E-1027—Building alongside
Villa E-1027, Roquebrune-Cap-Martin, 1926–1929 / Cabanon Le Corbusier, Roquebrune-Cap-Martin, 1952
Eileen Gray & Jean Badovici, architects / Le Corbusier, architect

06_Fall 2009
VOIR.IE—Redevelopment of a public building
Vernets Center, Geneva Public Roads Department (warehouse), Geneva, 1964–1967
Jean-Pierre Dom & François Maurice, architects

07_Spring 2010
VOIR.IE—Redevelopment of a public building
Vernets Center, Geneva Public Roads Department (administrative building and depot), Geneva, 1964–1967
Jean-Pierre Dom & François Maurice, architects

08_Fall 2010
FLAINE—Renovation and extension of a hotel
Winter sports resort (Les Gradins Gris and Le Totem hotels), Flaine, 1969–1971
Marcel Breuer, architect

09_Spring 2011
CERN—Redevelopment and extension of the power and heating plant
CERN power and heating plant, Meyrin, 1954–1960
Rudolf & Peter Steiger, architects

10_Fall 2011
FIR UN—Redevelopment of the Firminy Unité d'habitation nursery school
Unité d'habitation, Firminy, 1959–1967
Le Corbusier & André Wogenscky, architects

11_Spring 2012
EPFL—Extension of the École polytechnique fédérale de Lausanne campus
Buildings from the first stage of EPFL, Lausanne, 1970–1982
Jacob Zweifel, Heinrich Strickler & Associates, architects

12_Fall 2012 / Spring 2013
RIUSO?—Palazzo del Lavoro
Palazzo del Lavoro, Turin, 1959–1961
Pier Luigi Nervi, architect and engineer

13_Fall 2013 / Spring 2014
CD SD—Redevelopment and extension to the Claude & Duval factory in Saint-Dié
Claude & Duval factory, Saint-Dié, 1946–1950
Le Corbusier, architect

14_Fall 2014 / Spring 2015
PESSAC—Conservation and extension of a housing complex
Quartiers modernes Frugès, Pessac, 1924–1927
Le Corbusier & Pierre Jeanneret, architects

15_Fall 2015 / Spring 2016
M.MI NRE BRF FIR CHA—Les Unités d'habitation: analyses and transformations
Unités d'habitation, Marseille / Rezé-lès-Nantes / Briey-en-Forêt / Firminy / Berlin, 1945–1967
Le Corbusier, architect

16A-B_Fall 2016 / Spring 2017
RON LC ZH—Two Le Corbusier sites in development
Chapelle Notre-Dame du Haut, Ronchamp, 1950–1955 / Maison de l'Homme, Zurich, 1961–1967
Le Corbusier, architect

17A-B_Fall 2017 / Spring 2018
CU CUB—Le Corbusier at the Cité internationale universitaire de Paris
Pavillon suisse, Paris, 1929–1933 / Maison du Brésil, Paris, 1953–1959
Le Corbusier & Pierre Jeanneret, architects / Le Corbusier & Lucio Costa, architects

18_Fall 2018 / Spring 2019
FRANZISKUHAUS—Conversion of a brutalist structure
Franziskushaus, Dulliken, 1964–1969
Otto Glaus, architect

19_Fall 2019 / Spring 2020
SFRA Changins – Extension to the "shared space"
Swiss Federal Agricultural Research Station, Changins, 1969–1975
Heidi & Peter Wenger, architects

20_Fall 2020 / Spring 2021
CIP Tramelan—Transformation and extension
Centre interrégional de perfectionnement, Tramelan, 1979–1991
Heidi & Peter Wenger, architects

21_Fall 2021
POSTGARAGE—Conversion of the Postgarage
Postgarage, Brig, 1966–1974
Heidi & Peter Wenger, architects

22_Spring 2022
VIDY 67—Extension to the wastewater treatment service building in Lausanne
Wastewater treatment service building in Vidy, Lausanne, 1963–1967
Jean-Pierre Desarzens, architect

THE STUDIOS

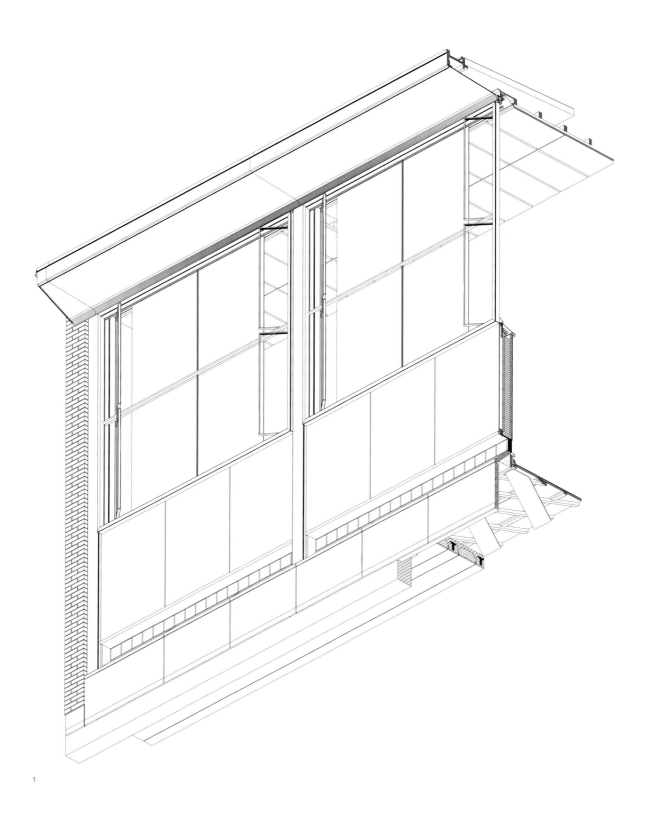

1 Axonometric construction drawing (cutaway view) of the façade of the large sports hall (view from below)
Following page Project models (1:50) and studio poster

TEACHING THE PRESERVATION 66

01_RUE DU STAND

Winter 2005–2006

Preservation and extension
of the sports halls
Rue du Stand
Geneva, 1951–1953

Paul Waltenspühl
architect

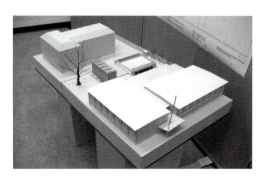

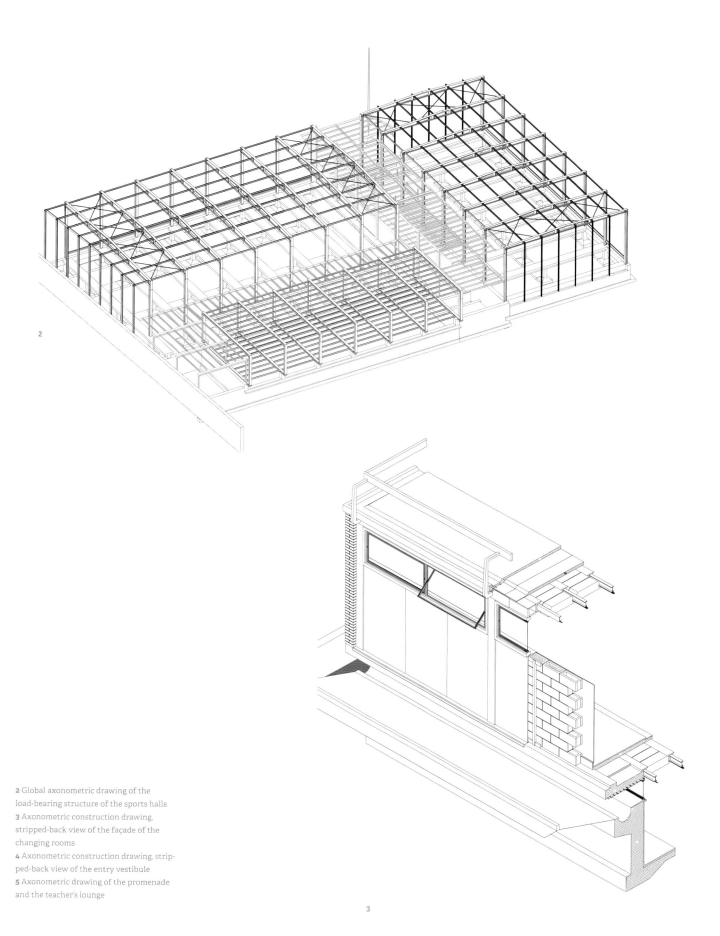

2 Global axonometric drawing of the load-bearing structure of the sports halls
3 Axonometric construction drawing, stripped-back view of the façade of the changing rooms
4 Axonometric construction drawing, stripped-back view of the entry vestibule
5 Axonometric drawing of the promenade and the teacher's lounge

TEACHING THE PRESERVATION 68

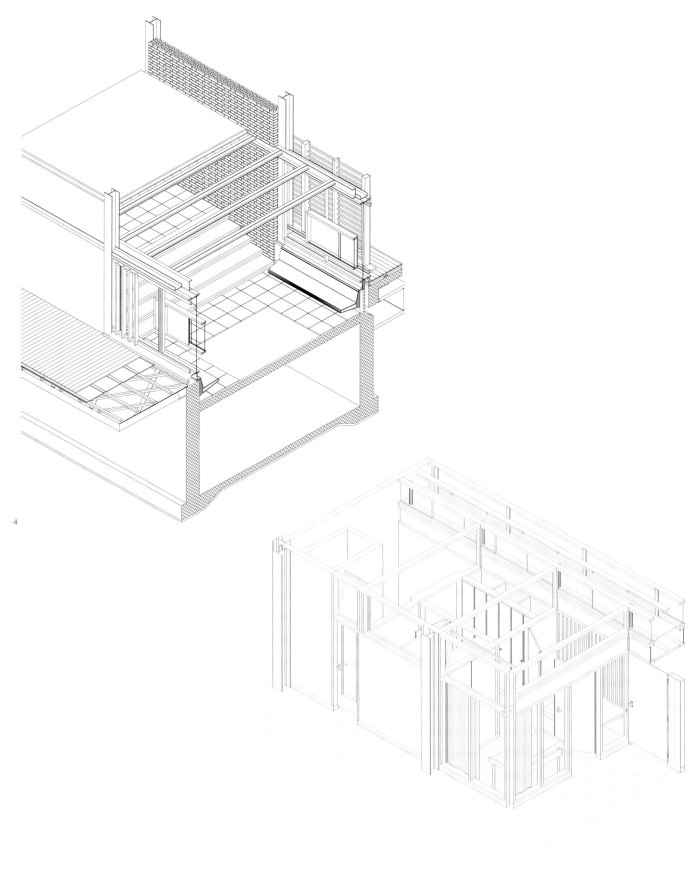

4

5

69 THE STUDIO, OR TEACHING THE PRESERVATION PROJECT

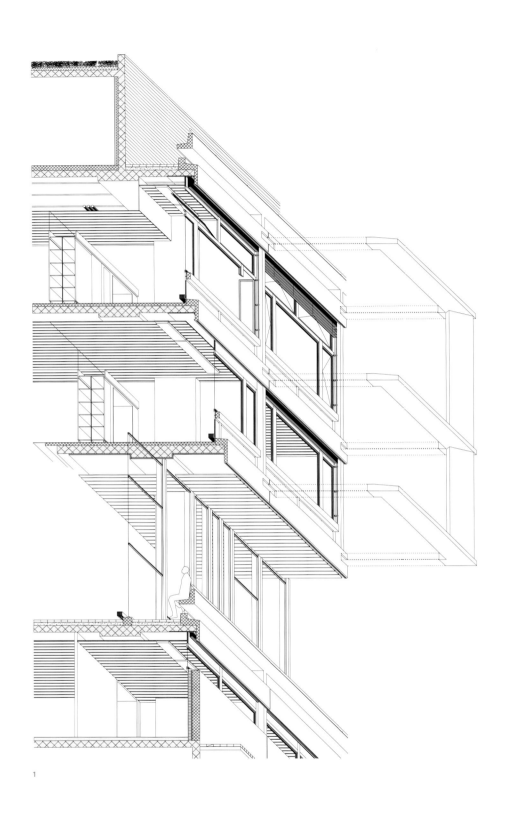

1

1 Axonometric construction drawing of the south façade of the administrative building
Following page Project models (1:100) and studio poster

TEACHING THE PRESERVATION   70

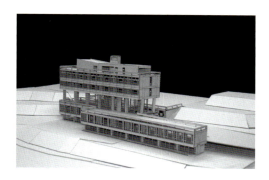

02_STEP AÏRE 1

Fall 2007

Redevelopment of the Aïre wastewater treatment plant (administrative building) Geneva, 1962–1967

Georges Brera & Peter Böcklin architects

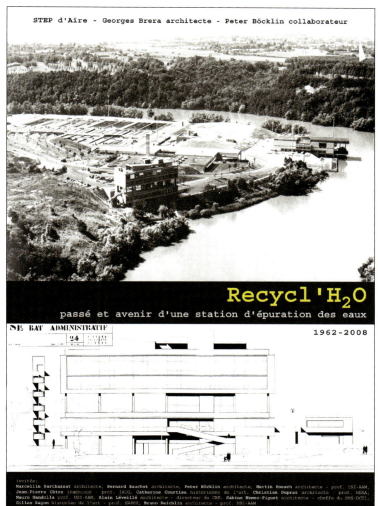

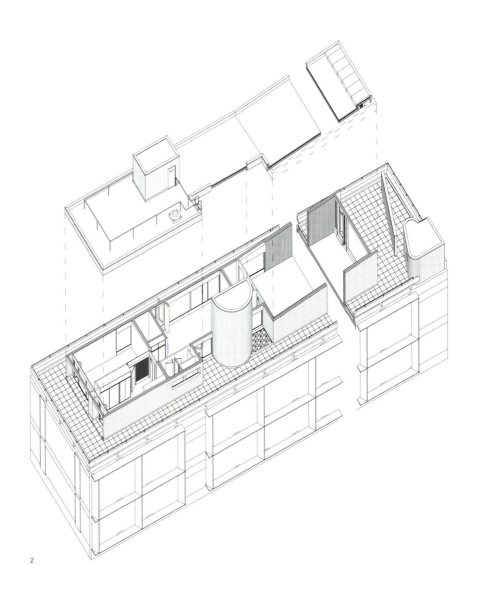

2

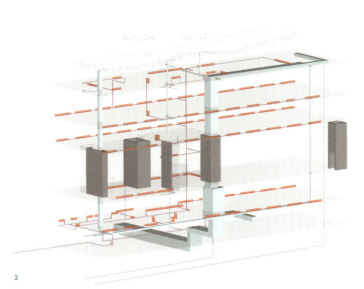

3

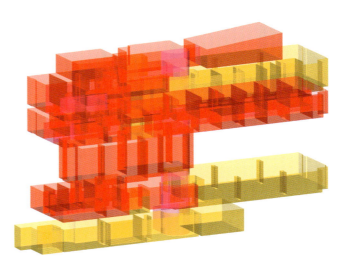

4

TEACHING THE PRESERVATION 72

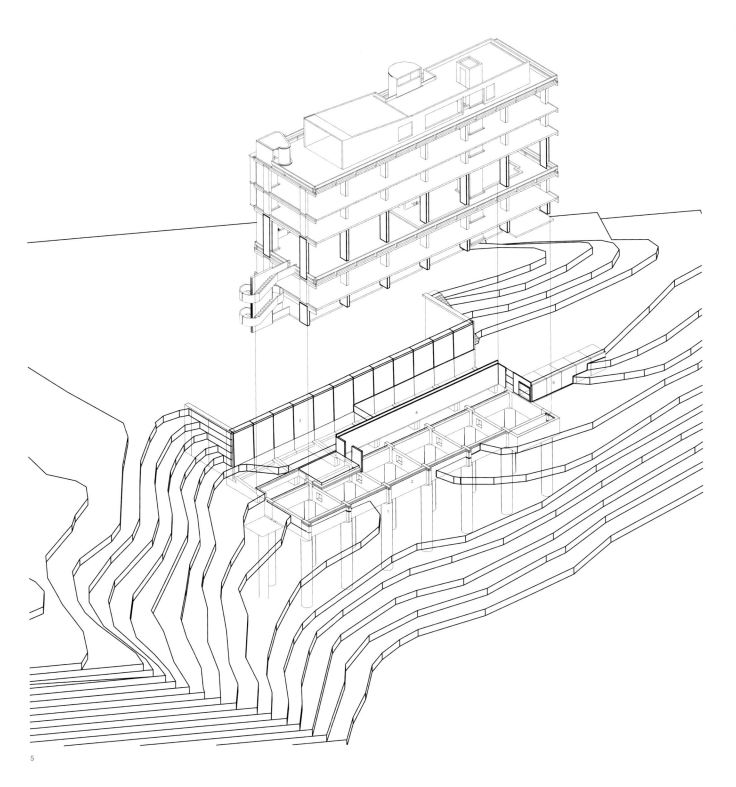

2 Axonometric drawing, exploded view of the attic
3 Axonometric drawing of the heating and ventilation system
4 Axonometric drawings of the different kinds of heated spaces in the building
5 Axonometric construction drawing, exploded view of the foundations

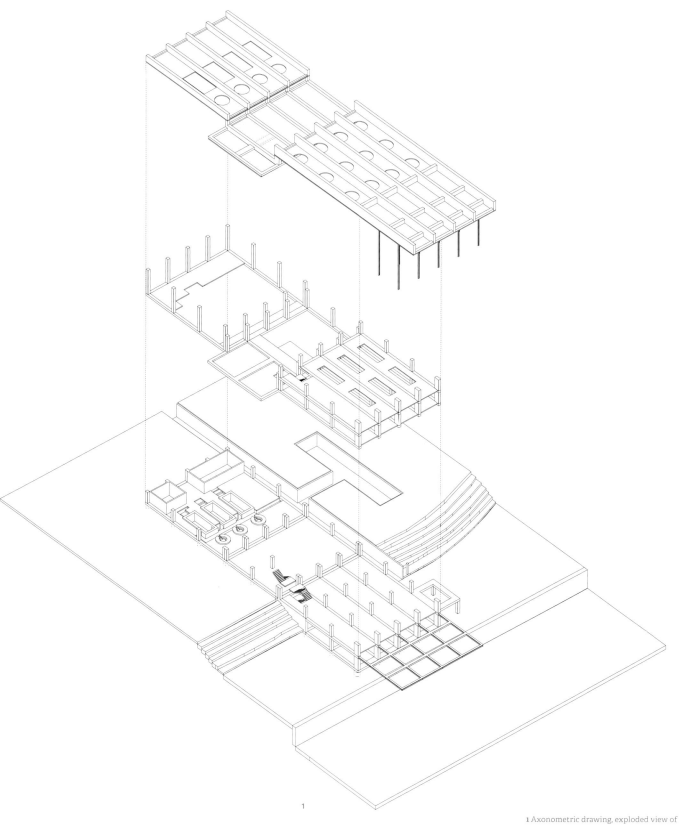

1 Axonometric drawing, exploded view of the load-bearing structure of Porteous
Following page Project models (1:100) and studio poster

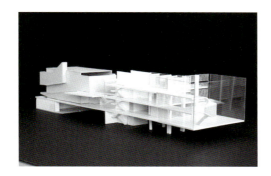
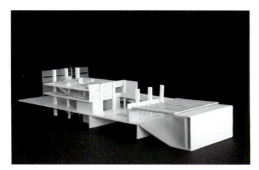
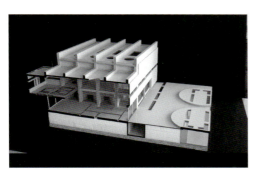

03_STEP AÏRE 2

Spring 2008

Redevelopment of the Aïre wastewater treatment plant (Porteous building) Geneva, 1962–1967

Georges Brera & Peter Böcklin architects

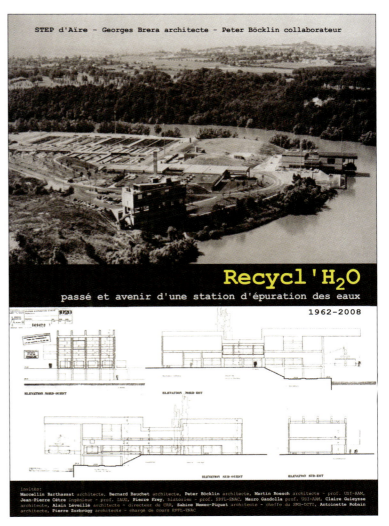

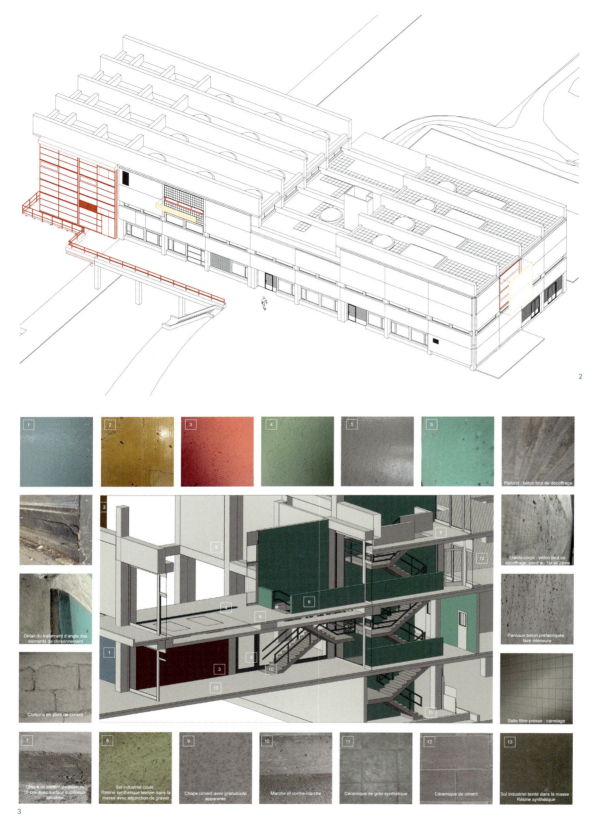

TEACHING THE PRESERVATION 76

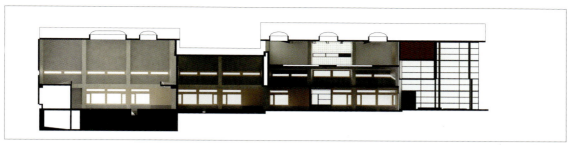

Coupe longitudinale Sud-Ouest | 1:100

Plan niveau 1 | 1:100

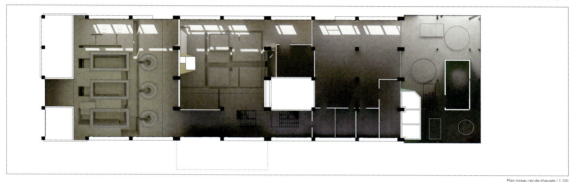

Plan niveau rez-de-chaussée | 1:100

Rendus photoréalistes

Les plans et la coupe ci-dessus ont été obtenus après modélisation en 3 dimensions du bâtiment. Des rendus photoréalistes ont ensuite été calculés avec AutoCAD, pour la date du 20 mars 2008 à 14h00. Cette technique permet ainsi de prédire de manière assez réaliste les qualités de la lumière à une date et une heure donnée. Il faut toutefois souligner que cette technique est onéreuse: il faut que la modélisation soit au plus près de la réalité et surtout le temps de calcul des rendus est très élevé.

Mesure photométrique de la lumière

Les trois plans suivants indiquent, sur une double échelle, la quantité de lumière aux trois niveaux du bâtiment. Ils doivent permettre, en un coup d'œil, de déterminer les zones qui bénéficient insuffisamment ou excessivement de lumière naturelle. L'échelle de représentation est établie de manière à ce que les zones à 500 Lux (quantité optimale de lumière pour une place de travail) ressortent en blanc. L'absence de lumière, à 0 Lux, est signifiée en noir, alors que la valeur maximale, l'éclairement extérieur (7 mars 2008 à 10h30 = 22'800 Lux) est indiqué en rouge.

Toutes les mesures ont été prises à environ 80cm du plancher, hauteur approximative d'une table. Tous les points de mesure sont inscrits sur une trame d'une demi-portée entre deux poteaux. Ces points correspondent au centre de chaque rectangle du plan. Les hachures obliques représentent les zones pour lesquelles aucune mesure n'a été prise.

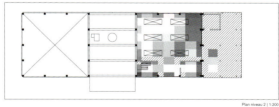

Plan niveau 2 | 1:200

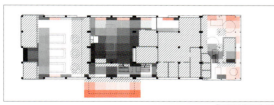

Plan niveau rez-de-chaussée | 1:200

Plan niveau 1 | 1:200

4

2 Global axonometric drawing of Porteous with transformations indicated
3 Axonometric drawing showing the materiality and the polychrome elements of the interior spaces of Porteous
4 Natural light study, plan drawing, and cross-section of interior spaces

77   THE STUDIO, OR TEACHING THE PRESERVATION PROJECT

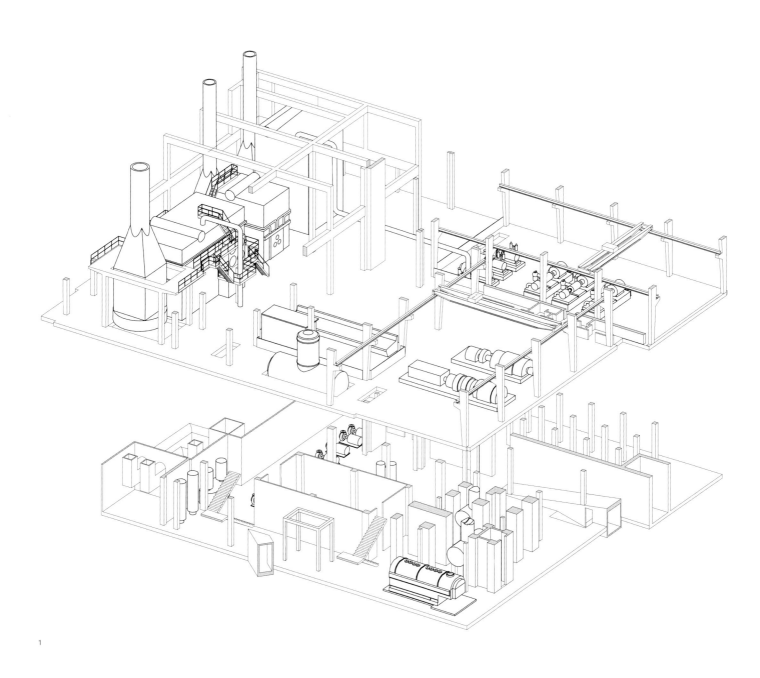

1 Axonometric drawing, exploded view of technical equipment of the thermoelectric power plant
Following page Project models (1:50) and studio poster

TEACHING THE PRESERVATION 78

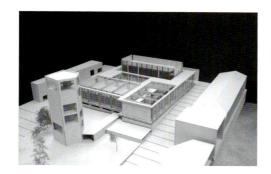

04_IVREA

Fall 2008

Redevelopment of the Olivetti thermoelectric power plant
Ivrea, 1956–1959

Eduardo Vittoria
architect

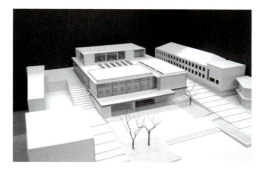
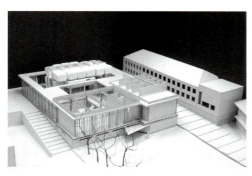
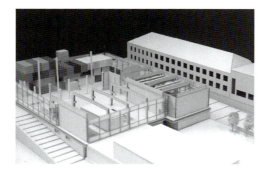

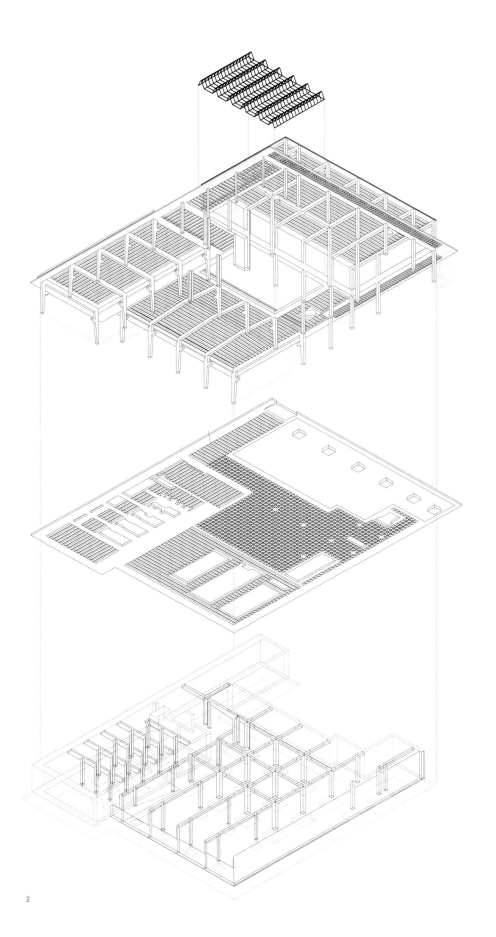

2 Axonometric drawing, exploded view of the load-bearing structure of the power plant (view from below)
3 Axonometric construction drawing showing the angle of the north and east façades (view from below)
4 Axonometric drawing of the interior partitions of the control room (view from below)

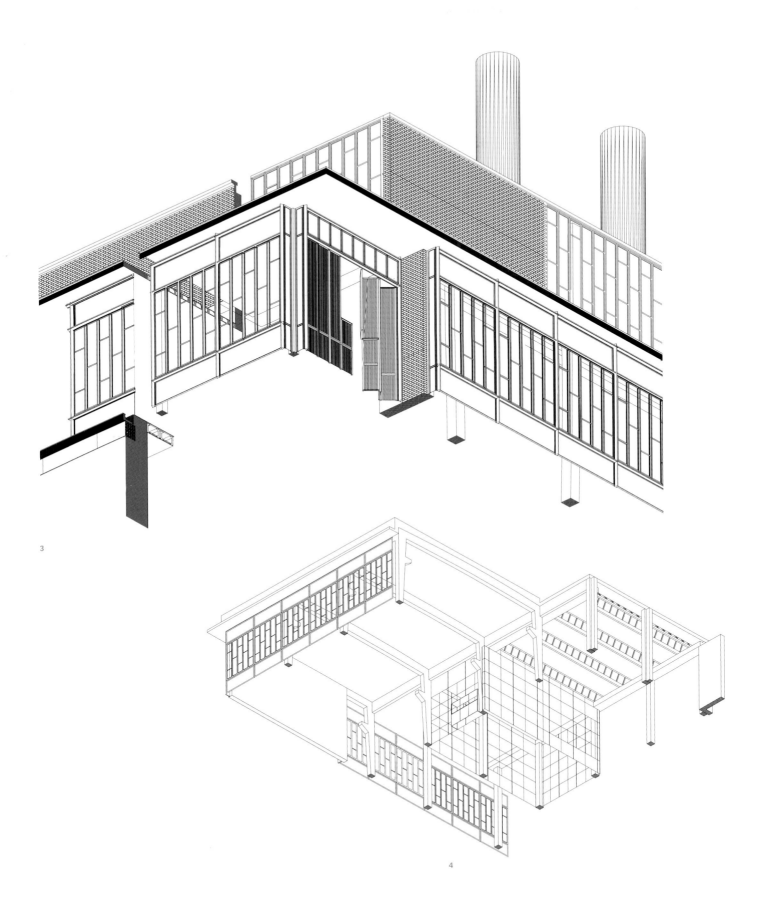

81 THE STUDIO, OR TEACHING THE PRESERVATION PROJECT

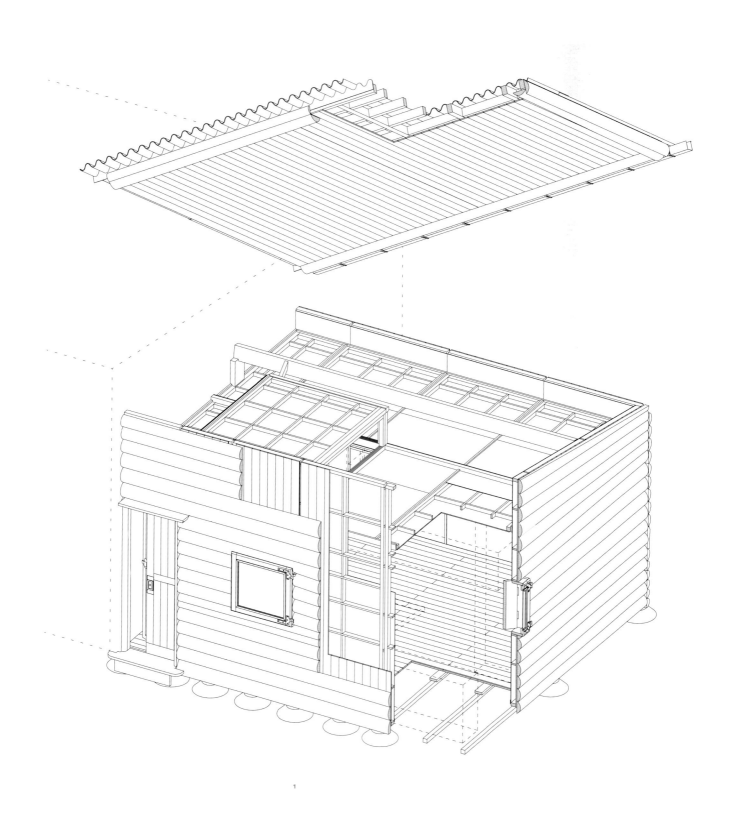

1 Axonometric construction drawing, exploded view of the Cabanon
Following page Project models (1:50) and studio poster

TEACHING THE PRESERVATION 82

05_LC E-1027

Spring 2009

Villa E-1027 and Cabanon Le Corbusier:
Building alongside
Roquebrune-Cap-Martin,
1926–1929 and 1952

Eileen Gray & Jean Badovici
Le Corbusier
architects

83 THE STUDIO, OR TEACHING THE PRESERVATION PROJECT

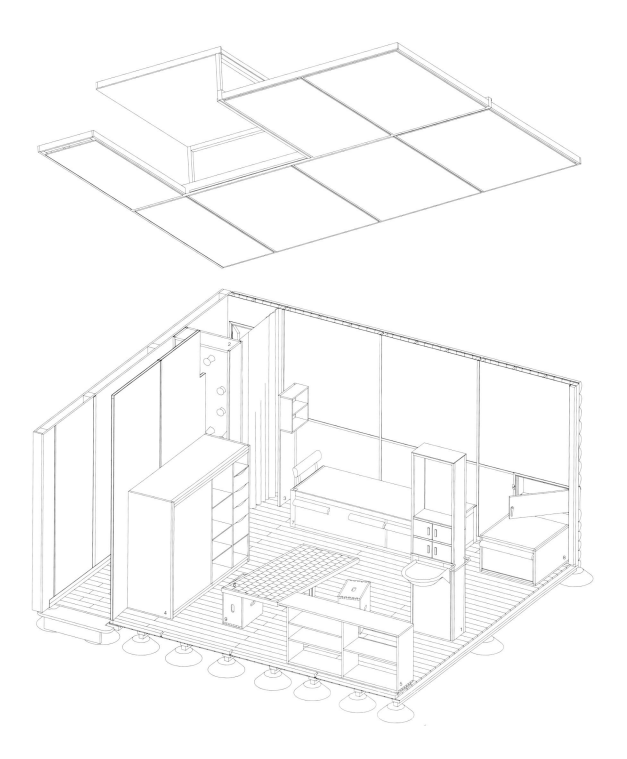

2 Axonometric drawing of the interior of the Cabanon with its furnishings
3 Global axonometric drawing of Villa E-1027
4 Detail drawing of the living room's sliding window and its solar shading device (view from interior)

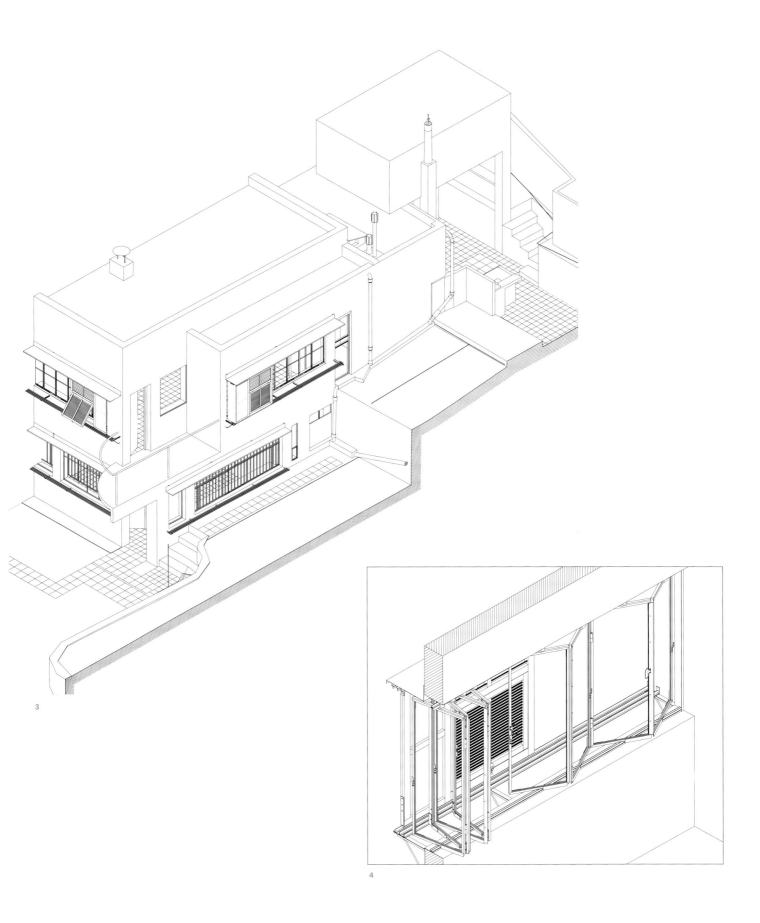

3

4

85 THE STUDIO, OR TEACHING THE PRESERVATION PROJECT

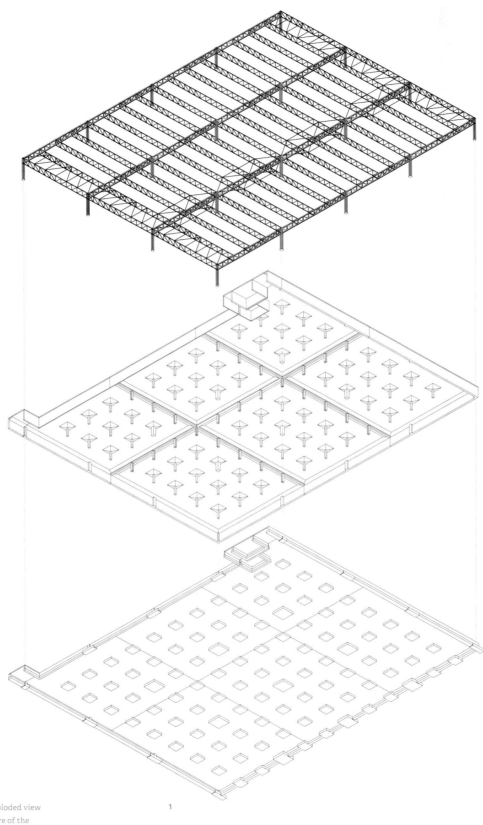

1 Axonometric drawing, exploded view of the load-bearing structure of the warehouse
Following page Project models (1:200) and studio poster

TEACHING THE PRESERVATION   86

06_VOIRIE 1

Fall 2009

Redevelopment of the Vernets Center, Geneva Public Roads Department (warehouse)
Geneva, 1964–1967

Jean-Pierre Dom & François Maurice architects

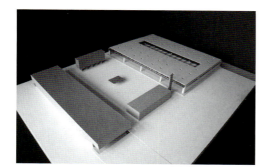
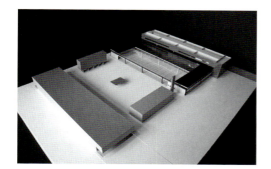
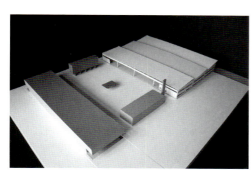
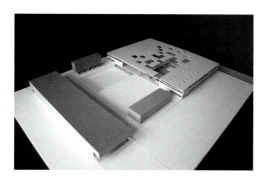
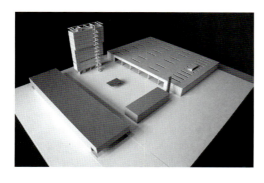
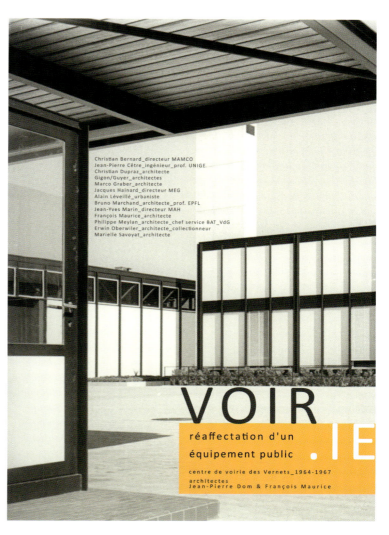

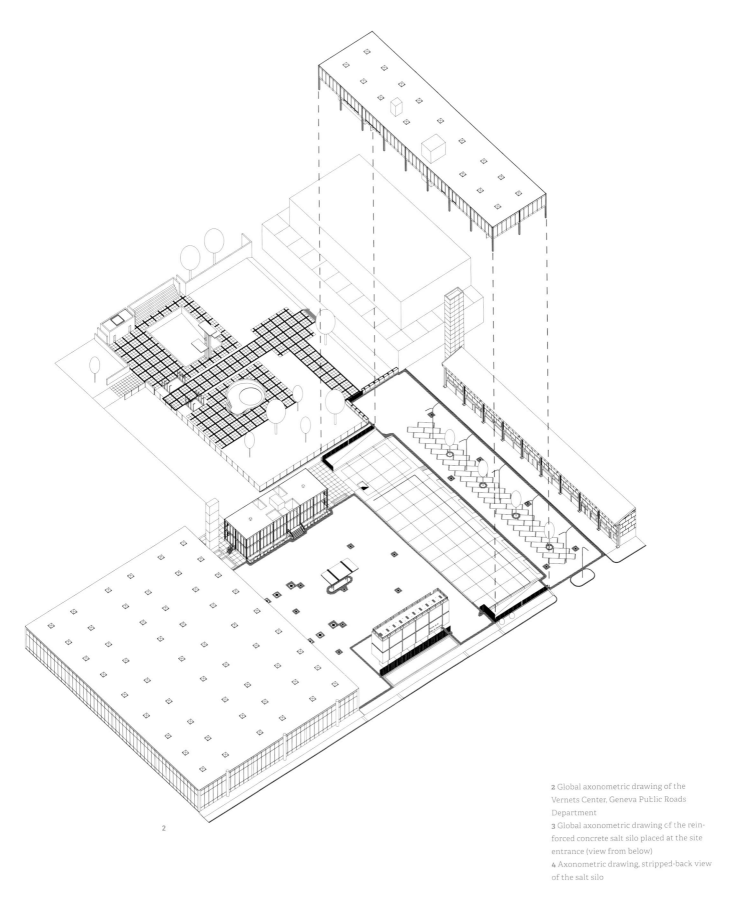

2 Global axonometric drawing of the Vernets Center, Geneva Public Roads Department
3 Global axonometric drawing of the reinforced concrete salt silo placed at the site entrance (view from below)
4 Axonometric drawing, stripped-back view of the salt silo

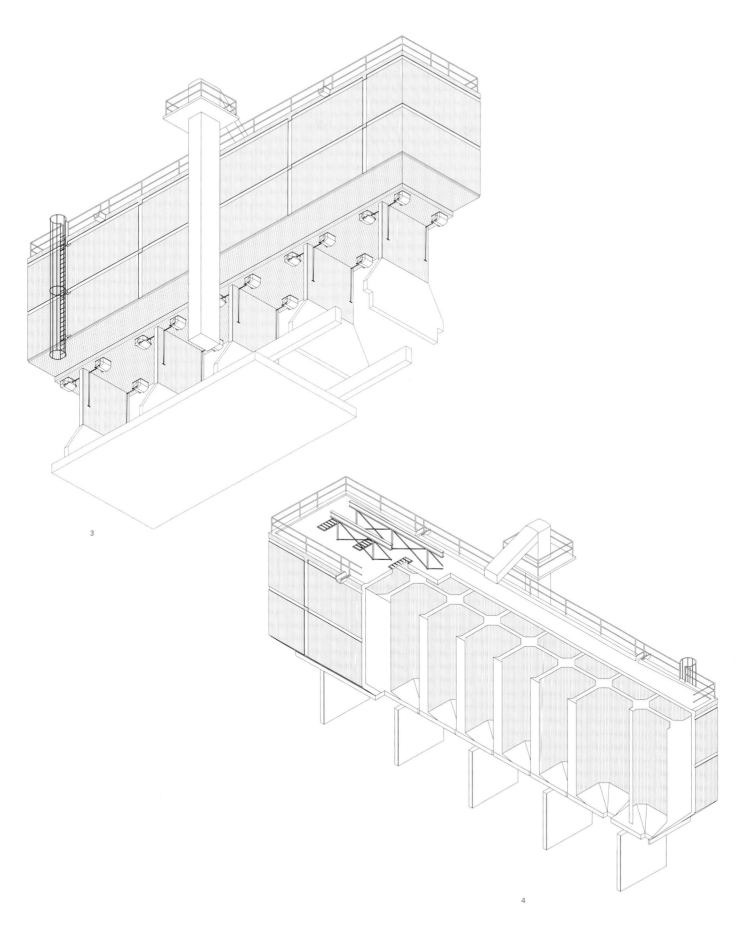

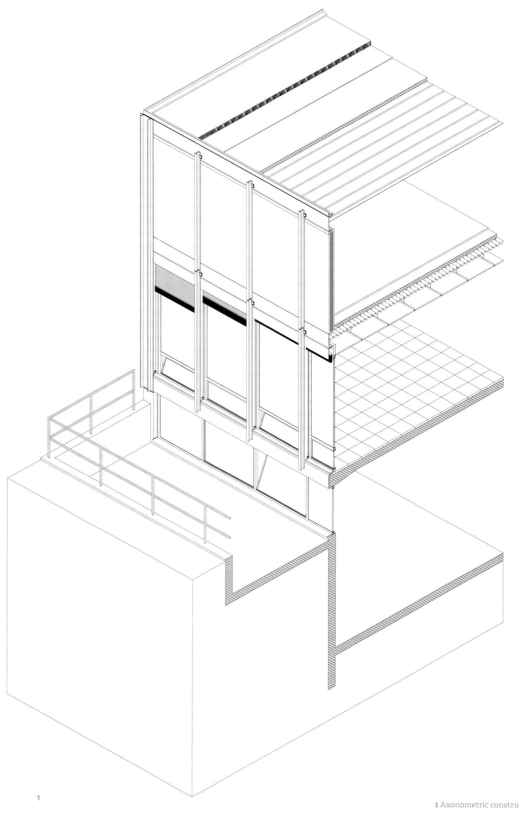

1 Axonometric construction drawing, stripped-back view of a fragment of the façade of the administrative building
Following page Project models (1:200) and studio poster

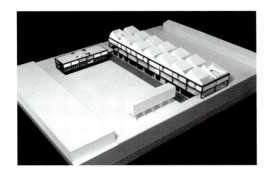
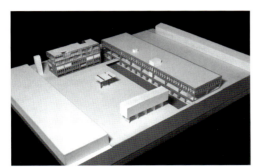
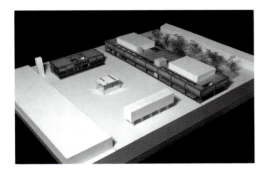
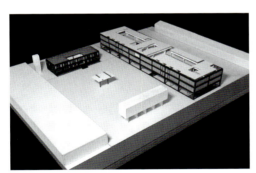
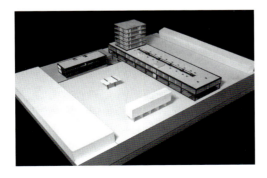

07_VOIRIE 2

Spring 2010

Redevelopment of the Vernets Center,
Geneva Public Roads Department
(administrative building and depot)
Geneva, 1964–1967

Jean-Pierre Dom & François Maurice
architects

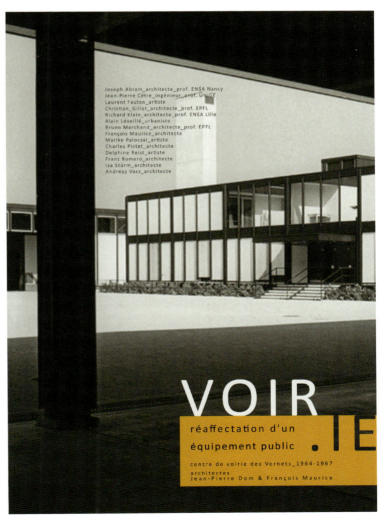

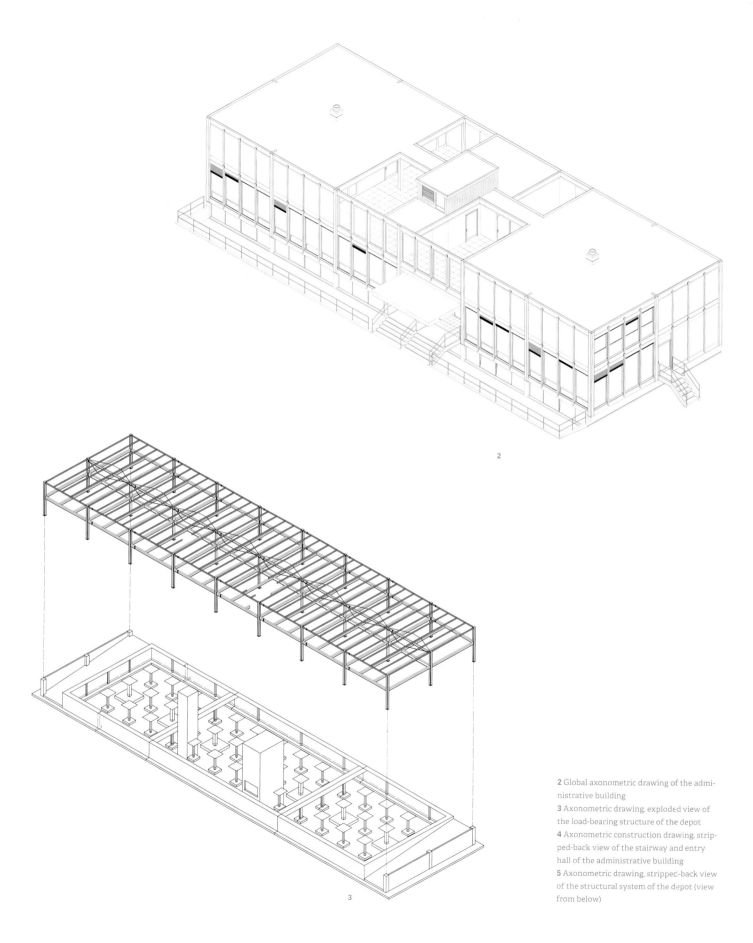

2 Global axonometric drawing of the administrative building
3 Axonometric drawing, exploded view of the load-bearing structure of the depot
4 Axonometric construction drawing, stripped-back view of the stairway and entry hall of the administrative building
5 Axonometric drawing, stripped-back view of the structural system of the depot (view from below)

TEACHING THE PRESERVATION

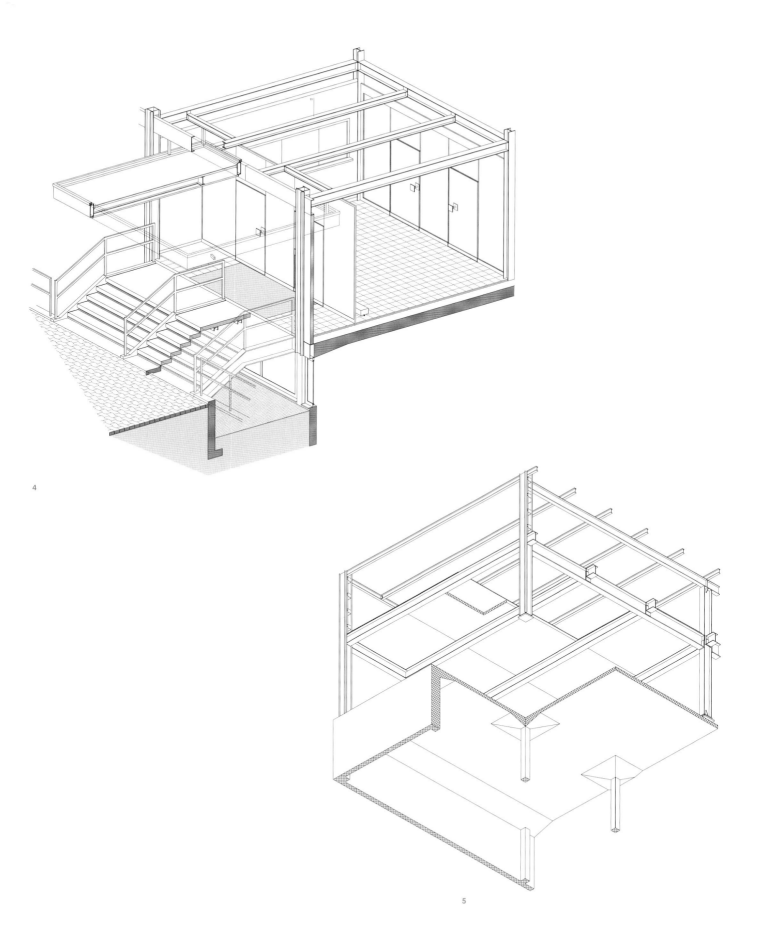

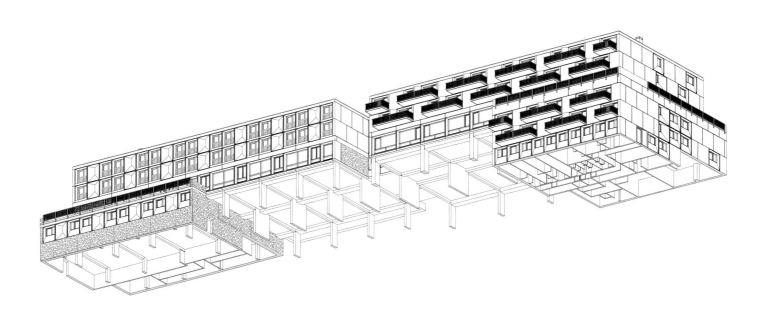

1 Global axonometric drawing of the building housing the hotels "Les Gradins Gris" and "Le Totem" (view from below)
Following page Project models (1:200) and studio poster

TEACHING THE PRESERVATION 94

08_FLAINE

Fall 2010

Renovation and extension of
Les Gradins Gris and Le Totem hotels
Flaine, 1969–1971

Marcel Breuer
architect

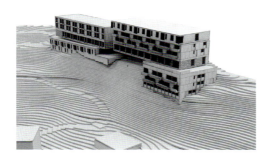

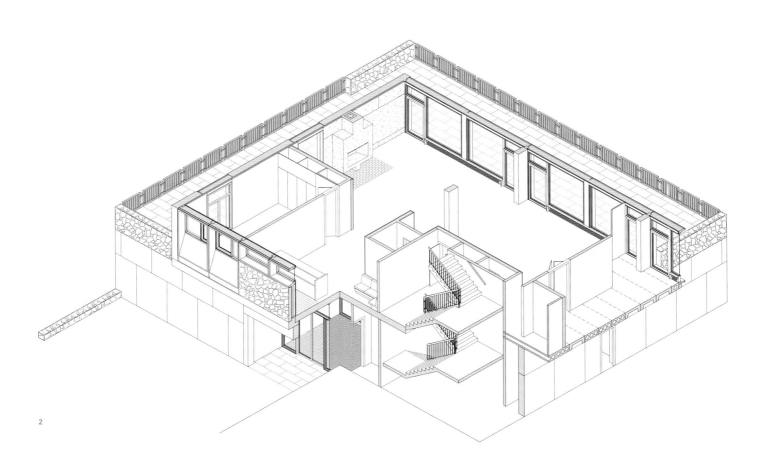

2

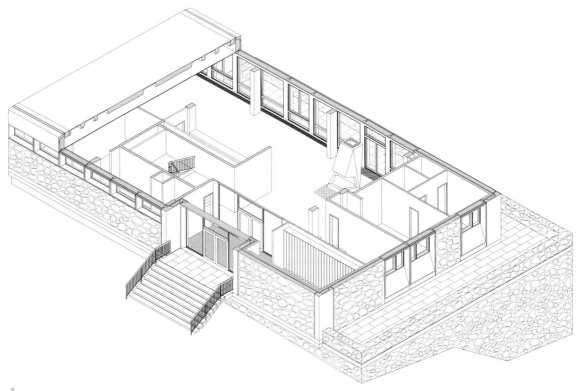

3

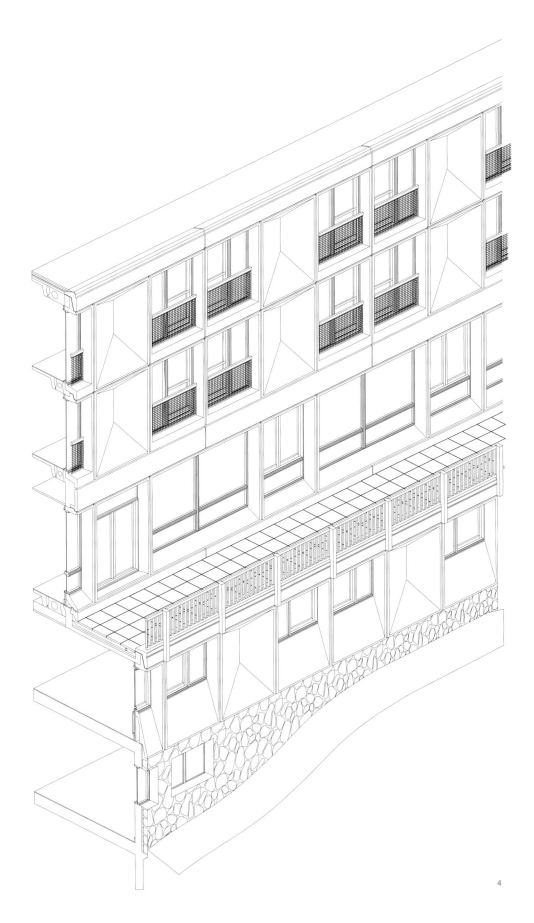

2 Axonometric drawing, stripped-back view of the entrance and the living room of the hotel "Le Totem"
3 Axonometric drawing, stripped-back view of the entrance and reception area of the hotel "Les Gradins Gris"
4 Axonometric drawing, stripped-back view of the south façade of the hotel "Les Gradins Gris"

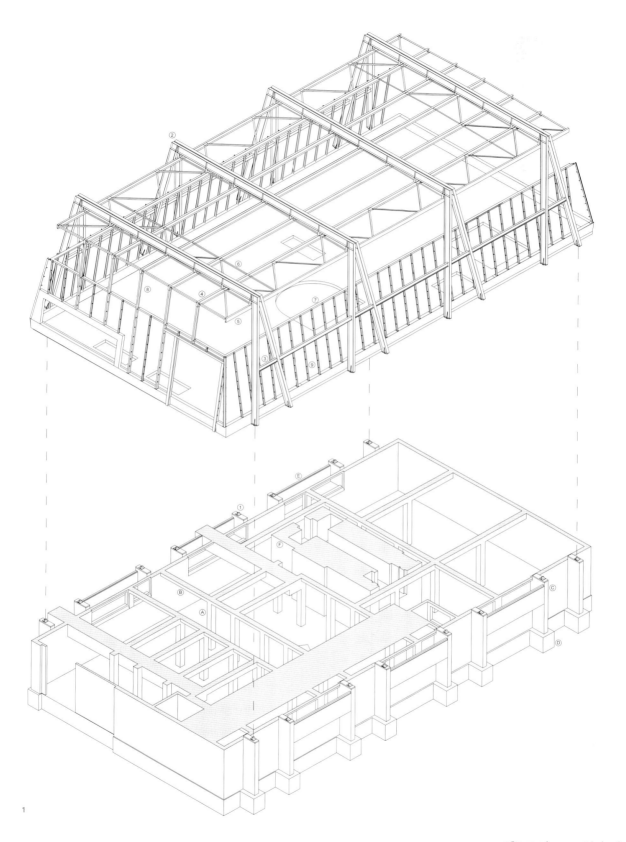

1 Structural axonometric drawing of the thermoelectric power plant
Following page Project models (1:100e) and studio poster

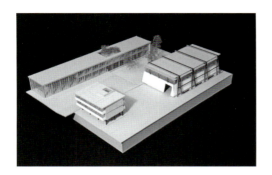
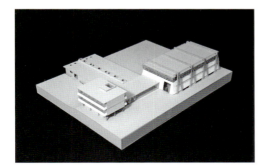
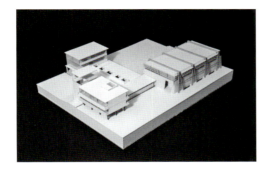
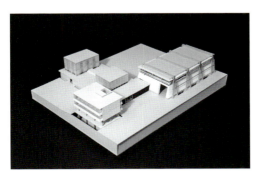
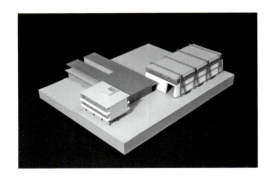

09_CERN

Spring 2011

Redevelopment and extension
of the CERN power
and heating plant
Meyrin, 1954–1960

Rudolf & Peter Steiger
architects

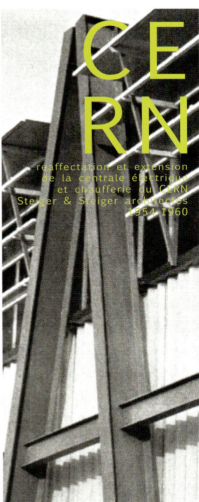

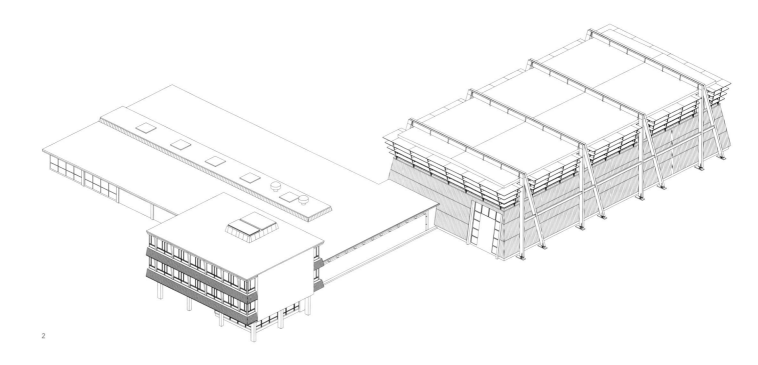

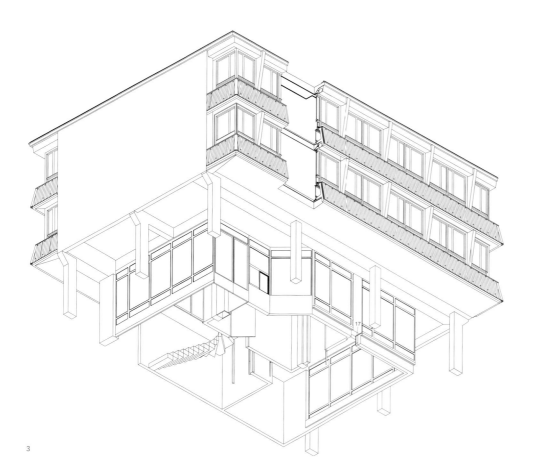

2 Global axonometric drawing of the CERN entrance buildings (administrative building, studios, and thermoelectric plant)
3 Axonometric drawing, stripped-back view of administrative building (view from below)
4 Study of natural (day) and artificial (night) light

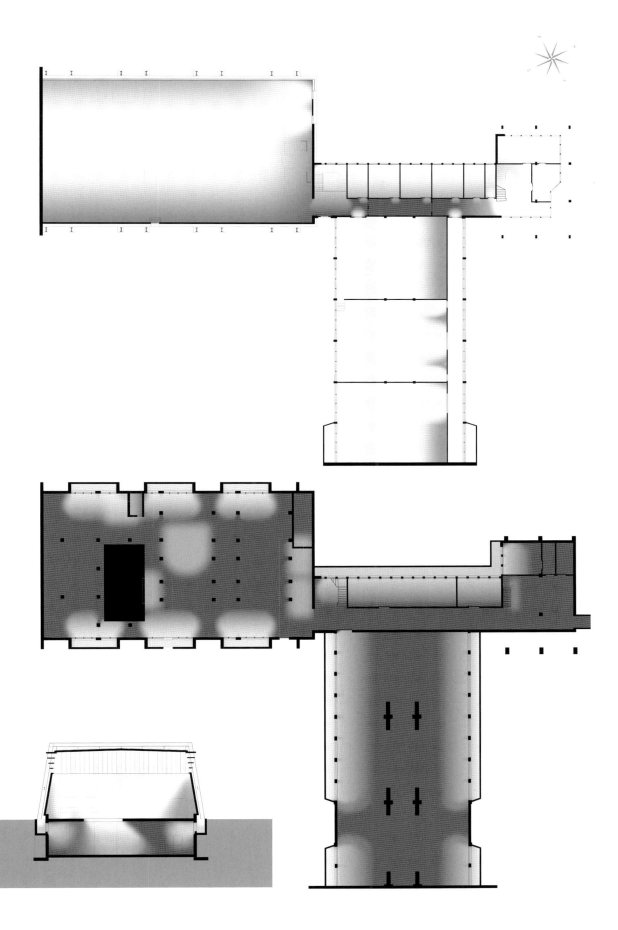

4

101 THE STUDIO, OR TEACHING THE PRESERVATION PROJECT

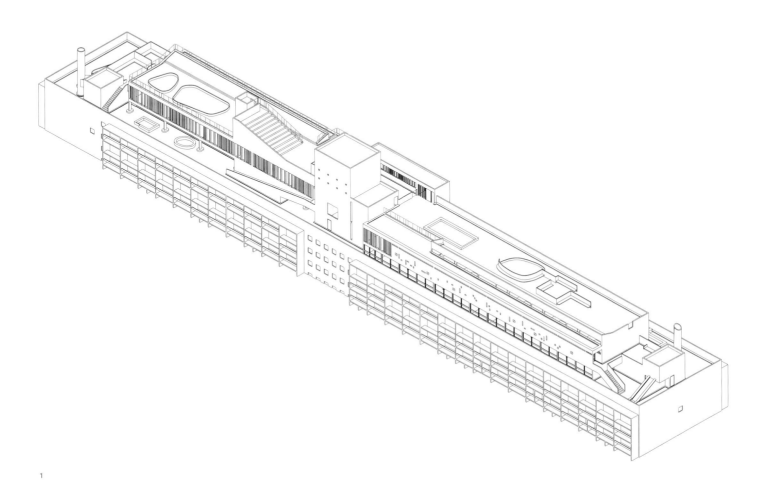

1 Global axonometric drawing of the nursery school on the roof of the Firminy Unité d'habitation
Following page Project models (1:100e) and studio poster

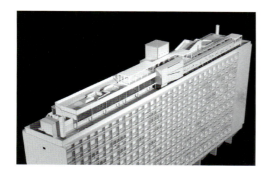
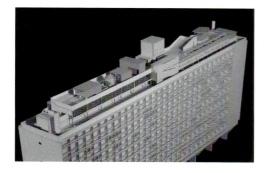

10_UH FIRMINY

Fall 2011

Redevelopment of the Firminy
Unité d'habitation nursery school
Firminy, 1959–1967

Le Corbusier & André Wogenscky
architects

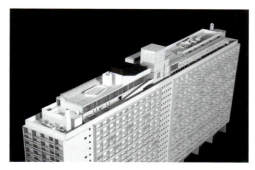

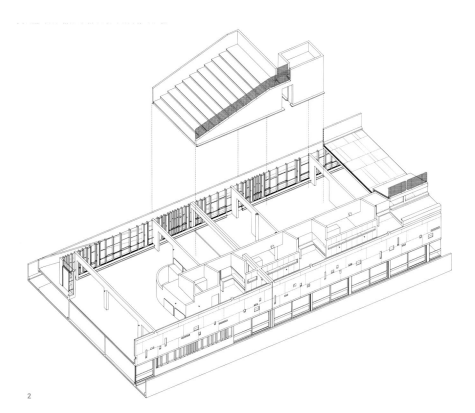

2

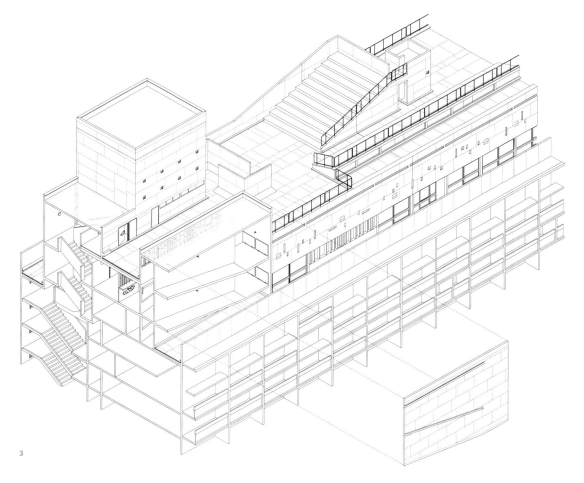

3

TEACHING THE PRESERVATION 104

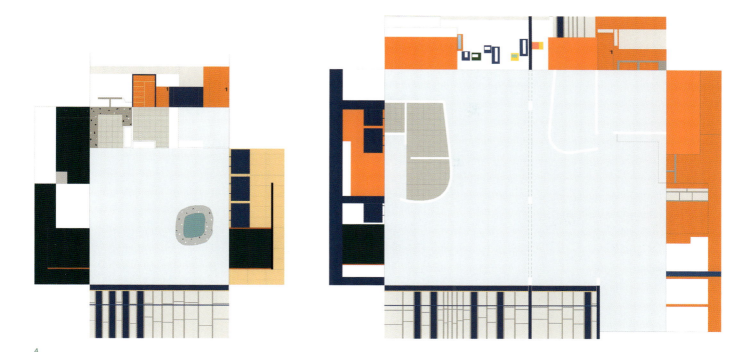

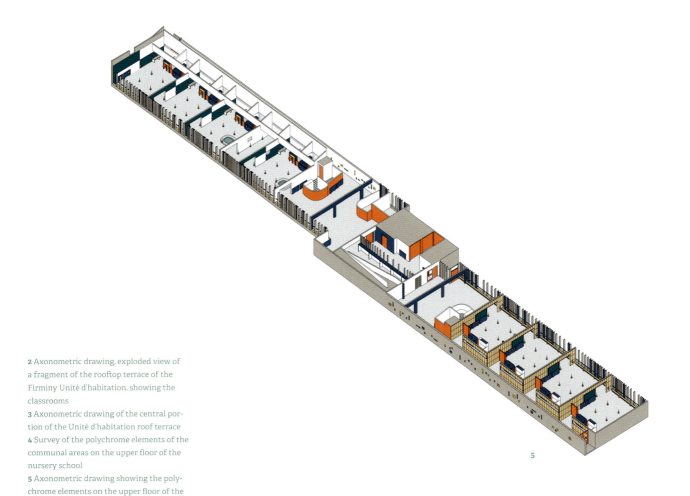

2 Axonometric drawing, exploded view of a fragment of the rooftop terrace of the Firminy Unité d'habitation, showing the classrooms
3 Axonometric drawing of the central portion of the Unité d'habitation roof terrace
4 Survey of the polychrome elements of the communal areas on the upper floor of the nursery school
5 Axonometric drawing showing the polychrome elements on the upper floor of the nursery school

105 THE STUDIO, OR TEACHING THE PRESERVATION PROJECT

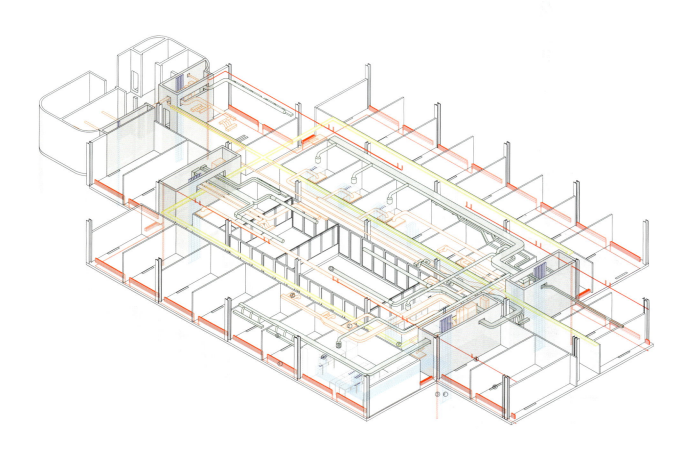

1 Axonometric drawing of the technical equipment of the GR building, standard floor
Following page Project models (1 500) and studio poster

11_EPFL

Spring 2012

Extension of the École polytechnique fédérale de Lausanne campus Lausanne, 1970–1982

Jacob Zweifel, Heinrich Strickler & Associates architects

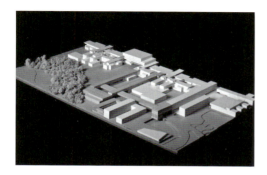
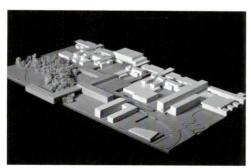
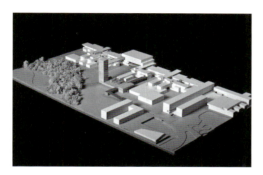
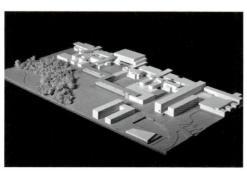
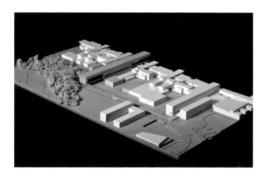

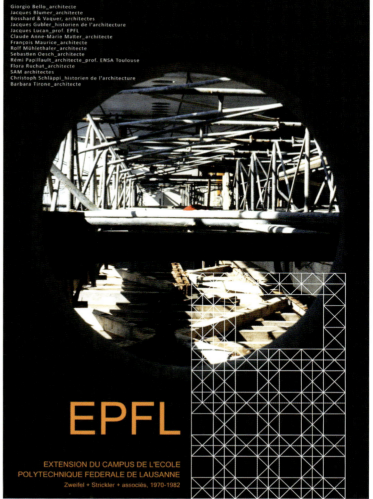

Giorgio Bello_architecte
Jacques Blumer_architecte
Bosshard & Vaquer, architectes
Jacques Gubler_historien de l'architecture
Jacques Lucan_prof. EPFL
Claude Anne-Marie Matter_architecte
François Maurice_architecte
Rolf Mühlethaler_architecte
Sebastien Oesch_architecte
Rémi Papillault_architecte_prof. ENSA Toulouse
Flora Ruchat_architecte
SAM architectes
Christoph Schläppi_historien de l'architecture
Barbara Tirone_architecte

EPFL

EXTENSION DU CAMPUS DE L'ECOLE POLYTECHNIQUE FEDERALE DE LAUSANNE
Zweifel + Strickler + associés, 1970-1982

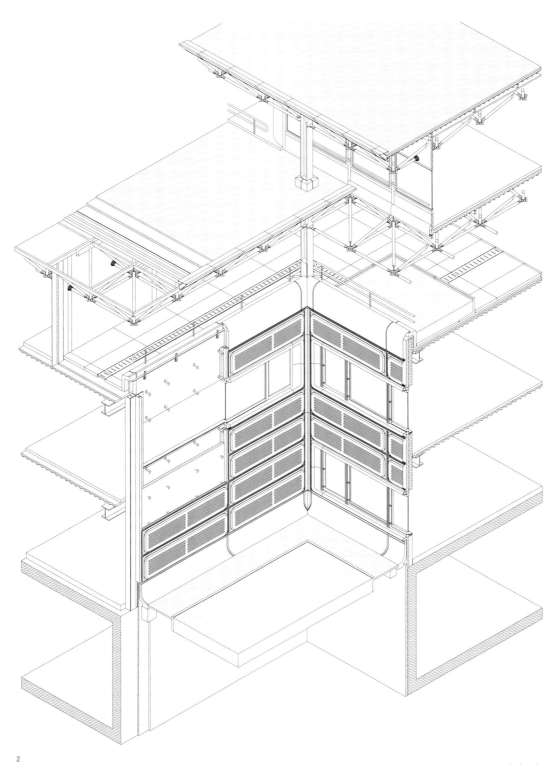

2 Axonometric drawing, stripped-back view showing the junction of the CM and GC buildings
3 Axonometric drawing, stripped-back view of an angle of the GC building

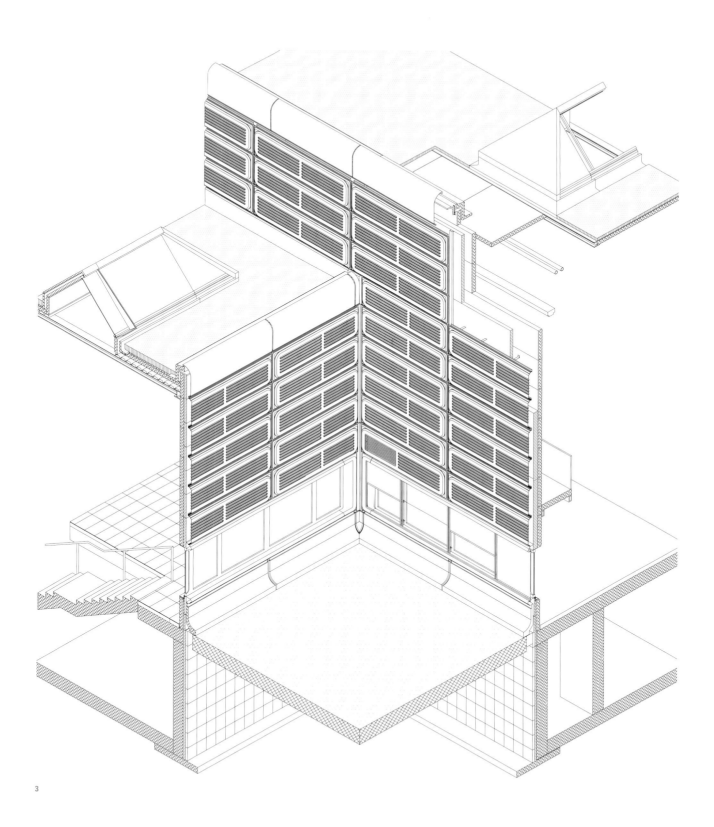

1 Model of the Palazzo del Lavoro, 1:100
Following page: Project models (1:200) and studio poster

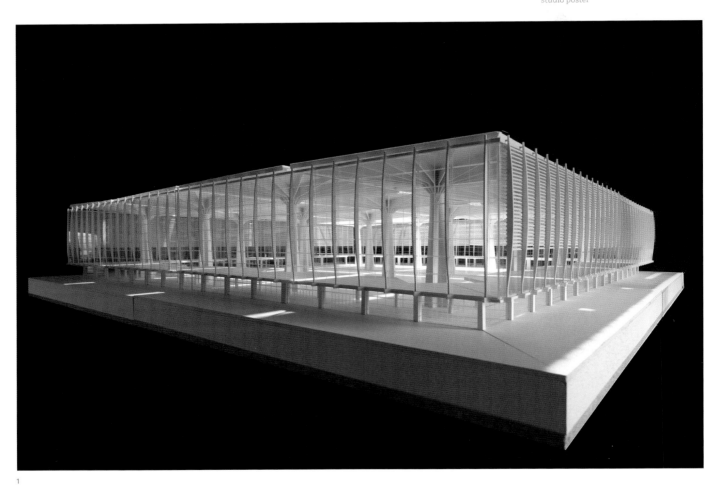

12_PALAZZO DEL LAVORO

Fall 2012 / Spring 2013

Conversion of the Palazzo del Lavoro
Turin, 1959–1961

Pier Luigi Nervi
architect and engineer

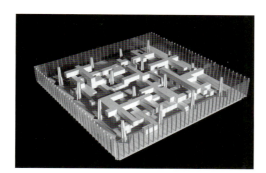

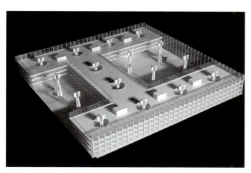
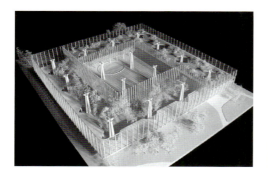

2 Axonometric drawing of the load-bearing structure at the Palazzo del Lavoro (view from below)
3 Axonometric construction drawing of a building corner (view from below)
4 Axonometric details of the fastenings of one of the façade stiffeners

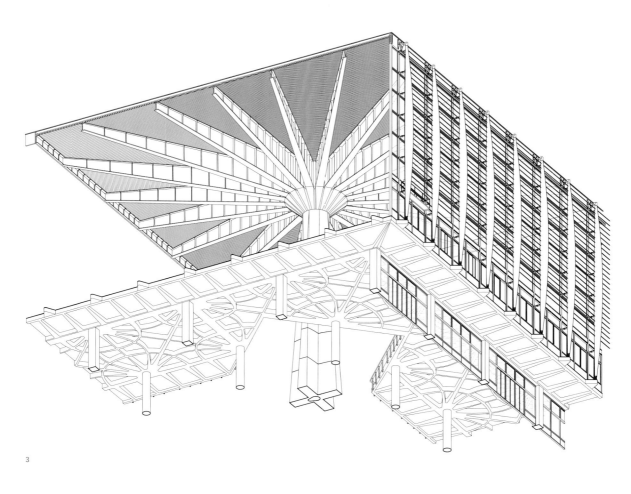

3

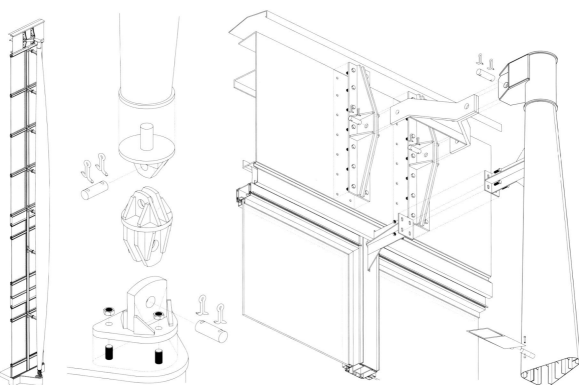

4

113   THE STUDIO, OR TEACHING THE PRESERVATION PROJECT

1,2 Model of the Claude & Duval factory, 1:50
Following page: Project models (1:200) and studio poster

13_CLAUDE & DUVAL

Fall 2013 / Spring 2014

Redevelopment and extension
to the Claude & Duval factory
Saint-Dié, 1946–1950

Le Corbusier
architect

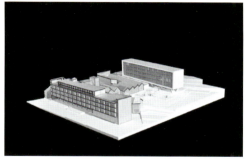

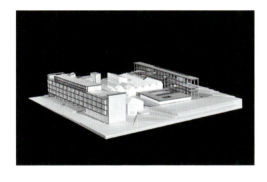

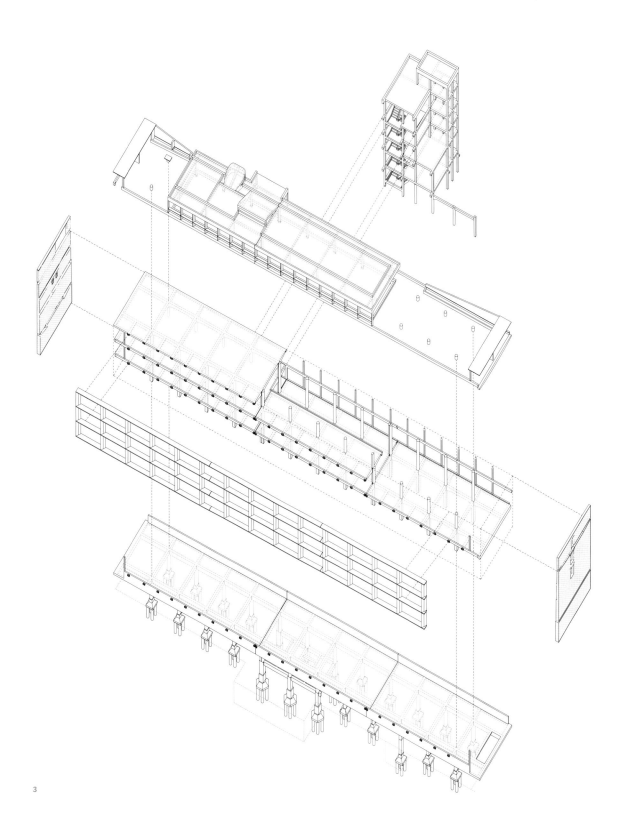

TEACHING THE PRESERVATION 116

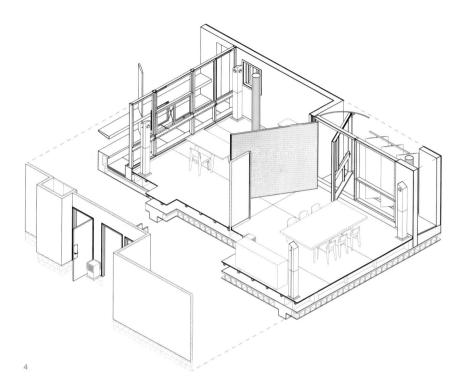

4

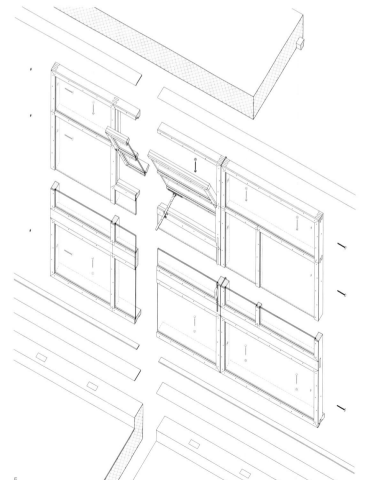

3 Axonometric drawing, exploded view of the load-bearing structure of the Claude & Duval factory
4 Axonometric drawing of the conference room and Paul Duval's office
5 Axonometric drawing, exploded view of the wood joinery (type 2b) on the south façade

5

1, 2, 3, 4 Models of the various house types at the Cité Frugès, 1:50
Following page: Project models (1:200) and studio poster

1

2

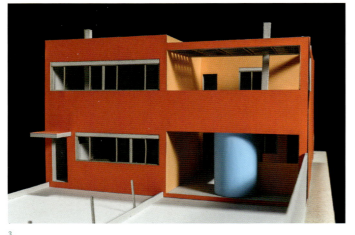
3

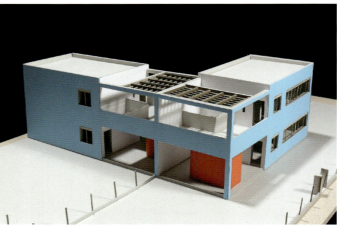
4

TEACHING THE PRESERVATION   118

14_PESSAC

Fall 2014 / Spring 2015

Extension and conservation
of the Quartiers modernes Frugès
Pessac, 1924–1927

Le Corbusier & Pierre Jeanneret
architects

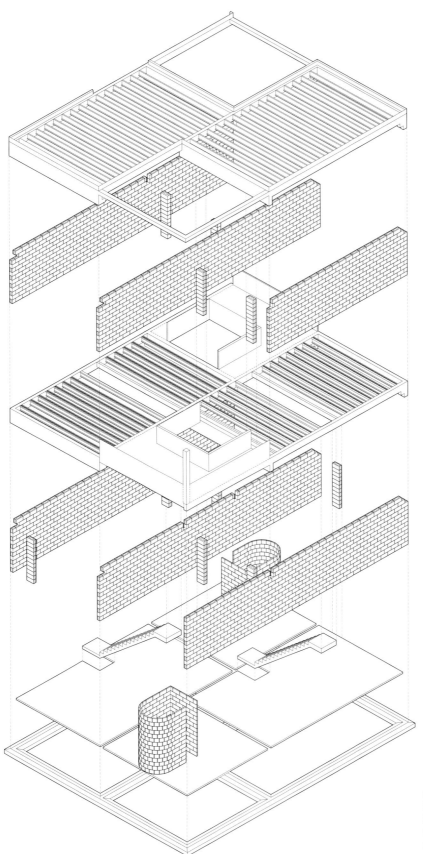

5 Axonometric drawing, exploded view of the load-bearing structure in a "quincunx" type house, 1:50
6 Axonometric construction drawing, stripped-back view of the corner of a "quincunx" type house, 1:50

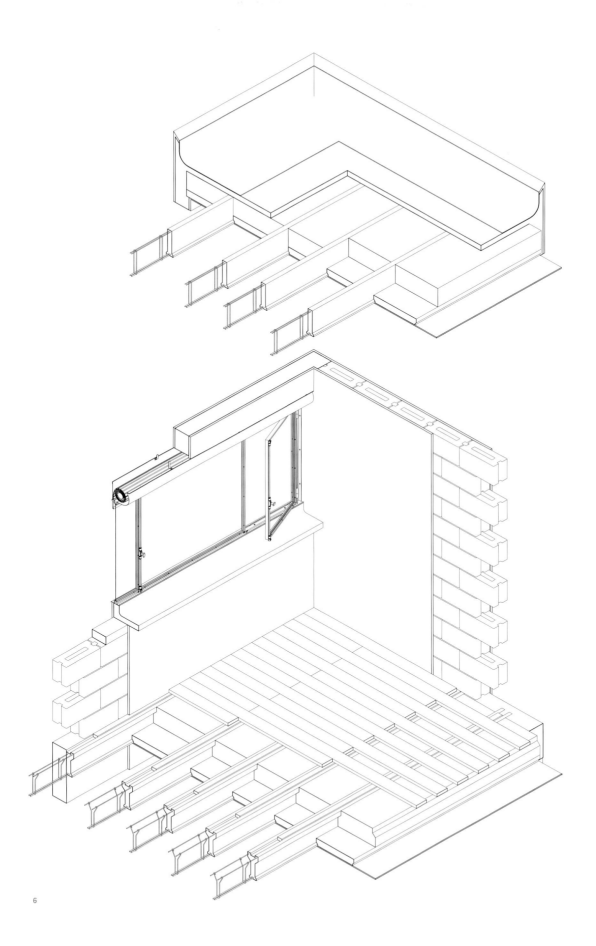

1 Model of the load-bearing structure at the Unité d'habitation in Marseille
Following page: Models of the micro-projects for various Unités d'habitation (various scales) and studio poster

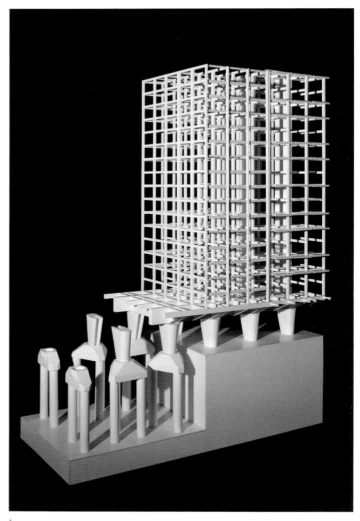

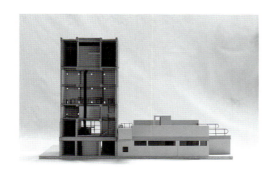
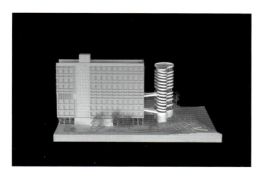

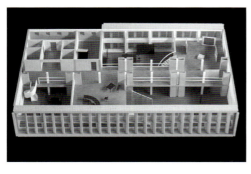

15_UH LC

Fall 2015 / Spring 2016

Conservation and transformation of Le Corbusier's Unités d'habitation Marseille / Rezé-lès-Nantes / Briey-en-Forêt / Berlin / Firminy, 1945–1967

Le Corbusier & André Wogenscky architects

Joseph Abram, architecte, ENSA Nancy
Dominique Amouroux, historien de l'architecture, Nantes
Martin Boesch, architecte, Zurich
François Botton, architecte en chef des Monuments historiques, Lyon
Eugen Brühwiler, ingénieur, EPFL
Jean-Pierre Cêtre, ingénieur, Genève
Diener & Diener, architectes, Bâle
Gabriele Dolff-Bonekämper, historienne de l'architecture, TU Berlin
João Pedro Falcão de Campos, architecte, IST Lisbonne / EPFL
Thierry Mariasseh, architecte, EPFL
Yvan Mettaud, conservateur du patrimoine, Firminy
Maryline Monnier, architecte, Rezé
Gilles Ragot, historien de l'architecture, Université de Bordeaux
Arthur Rüegg, architecte, Zurich
Jacques Sbriglio, architecte, ENSA Marseille
Danièle Voldman, historienne de l'architecture, CNRS Paris

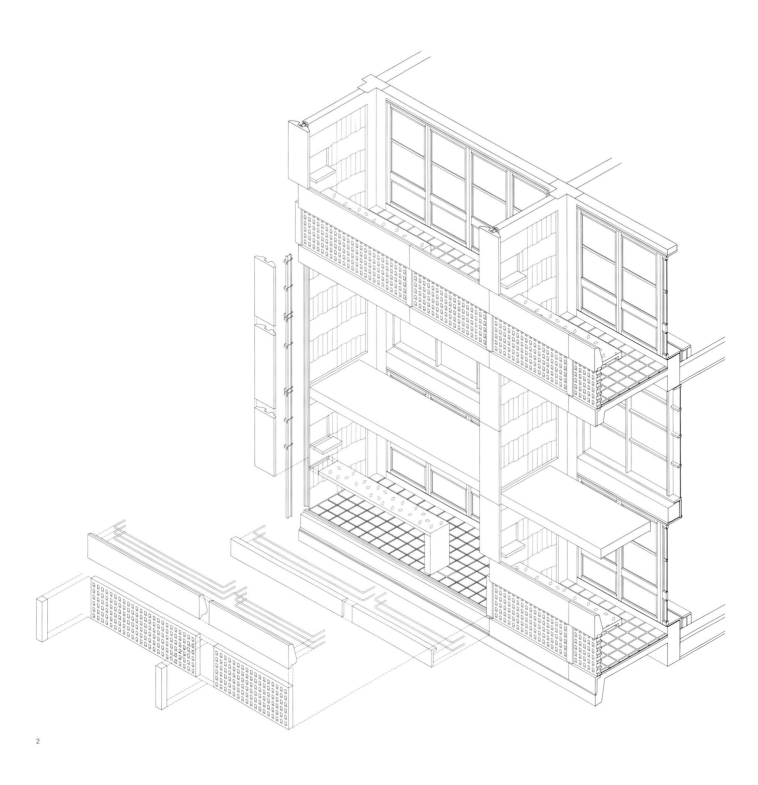

2

2 Axonometric construction drawing, exploded view of the façade envelope of the Unité d'habitation in Marseille (1945–1952)
3, 4 Model of the roof terrace on the Unité d'habitation in Marseille, 1:100
5 Model of a floor-through apartment (duplex) in the Unité d'habitation in Marseille, 1:50

TEACHING THE PRESERVATION   124

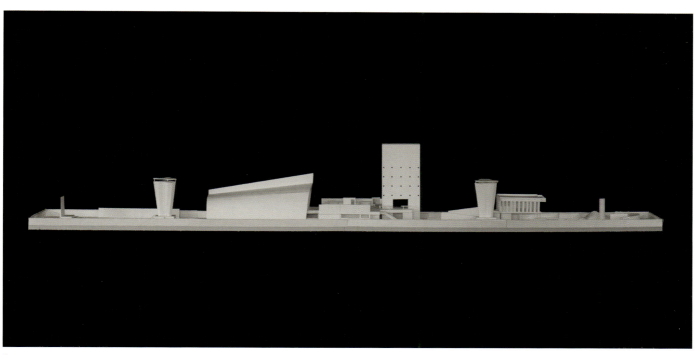

3

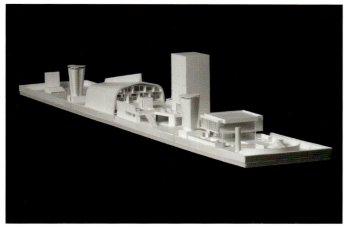

4

5

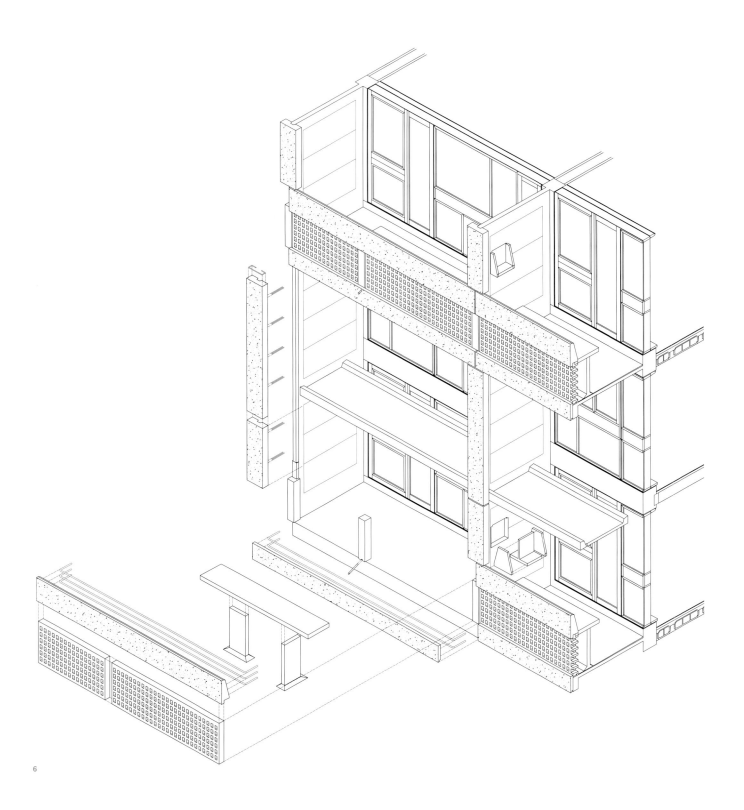

6 Axonometric construction drawing, exploded view of the façade envelope of the Unité d'habitation in Rezé (1948–1955)
7, 8 Model of the roof terrace on the Unité d'habitation in Rezé, 1:100
9 Model of a floor-through apartment (duplex) in the Unité d'habitation in Rezé, 1:50

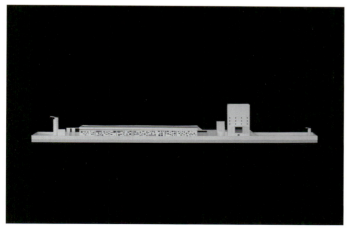

7

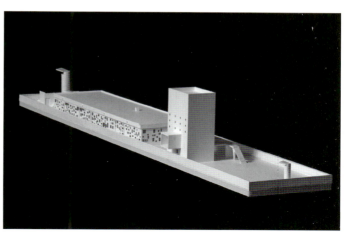

8

9

127   THE STUDIO, OR TEACHING THE PRESERVATION PROJECT

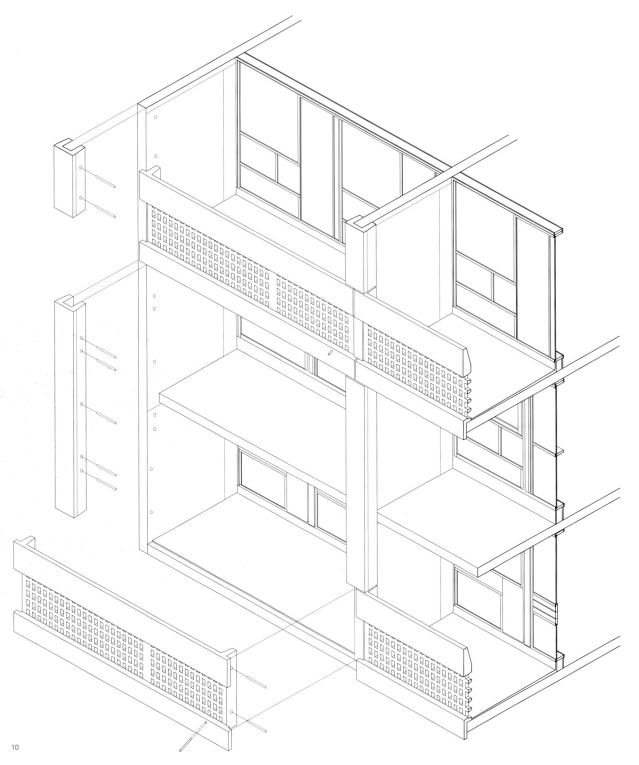

10 Axonometric construction drawing, exploded view of the façade envelope of the Unité d'habitation in Briey-en-Forêt (1953–1961)
11, 12 Model of the unbuilt project for the roof-terrace of the Unité d'habitation in Briey-en-Forêt. 1:100
13 Model of a floor-through apartment (duplex) in the Unité d'habitation in Briey-en-Forêt. 1:50

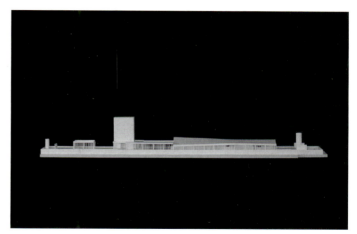

11

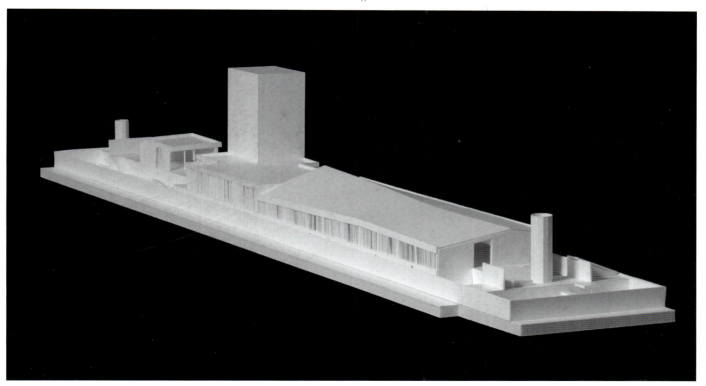

12

13

129   THE STUDIO, OR TEACHING THE PRESERVATION PROJECT

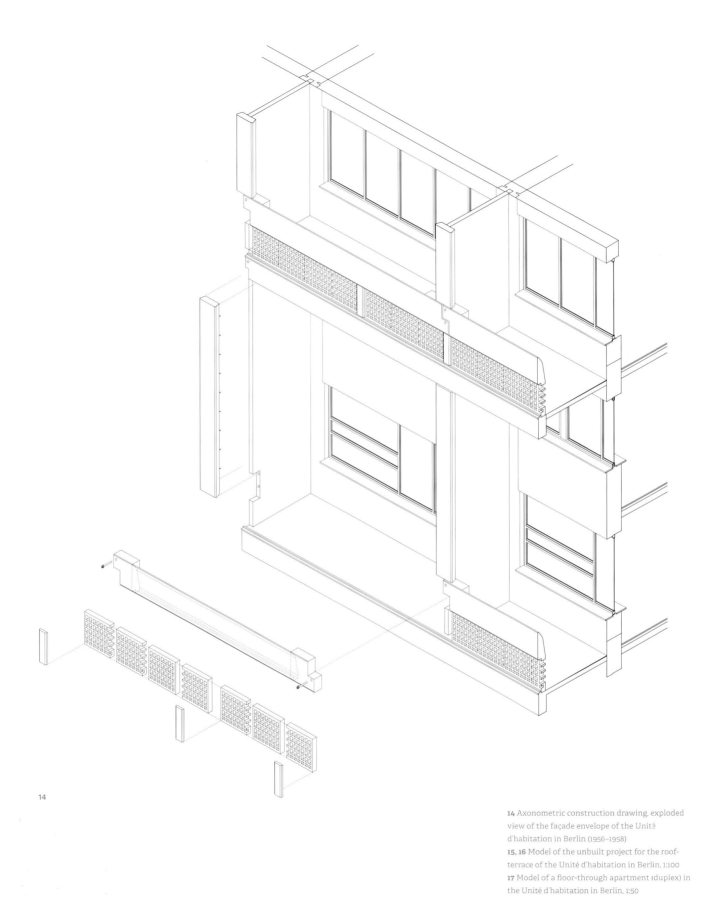

14 Axonometric construction drawing, exploded view of the façade envelope of the Unité d'habitation in Berlin (1956–1958)
15, 16 Model of the unbuilt project for the roof-terrace of the Unité d'habitation in Berlin, 1:100
17 Model of a floor-through apartment (duplex) in the Unité d'habitation in Berlin, 1:50

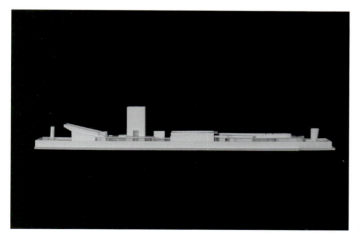

15

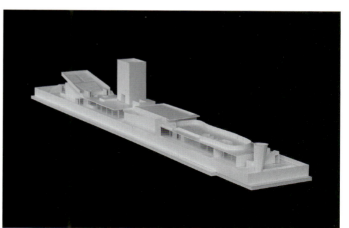

16

17

131 THE STUDIO, OR TEACHING THE PRESERVATION PROJECT

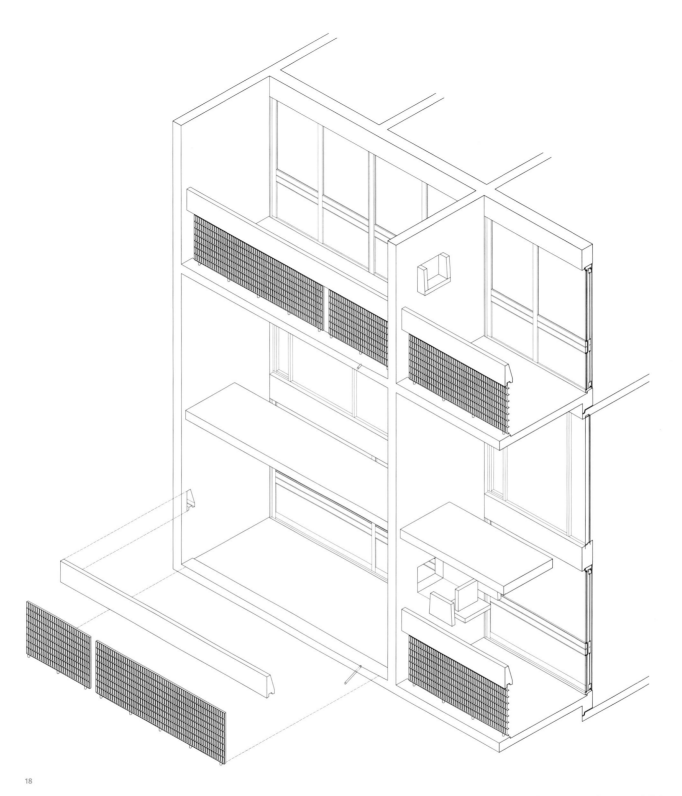

18 Axonometric construction drawing, exploded view of the façade envelope of the Unité d'habitation in Firminy (1959–1967)
19, 20 Model of the unbuilt project for the roof-terrace of the Unité d'habitation in Firminy, 1:100
21 Model of a floor-through apartment (duplex) in the Unité d'habitation in Firminy, 1:50

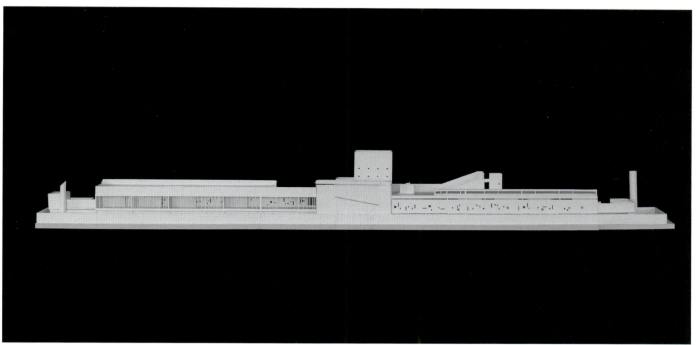

19

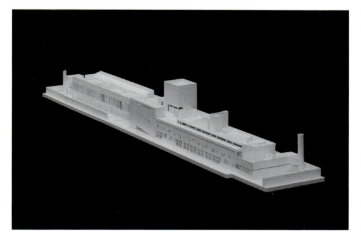

20

21

1 Model of the reinforced concrete load-bearing structure for the Ronchamp chapel, 1:50
Following page: Project models (1:200) and studio poster

16A_RONCHAMP

Fall 2016

Revitalization of the
Ronchamp village, along with the
Notre-Dame du Haut chapel
Ronchamp, 1950–1955

Le Corbusier
architect

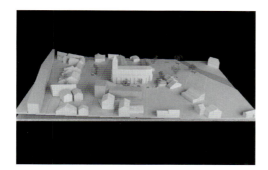
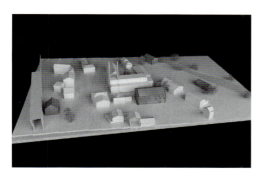
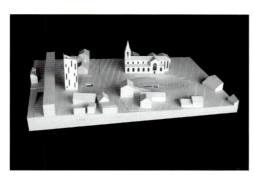
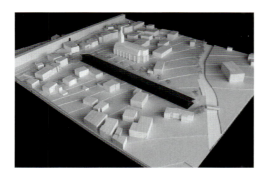

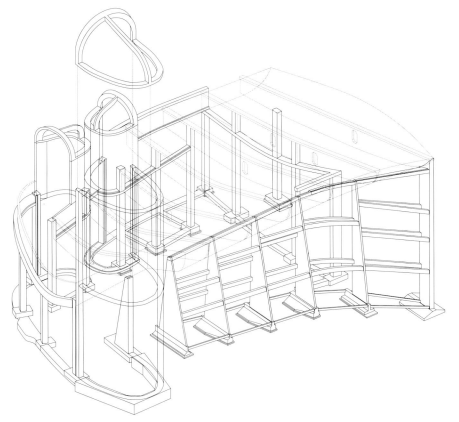

2

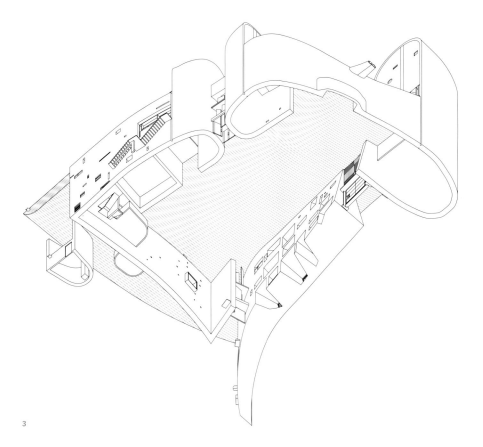

3

TEACHING THE PRESERVATION 136

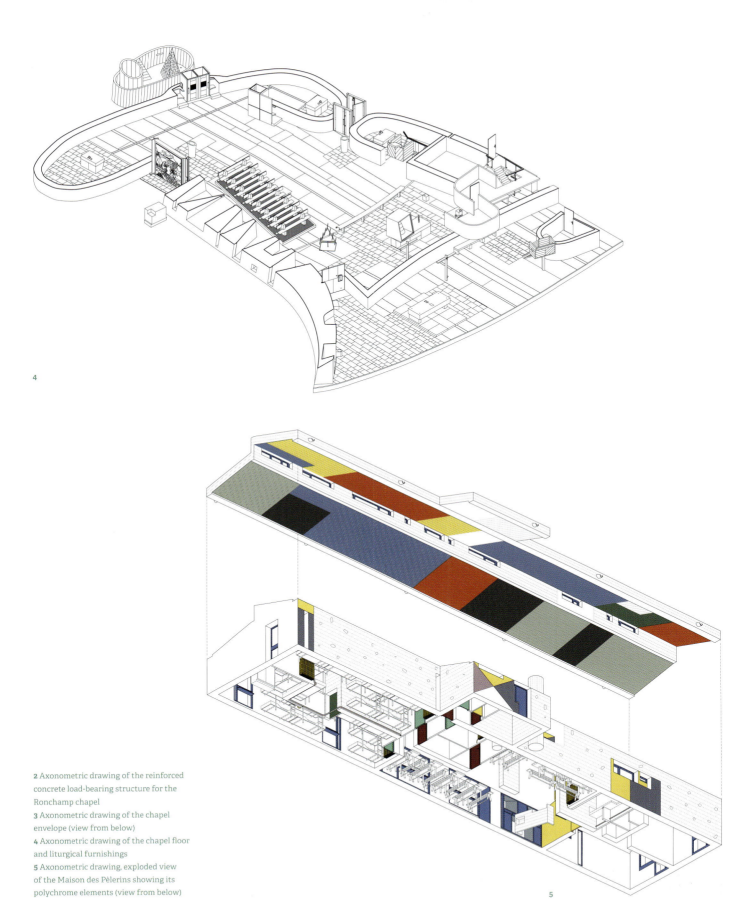

2 Axonometric drawing of the reinforced concrete load-bearing structure for the Ronchamp chapel
3 Axonometric drawing of the chapel envelope (view from below)
4 Axonometric drawing of the chapel floor and liturgical furnishings
5 Axonometric drawing, exploded view of the Maison des Pèlerins showing its polychrome elements (view from below)

1 Model of the Maison de l'Homme, 1:50
Following page: Project models (1:200) and studio poster

16B_LCZH

Spring 2017

Maison de l'Homme: Building alongside
Zurich, 1961–1967

Le Corbusier
architect

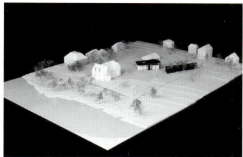

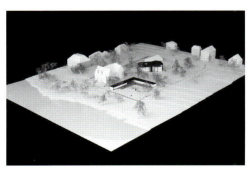

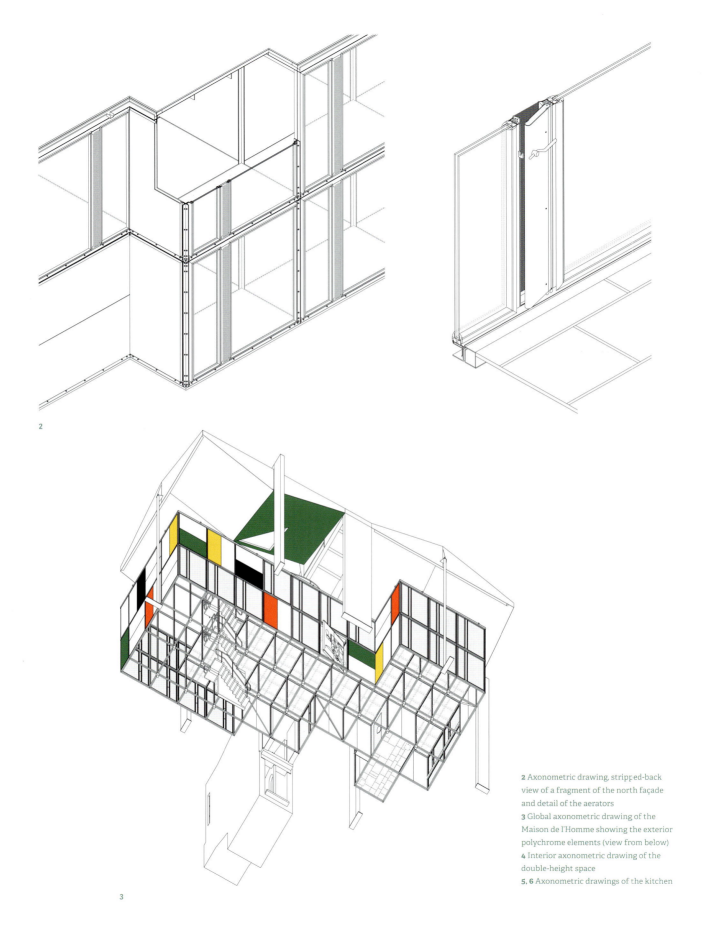

2 Axonometric drawing, stripped-back view of a fragment of the north façade and detail of the aerators
3 Global axonometric drawing of the Maison de l'Homme showing the exterior polychrome elements (view from below)
4 Interior axonometric drawing of the double-height space
5, 6 Axonometric drawings of the kitchen

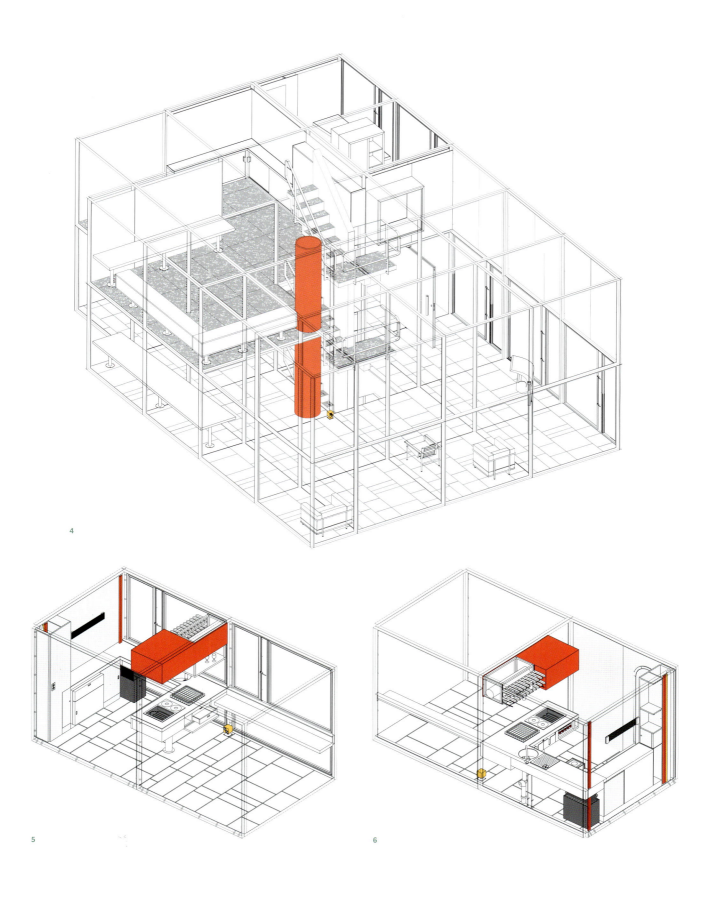

141   THE STUDIO, OR TEACHING THE PRESERVATION PROJECT

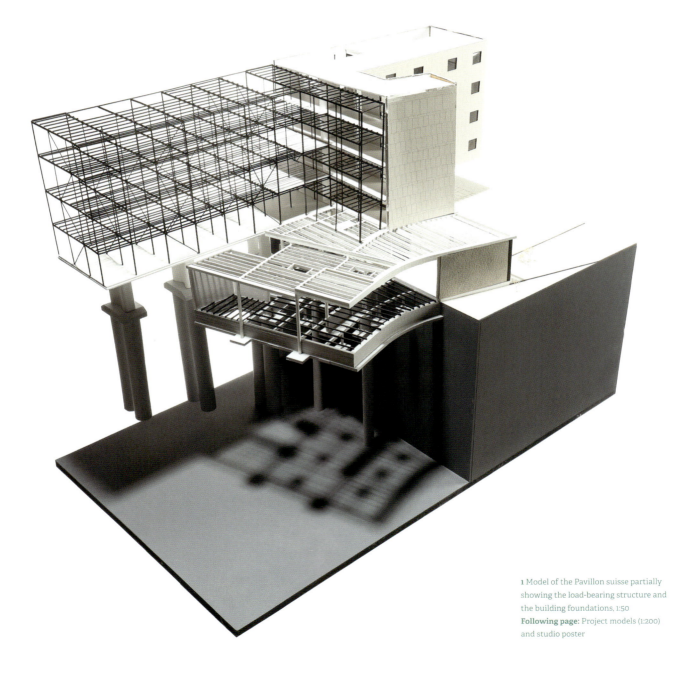

1 Model of the Pavillon suisse partially showing the load-bearing structure and the building foundations. 1:50
Following page: Project models (1:200) and studio poster

TEACHING THE PRESERVATION 142

17A_CIUP SUISSE

Fall 2017

The Pavillon suisse
at the Cité internationale universitaire
de Paris: Building alongside
Paris, 1929–1933

Le Corbusier & Pierre Jeanneret
architects

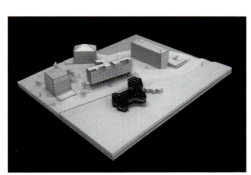

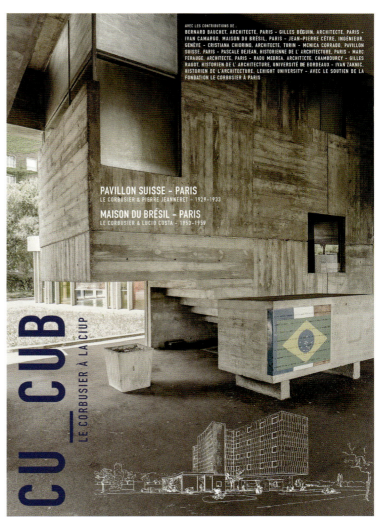

2, 3 Axonometric drawing of the polychrome elements (original state 1933 and modified state 1948)
4 Axonometric construction drawing of the south façade (original state 1933)

TEACHING THE PRESERVATION   144

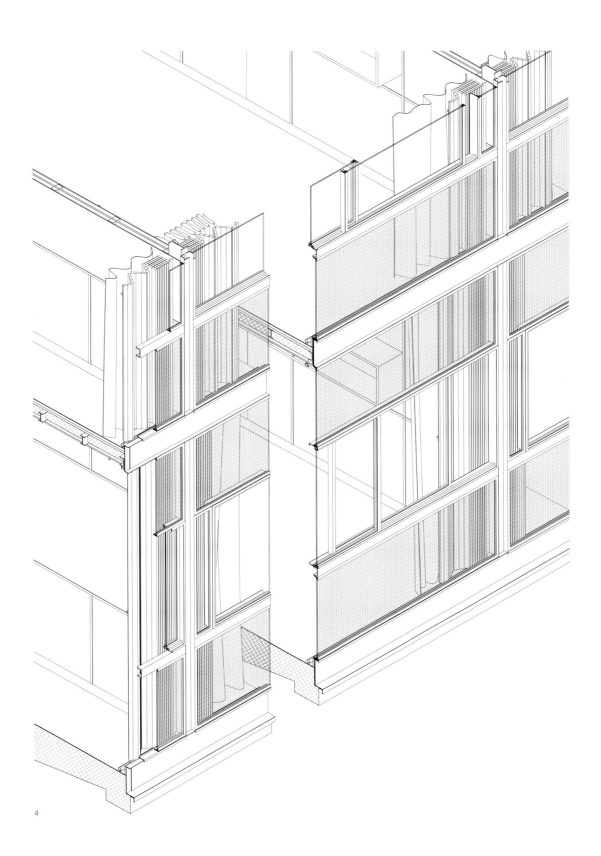

4

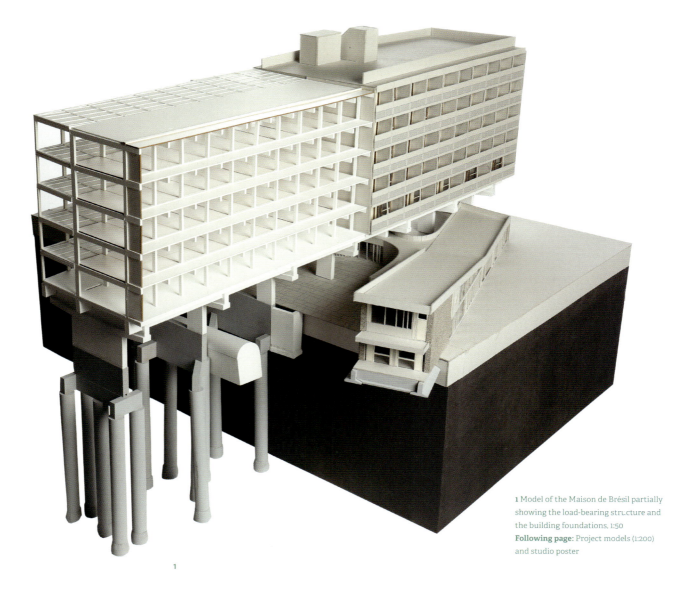

1 Model of the Maison de Brésil partially showing the load-bearing structure and the building foundations, 1:50
Following page: Project models (1:200) and studio poster

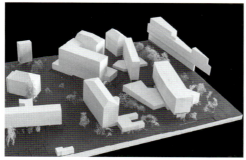
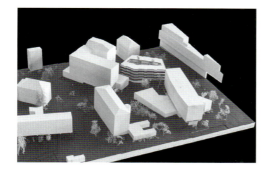

17B_CIUP BRÉSIL

Spring 2018

The Maison du Brésil
at the Cité internationale universitaire
de Paris: building alongside
Paris, 1953–1959

Le Corbusier & Lucio Costa
architects

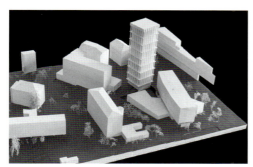
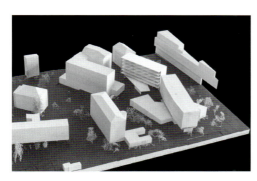
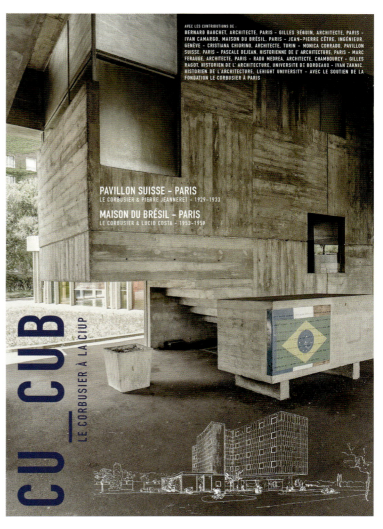
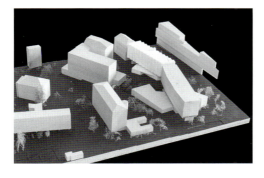

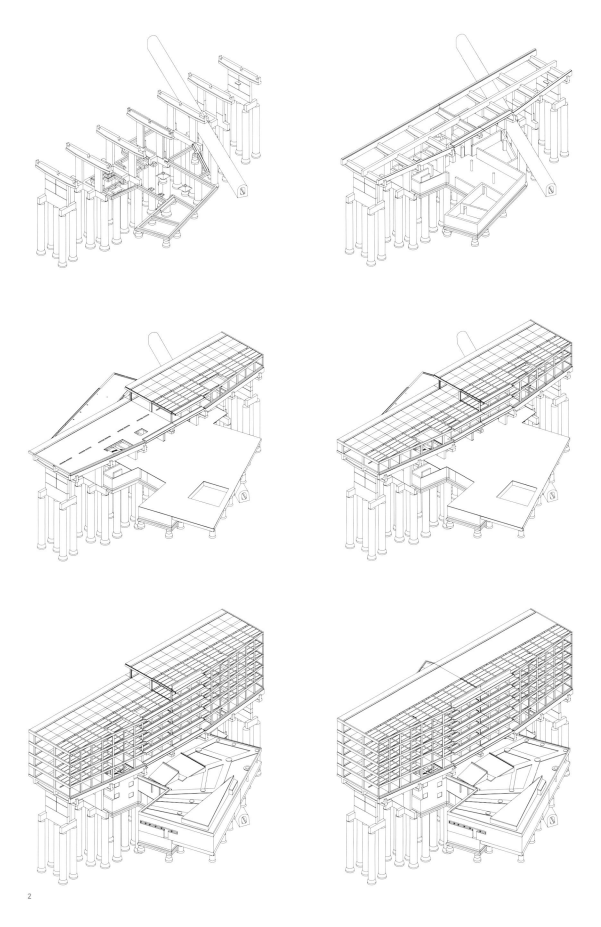

2

TEACHING THE PRESERVATION   148

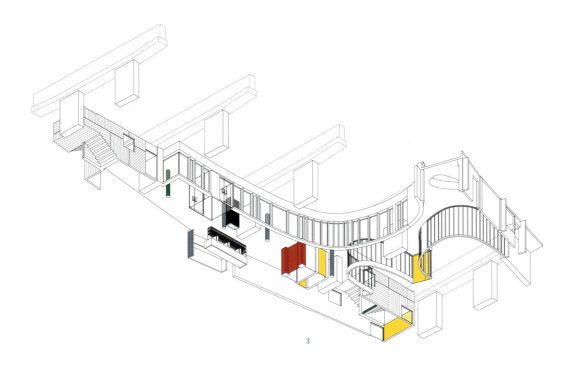

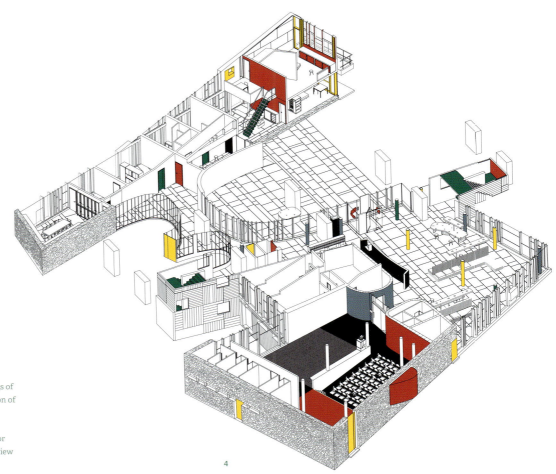

2 Axonometric construction drawings of the various phases in the construction of the Maison du Brésil
3 Axonometric drawing of the distribution space on the ground floor showing the polychrome elements (view from below)
4 Axonometric drawing of all the spaces of the ground floor showing the polychrome elements

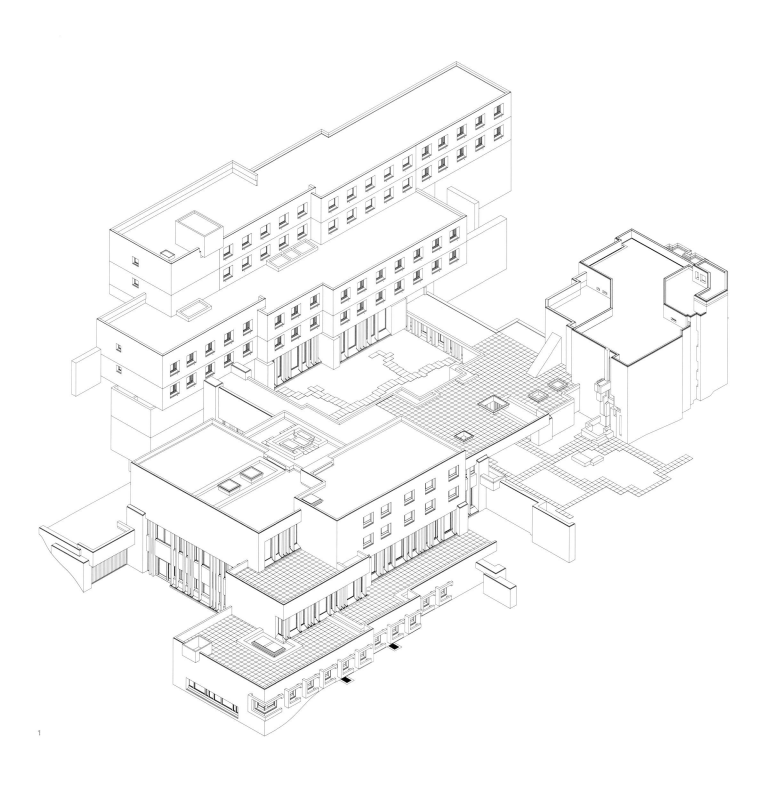

1 Global axonometric drawing of the Franziskushaus
Following page: Project models (1:250) and studio poster

TEACHING THE PRESERVATION 150

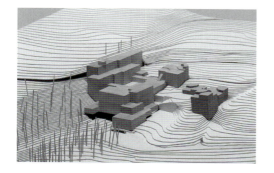
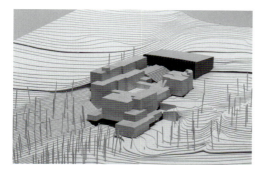
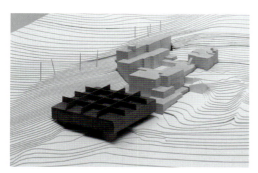
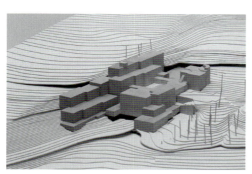

18_FRANZISKUSHAUS

Fall 2018 / Spring 2019

Conversion of the
Franziskushaus
Dulliken, 1964–1969

Otto Glaus
architect

[survey of the Sainte-Marie
de La Tourette convent, Éveux,
1953–1960, Le Corbusier, architect]

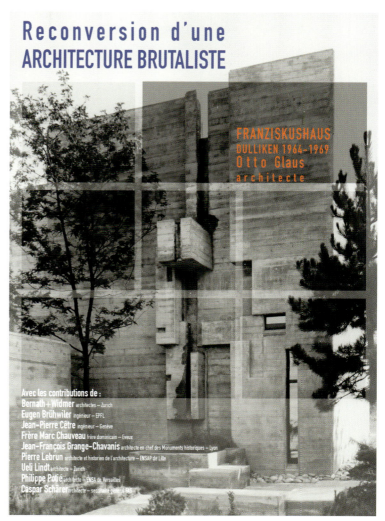

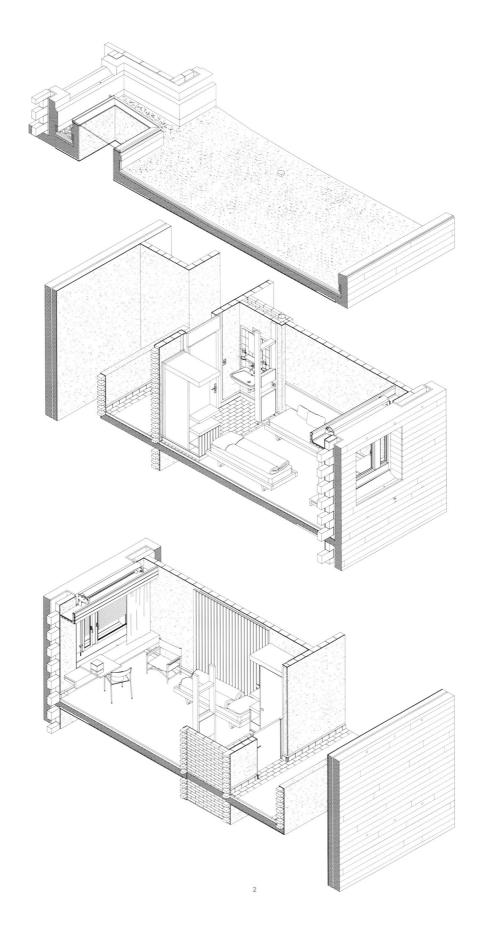

2

TEACHING THE PRESERVATION 152

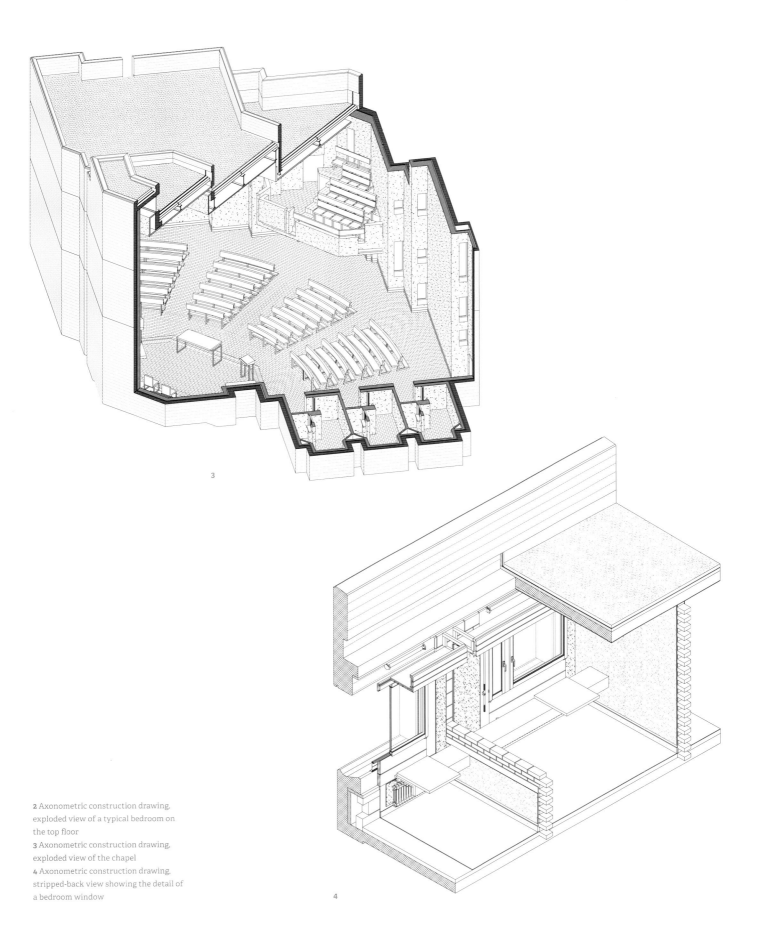

2 Axonometric construction drawing, exploded view of a typical bedroom on the top floor
3 Axonometric construction drawing, exploded view of the chapel
4 Axonometric construction drawing, stripped-back view showing the detail of a bedroom window

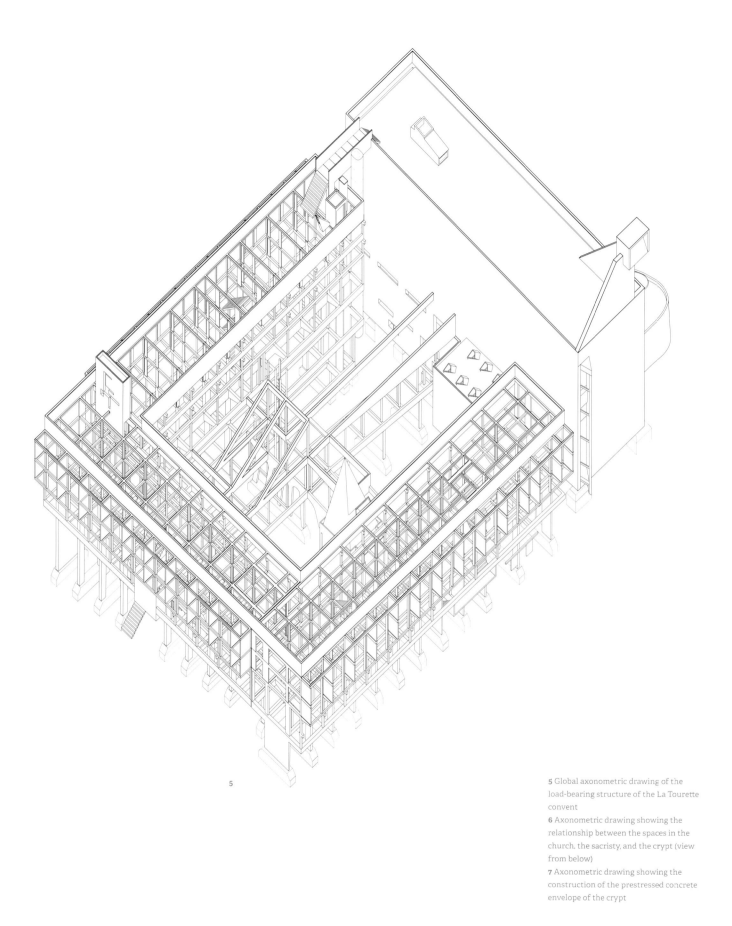

5 Global axonometric drawing of the load-bearing structure of the La Tourette convent
6 Axonometric drawing showing the relationship between the spaces in the church, the sacristy, and the crypt (view from below)
7 Axonometric drawing showing the construction of the prestressed concrete envelope of the crypt

TEACHING THE PRESERVATION

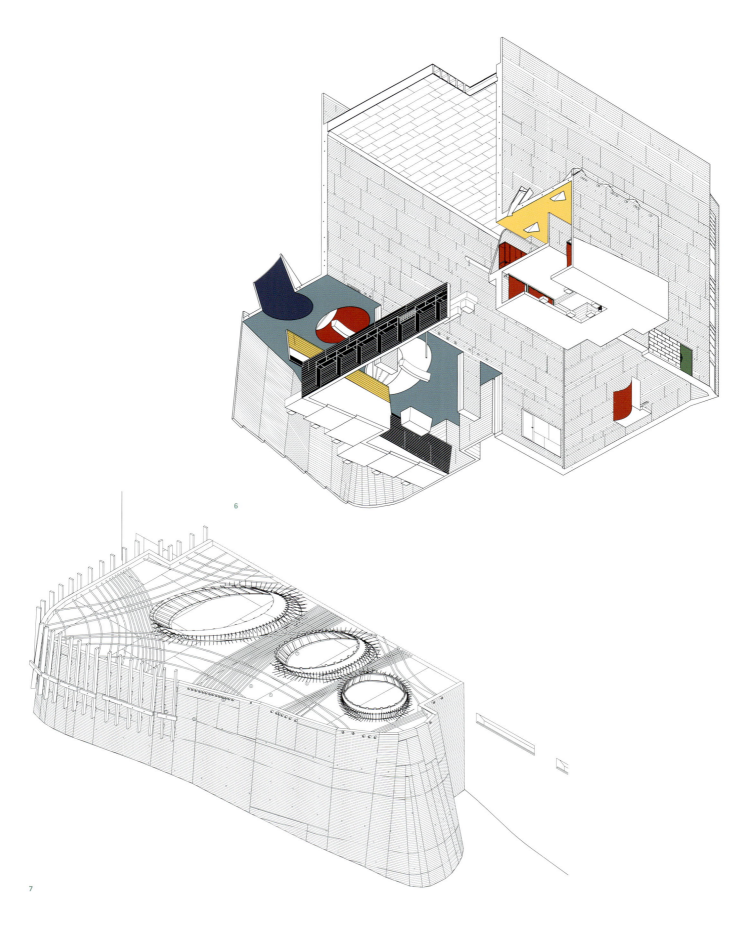

155 THE STUDIO, OR TEACHING THE PRESERVATION PROJECT

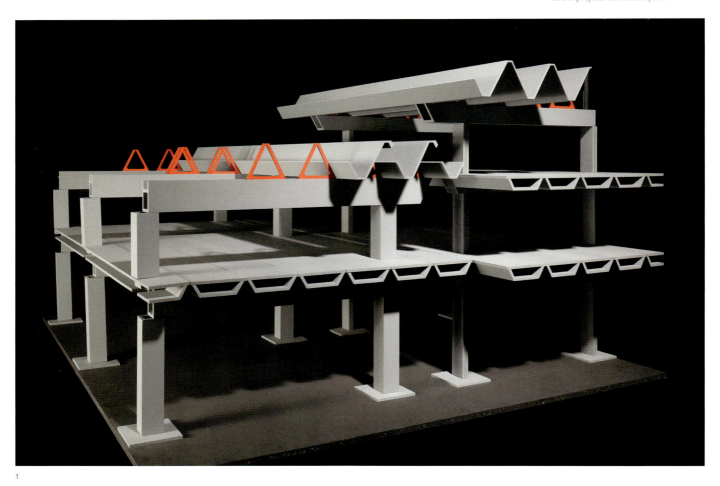

1 Structural model showing the assembly of various prefabricated concrete elements from the "shared space" in the SFRA, 1:20
Following page: Axonometric drawings of the projects and studio poster

19_SFRA

Fall 2019 / Spring 2020

Extension of the "shared space" in the Swiss Federal Agricultural Research Station (SFRA Station fédérale de recherche agronomique) in Changins Nyon, 1969–1975

Heidi & Peter Wenger architects

[Survey of the Wengers' house-studio, Brig, 1952–1955, H. & P. Wenger, architects]

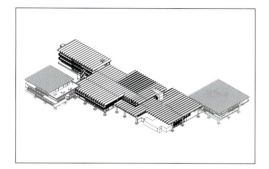

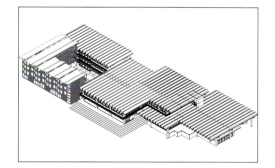

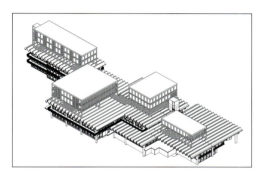

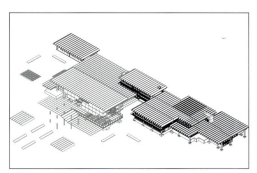

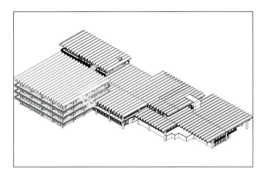

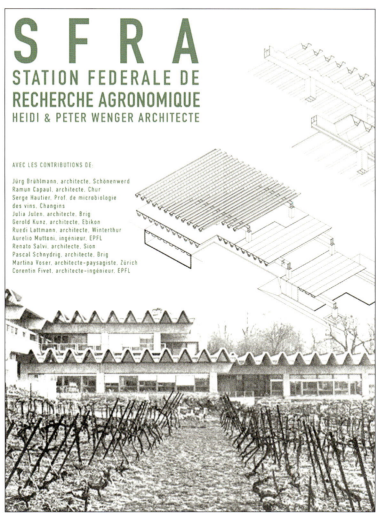

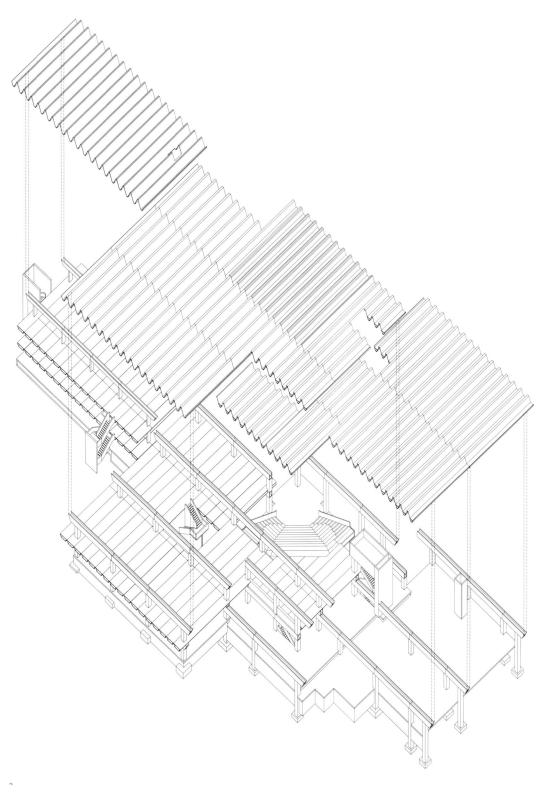

2 Axonometric drawing, exploded view of the load-bearing structure of the "shared space" in the SFRA
3 Axonometric drawing of the boarding hostel envelope (north-east and north-west façades, views from below)
4 Global axonometric drawing of the ventilation network

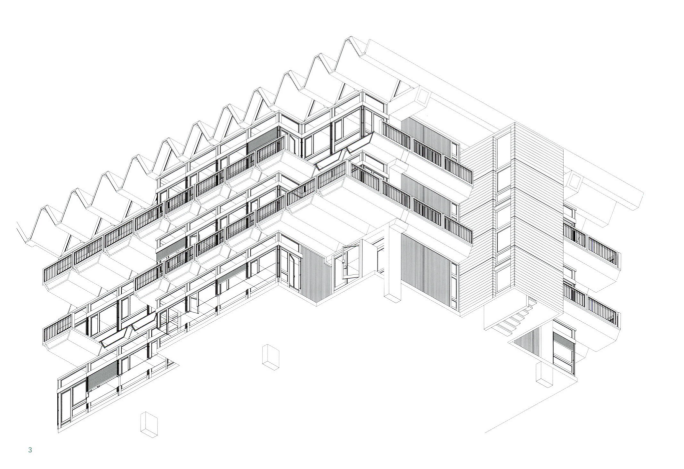

3

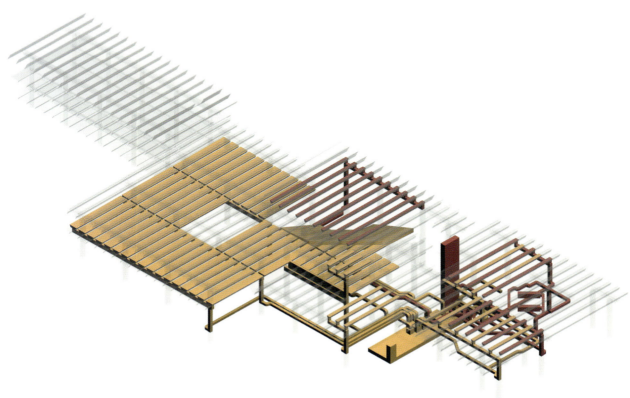

4

159   THE STUDIO, OR TEACHING THE PRESERVATION PROJECT

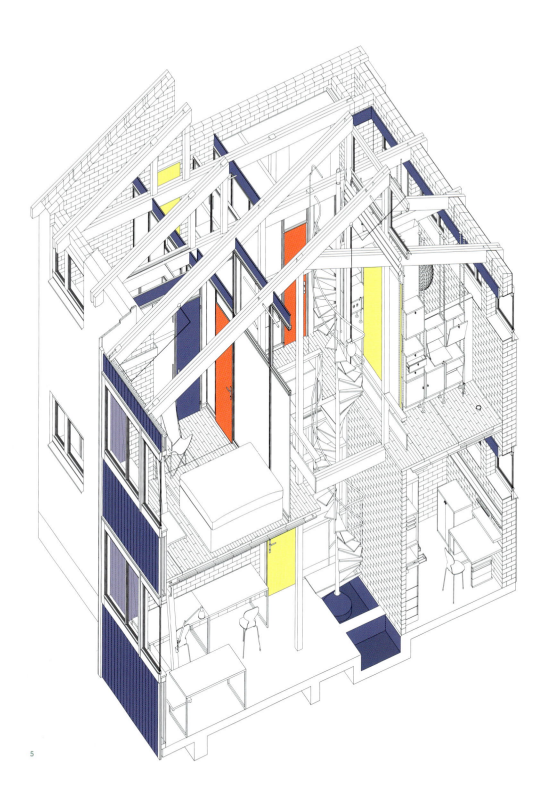

5, 6 Axonometric drawing, stripped-back view showing the inside space and the polychrome elements of the Wengers' house-studio

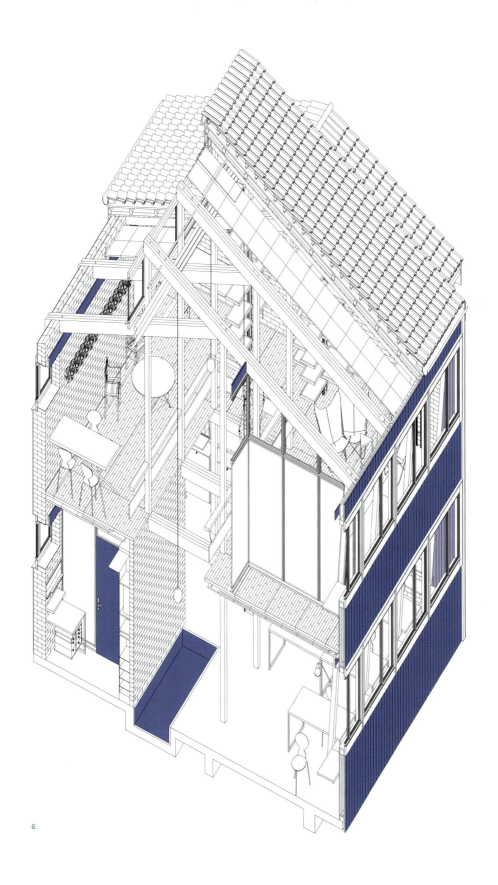

1 Model of part of the CIP, 1:33
Following page: Project models (1:200) and studio poster

TEACHING THE PRESERVATION 162

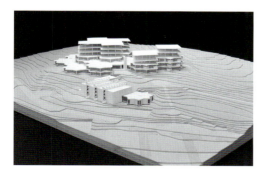
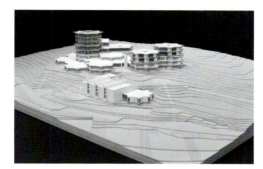
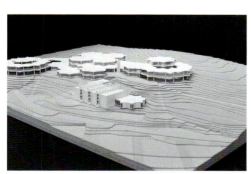
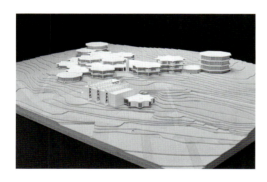

20_CIP

Fall 2020 / Spring 2021

Transformation and extension of the Centre interrégional de perfectionnement Tramelan, 1979–1991

Heidi & Peter Wenger architects

[Survey of the Trigon chalet, Rosswald, 1955–1956, H. & P. Wenger, architects]

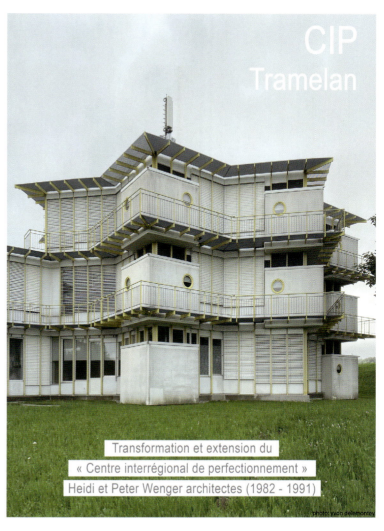

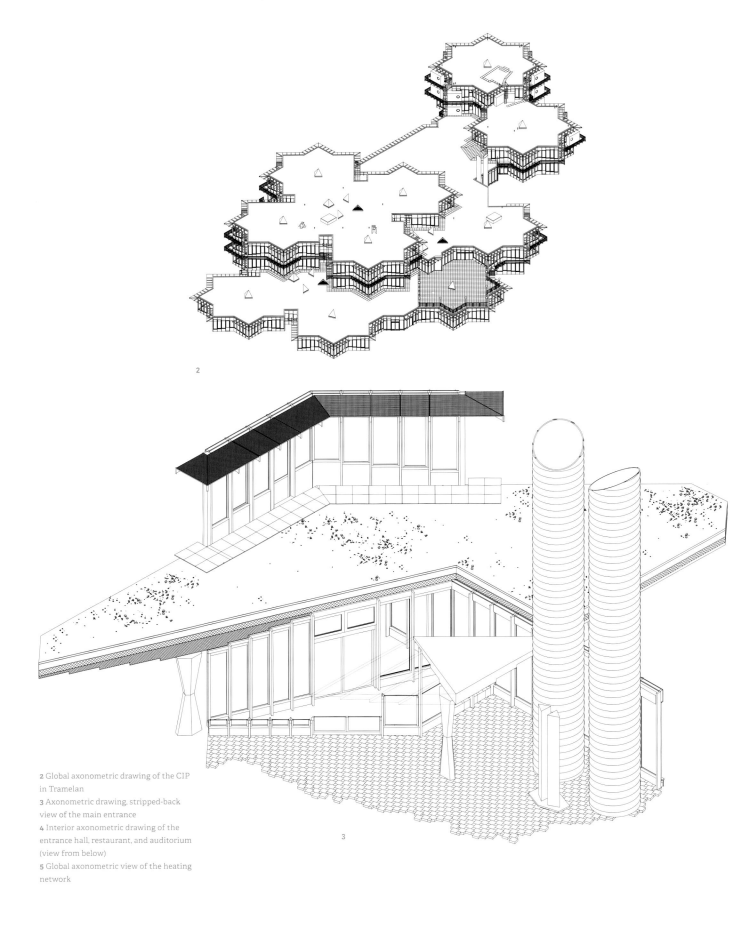

2 Global axonometric drawing of the CIP in Tramelan
3 Axonometric drawing, stripped-back view of the main entrance
4 Interior axonometric drawing of the entrance hall, restaurant, and auditorium (view from below)
5 Global axonometric view of the heating network

TEACHING THE PRESERVATION   164

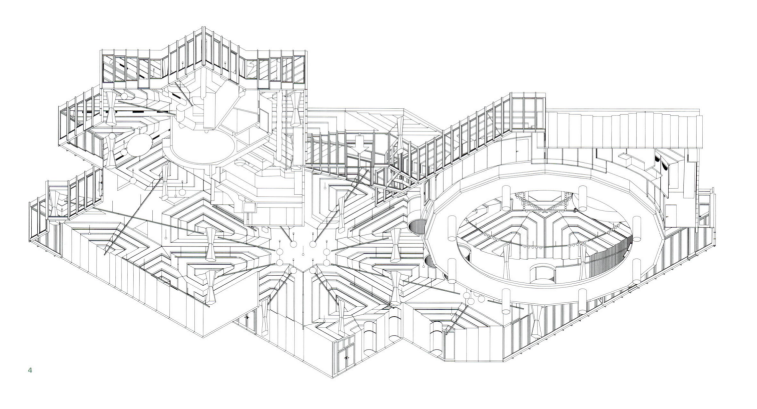

4

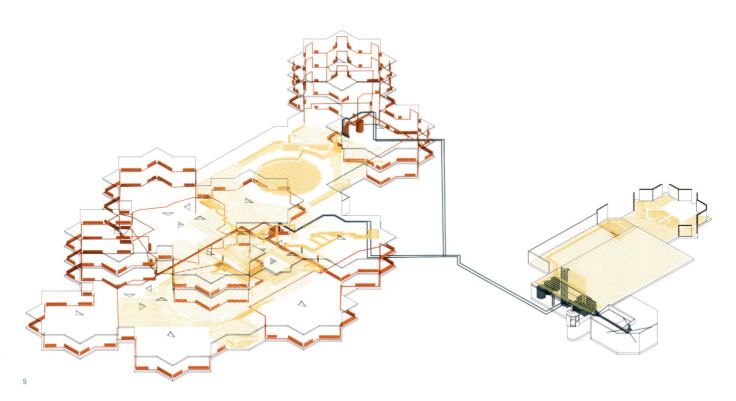

5

165   THE STUDIO, OR TEACHING THE PRESERVATION PROJECT

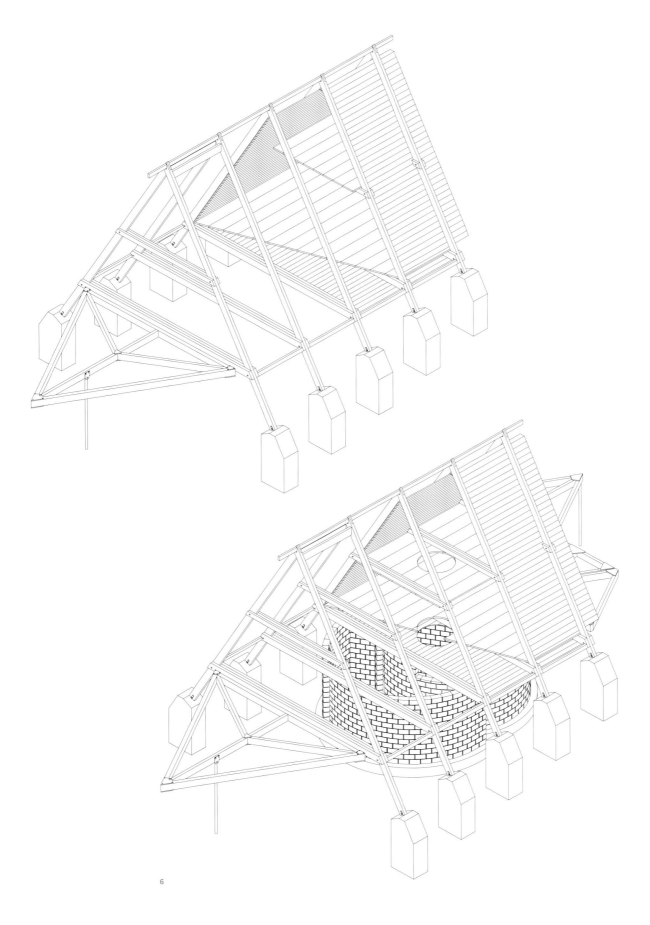

TEACHING THE PRESERVATION   166

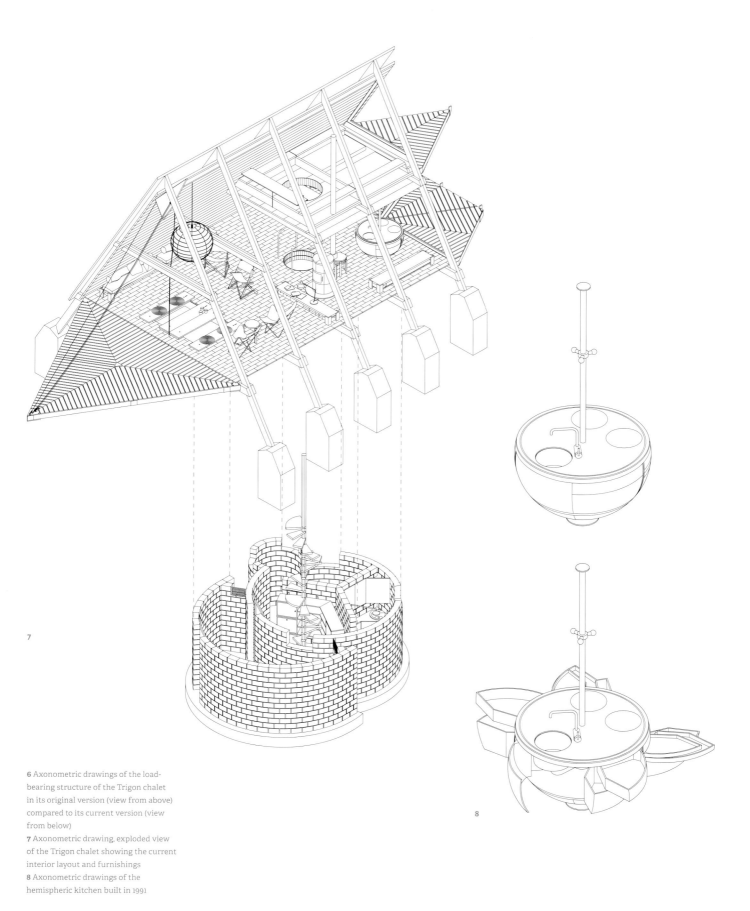

6 Axonometric drawings of the load-bearing structure of the Trigon chalet in its original version (view from above) compared to its current version (view from below)
7 Axonometric drawing, exploded view of the Trigon chalet showing the current interior layout and furnishings
8 Axonometric drawings of the hemispheric kitchen built in 1991

1 Model of the Postgarage, 1:50
Following page: Project models (various scales) and studio poster

21_POSTGARAGE

Fall 2021

Conversion of the Postgarage
Brig, 1966–1974

Heidi & Peter Wenger
architects

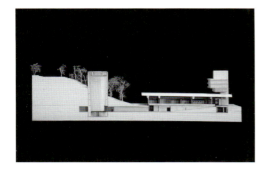
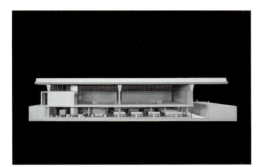
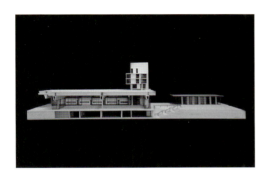

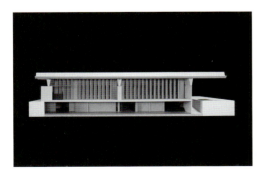

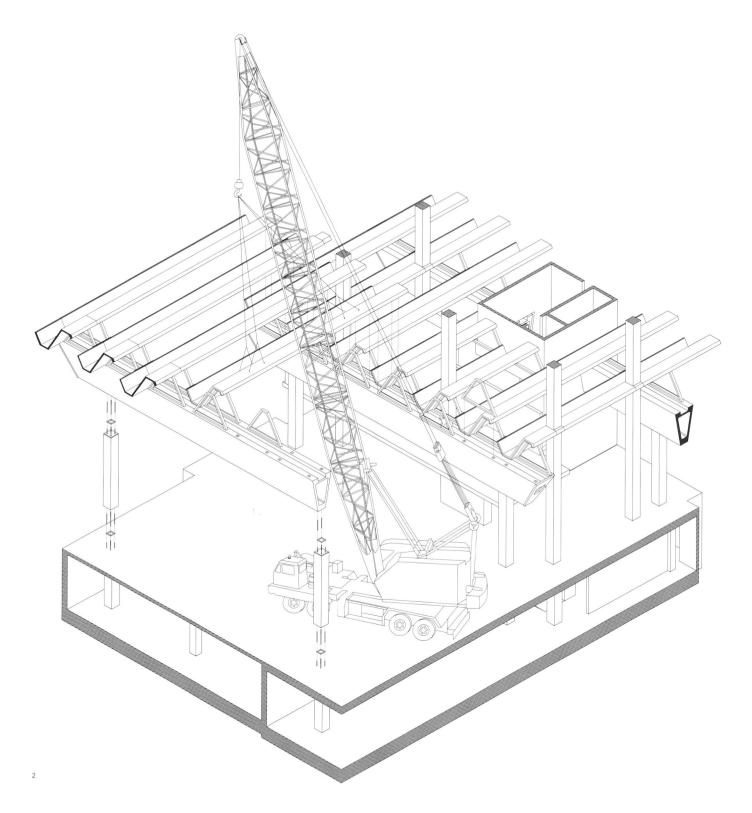

2 Axonometric construction drawing of the installation and assembly of the hall's structural elements (columns, beams, and shed)

3, 4 Global axonometric drawings (views from above and below)

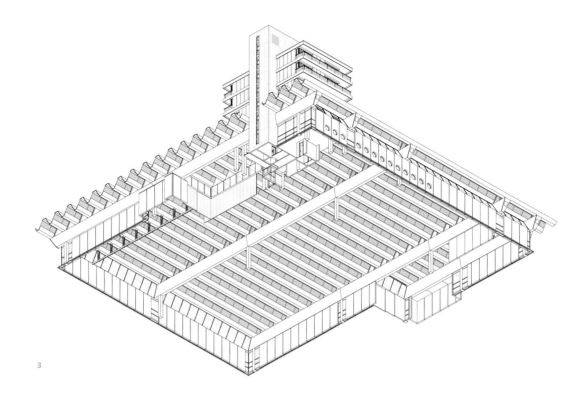

3

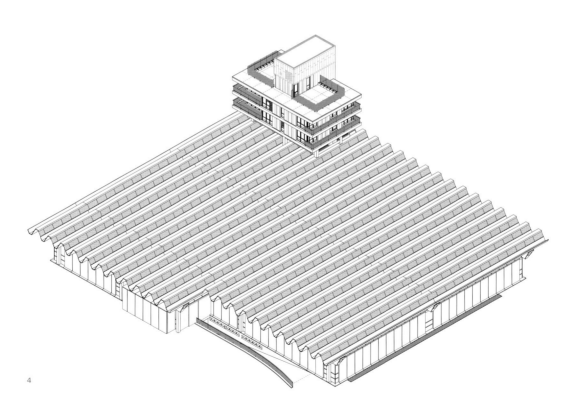

4

1 Model of the wastewater treatment service building in Lausanne, 1:100
Following page: Project models (1:200) and studio poster

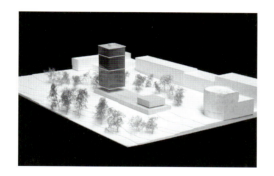
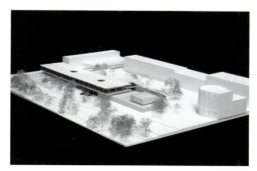

22_STEP VIDY

Spring 2022

Extension to the
Lausanne wastewater treatment service building
Lausanne, 1963–1967

Jean-Pierre Desarzens
architect

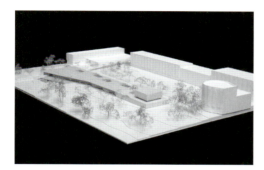
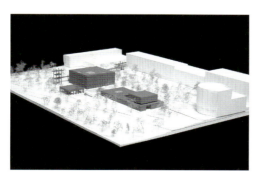
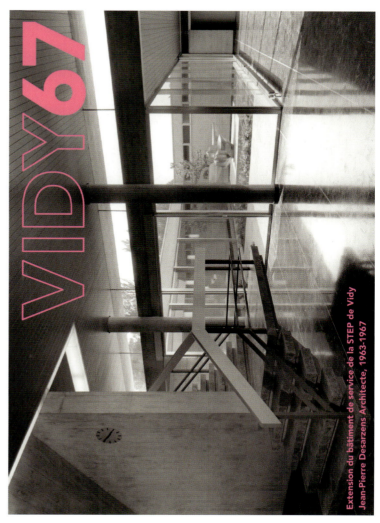

173   THE STUDIO, OR TEACHING THE PRESERVATION PROJECT

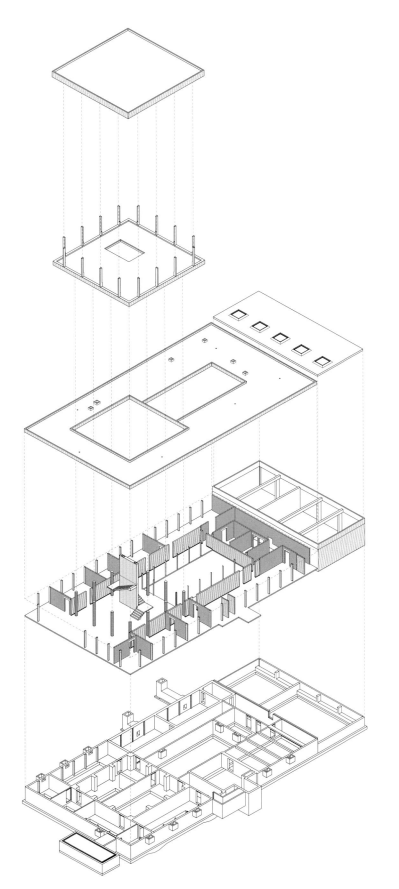

2 Axonometric drawing, exploded view of the load-bearing structure of the service building
3 Axonometric drawing, stripped-back view of the base envelope and the floor volume
4 Axonometric drawing of the internal partitions, coating, and furnishings on the ground floor (base)

TEACHING THE PRESERVATION 174

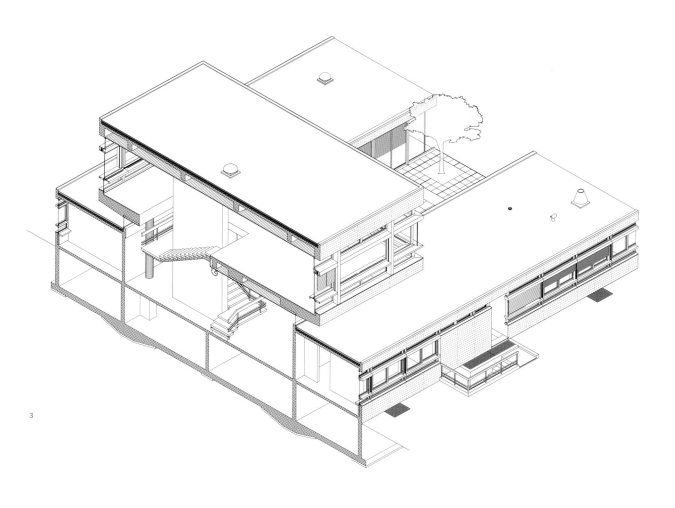

3

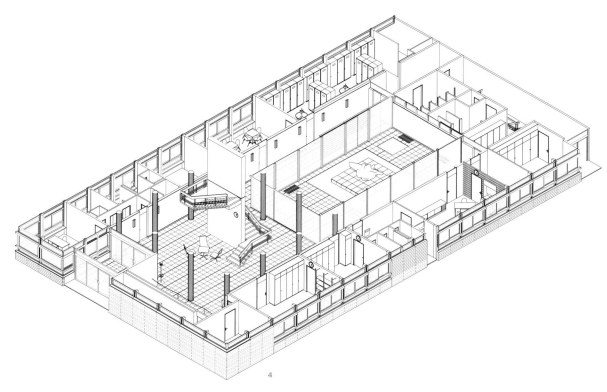

4

175   THE STUDIO, OR TEACHING THE PRESERVATION PROJECT

AUTHOR
ACCOUNTS

1 See Franz Graf, "Histoire matérielle du bâti et projet de sauvegarde, un rappel," and Gilles Ragot, "Se tenir hors de l'histoire," in Richard Klein (ed.), *À quoi sert l'histoire de l'architecture?* (Paris: Éditions Hermann, 2018), pp. 69–74 and 133–37.

TO UNDERSTAND IS TO IMAGINE

GILLES RAGOT

Professor of contemporary art history, Université Bordeaux Montaigne
Former professor of architectural history and culture at the École Nationale Supérieure d'Architecture et de Paysage in Bordeaux

> "I do not think that it is essential for architecture critics to know how to build—any more than it is essential for professional birdwatchers to know how to lay an egg."
> Peter Blake, *Form Follows Fiasco* (Boston: Little Brown and Company, 1974)

If we swap historian for critic, Peter Blake's witticism retains all its pertinence. He is questioning his own right to speak about architecture compared to the architect who knows how to build—in other words: "lay an egg." But although the words of architects and historians enrich each other, they do not actually speak of the same thing. Putting the critic to one side, let's consider the respective contributions of the historian and the architect, which we were spurred to consider during the interventions of Franz Graf and his team at the Preservation Project between 2009 and 2017.

Each session involved shedding historic light on the genesis or conditions in which Le Corbusier developed his projects and upon which the students were then asked to intervene. Graf and I had not outlined a theory on these contributions ahead of time, but we are both very comfortable with the subject matter in our respective fields. Our understanding of the role of the historian within the studio approach was tacit, until we were invited to clarify our positions on this question as part of a book with several authors entitled: *A quoi sert l'histoire de l'architecture?*[1] Among the twenty-eight contributors to the book, there was a sharp divide between those who believe that history must serve the project and protect heritage, even at the risk of sometimes instrumentalizing it, and my own position: that a distance should be maintained from the carrying out of the project (both a new or preservation project). My response—paradoxically called "Se tenir hors de l'histoire," was articulated around a sentence by Roland Barthes that Françoise Choay brought to a new audience in *L'Allégorie du patrimoine* (1998): "[History] is constituted only if we consider it, only if we look at it—and in order to look at it, we must be excluded from it."

The studies of built heritage that were entrusted to me after the completion of the Saint-Pierre de Firminy church (2003) or prior to the renovation/restoration of the Maison des Jeunes et de la Culture in the same neighborhood (2007)—two projects by Le Corbusier—but also that of the CHU Necker Hospital by André Wogenscky (2011), led me to define my role as a historian to practicing architects. My first belief is that the study of an edifice can only

2 Graf, "Histoire matérielle du bâti et projet de sauvegarde, un rappel," p. 74.
3 Philippe Bruneau and Pierre Yves Balut, "Positions," *Ramage. Revue d'archéologie moderne et d'archéologie générale*, 1982–1, p. 7.
4 Graf, "Histoire matérielle du bâti et projet de sauvegarde, un rappel," p. 71.
5 Ibid., p. 74.

take place over the long term. Unlike other creative fields—painting, sculpture, decorative arts—architecture is inherently an uncompleted work. As Graf highlights in his own contribution in the book mentioned above, "regular maintenance is the most effective method of prevention."[2] But it does not prevent the alterations that result from transformations, extensions, adaptations to new uses or to the new standards to which many buildings are subject. All interventions contain within them the seed of a modification to the work's heritage value and its original materiality. As with archaeology, where the role of the dig is to "understand the effect of successive eras on a continuous space,"[3] the history of architecture can only be understood by considering the effects of time on the edifice. This approach is in line with that of the preservation studio, when Graf, defining the material history of the built environment, reiterated the importance of taking a long-term view of the building and establishing "the way the intervention operates on it."[4] In his role as architect and lecturer on project design, he goes on to add that this involves shifting from "knowledge that acts to knowledge that informs the preservation project."

The second element that I have gathered from my work on contemporary heritage emerges out of this very shift from knowledge to application. The study of history and heritage allows us to distinguish between what Graf has called the "hard"—or intangible— parts and "soft" parts—those which may undergo possible transformations. And in his role as the director of the Preservation Project, whose aim is to teach students to fly with their own wings (to continue Peter Blake's well-loved animal metaphor), he invites them to adopt a design stance and use their imagination, providing it is "appropriate."

My role as a historian is not to prescribe but to bring, with the greatest possible rigor and total inclusivity, the most possible knowledge and elements for understanding the existing built environment, in other words, tools that help in the decision-making process. This approach of maintaining a distance regarding the object in question found favor during my lectures to the Preservation Project. Seeking to understand and immersing oneself in the past do not, as many architects and teachers of architecture would seem to have it, act as a brake on one's imagination. Which was most aptly summarized by Graf when he wrote: "Remaining as close to things as one possibly can has never implied a lack of imagination. Instead, it opens up fields that objectively are possible."[5]

ENGINEERING

JEAN-PIERRE CÊTRE
Civil engineer, EPFL
Former professor at the Institute of Architecture of the University of Geneva (IAUG)

When examined by the architectural students of the project studio with an eye towards its preservation, an existing building, commonplace or precious, with many uses and not so old, is the very opposite of a blank page. It's more of an enigmatic and original chaos of materials, uses, and architectures, superimposed in time and space. The "survey drawing"—in fact a diagnostic in view of an intervention project which has generally already been presented to the students—drives them to an intimate understanding of the existing built environment in all its dimensions, as much material as cultural or historic. The fields of knowledge that are intelligently formulated in the architectural teaching programs are not yet clearly distinguished. They constitute an enigma that the students passionately attempt to resolve. The students succeed, and propose a project, a new life for the building. Whether that proposition is in continuity with or breaks away from its previous history, it certainly takes that prior history into account.

I have had the pleasure, semester after semester, of accompanying these students in over twenty passionate and fruitful archeological adventures. For years, I had already been faced with the challenge of teaching architecture as a professor of materials and structures, both in the second cycle—so, still rather general instruction—and in the third cycle at the IAUG on the subject of preservation of the modern and contemporary built heritage. The preparatory research for these courses taught me a great deal, but the students, and those to follow, benefitted much less! I was perfectly conscious of the pedagogical vanity of this practice, but I had not yet escaped the well-known curse that strikes construction classes in architectural schools. I had made the decision, however, which I still stand by, to insist on teaching the elements of construction or engineering in their historical and architectural context. A wise precaution, but completely insufficient. In contrast, the framework of the EPFL preservation studio itself provides this contextualization of construction problems, something the students clearly appreciate. How wonderful for an old retired professor, and what's more, to be surrounded by friends both old and new!

Knowledge that was useful and questioned knowledge often concerned the basic knowhow covered in the architectural curriculum. What continually resurface are basic questions relating to foundations and geotechnics, seismic bracing, loads and load lowering, stability, deformations, and cracks or various forms of deterioration. And yet the practitioner's commentary, at least so far as structural engineering is concerned, is often necessary in order to interpret the rationality or incongruity of the choices made during the construction or successive modifications. It was often necessary (and always enlightening) to exchange with the architectural colleagues who were present; the value in having a close relationship between the architect and the engineer was clear, not only for its fruitfulness but also for its placing of limits. Theoretical knowledge of structural mechanics was rarely called upon, but the research at the time on the conservation and durability of materials, whether wood, metal, or concrete, was sometimes relevant or even decisive for the outcome of the diagnosis. In the modern and even contemporary buildings that we visited, the analysis of cracks played only a small but unfortunately repetitive role in the study of deterioration by concrete carbonation: this was the opportunity to remind the students of possibilities of repairing and preventing, as well as of the need for a thorough diagnosis. Pedagogically more interesting, the shrinkage cracks are related to the survey of the expansion joints which condition the project. Of course, the most frequent questions concerned the foundations and the geotechnical knowledge of the site, as well as its susceptibility—or lack thereof—to the overload resulting from building heightening. Which ultimately, for the students meant a growing awareness of the natural and long-term workings of different constructions. The historic evolution, even over a short period of time (contemporaneity) of architecture, in relation to the modes of construction, always appeared. The clearest example is prefabrication.

All in all, each exercise turned out to be a tremendous lesson, touching on all aspects of the building. Although it is more of a distant pedagogical preoccupation for the civil engineer, the understanding of urban sites crowned each analysis in a significant way: putting the students into a real-life situation. There is nothing inconsequential or random about that! It is instead a call to imagination and innovation for the development of a project.

1 See Luc Ferry, *L'innovation destructrice* (Paris: Plon, 2014).

IMPLIED VALUES

RENATO SALVI
Architect, ETHZ FAS-SIA

The students from the project studio run by Professor Graf and his collaborators are busy discussing and sharing their impressions and research, in a room packed with models, the fruit of their analyses. Sharing the knowledge they have gleaned is what brings them together.

The chosen building is dissected, analyzed, measured, redesigned, and recreated, over the course of several semesters. A lengthy and meticulous task, requiring careful work. A face-to-face encounter with the work of an architect, sometimes a few architects, from which to draw a culture of constructing. The architectural work is placed back into its original historical and spatial context using techniques that were available and developed to fulfill their purpose. This studied heritage, often little-known, is at the heart of the studio; rediscovering the interest of a past work in order to prolong it into the present so that it can be a part of an envisageable future, opens a new field of possibilities. The choice is not necessarily for prestigious works, but more often buildings that possess a certain construction logic, or intrinsic proportions, and the multiple beauty that comes with it. This is not a stripped-back, purely technological studio, but a poetic, sensitive space, which tries to instill the pleasure one feels when culture invites itself into one's path.

Once the investigations and diagnoses have been completed, the second part of the studio's work begins. The students are asked to imagine a project where the existing built environment must be integrated into a sizable extension program requiring a total upgrading. The result is surprising, and the strategies developed are rich; this is what sustainable development is all about. We do not give in to the "destructive innovation"[1] of replacing the building, rather it is recognized as the expression of a common asset that nourishes architectural culture. A culture of the past that teaches us not only about the constructive techniques involved, but also about the visions that created them, the existence or absence of societal ambitions, or about the climatic conditions that shaped them (sunshine, wind, flood risk, earthquakes, security, etc.): a kind of X-ray of the time period. The studio does not train future professionals who will build structures as a "service" but offers an approach that will be sensitive to continuity in order to slip into the footsteps of their predecessors. Learning to look at the "ordinary" on different scales, to be confronted with one's own doubts, to have the courage to take a different path, to work with a certain humility; these are the studio's values.

To intervene or on the contrary to show a certain restraint, or even to decide nothing at all—which is the right attitude to adopt? And what if the initial survey contained most of the answer?

I have always agreed with this approach. And it is thus with great emotion that I have found here this practice, nearly forgotten today. I have always loved this necessary "prelude" and often recorded it in my travel diaries. I have measured numerous spaces, in order to depict them, discover their characteristics, appropriate them. I remember the transformation of an old farmhouse where I unfortunately wasn't able to keep the interior walls themselves but only their exact dimensions. That said, by keeping the small measurements, their low ceilings, their rooms laid out in succession, and their small openings, the rooms were able to preserve the shadowy quality they had always had.

A wish? That this teaching continues, that it takes root in the student curriculum, and that it takes an ever-larger role in shaping future abilities and a way of looking at things related to built heritage and the landscapes containing it, and that it continues to question the paralyzing injunctions of our society.

THIERRY MANASSEH

DIVERSITY AND CONVER-GENCES:
PROJECT TEACHING IN THE "PRESERVATION" ORIENTATION

In 2012, the "orientation" system became part of the EPFL master's in architecture. In this system, two courses—one theoretical and the other practical—complement the teaching of the preservation project. Based on the same general subject, but not directly connected, they introduce new questions to the design project and develop tools for answering them. This approach becomes part of the course program once students have carried out their three-year bachelor's degree and a twelve-month professional internship.

As part of the preservation orientation, guest lecturers are invited to teach project design for two consecutive semesters. They are chosen for their abilities as practicing professionals, demonstrated through their built projects and sometimes also through their written work and academic experience.

As Franz Graf provides an overview of preservation studies in the third year of the bachelor's course, the master's program further develops the subject by looking at different cultures, with architects who work outside of the French-speaking part of Switzerland, including France, Spain, Portugal, and the United States. The studio also provides an opportunity to open up to other disciplines, such as Landscape, which in 2020–2022 was taught by Martina Voser.

The concepts of interaction and exchange are therefore present throughout. The lecturers are able to learn more about a school with its own ways of teaching and its own students, while the latter are given the opportunity to discover other built heritages, through the study topic and associated site visit.

This intercultural aspect is sometimes reinforced by the subject itself, as with that taught by Professor João Pedro Falcão de Campos: a school in Lisbon in the first semester and a school in Geneva in the second, built by two architects born in the same year who respond to the same demands in two different cultural, economic, and political contexts.

Topics: Diversity

Whether the topic is the preservation of a building, an ensemble of buildings, or part of a town or landscape, each lecturer's choice of research topic is always representative of a multitude of elements.

It includes information on the historic context in which the architect usually works, as, for example, in the study project offered by Andreas Vass: the rehabilitation of two "Flaktürme," and Augarten park in which these two anti-aircraft towers are located.

It sometimes communicates knowledge of the social and cultural framework of a place, for example, Los Angeles, where Frank Escher and Ravi GuneWardena work. In this research topic, the idea of an opening towards the exterior, much appreciated in warmer climates, is broadened to include the lifestyle and ways of inhabiting buildings in California in the twentieth century.

In other examples, it bears witness to issues in preserving local heritage, such as in the Grisons, birthplace of Ramun Capaul and Gordian Blumenthal, where students were encouraged to think about adapting a typology based on contemporary uses and the development of building techniques.

It may also focus on architecture on the margins of the Modern movement that has a rich but little-known built heritage, pushed to the fore in the history of architecture. The work of Hans Döllgast, the architect of several reconstruction projects in Munich after the Second World War, provided precious learning opportunities in José Ignacio Linazasoro's studio, in which students developed a "preservation project for a preservation project," thus demonstrating the theoretical depth of working with existing structures.

The selected topics are firmly based in the political context and reality in which they are located. The rehabilitation of the Musée National des Arts et Traditions Populaires (MNATP) in Paris, was also put forward as a subject by Denis Eliet and Laurent Lehmann, as these two architects had realized how uncertain its future was following the transfer of its collections to the Musée des Civilisations de l'Europe et de la Méditerranée, an iconic new cultural building in Marseille. The purchase of the MNATP building by Louis Vuitton after it built its Fondation on the neighboring section marked the beginning of a major transformation and change in image, without any consideration of its heritage values, which had been examined some years earlier by students at the EPFL studio.

Method: Convergences

Among the many topics and objects of study, convergences have begun to appear in the manner in which the subjects are dealt with, no doubt partly due to the methodology developed at the TSAM, but also due to the professional practice of each teacher-architect.

The constant element is the consideration and attention brought to the existing built environment, the respect for it. The first stage in this approach is always understanding the existing environment—its context, its place in the collective imagination, and its built reality.

Students learn from another architect, understand that architect's choices, and attribute a value to them, which finally helps them make their own decisions as part of the preservation project. The study of archives, the survey, site visits, and redrafting are some of the tools required for building knowledge.

This know-how is constructed by groups of students and then reproduced in several different formats: synthetic drawings, detailed models, comparative analyses, "Raumbuch," or even extremely detailed "inventories," such as those produced by students attending the Lacaton Druot studio on a section of the city south of the Renens train station. Tree species are identified and recorded in the same way as wastewater or the noise register.

In all these studios, the initial stage is not carried out in the way a historian would, by studying and recounting, but by using the forward-looking eyes of an architect to make a plan based on the qualities and shortcomings that can be seen and by learning to understand the object through the lens of the project. In order to further reinforce this aspect, Martina Voser suggests, for example, that her students develop an initial idea, an initial intuition, before visiting and becoming familiar with the site.

Projects: Diversity, once again

Interventions occur on our built heritage through a cultural attitude that evolves over time. Free of all constraints, the university environment is the ideal place for exploring and developing these attitudes through a project (at least, this is what the work carried out by students, guided by various guest lecturers, indicates).

Many project strategies are studied; some are well known but others are also surprising. No matter the approach to tackling the program (pre-determined in some studios and left up to the student in others), it is always an integral part of the project. It was a vital component of one of the projects in Falcão de Campos's studio, where students worked on the reorganization and distribution of the functions of various schools in Lancy, within their existing buildings, in order to avoid an extension to one of the schools.

In other cases, the strategy may be determined by the existing environment, in particular its alterations. This was the case for a project carried out as part of the Capaul & Blumenthal studio, where the typology preserved and took advantage of the space that was created across all levels of the *Waldhaus* when floors collapsed after the building had fallen into disrepair over many years. Another project fitting thermal baths into the exhibition hall of the MNATP also took advantage of the existing surroundings, or rather the memory of them, when the new pools were drawn using the old exhibition plans.

When it is not based on the existing environment, the approach may be drawn from the practices of the architect who designed the building in question. In the case of the St. Bonifaz church in Munich, preserved and transformed by Hans Döllgast, the architect switched a roof to provide room for a new stairway and create a new front façade overlooking the street. He carried out this intervention in several projects, as part of various transformations, thereby radically changing the typology and meaning of the building with only a slight intervention. This strategy was adopted as part of a project by the Linazasoro studio, which was focused on the idea of the extension—as with the *Weiterbauen*—in this case, however, not of the building itself, but of the architect's project method.

Photograph Exhibition of the case study models, Escher GuneWardena studio, EPFL, 2017

The approach may also be echoed in the collective imagination of architects, as in the case of the Eames and their "Solar Do-Nothing Machine," used as a reference in a project by the Escher GuneWardena studio, to transform the program for the reception building into various pavilions, which were designed like games in the grounds of the Eames' house.

Whatever strategy is used, the projects developed in the preservation studios demonstrate a theoretical depth and diversity that is undeniably embedded in culture. The existing environment, in its material state and in its immaterial dimensions, and of course lecturers' and students' perception of it, provides the necessary resources for the creation of the project. The few examples given here are only a preliminary—they represent but a tiny fraction of the multifaceted work undertaken, and in each studio there are as many different solutions to a given situation as there are students.

Relevance of preservation teaching (and of the discipline)

Briefly introduced with this text and further developed by the contributions following it, the topics that have been proposed over the years, with their connected and inter-related themes, give an indication of the issues at play in contemporary architecture around the world. They demonstrate the broad range of work an architect may be involved with and the tasks awaiting the students in the profession. They are unique to our time but as part of the teaching program are explored with an approach that is both universal and timeless, bringing to the fore the need for critical thinking and sensitivity to the existing environment, to what has already been developed and built, and of course to those who inhabit it.

The pedagogical value of this teaching first of all resides in the possibility of learning through the work of another. Once this knowledge, both technical and sensorial, has been acquired, in a second phase a project with a certain theoretical depth can be planned—the word "depth" is used here in opposition to the surface or the image, which could be used to describe many contemporary projects.

The architect, whether a student or professional, remains in the background (at least temporarily) and is thus freed from his or her own restrictions, able to widen the imaginative possibilities to match that of another person or another time. This freedom in the design of a project, regarding standards, the accepted uses and norms, is made possible by what is already there, thus allowing or even requiring greater creativity than in a new design project.

The existing environment as a learning aide—especially when of a high quality—allows issues of the materiality, construction, and detail of a project to be covered as soon as the semester starts and with all students, whatever their personal ability to plan a project may be. It allows the complexity of the issues surrounding contemporary project planning to be treated, as well as the priorities to be integrated or challenged, with the critical spirit mentioned by Daniel Bosshard and Meritxell Vaquer in their contribution.

Through its needs in terms of the current economic and environmental issues at stake, through the scope of competences required, and through the abundance of theoretical levels it employs, preservation—and broadly speaking any project in an existing situation—is a discipline that gives even greater credibility to the role of the architect in our contemporary society. As Anne Lacaton confirms in the interview in the following pages, most students are already entirely convinced of that.

"WIENER MELANGE"
Monuments et tracés I

Prof. invités Erich Hubmann + Andreas Vass
EPFL 2012-2013

"CAMPUS CRÉATION SONORE - L'ISLE" CCSL
Monuments et traces II

Prof. invités
Erich Hubmann + Andreas Vass
EPFL 2012-2013

HUBMANN & VASS

Fall 2012

WIENER MELANGE—Monuments and Traces I –
Anti-aircraft towers (Flaktürme) in Augarten park in Vienna 1939–1945

Professors: Erich Hubmann and Andreas Vass
Teaching assistants: Oliviero Piffaretti and Stephan Rutishauser

Reviewers: Hermann Czech, Peter Neitzke
Guest professors: Maria Auböck (Augarten), Hermann Czech (Urban
history in Vienna)

Visits: Vienna

Spring 2013

CAMPUS CRÉATION SONORE L'ISLE / CCSL—
Monuments and Traces II
The historic village center of L'Isle (VD)

Professors: Erich Hubmann and Andreas Vass
Teaching assistants: Oliviero Piffaretti and Stephan Rutishauser

Reviewers: Pierre-Alain Croset, Monique Ruzicka-Rossier
Guest lecturers: Blaise Arlaud (acoustic),
Dragos Tara (SMC–concert hall),
Christoph Theiler (composition and contemporary music techniques)

Visits: L'Isle

MONUMENTS AND TRACES: PROJECTING MEMORY

ERICH HUBMANN
ANDREAS VASS
Hubmann Vass Architects, Vienna

Every architectural project produces its own future memory.

This is the thesis that was proposed to the master's students as a starting point for their projects, which were meant to use existing architecture to bring the students into contact with structures loaded with history that we have called landscapes. In the Fall semester, we looked at Vienna and its still-visible vestiges of National Socialism and the Second World War: the system of defensive anti-aircraft towers constructed towards the end of the war around the center of town. In the Spring semester, we traveled to the Jura Vaudois, to a seemingly more peaceful, almost idyllic small village whose name, L'Isle (the Island), hints at a complex history that, when looked at more closely, reveals its own tensions and ruptures, between domination and incidents, between disruptive and interrupted development, and a low level of social organization.

The starting postulate required us to closely examine a dimension of the architecture that in our work is usually relegated to the background, as a self-evident fact that architecture usually tends to endure, and which isn't usually the object of our thoughts and concerns: the dimension of time. On the one hand, when we work with existing constructions this dimension is inescapable, but, on the other hand, it is a source of questions and difficulties for those who integrate it into the project. The metaphor that we propose as a means of identifying or imagining the dimension of the ephemeral or the fleeting is that of memory.

But how to become aware of this potential memory, this ability to remember? And how to take advantage of this awareness in order to elaborate projects that go beyond simple functionality, without claiming an illusory autonomy?

These questions touch on the paradoxes of architecture's temporality: however contemporary it might be at the moment we perceive it, it seems to come from far away, from another time, from a past that it seems to carry along with it. But which past? Were cathedrals ever "white" like Le Corbusier wanted us to believe? Is it their novelty that works of architecture carry with them through time? Is it the idea, which remains present at all times—immortal—in architecture as it ages? Is it the shape, in fact, that it was meant to take and that it perhaps never took? Or, on the contrary, is the past made up of all these periods that the work of architecture has gone through, of all the transformations that it has undergone, up until it reaches us? Is it precisely the aging that emerges as the past of the work of architecture? The traces of aging, which led Aloïs Riegl to call the "value of oldness" the cardinal value of monuments?

1 See Maurizio Ferraris, "Quel che resta dell'architettura," *Rassegna (Minimal)*, 36, no. 10 (1988): 9–14.

2 Georg Wilhelm Friedrich Hegel, *Ästhetik*, vol. 1 (Berlin: 1984), 89 (citation translated by author).

The third position that may help us grasp the paradoxes of the temporality of architecture is that which Italian philosopher Maurizio Ferraris developed in 1988 in a text on architectural minimalism.[1]

Starting from Hegelian theses on the "symbolic" architecture of the pyramids, Ferraris believes that the privilege of architecture is to offer, in relation to the pure idea, a "minimal" surplus, its materiality, which allows it to survive the death of the idea in the void. For Ferraris, who is far from claiming that architecture is autonomous, it is neither the idea nor the value in the age of the patina that allows architecture to move from one period to another—similarly for Hegel, who distinguishes his views from those of Kant, it is not the pleasant decoration, not some aesthetic supplement to a changing functional and practical basis, that legitimizes and anchors it as the first of the arts. There is no assigned meaning, no connotative "second function" or ancient message allowing architecture to transcend time, rather its vocation as an abstract symbol, of preparation and material reference to a meaning that has not (yet) occurred: the task of "beautiful architecture ... lies in working the inorganic exterior nature in such a way that this latter, as an exterior world that conforms to art, resembles the spirit."[2] Questioning the paradoxical temporality of architecture—which is indispensable when one develops a project involving existing buildings—also implies concentrating on the work of architecture, on its persistence and its material surplus: the overdetermination of its materiality.

Now, for a project to be conscious of its future memory, these three attempts to grasp the diachrony of architecture—the idea of the original, the unrolling of the metamorphosis, and the resilience of the materials—become operative only if we accept that the project has already begun before us and that the very purpose of such a project creates a distance between us, at the moment when we begin the studies, and this same project, which is its own past. The project is made up of things and stories that are found on-site, material and immaterial data that need to be discovered, "prehistory" that we will transform into history when we develop the project. As a result, only a laborious empirical and hermeneutic search allows to move from this prehistory to the as-yet-unwritten history that the project generates. When we ask ourselves how a project can or should "refer" to a determined context, it means first measuring this distance, which presupposes that we are clear about our own position and our own interests regarding the context, then defining a basis or a support to signal or "make visible" this prehistory as an absence. This basis, which opens up to a reality, is simultaneously material and fictive, much like the symbol mentioned by Hegel.

This way of producing the project thus gives the architecture no room for autonomy, no memorial authority, but postulates instead the openness of the project to the social constitution of memory and to the memory materialized in its concrete and current context. The monuments and the traces constitute two different scales for the architectural space of reference.

These intentions were decisive for the didactic structure of the master's level studio, as much in the choice of sites and themes as in the specific programs and work stages. The Viennese anti-aircraft defensive towers from the Second World War (more specifically, one of the sites having two such towers, the Baroque Augarten Park, which is important for Vienna in more ways than one), but also the complex morphology of the village of L'Isle offered numerous occasions for searching and interpreting the traces and for coming into contact with the apparent monumental elements of the history inscribed in these places. The programs were, however, anchored in the present, even if there was no lack of potential historical references.

We suggested that grasping these two parallel planes of design work be understood as an "immaterial" and "material" project, respectively. The level of the "immaterial" project included relationships on a large scale—landscape and town—while for those on the "material" level, the discussion was focused on the constructive and spatial interventions on a relatively small scale.

The first (and completely essential) step was to carry out a large-scale interpretive analysis: comparing the facts from available historical documents—texts, images, and maps—with the concrete and individual observations made on-site, and to select, interpret, and categorize—that is, carrying out a systematic reading of the facts in their spatial and temporal dimensions.

The next step was to study what relationship the concrete program of the spaces—each with about 1,500 to 2,000 square meters dedicated to various uses—could have to these interpretive sketches: could these programs have been designed as devices and direct references, as affirmation or antithesis, or did they need to be superimposed on preexisting structures and stratifications as new temporary or permanent layers?

A small study center for the Austrian Film Archives (Filmarchiv Austria) and a building for the Documentation Center of Austrian Resistance (Dokumentationsarchiv des Österreichischen Widerstandes) in the Augarten in the Fall semester, and a center for contemporary music with a small concert hall, classrooms, and housing for artists in residence around the castle and in the center of the village of L'Isle during the Spring semester—these two programs offered numerous possibilities for interpretation. Some of the existing buildings lent themselves to transformations or enlarging, and certain unbuilt surfaces to the installation of new volumes. When placing the different programs and relating them to the existing constructions, the exterior spaces and built volumes had to be approached in an integrative way and treated with the same care.

It was then necessary to develop the material and constructive elements of the selected parts with the help of plans, images, and models, and to develop them up to the scale of the representative details.

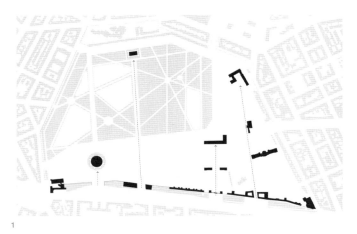

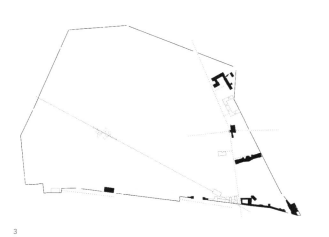

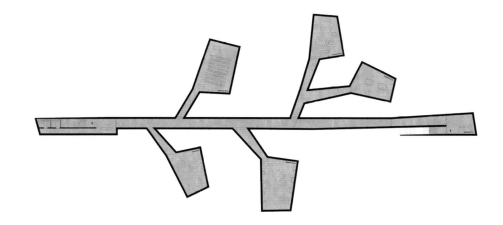

TEACHING THE PRESERVATION 196

1, 2 Analysis of the "boulevard" as a typology in the history of the city of Vienna, and a project that explores the link between the boulevard "Obere Augartenstrasse" and the park, with its existing monuments and the new program

3, 4, 5, 6 The axial connection of three anti-aircraft towers constructed on the city's territory is materialized by different interventions in Augarten. The above-ground program is situated on the outskirts of the park, while an underground commemorative hall is created near the anti-aircraft tower

7, 8, 9 As the towers were constructed without being integrated into the layout of the park, the project proposes to let water flow down the entire height of one tower, representing the trace of a river branch at the exact spot it passed in the eighteenth century and symbolizing both the link and the distance between the park and the tower

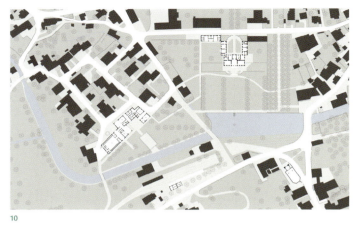

10

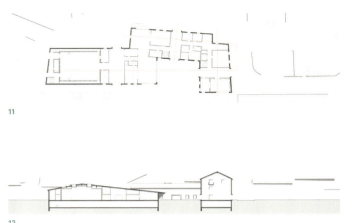

11

12

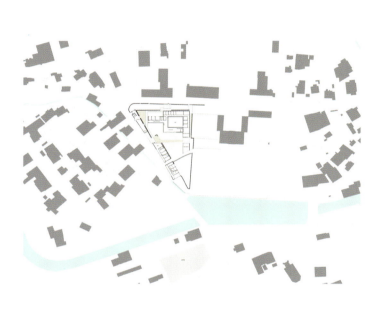

13

14

15

16

TEACHING THE PRESERVATION 198

17

10, 11, 12 The transformation of the extension of an existing house in the structure of the village broadens the zone of the public buildings on the waterfront and links the station (arrival place) to the historic center (castle)

13, 14, 15, 16 The precise positioning of new volumes and the integration of existing buildings on the triangular parcel to the west of the castle gives the park a new setting

17, 18, 19 The project occupies an abandoned parcel of land belonging to the SAPJV postal bus garage. New partially mobile structures occupy the no-longer-used buildings and integrate the CCSL program

18

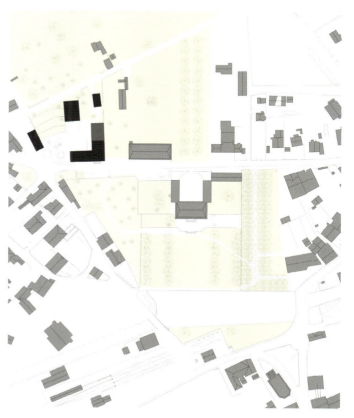

19

[FAU]BOURG

We will build castles in the air and test the utopian as parallel thought to the established. The town as answer to a desperate attempt to achieve city or the romanticised rurality in an endless suburbia.

Picture: Wappenbuch Gerold Edlibach, 1493, Staatsarchiv Zürich

El Quadrat d'Or

Built on a very rational urban plan, we will look at the eclectic growth of one of Barcelona's Eixample city blocks. Your proposals for extension or renewal will develop out of understanding and rethinking this complex cultural context that includes a house like Casa Milà from Antoni Gaudí i Cornet.

TEACHING THE PRESERVATION   200

BOSSHARD & VAQUER

Fall 2013

Greifensee

Professors: Daniel Bosshard and Meritxell Vaquer
Teaching assistants: Esther Elmiger, Csaba Tarsoly

Reviewers: Franz Graf, Philip Ursprung

Visits: Greifensee and Zurich

Spring 2014

El Quadrat d'Or

Professors: Daniel Bosshard and Meritxell Vaquer
Teaching assistants: Esther Elmiger, Csaba Tarsoly

Reviewers: Jean-Pierre Dresco, Joaquim Rosell

Visits: Barcelona

1 Climate Strike, "Climate Action Plan," accessed December 16, 2022, https://www.climatestrike.ch/fr/crisis#solutions.

THOUGHTS ON PERSISTENCE AND INVENTION

DANIEL BOSSHARD
MERITXELL VAQUER
Bosshard Vaquer Architekten, Zurich

Preservation

Any action is in reality an intervention in the existing environment, and deserves to be preserved for many reasons.

Today, in 2022, our societies are on the cusp of a new way of understanding the world. The human presence permeates everything and is continuing to spread. Temperatures around the world are increasing. There is an urgent need to go beyond our modern ideals, corrupted by capital—the idea of freedom and a new start, the *tabula rasa* with its immanent distinction between nature and culture, as the past one hundred years have too often celebrated, while simultaneously perverting this distinction by favoring profit and growth at the cost of high-quality densification. The paradigm shift that is taking place right now is particularly stimulating for architects. We are questioning the teaching of architecture; the pendulum has already begun to swing towards a design approach that protects our resources. In universities and in practice, the analysis and management of CO_2 emissions and construction-related gray energy are central concerns. The Climate Action Plan developed by the Climate Strike movement in Switzerland[1] goes even further: a temporal pause in the form of a moratorium on new constructions. Understanding the whole of the built environment as a precious resource, and not just in terms of energy, provides us with the opportunity for a renewed and broadened collective appreciation for preservation and our built heritage. Interesting buildings that have not been listed and are not protected can then be preserved and transformed, rather than demolished as has been the case, even recently. Our teaching approach takes into account the existing environment and we emphasize the benefits of good maintenance. Heritage monuments shall not be sacrificed to the transformations that are underway.

The approach taken towards the existing built environment must be adapted to each situation. In order to define this method of working and make it usable in a classroom context, we will attempt first of all to describe our understanding of the profession and the meaning of the concept "existing built environment." We will then outline how as guest professors we have applied the concept of intervention on the existing built environment into our classes on project design.

These classes are designed to develop students' critical thinking so that they are capable of putting forward new and concrete approaches within a complex reality and so that through their work they can creatively contribute to our culture while also challenging it.

2 "architect (n.): person skilled in the art of building, one who plans and designs buildings and supervises their construction, 1560s, from French *architecte*, from Latin *architectus*, from Greek *arkhitekton* 'master builder, director of works,' from *arkhi-* 'chief' (from *arkhein*, 'to lead the way, govern') + *tekton* 'builder, carpenter' (from PIE root *teks-* 'to weave,' also 'to fabricate')." (Online Etymology Dictionary, "architect (n.)," accessed December 6, 2022, https://www.etymonline.com/word/architect)

3 For Gottfried Semper, tectonics relates to the art of assembling in the field of carpentry, and, partly, the fields of stone construction, metalworks, and surfacing and coating. (See Semper, *Der Styl in den technischen und tektonischen Künsten*, [Frankfurt: Verlag für kunst un wissenschaft, 1860]).

Tektōn

When we began our careers as architects in the 2000s, we decided to stop worrying about issues of style and instead shape our philosophy around what was physically present on site, so that we could work in total independence. We wanted—and still want—to develop a keen and curious view on things, capable of building clear relationships between open spaces, eras, and architectures. As *tektonoi*, we were determined to make constructive decisions based on form, volume, and terrain, and thus find the exact answer to the particular problem we were facing. For us, architectural thought has always been unreservedly connected to what came before, and our practice must also develop out of this. In all our projects we adhere to the notion of the existing built environment—in the sense of *Weiterbauen*—independently of the fact that the context must be considered as more or less worthy of preservation. We feel the need to identify on each site the elements that provide continuity, that for us fulfill the requisite condition for invention. We endeavor to determine the potential for permanence and quality, activating them for the benefit of the community through meticulous and precise work, thus also considering the present as well as past eras, and more or less natural open spaces, architectures, and landscapes.

Over such a long period of study and on-site work, the *arkhi-tektōn*[2] takes on a large amount of responsibility. In practice, he or she works with specialists from multiple disciplines to find concrete solutions that are more than just answers to problems of statics and hygiene. From the earliest days of our professional career, both the technical and constructive complexity caused by questions of energy and the need to take into account environmental and heritage issues are inherent to our project work. Until only recently, however, ensuring a sparing use of construction materials was not a major preoccupation. The legal framework within which we act, rules governing urban design, construction standards, fire protection and earthquake safety legislation, and the laws concerning parking must all be revised in order to radically change our excess consumption of gray energy. This is the responsibility of politicians and political organizations.

While thanks to the writings of Gottfried Semper[3] the issue of tectonics has already been defined and integrated into traditional teaching of project design, the issue of responsibility can only be learned through practice. The impossibility of dissociating our professional activity from social and political concerns is clearly illustrated through our choice of semester topics. The interdisciplinarity and manifold points of view are visible in the collaboration between laboratories and in the various working groups.

For our first semester at the EPFL, we chose to study Greifensee, a small town in the countryside outside Zurich, reflecting on ways to develop spaces for living and activities that would generate a denser built fabric, while still preserving and highlighting the location's rural and suburban qualities. The second semester was devoted to one of the most popular attractions in Barcelona, Antoni Gaudí i Cornet's Casa Milà, known as "La Pedrera" (the "stone quarry"). Over time, this iconic housing block has gradually lost its strictly residential purpose. The few remaining tenants live their day-to-day lives as if in a show, and in neighboring buildings, the effects of online temporary rental platforms are strongly felt. This monument, a UNESCO world heritage site that is losing importance for the city due to increased tourism, also provided us with the opportunity to study new modes of living and working in this small area in the Eixample neighborhood.

4 "exist (v.) to have actual being of any kind, actually be at a certain moment or throughout a certain period of time, c. 1600, from French *exister* (17c.), from Latin *existere/exsistere* to step out, stand forth, emerge, appear; exist, be" (Online Etymology Dictionary, "exist (v.)," accessed December 6, 2022, https://www.etymonline.com/search?q=exist); "**persist** (v.)

continue steadily and firmly in some state or course of action, especially in spite of opposition or remonstrance; persevere obstinately, 1530s, from French *persister* (14c.), from Latin *persistere* 'abide, continue steadfastly,' from *per* 'thoroughly' [...] + *sistere* 'come to stand, cause to stand still'" (Online Etymology Dictionary, "persist (v.)," accessed December 6, 2022,

https://www.etymonline.com/search?q=persist); "**consist** (v.) 1520s, 'to be, exist in a permanent state as a body composed of parts,' from French '*consister*' (14c.) or directly from Latin *consistere* 'to stand firm, take a standing position, stop, halt,' from assimilated form of *com* 'with, together' [...] + *sistere* 'to place,' causative of *stare* 'to stand, be standing.' From 1560s,

with *of*, as 'be composed, be made up.' From 1630s as 'be consistent.' (Online Etymology Dictionary, "consist (v.)," accessed December 6, 2022, https://www.etymonline.com/search?q=consist)
5 Regarding the notion of landscape, see John Brinckerhoff Jackson: "Landscape is not scenery; it is not a political unit; it is really no more than a collection, a system of man-

made spaces on the surface of the Earth. Whatever its shape or size, it is never simply a natural space, a feature of the natural environment; it is always artificial, always synthetic [...] A landscape is where we speed up or retard or divert the cosmic program and impose our own." *Discovering the Vernacular Landscape* (New Haven, CT: Yale University Press, 1984), 156–57.

Greifensee and Barcelona both play an important role in each of our lives, which made it easier to prepare our teaching units. As part of this thought process around Barcelona's cultural context, the collaboration with Philippe Block, professor of structure at the EPFZ, opened up interesting paths with regard to the possibility of including historical arched constructions into the project using computer-assisted research methods.

The existing built environment

The verb "exist," referring to something that is (already) there, shares the same Latin root as the words "persist" and "consist."[4]

This common root suggests that what already exists, in the architectural sense of the word, may be understood as being that which persists across time and that is part of architecture's "capital"—both permanent and continually renewed, just like that which is present, through its ability to last as part of a whole, of a larger unit.

Architectural heritage is first of all made up of what is physically there, and it changes with each project. Architecture's contribution to space is manifested as form—it can therefore learn from pre-existing forms. The logic of a building or a landscape[5] or a city is best understood through each of their own forms. Built objects are seen as authentic and without falsification. But they are produced within a specific era and society, in which they participate as a cultural asset and to which they are subject. A certain amount of contextualization is needed in order to better understand how the decisions made are contained in this "form."

Intervening in an existing building, landscape, or city requires a design approach that is attentive and rational. It is a question of studying what already exists, but also the context in which it developed, in order to better understand the construction techniques that were employed, as well as the decisions and original project principles. Kept records and an often non-exhaustive list of authors, specialists, sponsors, and other historians that the architect can gather together will provide a valuable source of information that helps in the development of the project, but that may also provide a distraction from the final goal.

Working with the existing environment and analyzing the complex reality of each job are more than simply rational processes; they require empathy.[6] In the field of heritage preservation, the framework for the physical intervention is established in a more narrowly focused manner. Here, what already exists is defined by its attributes, and by a specific, or even exceptional, cultural worth that is rich and diverse. Maintaining these attributes is an obligation that as architects we carry out with joy. Changing eras involves new requirements and a new form of interpretation or even invention that is capable of reconciling the old and the new, and "reconfirming" the existing environment. The principles remain valid and can also be applied to unremarkable examples that must be preserved for other reasons. The idea of something that comes back or something that lasts, can be extended, and the empathy that is developed over the course of one's work brings additional value through the attribution of an appropriate meaning and place to each thing.

The survey as a means of research and interpretation

During the long phase of work that precedes the site visit as part of the study trip, the students collect a great deal of information. The whole group participates in the creation of models that

6 In psychology, empathy refers to the ability to share another person's feelings and emotions. In the field of architecture, empathy can be understood as the ability to perceive and identify the attributes and potential of an existing work, ensemble, or system.
7 Catalan modernism is an artistic and architectural movement that developed towards the end of the nineteenth century, out of an aspiration for modernity.

Art Nouveau, Modern Style, Jugendstil, Stile Liberty, and Sezessionsstil are other European expressions of the same movement.
8 "interpret (v.) late 14c., 'expound the meaning of, render clear or explicit,' from Old French *interpreter* 'explain; translate' (13c.) and directly from Latin *interpretari* 'explain, expound, understand,' from *interpres* 'agent, translator.'" (Online Etymology Dictionary, "interpret (v.)," accessed December 6, 2022, https:// www.etymonline.com/word/ interpret#etymonline_v_9429)

have a strong physical presence: the neighborhood block at a 1:50 scale for the semester in Barcelona, and a textured physical map and axonometric drawing of the whole built territory for the town planning study at Greifensee. The students then choose a one-kilometer strip to survey during the study trip. In order to be able to work effectively once on site, they must gather information in groups about such topics as infrastructure, building typology, protected buildings, or topography, and get a clear idea about the work that will later be required. For Greifensee, each group focuses on a specific period in the history of the area, synthesizes the information in an essay, and then presents the results to the rest of the class. For Barcelona, the students make detailed drawings of architectural works that are typical of Catalan modernism,[7] drawn from criteria such as type, façade construction, or general construction principles, then, before they begin the design, they outline together the functions of several buildings within the block.

At the beginning of each semester, students receive a reading list. They each choose a text depending on their interests and then present their own interpretation to the group to discuss. Throughout the semester, historical examples with the particularly successful expression of a style are also presented. For Greifensee, this includes English landscaped gardens that made an appearance during the agricultural revolution of the eighteenth century, Palladian villas from the Republic of Venice, the medieval monastery, and, in the canton of Zurich, traditional regional types such as the *Flarzhäuser* (adjoining farmhouses), and the traditional layout of market towns as they currently are. For Barcelona, this includes Catalan modernist buildings and those with *volta catalana* (traditional arches built without an intrados), which form part of substantial preparatory documentation work and which the students later draw while on site, as well as the buildings that will be visited during the study trip.

The students begin the semester by drawing, photographing, and describing the place or the buildings that have been chosen as a basis for the project. This task is not a simple formality, but requires interpretation, and is carried out in groups and through mutual exchange. It is a process of understanding, whose aim is to create a project for today's world and for a specific site. The approach is critical and selective.

The groups lay out the observed features and the experiences gained from the site visits. The study of the historical and typological development of the space is carried out in parallel, fueling the interpretative work.

To be able to interpret,[8] one has to be able to understand, and this understanding grows from the empathy that is required for drawing: drawing helps us perceive, understand, and remember. This task is not always exhaustive; as a critical interpretation it can be intentionally targeted or instead focus on specific features.

This survey stage nevertheless remains close to reality and, in an attempt to both test and evaluate, brings to light what will be instrumental for the project and what in the end will be used for its representation.

Teaching design: Imagination and *designare*

Hermann Czech's "everything is transformation"[9] and the idea of "replay"[10] are the two guiding principles for teaching design. They imply the acquisition of knowledge—especially historical knowledge—and the establishment of rules. Just as in the field of preservation it is a question

9 See Hermann Czech, "Alles ist Umbau," *Werk, Bauen+Wohnen*, no. 3 (1998). "Transforming an existing building a new one – because, in essence, everything is transformation (1973). Yesterday's large city is an entity made up of different levels. [...] Each one of these levels is the for-

malization and specification of the previous level. Order issues from the decisions made in the previous levels, while diversity occurs in the subsequent levels. Different time frames are ascribed to the different levels, with large-scale decisions having a longer time span than small-scale ones. Neither

urban development nor urban life itself is possible without transformation."
10 See Franz Graf and Giulia Marino, "Conservation et réutilisation de l'architecture du XXᵉ siècle – Replay et projet de sauvegarde,"; and Daniel Bosshard and Meritxell Vaquer, "Replay," in Marco Bakker, Alexandre Blanc,

Pauline Seigneur, *Architectura ludens – Magma & Principes* (Lausanne: Manslab Edition, 2015).
11 On June 17, 2012, 54.5% of voters in the canton of Zurich approved the proposed cantonal referendum (in the form of a general, rather than legislative, proposal) aiming to preserve areas with great agri-

cultural and ecological value ("Kulturlandinitiative").
12 The Quadrat d'Or (Golden Square) is a square area straddling the Passeig de Gràcia. It contains many remarkable buildings built in the Catalan modernism style.

of continuing the built heritage by drawing on an in-depth study of the architectural "capital," the creation of new architecture must also be at the service of the urban context, whose definition fades under the influence of uncontrolled development.

To portray an idea, the design drawings use the same graphic techniques and codes as survey drawings. The situation models previously made help the design process. Drawings and models enable the students to first of all study and then demonstrate the selected architectural installation and language. The models present the projects from the outside and the inside, while photographs produce visualizations in the form of collages. Students are not allowed to use computer-generated images.

In Greifensee, certain projects put forward concrete ideas for a contemporary town, through careful interventions on existing urban structures. Greifensee has a typical old town center, overlooked by a castle, prefabricated housing complexes, and a huge anonymous intermediary zone within which the uncertain life of a typical country town takes place. The visual impression one may have of the town is created in part by the historic center but also, in sharp contrast, by the prefabricated buildings. While density alone does not create a town, neither does low density guarantee a rural life. Instead, it creates an urban sprawl that destroys the original intention, as can be seen in neighborhoods with individual houses. Given that in the canton of Zurich, agricultural areas are now protected,[11] the design projects explore different ways to reduce the built footprint in this era of population growth, while promoting urbanism and enriching daily life through the inclusion of specialized trades and commercial activity.

In groups, students choose the sites and define the framework of the relevant functions The projects have names such as *Sawmill Two: Inhabiting, Enlarging, and Transforming the Modern Vernacular; Burg-am-Greifensee; Plattenbau for the Country Town: Göhner Revisited; The Market Road: New Interpretations of the Flarzhouse; The Cluster at the Hamlet: The Square as Threshold to the Town; The Tower, the Bourg.*

The formal and urban connections between the suggested and existing ensembles are at the very heart of the issue. The physical map, axonometric drawing, detailed plans, and general models depict—including in terms of materialization and construction—the students' propositions for housing and contemporary working areas in a small country town like Greifensee.

In their interventions on the Quadrat d'Or,[12] which is the central zone of the Eixample neighborhood in Barcelona, the students begin with the existing environment and reflect on how to integrate housing and studios for artists, musicians and researchers, and offices for two foundations, as well as additional rental accommodation. Part of the complex for the foundations is also used as a hotel, with function and exhibition rooms, a café-bar, restaurant, auditorium, and meeting and conference rooms.

The students choose the specific area in the neighborhood they wish to study and develop the accompanying design. To do this, they split into three groups that each must produce a masterplan: two of these plans focus on half of the neighborhood, including the remarkable buildings that are present (La Pedrera, Casa Josep Codina, Casa Ramon Casas, Casa Josep Ferrer i Vidal), while the third focuses on the square. Plans of the floors and detailed sections incorporating the whole neighborhood, as well as elevations produced using collage techniques, form the basis for students to maneuver within and develop their designs. They create their propositions in small groups and regularly insert them into the overall master-

13 "invention (n.) early 15c., *invencioun*, 'finding or discovering of something,' from Old French *invencion* (13c.) and directly from Latin *inventionem* 'faculty of invention,' noun of action from past-participle stem of inve-nire 'to come upon, find; find out; invent, discover, devise; ascertain; acquire, get, earn.' The sense of 'thing invented' is first recorded 1510s; that of 'act or process of finding out how to make or do' is from 1530s." "invent (v.) c. 1500, 'to find, discover' (obsolete), a back-formation from invention or else from Latin *inventus*, past participle of *invenire* 'to come upon; devise, discover.' The general sense of 'make up, fabricate, concoct, devise' (a plot, excuse, etc.) is from 1530s, as is that of 'produce by original thought, find out by original study or contrivance.'" (Online Etymology Dictionary, "interpret (v.)," accessed December 6, 2022, https://www.etymonline.com/word/interpret#etymonline_v_9429)

plan. The various formats ensure that students can seamlessly move from the survey phase to the design phase. Photographs of the large-scale interior models show how the interventions interact with the existing environment.

Propositions for extension or renovation develop out of the understanding students have of the built context and its rearrangement through various spatial and tectonic approaches. A harmonious cohabitation between housing, workspaces, shared premises, and tourism activities can thus take shape. With its density and strong character, the existing environment provides the ideal substratum.

In a manner of speaking, our imagination places before us the idea in the form of a built object or space, of an entity that demands to be thought of and worked on. The representation is physical and requires us to employ all our senses. It is connected in a certain way (a way that we need to analyze) with the field of actual activity. Our professional knowledge affects its representation. Imagining is a permanent, kaleidoscopic, and inductive process that tends to enhance the project; it creates more complexity.

In Latin languages, and French in this case, the verb "entendre" can mean "perceive," "understand," and "intend." The first stages of the project take place thanks to what we have perceived and understood, and thanks to knowledge coupled with intention. The word "design," from the Latin *designare*, also means a general plan or intention. To design, therefore, is to combine perception and intention, through representation and professional knowledge. It is an iterative process that emerges from one's imagination and that brings into play all the discipline's various aspects in order to produce a reinvented reality[13]—out of and for the existing environment.

1 Burg-am-Greifensee; wooden vertical extension of the town's commercial center, with housing and open-air theater; model
2, 7 An esthetic transition between agriculture and habitat; housing and greenhouse, wooden horse-riding stables, and events pavilion; model and plan
3 *"Plattenbau" for the Country Town: Göhner Reworked*; prefabricated concrete housing, model
4 Physical map
5 Housing tower, the village; two housing towers with boat shed, sailing clubs, fishpond, and cafe; image
6 Axonometric drawing

TEACHING THE PRESERVATION 208

209 PROJECT TEACHING IN THE "PRESERVATION" ORIENTATION

8

9

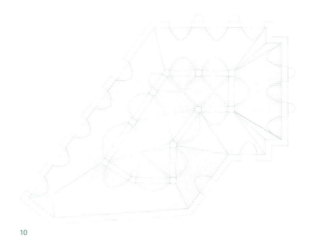
10

11

12

13

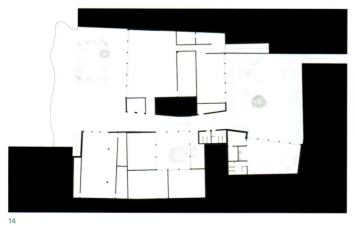
14

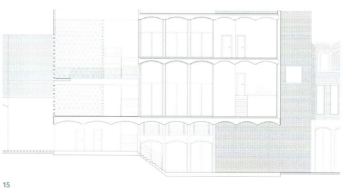
15

8 Casa Planells, Josep Maria Jujol, 1924, elevation
9 Casa Amatller, Josep Puig i Cadafalch, construction from 1898 to 1900, elevation
10 Manhattan municipal building, Rafael Guastavino, ceramics on the ceiling of the south arcade
11, 12, 13, 14, 15 Project organized around a courtyard; model and section inserted into overall context, image, plan of ground floor, section
16, 17 Casa Josep Codina; detail of façades overlooking courtyard and street
18 Model of block
19, 20, 21, 22 Project for the Casa Milà and Casa Josep Codina; section, elevation, general plan, plan of one appartment building in the roof

TEACHING THE PRESERVATION   210

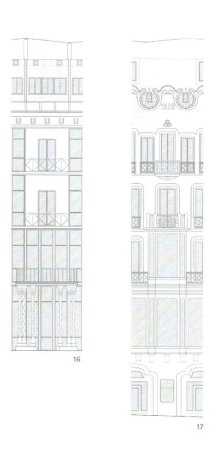

16

17

18

19

20

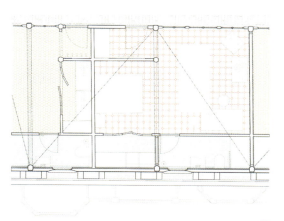

21

22

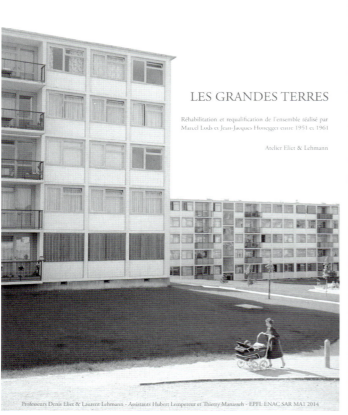

LES GRANDES TERRES

Réhabilitation et requalification de l'ensemble réalisé par
Marcel Lods et Jean-Jacques Honegger entre 1951 et 1961

Atelier Eliet & Lehmann

Professeurs Denis Eliet & Laurent Lehmann - Assistants Hubert Lempereur et Thierry Manasseh - EPFL ENAC SAR MA1 2014

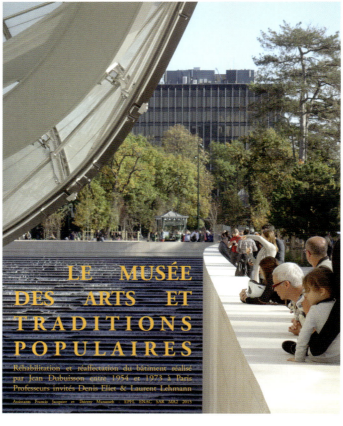

LE MUSÉE DES ARTS ET TRADITIONS POPULAIRES

Réhabilitation et réaffectation du bâtiment réalisé
par Jean Dubuisson entre 1954 et 1973 à Paris
Professeurs invités Denis Eliet & Laurent Lehmann

Assistants Francis Jacquier et Thierry Manasseh - EPFL ENAC SAR MA2 2015

ELIET & LEHMANN

Fall 2014

Les Grandes Terres—
Rehabilitation and re-qualification of overall complex
Marcel Lods & Jean-Jacques Honegger architects, 1951–1961

Professors: Denis Eliet, Laurent Lehmann
Teaching assistants: Hubert Lempereur, Thierry Manasseh

Reviewers: Benoit Carrié, Jean-François Cabestan, Franz Graf
Additional Lecturers: Bernadette Blanchon, Hubert Lempereur,
Sergio Grazia, Vincent Thiesson

Visits: Geneva and Paris

Spring 2015

The Musée des Arts et Traditions Populaires—
Rehabilitation and conversion
Jean Dubuisson architect, 1954–1973

Professors: Denis Eliet, Laurent Lehmann
Teaching assistants: Francis Jaquier, Thierry Manasseh

Reviewers: Aurore Dubuisson, Sylvain Dubuisson,
Franz Graf, Elise Guillerm
Guest lecturers: Elise Guillerm, Pierre-Yves Brunaud,
Jean-Michel Derex, Didier Mignery

Visits: Paris

TEACHING FRAGMENTS

DENIS ELIET
LAURENT LEHMANN
ELIET&LEHMANN, Paris

MNATP—February 2021

The carcass of Jean Dubuisson's masterpiece looms, much like a reproach, in the Bois de Boulogne.

Reduced to its steel skeleton, the building is now no more than a shadow, pierced by the wind and rain.

The irony of its fate—a thanatomorphosis carried out by the creator's own grandson—doesn't take away from the tragedy of the moment.

In the generalized indifference, the remains of the masterpiece of French modern architecture stand rustily, just across from the opulent Fondation Louis Vuitton.

And its name is added to the long list of its peers, who have also left us too soon.

Modern architecture and heritage

While the passing of time ends up reestablishing natural hierarchies in the artistic domain, modern architecture seems almost to have been touched by a curse.

While modern furniture flies out of sales rooms, and even the least known visual artists see their works reevaluated and their ratings soar, ordinary modern architecture—not including iconic structures (but even those)—follows the opposite path.

In Paris, the price difference between one square meter of an uncomfortable Haussmann building and that of an honest post-war building is often more than 20%.

The reasons for this disenchantment with modern architecture are greatly debated by specialists.

The rigor and the simplicity of the material reality have a hard time resisting the effects of passing time and the incessant attacks justified by evolving uses.

Technical materials and equipment, which used to be the most avant-garde of the industry, are difficult to maintain and impossible to replace with identical ones, as they are simply no longer produced.

Evolving norms—particularly those concerning energy efficiency—require transformations which often complete the process of architectural exhaustion.

The loss of readability as a result of these uncoordinated attacks often makes it indefensible to restore or preserve that which—to the common eye—seems now an incongruity of the landscape.

Reglementary requirements are used as a welcome pretext for a crude refurbishment which seals the fate of the condemned; or its demolition (often architecturally preferable).

1 "Simplifying does not consist so much in neglecting what is complex, as it does in clarifying what is important," words of Glenn Murcut,

cited in Françoise Fromonot, *Glenn Murcutt. Projets et réalisations, 1932–2002* (Paris: Gallimard, 2003).

2 Creation of E&L INGENIERIE in 2009.
3 Creation of E&L PROMO-TION in 2016.

Resistance

The implications of these disappearances are barely felt. Few people are bothered.

A few residents, architects, historians… Sometimes a slightly oblivious aedile.

They talk and comfort one another. Sometimes they mount an attack; and lose… Friendships are created.

The subject is not actually very profitable.

Difficult to theorize, except when simplifying. Difficult to monetize, except when tackling the exceptional. Difficult to garner interest, except when making a caricature.

We became involved with it only by chance.

Eliet & Lehmann—August 2002

We met in 1996 while working with architect Christian Devillers (a student of Louis Kahn) and opened our office in 2002 in Paris.

Like all young professionals, we went from one meager suburban commission to another.

Commissions that were most often without any architectural desire. Carried out in spite of the project owner, sometimes against.

Working without a significant budget, in increasingly difficult working conditions, this practice on the margins forced us to learn how to create architecture with very little.

We wanted to simplify.[1] To save on the unnecessary.

Interested by the procedures of transforming matter, protective of the few meager prerogatives we did have, we became a design office[2] and then a project manager. We wanted to further develop our practice by changing it.[3]

La Faisanderie—September 2008

In the little meeting room of the public housing commission of Fontainebleau, we have ten minutes to deliver our proposal.

The challenge isn't clearly formulated. The project is to redo the 200 housing units of "La Faisanderie" or rather, the "SHAPE Village de Fontainebleau" by Marcel Lods.

In the hallway, we ran into our competitors: well-known Parisian architects, established colleagues from Fontainebleau, and a whole host of well-heeled design firms.

Our chances were slim. We were on our own. We won the bid.

In response to vaguely formulated questions (What would we do with this strange structure, these damaged façades, this obsolete technical equipment? How would we meet the challenges of acoustics and energy efficiency?), we brought clear answers and precise propositions.

But above all, we brought our conviction that this complex is—or was—magnificent; and that it would be again.

Not a simple conviction; an ambition. An ambition, not a doctrine.

What must we, what can we conserve? And at what price?

What is architecture, unquestionably?

What is weak and can be discussed?

This last question is central to our intervention, as it is in the rest of our work.

4 Sergio Grazia, 'Photographier le construit"; Hubert Lempereur, "L'invention du grand ensemble"; Bernadette Blanchon, "Pratiques paysagistes dans les grands ensembles"; Vincent Thiesson, "Paysages urbains, enjeux nocturnes."

Curiously it has never been directed at us. And yet there would have been good reason to.

That is where there's no more doctrine and where you have to decide on your own what architecture is already and decide what the project will be and do.

Another important angle of our work consists of re-questioning the initial monofunctional uses (social housing) and convincing the project owner and local elected officials of the capability of these buildings to be adapted to other uses. We will come back to this.

EPFL—July 2011

Our work on La Faisanderie was published, a little.

The TSAM asked us to speak at the "Industrialized and Prefabricated Architecture: Knowledge and Preservation" study days organized in Lausanne.

Many researchers and historians were invited.

We aren't well-acquainted with the world of academic research in architecture. We don't have any special training in heritage.

Our presentation is certainly not a model of its kind.

It can't have been a total disappointment, as two years later we were invited to participate in a panel judging third-year students, where we discovered the uniqueness and the efficiency of the TSAM teaching methods.

The subject for the semester was Le Corbusier's factory in Saint-Dié.

We attended the presentation of the analysis and a short exercise, and then a few months later, the exercises from the project.

By exploring this exceptional heritage, the student learns simultaneously to look at what is built (identify, report, analyze), to study in detail the work of a master and learn the art of project design under the absent but strict gaze of that master.

It's a good exercise.

Growing is only possible by climbing onto the shoulders of those who have gone before us.

Two years later, we were surprised and honored to be invited for a year of teaching.

EPFL—2014 / 2015

It didn't start well.

We hadn't taken the time to learn beforehand about how the EPFL works, and we hadn't prepared sufficiently for teaching our project, so the lecture and presentation of our first topic (the "Grandes Terres" by Marcel Lods at Marly-le-Roi) was a failure.

A small group of motivated students was nonetheless tempted.

Using TSAM methods as our direct inspiration, we worked with those students to tackle a modest yet urgent project.

With the help of our assistants—Thierry Manasseh and Hubert Lempereur—we organized a visit to works by Marcel Lods and Eugène Beaudouin in Paris and Geneva. A series of lectures[4] on the construction of mass housing projects in post-war France was organized.

After a quick analysis of this immense site, we began in parallel short, detailed exercises and in-depth study, focusing on the malfunctions that had appeared with time.

5 Jean Dubuisson: housing and technical equipment at Rocquencourt and Courbevoie, in Paris at Boulevard Suchet, Avenue de la Bourdonnais, and Rue du

commandant Mouchotte; Villa Weil in Pontpoint; MNATP in the Bois de Boulogne. Le Corbusier: Villa Savoye. Alvar Aalto: Villa Carré.

6 Élise Guillerm, "Le MNATP"; Pierre-Yves Brunaud, "Révéler l'existant"; Jean-Michel Derex, "Le bois de Boulogne"; Didier Mignery, "Réhabilitation de l'ensemble La Méditerranée."

The short exercises gave structure to the semester and grounded the project in a manageable and commonplace (although ambitious) reality.

1. Mailboxes (replacing these under-dimensioned objects for new uses);
2. Densities (what densification is possible given the existing architecture);
3. Façade panels (how to ensure the evolution, notably in terms of energy efficiency, of these rather damaged prefabricated elements).

Alone or in pairs, the students tackled various issues: from the urban scale (parking, traffic flow, land development) to the question of residential organization (plantings, playgrounds, package and mail storage) and the bringing back to life of the shopping mall built by Marcel Lods and the work on the buildings themselves.

– Antoine Girardon and Jérémie Jobin: A Walk through the Territory, Landscape, and Parking Spaces
– Fanny Vuagniaux: Communal Spaces and Small Technical Equipment
– Florim Asani: Densification
– Chantal Blanc and Nathalie Grobéty: Urban Space and Reclassifying Basements
– Andrew Dragesco: The Shopping Mall

Intellectually speaking, the results of this first semester were very satisfactory.

However, the small group (reduced in size after the departure of a student for medical reasons) found it difficult to cover the entire site and the buildings. We missed the dynamics of a bigger group.

This disappointing result, which came from our initial clumsiness, was a learning point.

We started the second semester better prepared and with a more balanced subject—Jean Dubuisson's Musée National des Arts et Traditions Populaires (MNATP). We had a core group of several returning students and were joined by a motivated team of new arrivals.

Having mastered the teaching organization of the EPFL, we began with a carefully prepared visit to works by Jean Dubuisson in Paris. Thanks to the unrelenting efforts of our assistants—Thierry Manasseh and Francis Jacquier—doors that had previously remained firmly closed began to open. The four days visiting were rich in discoveries, intense, and exhilarating.[5]

Jean Dubuisson's work—of which we knew only part—revealed itself in all its splendor.

March 3, 2015, the visit and the lectures organized almost as a sort of happening inside the MNATP—opened specially for the occasion—were a shared moment of wonder for all present.

The lecture series[6] provided a framework and accompanied the different sequences of the semester with dynamism and efficiency.

The students—now sufficiently numerous—worked together for a rich and detailed analysis. The models built provided a more precise appreciation of the perfection of the work.

One spectacular model reproduced a scale version of its metallic structure. We couldn't have imagined that six years later this would be the very image of what now remains...

– Group 1: History, urbanism, and environment
– Group 2: Plans, sections and elevations, program, function
– Group 3: Structure
– Group 4: Envelopes and technical equipment
– Group 5: Furniture and lighting

In a second phase, greedily inventing possible uses (if they didn't want to follow the proposed hotel function), the students were confronted with one of those obstacles that can be spotted in many works of modern architecture: the difficulty in coordinating preservation and use.

This is an important subject, and a precise understanding of the existing structure is the key to imagining what can be done; and thus, what will be saved.

When working with a masterpiece like the MNATP, this difficulty (perhaps simple in theory) is in practice immense.

For our academic exercise, we accepted varied propositions, as long as their intentions were coherent.

With great appetite, the end of semester projects were coordinated around the explicit qualities of the existing built environment.

– Alexandre Jacot-Guillarmod: Hotel, Exhibition Hall, and Cinema
– Nicolas Chatelan and Andrew Dragesco: Hotel and Gastronomy School
– Johan Cosandey: Center for Artistic Creation
– Roxane Doyen: Hotel and Spa
– Katia Sottas Kacou: Hotel and Concert Hall
– Antoine Girardon and Jérémie Jobin: Apprenticeship Complex
– Timon Ritscher: Exhibition Center
– Lisa Robillard and Loïc Schaller: Casino Hotel
– Caroline Schartz: UNEP Headquarters and Museum of Climate Change
– Pierre-Henri Sévérac: Hotel, Aquarium, Spa, Conference and Exhibition Hall
– Rafaël Schneiter: School of the Chambre Syndicale de la Couture Parisienne

INHA—March 2016

The seminar organized by Jean-François Cabestan comes to an end.

A day of debates around the future of the MNATP. At this time, the building is still whole, abandoned but magnificent.

In the adjoining hall the students' models hold court. They are very proud. As are we.

Over the course of the day, rich with interventions and debates, we met Martine Segalen and we caught up with Élise Guillerm, Richard Klein, Giulia Marino, Bruno Reichlin, Benoît Carrié—friendships born out of this year of teaching.

Aurore and Sylvain Dubuisson, Jean's children, also joined us. It was the first time we'd seen each other since the final jury panel in Lausanne the year before. They were happy with the day, dedicated to one of their father's major works. As beneficiaries, they were torn between the admiration expressed by the room and fear for the future of the building, in the hands of Thomas, their son and nephew.

While in the end this day did not save the MNATP, it will remain in our memory, and in those of our students. The seminar minutes might serve as a support for future admirers of this work, which has now disappeared.

7 After the marvelous days of the year before in Lisbon, in the company of João Pedro Falcão de Campos and his students.

Palm Springs—February 2017

We are seated on a sofa in the home of californian architect Albert Frey.

An upheaval.

Thanks to our assistant for the year at the EPFL—architect Thierry Manasseh—we joined the group brought to the US by Frank Escher and Ravi GuneWardena—guest lecturers invited by the TSAM in 2016–2017.

We have just spent a week in Los Angeles visiting works that are often inaccessible.[7]

In addition to the enrichment that we owe to those students, to those met during this exceptionally rich and intense year, to the works of architects that we were lucky enough to get so close to, this year has made us custodians of the benevolent and luminous excellence driven by Franz Graf and the community of the TSAM.

It is a teaching.

1

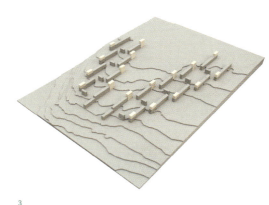

3

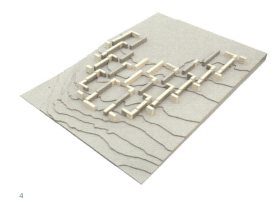

4

2

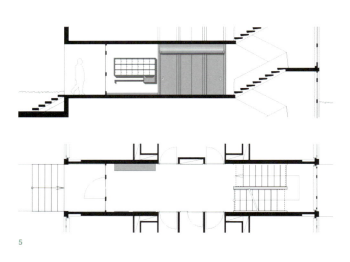

5

6

TEACHING THE PRESERVATION   220

1 The Grandes Terres, view of a neighboring unit from the square, 1961
2 Original façade with prefabricated bays, lightened by corrugated metal, and windows with functional divisions, model
3, 4 Exercises on density, adding 20% and 100% more housing, study models
5 Mailbox exercise, reuse of the existing carpentry to integrate new boxes, plans and section
6 Regeneration of a hall with a new wall to hold a large mirror on one side and the mailboxes on the other, model
7 Project to adapt the north entrance, rehabilitation of the existing housing units, extension, and adding businesses
8 Rehabilitation project for the exterior space, installation of lighting adapted to use, seasons, and time of day
9 Rehabilitation project for the housing units, densification, and addition of a public area on the northern part of the complex

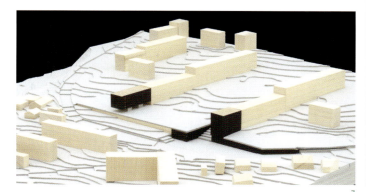

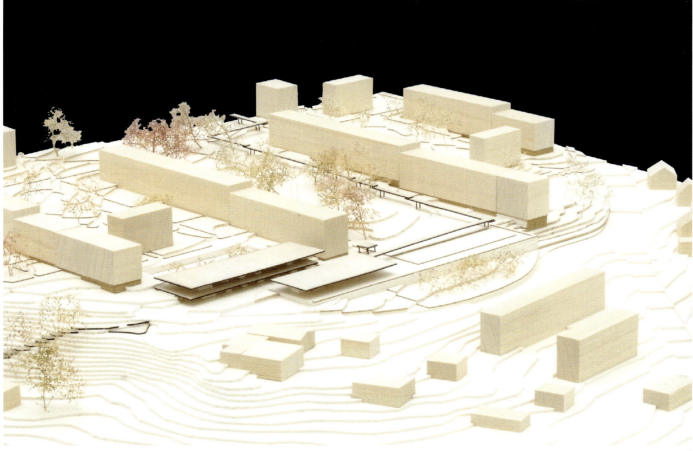

221 PROJECT TEACHING IN THE "PRESERVATION" ORIENTATION

10

11

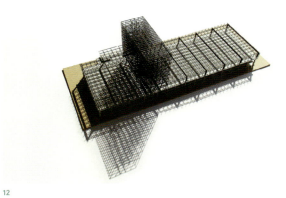
12

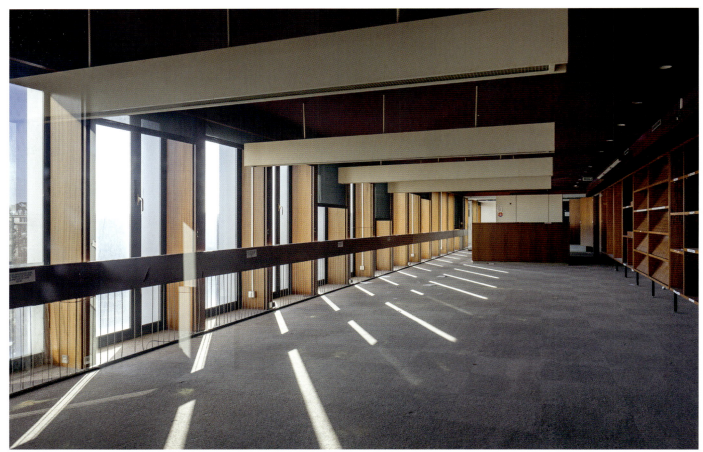
13

TEACHING THE PRESERVATION   222

10 Musée National des Arts et Traditions Populaires (MNATP), view from the entrance portico, exhibition in the horizontal part, and scientific research in the tower, 1973
11 Facing views between the MNATP and the Fondation Louis Vuitton at the border of the Jardin d'Acclimatation, model
12 Structure of the MNATP, analysis model
13 View of a floor of the office tower dedicated to scientific research, consultation hall, 2015

14, 15, 16 Project to transform the building into a hotel with swimming baths, organized according to the original plan drawing and taking advantage of the existing skylights, plan drawing and images
17, 18, 19 Project to transform the building into an apprenticeship complex, extension of the "galette" into a greenhouse, and adaptation of the tower usage to be as close as possible to the existing to conserve its spatial and material qualities, plan and images

14

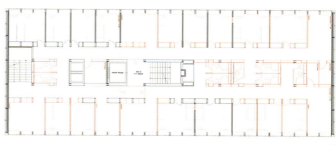

17

15

18

16

19

223 PROJECT TEACHING IN THE "PRESERVATION" ORIENTATION

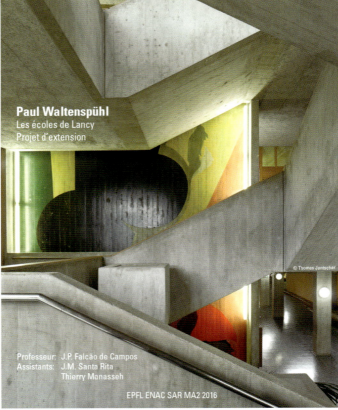

TEACHING THE PRESERVATION 224

FALCÃO DE CAMPOS

Fall 2015

Rehabilitation of the Teixeira de Pascoaes School
Ruy d'Athouguia architect, 1952–1956

Professors: João Pedro Falcão de Campos
Teaching assistants: João Santa Rita, Thierry Manasseh

Reviewers: Jean Gérard Giorla, Franz Graf, Eduardo Souto de Moura
Guest professors: Manuel Aires Mateus

Visits: Lisbon

Spring 2016

Lancy schools
Paul Waltenspühl architect, 1964–1995

Professors: João Pedro Falcão de Campos
Teaching assistants: João Santa Rita, Thierry Manasseh

Reviewers: Christian Bischoff, Gonçalo Byrne, Franz Graf
Lecturers: Christian Bischoff, Nuno Brandão Costa, Christian
Dupraz, Erwin Oberwiller, Stéphane Rudaz, Jean-Denis Thiry

Visits: Porto

1 He became a partner in 1985 in the office of Waltenspühl & Oberwiller SA, in Geneva.
2 Preface to the book by Graça Correia Ragazzi, *Ruy Jervis d'Athouguia: A modernidade* *em aberto* (Lisbon: Caleidoscópio, 2008). For the work of d'Athouguia, see Graça Correia Ragazzi, *Ruy d'Athouguia* (Porto: Edições Afrontamento, 2018).

PRESERVATION OF MODERN SCHOOLS: TWO EXAMPLES

JOÃO PEDRO FALCÃO DE CAMPOS
Falcão de Campos, Architect, Lisbon
Professor at the Instituto Superior Técnico, University of Lisbon
JOÃO SANTA RITA
Assistant Professor, Department of Architecture, Escola das Artes, University of Evora

We present here a brief account describing the academic experiment we carried out following Franz Graf's kind invitation to lead a studio as part of the "Theory and Critique of the Project—Preservation Orientation" class at the EPFL's ENAC, in collaboration with Thierry Manasseh, architect and assistant.

During this studio, students were asked to develop projects to preserve schools built in Lisbon and Geneva by two modern architects during the 1950s and 60s, respectively Ruy d'Athouguia (1917–2008) and Paul Waltenspühl (1917–2001).

During the Fall 2015 semester, Falcão de Campos' studio concentrated on developing a preservation project for the Teixeira de Pascoaes School. The school was designed in 1952 and built in 1956 by Ruy d'Athouguia in coordination with the Bairro das Estacas (1949–1954) and in collaboration with architect Formozinho Sanches. For the Spring 2016 semester, the studio proposed a project in the town of Lancy, preserving a school designed by Paul Waltenspühl and Erwin Oberwiller (1935–2017). Oberwiller was involved as a collaborator and then as a partner[1] for more than thirty years—from the competition in 1963 until the end of the construction of the Cérésole School in 1995.

The Teixeira de Pascoaes School

The Teixeira de Pascoaes School was designed by Ruy d'Athouguia, one of the best modern architects of his generation in Portugal. All of his work is well-known, but one example is particularly renowned: the Calouste Gulbenkian Foundation (1956–1959), carried out in collaboration with José Alberto Pessoa and Pedro Cid, and classed as a Portuguese national heritage monument in 2010.

Ruy d'Athouguia was an "absolutely modern" architect, in the words of Eduardo Souto de Moura,[2] and his work is distinguished by its pure, fine, and elegant design. He was a man with an impressive architectural culture, and his production resonated with the best architecture of the twentieth century. D'Athouguia followed the modern paradigm without being dogmatic. His conceptual source came from the architecture and urbanism of Le Corbusier, moderated by Brazilian modernism, and in agreement with the Portuguese context. His works

3 The citations are part of the descriptive memory of the project of the Teixeira de Pascoaes School (source: Archives of the City of Lisbon). **4** See Alfred Roth, *The New Schoolhouse / Das Neue Schulhaus / La Nouvelle Ecole*

(Zurich/Stuttgart: Girsberger, 1950). **5** According to the reference given by João Paulo Martins in his article "Aquitectura Moderna em Portugal: A Difícil Internacionalização. Cronologia," published in Ana Tostões

(ed.), *Arquitectura Moderna Portugesa 1929–1970* (Lisbon: Edições Instituto Português do Património Arquitectónico, 2004), p. 157. **6** See Franz Graf, "Costruire correttamenta," in Christian Bischoff, Isabelle Claden,

Erwin Oberwiler, *Paul Waltenspühl architecte* (Gollion: Infolio, 2007), pp. 162–175. **7** See Paul Waltenspühl, Georges Brera, "Commune de Lancy, Constructions scolaires, prévision et répartition," Study, May 1962.

were designed for the Mediterranean climate, in particular the region of Lisbon where nearly all of his creations are found.

D'Athouguia's architecture valorizes the play of forms under light, in a chiaroscuro composition punctuated by the planes making up the transition spaces between the exterior and the interior. He designed functionally without imposing anything, making the interior of buildings fluid, constructing with a simplicity of means that highlights the tectonic image of construction and the truth of natural materials, as much in their textures as in their chromatic values. But, above all, his architecture is characterized by the creation of interior spaces on a human scale, spaces that try to be in communion with the exterior spaces. In the Teixeira de Pascoaes School, d'Athouguia's main preoccupation was encouraging "direct contact with the exterior by perfectly integrating the ambiance of the school in nature," thus making "the school more human, and more adapted to the child."[3]

The functional organization of the Teixeira de Pascoaes School reflects the model of the "open-air school," where classrooms are directly connected to exterior patios. This typology follows the pedagogical project, which is based on maintaining the proximity of children to nature. These "open-air schools" were first created using Hannes Mayer's research for the city of Frankfurt and then followed by a whole generation of modern European and North American architects. The model later became famous thanks to the Munkegaard school (1951–1958) in Copenhagen, constructed by Danish architect Arne Jacobsen.

The schools in Lancy

In the Spring semester, the Portuguese experience was followed up by the preservation project of the schools in the Lancy neighborhood (1964–1999), built in Geneva by Swiss architect Paul Waltenspühl, born the same year as Ruy d'Athouguia. In modern school projects, these two architects were able to integrate the best practices as documented in the work of Swiss architect Alfred Roth—*La Nouvelle École*[4]—which revealed and explained new methods of teaching. It should be noted that d'Athouguia knew Roth's written work, since he had been part of the first summer course of the UIA (Union internationale des architectes) dedicated to the theme "school constructions," which Roth directed in 1957. Roth had been invited by Carlos Ramos, at the time director of the School of Fine Arts in Porto.[5]

For our studio, the work of Waltenspühl reflects the discovery of a modern architecture free from the dogmatism of the Modernist movement, one characterized by a pure architectural composition serving as a support for human ambiances, simultaneously comfortable and welcoming. With his attentive and informed regard, Franz Graf led us to discover the work of Waltenspühl, an architect who "correctly built," showing us some of his more notable creations, such as the "*opera prima*" of the gymnastics halls in the Rue du Stand (1951–1953) or the Geisendorf School (1952–1956), both associated with a "refined tectonic" construction.[6]

The schools in Lancy were part of a model project, designed to evolve in response to the town of Lancy's needs for basic schooling (primary and nursery). They were designed during the 1960s to house the youth of a town with a population of around 50,000. The process began in 1961, when the municipality commissioned a provisional study of the demographic evolution of the town, specifically its future needs for "nursery, primary, and secondary schools"[7] from Paul Waltenspühl and Georges Brera, his associate at the time. Following this study,

8 On the life and work of Paul Waltenspühl, see Christian Bischoff et al., *Paul Waltenspühl architecte*.
9 See Christian Bischoff in the introductory text of the class book from the Spring semester of the Falcão de Campos studio; see also Mélanie Delaune Perrin, Christian Bischoff, "Les écoles de Lancy : une suite de processus exemplaires," in Christian Bischoff et al., *Paul Waltenspühl architecte*, pp. 206–215.
10 See his lecture given on the Campus Ultzama in 2015.
11 See Franz Graf, Christian Bischoff, Giulia Marino, *Un chef-d'œuvre de l'architecture des années 1950 à Genève : les salles de sport de la rue du Stand, Paul Waltenspühl, architect, 1951–1953* (Lausanne: EPFL, 2008).

an invitation-based competition for Les Palettes School was opened in 1963 to twelve Swiss architects, and won by Paul Waltenspühl. The Lancy schools project attempted to efficiently respond to the needs of a school population that was projected to increase, using a modular concept based on rapid and economical construction methods. For Christian Bischoff,[8] the most striking quality of this project came from the "aggregation of classes on the principle of rotative symmetry and according to a modular framework," which led him to conclude that "the schools built by Paul Waltenspühl in Lancy occupy a choice place in the history of school construction in Switzerland."[9]

The Lancy schools project integrated pedagogical concepts of "the New School," which places the child's needs and comfort at the center of the school project. For Roth, school needed to be seen as an extension of the home, democratic and open to the community. It must be made on the child's scale and accompany his or her cognitive and physical development. It must promote a varied teaching program of intellectual and physical activities, and encourage the differentiation of spaces that allow individual teaching and group work. The functional organization of the school must obey these pedagogical precepts thanks to varied and flexible spaces, and offer comfortable and joyous atmospheres in permanent contact with the sun, air, and nature.

The projects carried out in Falcão de Campos' studio

The initial idea emerged from Wilfried Wang's proposition: *"Before you contribute, construct your culture,"*[10] which (in our opinion) is consistent with the approach developed since 2007 by the TSAM for the preservation of modern architectural heritage.

According to Franz Graf,[11] any intervention in the modern built environment is characterized by:
— a project that begins with a thorough historical investigation into the object studied;
— a project that reverses the chronological process of genesis, which generally goes from programmatic objectives to the creation of a new construction, and instead begins with the existing architectural work, adding a new mode of existence that is in line with its own preservation;
— a project that is based on the rule of restraint and self-effacement where the designer adopts an attitude similar to that of a doctor or a lawyer, voluntarily remaining on the fringes of the "entertainment culture."

The specificity of the preservation project's approach to a work is in its "observation, analysis, research, learning, deduction, and questioning of a studied object, which is a constructed work, and which plunges the person designing the work into the immanence of the architectonic discipline." The preservation project must also consider, on the one hand, a collection of possible strategies of intervention, either of conservation which maintains the material substance of the original work, or of a new graft, a prolonging or superimposing of new interventions; on the other hand, the preservation project must not indicate specific paths or impose particular methods to be applied indiscriminately to modern heritage.

A project that begins with a thorough historical investigation into the object studied

At the beginning of the two-semester studio, the students carried out a major group project to identify the existing schools and analyze documentary and bibliographic sources. Groups of students were formed with the double responsibility of redesigning each of the schools—the Teixeira de Pascoaes School in the first semester and the schools in Lancy in the second—Les Palettes (1963–1969), Caroline (1964,1967), Bachet-de-Pesay (1968–1970), Morgines (1968–1969), En Sauvy (1971–1074), and Tivoli (1975–1978). The students also carried out thematic analyses according to the work being studied. During the first semester, works studied included the Alvalade plan, Cellule 8 of the Alvalade plan, the Bairro das Estacas, the Teixeira de Pascoes School, a classroom in the school, the diachronic study of twentieth-century schools, and, to finish, the diachronic study of schools of the twenty-first century. In the second semester, the analysis of each of the schools was carried out in parallel with the analysis of the following themes: environment and exterior organization, framework and modulation, structure, envelopes, art and communal spaces, comfort, and classrooms.

The main objective of the analytical work was understanding the project in detail and materializing each school. Its secondary objective was putting into evidence the functional transformations carried out up until that point and designing a project program that answered the needs for improvement and growth observed during the visits.

In both cases, the program defined by the studio consisted of renovating the schools as well as adding new communal spaces such as a school restaurant, a gymnastics hall, administrative offices, as well as classrooms for specialized teaching according to current standards, that is to say, flexible and accessible teaching spaces for people with reduced mobility. In the case of the schools in Lancy, in relation to their modular character, we anticipated their need for growth by adding teaching rooms for primary and nursery, in a ratio of three to one, identical to those ratios pre-established by Waltenspühl.

Each semester, visits to Portugal were organized: in the first semester to Lisbon, to make possible a detailed visit of the Teixeira de Pascoaes School and of the constructed work of Ruy d'Athouguia in Lisbon and Cascais (from September 26 to 29, 2015), and in the second semester to Porto, to visit the major works built by architects Álvaro Siza Vieira and Eduardo Souto de Moura (from March 19 to 22, 2016).

An intermediary review was organized each semester, by inviting Portuguese architects Manuel Aires Mateus (November 16–17, 2015) and Nuno Brandão Costa (May 2–3, 2016), who presented their recent work in two lectures at the EPFL on this occasion. The final reviews of the projects from the students of the two semesters were carried out by a jury composed respectively of Jean Gérard Giorla, Eduardo Souto de Moura, and Franz Graf (December 14–15, 2015), and by Christian Bischoff, Gonçalo Byrne, and Franz Graf (May 30–31, 2016).

A project that begins with the existing building in order to end up with a functionality that is conformed to it

As evoked earlier, we have sought to use the survey in order to understand the foundations of the original projects, thanks to the analysis of documents, bibliographic sources, and publications of the time. Guided visits of the schools and lectures on the work of the two architects were also organized. In the first semester, the visit of the Lisbon schools by Ruy d'Athouguia was complemented by visits to schools in Geneva—Budé School (1961–1963) by Georges Addor and Jacques Bolliger, the École française de Genève (1961–1962) by Georges Candilis and Arthur Bugna, Les Palettes School by Paul Waltenspühl, and Geisendorf School by Waltenspühl and Georges Brera. In the second semester, several lectures were organized to get to know the work of Waltenspühl. The first, by Christian Bischoff, introduced us to the architect's work in a monographic way. The second, by Stéphane Rudaz, architect in charge of work on the schools in Lancy, was held at Les Palettes School in the presence of architect Erwin Oberwiller. The current projects were presented to us with a special accent on the functional and legal necessities (energy efficiency, acoustics, security, and lighting). The last lecture was given by doctoral candidate Jean-Denis Thiry, who presented a diachronic study of the modern schools constructed in Switzerland between 1920 and 1975.

A project based on a discipline of restraint and self-effacement.

After the survey and analysis of the Teixeira de Pascoaes and Lancy schools, the students were free to work individually or in pairs to propose a preservation project for one of the schools.

Two intervention strategies emerged from the work presented: there were those who worked within the built core of the schools, seeking to minimize the presence of the intervention, and those who worked outside the schools, seeking a formal independence integrated in the system of composition of each of the schools and in the urban systems or neighboring landscapes.

Generally, the projects carried out presented propositions that were "invisible and respectful of the matter," always with a process of "creative abstraction." Abstract theoretical references exterior to the world of the schools were avoided and the propositions favored a formal restraint, based on the precise gesture of each intervention on the existing construction.

In conclusion

The invitation addressed to us followed the experience and achievements of architect João Pedro Falcão de Campos, particularly the preservation project of the Bank of Portugal (2007–2012), based on recovering a block from the Pombalin Center in Lisbon, carried out in collaboration with architect Gonçalo Byrne, as well as the renovation project of the Camões High School (begun in 2009) designed by architect Ventura Terra and currently in construction.

At the end of the experience shared with the students, we noticed that the methodology applied in an intuitive fashion in the framework of the creations of Falcão de Campos's

12 We were very pleased to learn that the Docomomo Rehabilitation Award 2021 was awarded to Franz Graf and Giulia Marino, in the category "Engaged Societies," for the preservation project of Le Lignon housing complex in Geneva (1963–1971).

office is similar to that used by the TSAM, because of its diverse interventions on built heritage, whether those are modern works or more ancient ones. Another observation is that the specificity of the TSAM's methods, having as a goal the preservation of modern heritage, is a multidisciplinary one and requires the presence of diverse specialists, coordinated around the architectural project. This observation leads to another conclusion, that of the benefits of sharing of knowledge in this field, between the academic world and professional practice,[12] as in the case of the TSAM, which could easily be replicated in other schools and in other countries.

1 The Teixeira de Pascoaes School in Lisbon, view from the central core and the two wings composed of classrooms with patio, around 1956
2 Les Palettes School in Lancy, view of the ground-floor nursery classrooms and the "towers" of the primary classrooms, around 1966
3 Rehabilitation of the Bank of Portugal, João Pedro Falcão and Gonçalo Byrne, architects
4 Rehabilitation of the Camões High School, João Pedro Falcão, architect
5 The Alvalade neighborhood in Lisbon with its schools situated at the highest point of each "cell," study model

6 Cell number 8 with the Teixeira de Pascoaes School and the housing built by Ruy d'Athouguia, study model
7 Teixeira de Pascoaes School, study model
8, 9 Classrooms in the Teixeira de Pascoaes School, study model
10 The town of Lancy with its six schools constructed by Paul Waltenspühl and Erwin Oberwiller, study model
11 The Morgines and Caroline schools, study models
12 Les Palettes School, study model
13 Bachet-de-Pesay School, study model
14 Envelope of a typical classroom of the Lancy schools, study model

1

2

3

4

TEACHING THE PRESERVATION   232

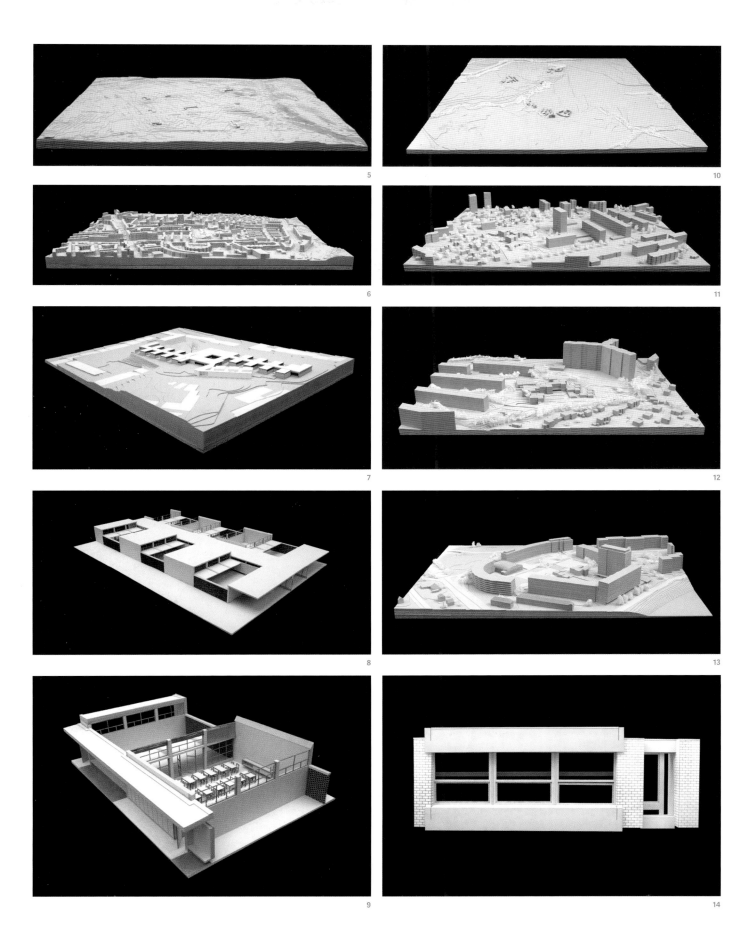

233 PROJECT TEACHING IN THE "PRESERVATION" ORIENTATION

15 Rehabilitation and extension project of the Teixeira de Pascoaes School with the construction of a detached gymnastics hall, site model
16 Rehabilitation and extension project of the Teixeira de Pascoaes School with daycare centers in the continuity of the housing, gymnastics hall, and school restaurant integrated into the pedestrian path of the schoolchildren, site model
17 Rehabilitation and extension project of the Teixeira de Pascoaes School with prolongation of the base to integrate the program and form a protected courtyard at the urban scale, site model
18 Rehabilitation and extension project of the Teixeira de Pascoaes School, image from the pergola structure towards the existing school
19 Rehabilitation and extension project of the Bachet-de-Pesay School, prolongation of the composition principles and the character of the school in brick, affirmation of the extension by a horizontal concrete band, elevation and image

TEACHING THE PRESERVATION

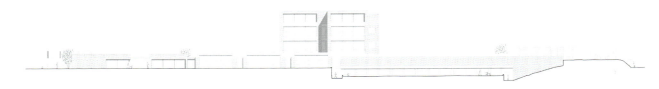

235 PROJECT TEACHING IN THE "PRESERVATION" ORIENTATION

Rudolph Schindler, Bubeshko apartments (1938/1940-41)

Los Angeles as a place of experimentation and laboratory of Twentieth Century Architecture

Studio Escher & GuneWardena
EPFL   ENAC   SAR   MA2   2016

ESCHER & GUNEWARDENA

Fall 2016

Eames House, Charles and Ray Eames, architects, 1949
Chemosphere House, John Lautner architect, 1960

Professors: Frank Escher and Ravi GuneWardena
Teaching assistants: Mounir Ayoub, Thierry Manasseh

Reviewers: Martin Bühler, Pascal Flammer
Patrick Heiz, Franz Graf

Visits: Los Angeles

Spring 2017

Bubeshko Apartments
Rudolph Schindler architect, 1938–1941

Professors: Frank Escher and Ravi GuneWardena
Teaching assistants: Mounir Ayoub, Thierry Manasseh

Reviewers: Anneke Abhelakh, Martin Bühler,
Catherine Dumont d'Ayot
Franz Graf, Gabriele Hächler, David Leclerc, Annette Spiro

Visits: Los Angeles

1 Franz Graf, "Teaching the Laboratory of the Techniques and Preservation of Modern Architecture (TSAM) at the École polytechnique fédérale de Lausanne," Docomomo Journal, no. 61, 2019/3, pp. 61–66.
2 Since the teaching experience at the EPFL, in addition to developing contemporary works of their own design, Escher GuneWardena continues to engage in a sizeable amount of historic preservation projects in the Los Angeles region. Current works include the restoration of the Paul R. Williams 1952 Residence, home of the first African American architect to be registered in the state of California and admitted to the American Institute of Architecture's College of Fellows (FAIA); the restoration of John Lautner's own home built in 1939; A. Quincy Jones and Whitney Smith's 1948 Pilot House and Frank Lloyd Wright's 1939 Eaglefeather Estate structures. Escher GuneWardena recently completed the restoration of the Greene Residence by Gregory Ain (developed in close proximity and resemblance to the 1950 MOMA Exhibition house by Ain), and the firm most recently embarked on the restoration of the iconic 1929 Lovell Health House by Richard Neutra.

CONSTRUCTION AND CONTINUITY: BUILDING THE TWENTIETH CENTURY IN LOS ANGELES

FRANK ESCHER
RAVI GUNEWARDENA
Escher GuneWardena Architecture, Los Angeles

Historic preservation is not only about saving buildings. It is about preserving our cultural history. Our past informs our present.

Engaging with our recent past as historians, academics, artists, or architects brings its own challenges: the lack of a critical distance, the difficulty of having an objective eye and mind, and, in the context of a learning institution, negotiating the boundaries between theory and practice. Preservation of a recent building, adaptively re-using it, or building within the immediate context of such an object, are three very different acts and they all bring their own sets of practical and intellectual challenges. But as a student of architecture, engaging with one's recent architectural past, its ambitions, experiments, miscalculations, successes, and failures, is both fascinating and essential to one's training.

The TSAM Laboratory addresses "the question of teaching the preservation of modern and contemporary buildings as a new discipline, specifically and radically different from that of new architecture, both in terms of theoretical courses and the contemporary architecture project. It has established a methodology and a practice based on its research that embrace the whole of polytechnic or university education, whether basic or advanced."[1] This is where the TSAM has begun to play an important role, a role one would like to see repeated at other schools.

As often cited, Los Angeles is a relatively young city developed largely in the twentieth century and with an interest in the experimental. For that reason, Los Angeles has an extraordinary legacy of twentieth-century architecture. Since establishing their office, Frank Escher and Ravi GuneWardena (of the eponymous firm Escher GuneWardena based in Los Angeles) have engaged frequently with preserving this legacy.[2]

With that in mind, in Fall 2016 and Spring 2017 Escher and GuneWardena conducted two studios with teaching assistants Thierry Manasseh and Mounir Ayoub in the TSAM Laboratory at the invitation of program director Franz Graf. With the premise of understanding Los Angeles as a place of experimentation, the studios explored two topics: Los Angeles as a Laboratory of Twentieth Century Architecture (Fall 2016); and Frugal Building—Exploring Ideas of Affordability and Simple Construction (Spring 2017). Both semesters began by examining a series of case study housing, including the project sites (for the course assignment) and various other important Los Angeles buildings. The students then developed a project of their own for assigned sites and building programs, incorporating their research material into the historic precedents.

Eames & Lautner

The Fall 2016 studio focused on building in the context of a historic monument, examining the dialog between a historic and contemporary work when adapting or expanding the program of a landmark building or site. Case studies for this semester included a selection from the works of Frank Lloyd Wright, Rudolf Schindler, Richard Neutra, John Lautner, Raphael Soriano, Gregory Ain, and Pierre Koenig, among others. Students were provided access to historic construction documents, photographs, and archival material from the various collections housing the archives of the architects. They then made individual research projects of specific case studies, examining construction techniques, the history of the architect's other works, and comparative models of the chosen houses at 1:100 scale.

In addition to monographs of the architects mentioned above, and books about the Case Study House program and California modernism, reading material for the course included four classic books analyzing the urban history of Los Angeles: Reyner Banham, *Los Angeles: The Architecture of Four Ecologies*, 1971; Doug Suisman, *Los Angeles Boulevard: Eight X-Rays of the Body Politic*, 1989; Mike Davis, *City of Quartz: Excavating the Future in Los Angeles*, 1990; William Fulton, *The Reluctant Metropolis: The Politics of Urban Growth in Los Angeles*, 1997.

Two projects, the 1949 Eames House and Studio, and John Lautner's 1960 Chemosphere were examined in greater detail with a proposed hypothetical project to expand the program on each of the large properties. For the Eames House (Case Study House #8 of John Entenza's *Arts & Architecture* magazine's "Case Study House Program"; 1945–1966), structures to accommodate the year-round program of visitors were proposed, either in a concentrated or scattered distribution of functions. For the Chemosphere, projects for a guest house and offices were developed to accommodate the expanding needs of the publisher client who currently owns the property.

The Eames House had recently completed Phase I restoration work with Escher GuneWardena as project architects as part of a multi-year conservation endeavor in collaboration with the Eames Foundation and the Getty Conservation Institute. Similarly, Escher GuneWardena had completed a major restoration of Lautner's Chemosphere project between 1998 and 2000, for which the architects had explored possible additions of other structures to the property.

Individual students developed a project for one of the assigned sites, employing construction techniques explored in the case studies, from tilt-up and cast-in-place concrete to steel frame and light wood frame structures. Examples included a project by student Amaya Corgodan-Gillet, who proposed a series of functional free-standing pavilions in the Eames garden inspired by the playful nature of the Eameses' works, such as the 1957 Solar Do-Nothing Machine. In contrast, a project by student Felip Aleix Subirà employed a series of vertical wall slabs, negotiating an entrance passage visitor center for the Eames House, descending the hillside embankment like a "Land Art" intervention.

At the Chemosphere site, a project by student Sebastien Fasel inserted a massive subterranean concrete structure into the landscape, including a tall and narrow library space, recalling John Lautner's later bold concrete building techniques.

Los Angeles study trip

A study trip to Los Angeles between the semesters allowed the students to visit the various case studies they had researched and further examine American construction techniques (often quite different from European norms) in closer detail. Project visits included Greene & Greene's 1908 Gamble House, Frank Lloyd Wright's 1917 Hollyhock House, 1923 Freeman House and 1939 Sturges House, R. M. Schindler's 1922 Kings Road House and 1941 Bubeshko Apartments, Richard Neutra's 1932 VDL House, Charles and Ray Eames 1949 House and Studio, Pierre Koenig's 1959 Stahl House, and several houses by John Lautner. The students were also able to visit the two project sites for the class assignment and assess how their proposed projects would integrate with the existing buildings.

Frugal building

The Spring 2017 studio focused on frugal construction techniques and multi-unit housing. Los Angeles has a rich history of commissions for modernist homes by bohemian artists, writers, and intellectuals with limited financial resources that drove their architects to find the most affordable forms of construction. Increasing the density of single-house residential lots was another means of achieving this goal, and it further challenged prevailing social middle-class norms in America of single-family home ownership. The studio explored numerous innovative examples of both frugal building and multi-unit housing in Los Angeles, such as R. M. Schindler's Kings Road Duplex, Richard Neutra's 1937 Strathmore Apartments, Craig Ellwood's Hollywood Courtyard Apartments, Gregory Ain's Avenel Cooperative and Dunsmuir Flats, and Frank Gehry's Indian Avenue Triplex and the Danziger Studio. Works by contemporary architects conceived in the idiom of affordable construction, including some projects by Lacaton & Vassal, Fred Fischer, Francois Perrin, and Escher GuneWardena, were also studied in detail.

Compared to European standard construction of structures intended to last for centuries (whether necessary or not), these Los Angeles buildings present pared-down techniques often built with the most basic necessity of shelter in mind. The temperate climate of Southern California certainly contributed to the range of possibilities, as well as to the long-term decay of these somewhat ephemeral structures.

Applying principles of "frugal building" philosophically, aesthetically, and in construction methodology extracted from these projects, students developed a multi-unit housing project on an affordable lot in Los Angeles. In this case, the project site was an empty steep hillside lot adjacent to R. M. Schindler's Bubeshko Apartments, originally intended for a third terraced housing project designed by Schindler. Students were zealous both in their research of case studies and in employing these alternative techniques in their own responses to the studio assignment. Contemporary environmentally sustainable building practices and collective or cooperative housing models were also employed, presenting a rich array of results.

Based on the idea of leaving the hillside as untouched as possible (to avoid costly grading and retaining walls) student Louis Desplanques developed a building that elegantly floated above its site, recalling site strategies employed by various modernist Southern California architects. Nina Haftka studied the idea of minimal and easily transformable units, combining the units' necessities into one organizing wall that ran through the building. Sebastian Fasel developed a project, lofted off the ground to reduce its footprint on the hill, with large communal areas for living and cooking, with minimal private spaces for sleeping and work. Finally, Louise Gueissaz combined a similarly innovative spatial program of large, shared spaces with minimally sized private compartments with an elegant, lightweight structure that touches the ground only as needed.

1 Eames House and Studio, Charles and Ray Eames, 1949, photograph of restoration work, Escher GuneWardena Architecture
2 Chemosphere House, John Lautner, 1961, photograph after restoration work, Escher GuneWardena Architecture
3 Bubeshko Apartments, Rudolph M. Schindler, 1938-41, photograph of the two first stages, as the third was not built
4 Pilot House, A. Q. Jones, Whitney Smith, Edgardo Contini, 1948, photograph after restoration work, Escher GuneWardena Architecture
5 Sheats Goldstein Residence, John Lautner, 1961–1994, model
6 Sturges House, Frank Lloyd Wright, 1939, model
7 Kings Road House, Rudolph Schindler, model
8 Frey House II, Albert Frey, 1964, model
9 Bubeshko Apartments, Rudolf Schindler, model
10 Danziger Studio and Residence, Frank Gehry, 1965, model
11, 12 Exhibition of the study models, EPFL, 2017

TEACHING THE PRESERVATION 242

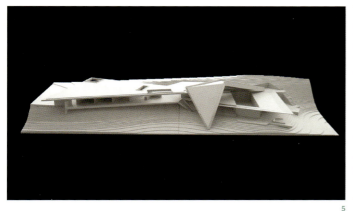

5

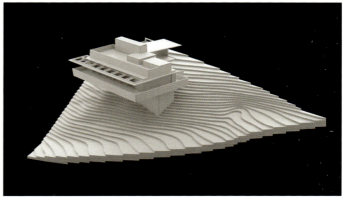

6

7

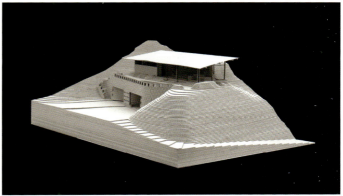

8

9

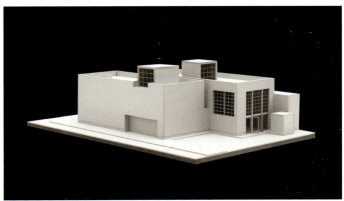

10

11

12

13, 14 Pavilions in the Eames House garden, inspired by the "Solar-Do-Nothing Machine" by Charles and Ray Eames, model, plans, and sections
15, 16, 17, 18 Extension to the Chemosphere House, with library and accommodation for the publisher's guests, model, section, and images
19, 20 Extension to the Bubeshko Apartments, with cantilevered communal housing above a car park dug into the section, section and model
21, 22 Light steel structure adjacent to the Bubeshko Apartments, section and model
23, 24 Communal housing supported by structural core, section and model
25, 26 Levels with communal housing stepped into the slope, section and model

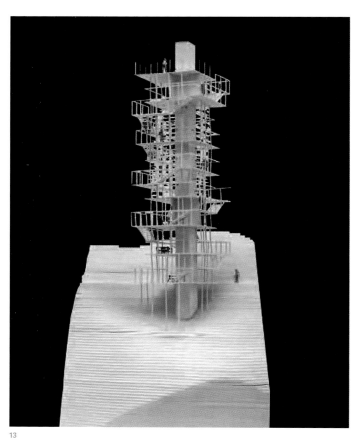

13

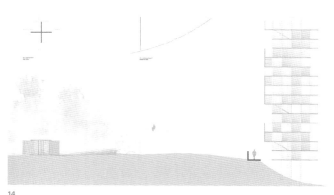

14

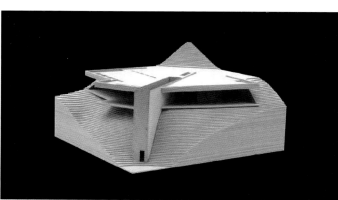

15

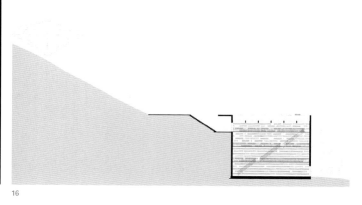

16

17

18

TEACHING THE PRESERVATION 244

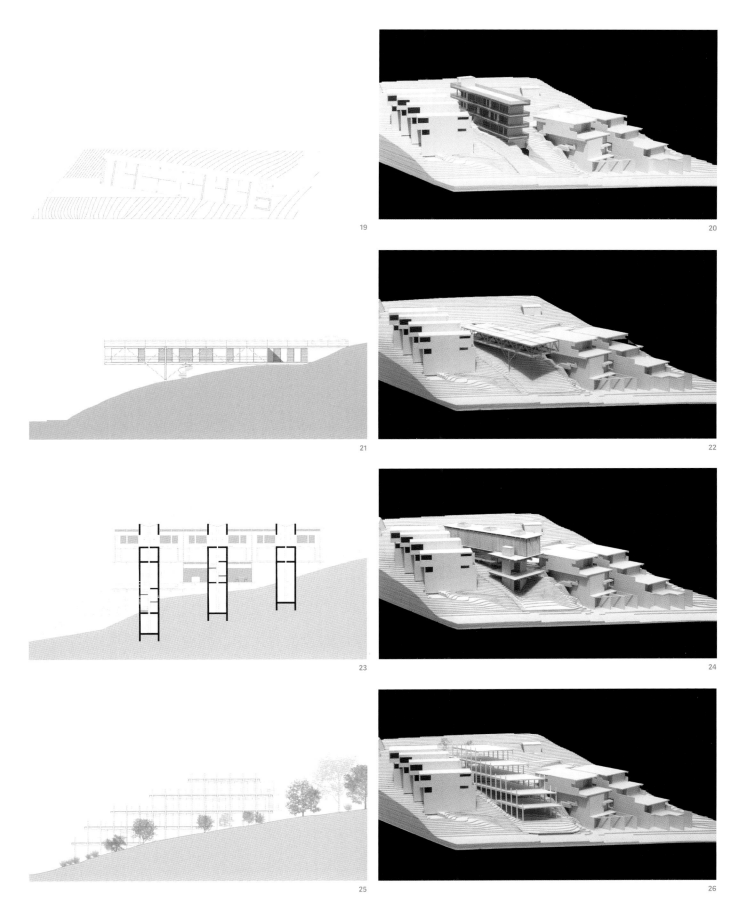

245 PROJECT TEACHING IN THE "PRESERVATION" ORIENTATION

TEACHING THE PRESERVATION 246

LACATON & DRUOT

Fall 2017 and Spring 2018

What and who is already there?
The existing environment is the primary structure
in any design project

Professors: Anne Lacaton and Frédéric Druot
Teaching assistants: Thierry Manasseh, Arabella Masson

Reviewers: Franz Graf, Éric Lapierre, Ariane Widmer

Visits: Bern

WHAT AND WHO IS ALREADY THERE?

OPEN CONVERSATION WITH ANNE LACATON (Lacaton & Vassal, Paris)
AND FRÉDÉRIC DRUOT (Frédéric Druot Architecture, Paris)

This conversation has been reconstructed from two meetings between Anne Lacaton, Frédéric Druot, Franz Graf, and Thierry Manasseh on December 13, 2021 and February 11, 2022.

On several occasions since 2006, Anne Lacaton has been invited to give lectures and teach at the EPFL. In 2017, as part of the preservation orientation, she taught project design with Frédéric Druot, an architect who often works closely with her and Jean-Philippe Vassal. Together they have developed several projects, including the PLUS study, the rehabilitation projects for the Bois-le-Prêtre housing tower in Paris, and the Grand Parc estate in Bordeaux.

Thierry Manasseh (TM): While deciding on the studio topic and project site, we visited a few places around Lausanne, but eventually we ended up selecting a seemingly ordinary part of the city, one we hadn't initially identified, near the Renens train station and the EPFL. Can you tell us about how you chose the studio topic and what was interesting about it?

Anne Lacaton (AL): The first thing I would like to say is that no one ever forced a choice upon us. Complete trust was placed in us and I thought that was quite remarkable. I think it is important for schools to be open to different ways of thinking, and even though I don't necessarily agree with them all, it's up to the students to decide on their individual approaches. Ours has always been the same—we have never wanted to come and teach what we know how to do ourselves, but instead we want to help students understand the complexity of architecture, of a site or a context, and to encourage them to see things "more broadly." In our profession, one of the most difficult things is being confined to a very limited work space. You are given a site, a function or use, and asked to construct a building without any discussion. This is something we have always found very restrictive, and when we begin a project, we always try to go backwards: where is the site, what context is it in, why have we been asked to work there, why has a specific function or use been defined, or not... and this drives us to re-situate the concept, and our thoughts around it, into something that is much broader, not just the creation of a form and function.

It is becoming increasingly clear that there is less need today for new major facilities. Broadly speaking, in Europe, there are enough big facilities, museums, etc. Building on an empty site is no longer the main focus nowadays either. It is more a question of extending, building onto something, reinforcing, strengthening. Not only is this more interesting, but it reflects the reality of the challenges we are facing. We have to take a wider view and understand what a site is capable of, define what is already there, what is of interest, what is lacking, what could be added. We have to deal with the site in a way that is appropriate and not let ourselves be carried away by masterplans that are still often established from a high-level viewpoint and are not grounded in reality. Today we are moving away from that kind of situation, unless the plan is to entirely remove what is already there, but this is in itself problematic, and we will be seeing less and less of it in the future.

Frédéric Druot (FD): We are always focusing on what in the end are similar themes—housing, the existing environment, and how to bring it up-to-date... This is what we have, what do we do with it, and who do we give it to. There are also the students—how do we provide them with a stance while trying to help them develop their own opinions. This is also a kind of a, perhaps general, criticism about teaching programs (and not just architecture), that is, knowing when the students have time to form their own opinions. It's also a question of knowing how to remove the hierarchy between teacher and student, a little, even though each has his or her own role to play. It means opening up a space for critical thinking in which the students are at ease, one that reflects our concerns (which are often in opposition to those on architecture), to look at what is already there and to think about what to do with it, rather than coming up with far-fetched inventions.

That's kind of an overall perspective, and then we have to put that in place. Essentially it's a matter of housing, how to inhabit a city. We try to find sites that are not exceptional, because the exceptional can upset the students' working methodology. So you might call this an "ordinary" part of the city, and that's what it is, but we could also say that it "has potential." It's trying to see what possible situations there are, without inventing anything. The first thing we tried to find in Lausanne were complex cases, with the aim of revisiting them and revealing their potential to become exceptional, not in terms of architecture, but in terms of how they could be livable in our current world. There are not really any dire situations in Lausanne. What we found interesting was not focusing just on housing but looking at how it fits into the city. The advantage with Renens is that it doesn't have any transport issues, as the area is already built up. Things are more or less stable and well-balanced, with a certain amount of diversity—subject, of course, to real estate pressure and the possibility that building projects will occur as developers try to capitalize on the property market. This diversity includes several activities, services, a factory—the neighborhood is actually very active, it has more potential than the word "ordinary" suggests. There is light, space, there's a bakery, everything you need.

So, we said to ourselves, let's learn as much as we can about this site, while paying attention to what is there, with an analysis that looks at things that may seem quite basic, like the sewerage system, but also so that we don't end up reinventing the wheel. It's also saying to students that in architecture there are lots of things to consider, it's not just a question of creating an iconic architectural model. So much needs to be done and considered. And that's what is so wonderful about teaching, we have a whole team that can look at thousands of things.

Franz Graf (FG): What is interesting about the site you chose is that, as you say, it's not a building, it's not one or several plots, but a whole area where everything can be found—roads, a mix of building types, etc.

AL: It's an urban entity that is broadly delineated by large urban elements where, as you say, everything can be found, but it is also part of a contemporary city where the issue of what it is to be a large city today is totally relevant. How can we ensure that within a city we have all the necessary conditions for density, without making the city sprawl? It is also a way of helping the students to get a feel for this subject—which makes everyone scared—with the basic principle that on the face of it nothing needs to be removed and that everything present must be seen as the starting point. There is a lot of confusion around what density means. It is almost as if living in housing blocks automatically implies density, while on the ground, there is much less density... When considering the site, the object in question, you also have to ask those questions, look carefully, analyze things in a positive light, and pull apart these preconceived ideas. That is why the inventory that we have put forward as the first step is absolutely vital. It is the prerequisite.

TM: With regard to the extremely detailed inventory that the students develop over almost a whole semester, I find it very interesting that there is no hierarchy between the subjects (history, vegetation, network and transport, amenities, housing).

FD: What I think is helpful for the students, to encourage this, is that the work must be spread among them. And so, as part of this allocation of tasks, the student dealing with networks might initially think that it is less interesting than, say, dealing with the built environment, but actually, not at all. It just demonstrates that there is a need for research, that you can find fascinating elements that are relevant for future projects, which themselves can begin from any point. It is the creation of a point of view. That is why the idea of an inventory is so essential—if we don't have an inventory, we cannot understand; if we cannot understand, we don't have any knowledge; if we don't have any knowledge, we cannot create a point of view; if we don't have a point of view, we cannot develop ideas, or at least not any ideas with a solid foundation.

I think that it is this series of steps that is so important. It is also a question of being open to them, to their ability to do things. Some things will strike a deeper chord than others, but we don't know the students. We have to establish a rhythm because they don't all have the same rhythm or level of ability—for some, their abilities develop at a different pace, and for others, their interest can drop because things progress too slowly, that's what is so fascinating about it...

The inventory is also a way of remaining focused on simple realities: counting, adding, making judgments.

FG: In terms of creating a point of view, making judgments is important. It means getting involved, even with something like the sewerage system. And then taking a stance on the subjects they study. They can't act like a detached technician who copies what the lecturer produces, they have to organize their own project, and I think that is a fundamental element of your approach and general way of doing things.

FD: Often while teaching, the students try to come up with a project with their teacher in mind, so yes, if you tell them to consider the sewerage systems, they can't think of anything else. So to start with, you remove that issue, the question of subordination.

AL: In our group, and in terms of their way of working, I find that the students have stuck to things pretty well: instead of each group doing its own independent analysis, they had to do an in-depth study and investigation of the site and then share this information with all the others in order to gather as much material as possible and create a form of exchange. This was sometimes difficult to achieve, because when we had meetings to share our data they felt as if they were wasting time. They were in a hurry to move on to the design phase. But it's an important step, because in just a short time it produces comprehensive data. The job of observing and inventorying is not set apart from design, it's part of the design process. The students begin to pay careful attention to everything, the ground, etc. and start to appreciate the imperfections, to admit that everything doesn't need to be perfectly straight everywhere, to accept what is already there. It's a question of learning to see and changing one's perspective. In every project, this process always teaches us a lot.

TM: The group that had been assigned vegetation had to analyze the number and species of trees on the site, and it's true that if you say you need to cut down "a tree," that's not the same as saying "a maple" or "a blue spruce."

AL: By the time you have identified each tree, one after the other, mapped them out, photographed, measured, and redrawn them, you can see that they are not all the same and that they are individual subjects, of different species, that they require specific conditions in which to develop—air, light, and soil. Once you have been through that process, it's not as easy to wipe them off the map. And it's the same for housing. Once you have seen how people live, the care they take of their interiors—even if you're not really a fan of their furniture or wallpaper, it becomes increasingly obvious that you can't dictate what is good or not good, nor that everything should be changed or replaced. This is all very important.

FG: We can certainly see this rich diversity in the summaries produced with the different groups, despite it being a sort of "ordinary" neighborhood.

AL: I don't actually think there is any such thing as an ordinary neighborhood. That's what we say when we look at something from far away, without really seeing it. And that's how decisions are often made—from far away, without getting a sense of the reality on the ground. When you are on site, right up close, you don't see the same things. And that is what architects must do today.

TM: From the summaries of the students' inventories, certain work themes appeared, each with their own exercises, and these ideas were put forward to the students. Was this to avoid working on a design project or specific function or use, in the way we are normally used to?

FD: I really like replacing the word "project" with "exercise"— the students are trying things out, they are not sure. We know what a project is, but an exercise is a little different, we test things out.

AL: They did some research; they analyzed projects by the Ville de Renens, as well as private projects, what is planned in terms of new housing, for example. There were also plans to renovate and increase the size of the school. And somewhere along the line, all this came together.

TM: In fact, there was a plan to demolish the factory and develop new housing on the basis of a neighborhood plan, and we suggested an exercise where the building was kept and a housing program was installed within it.

AL: Yes, there were some very interesting projects! Some also wondered if the existing carpark had the potential to be built onto, or added to with a building. We asked them to think about a transformation based on needs, but also by increasing density a little, or a lot; to establish the appropriate density for a site such as this one, which means it's not something that can be applied generally across the board, but in a more nuanced way, based on the actual possibilities. There are some places where nothing is possible and others where something or a lot can be done. This was why the mapping, where they overlaid analyses, was so interesting. In theory, you would say that density can be increased everywhere, in a regular, compact mass, but actually it can't. So we started by blocking off certain places: the proximity to existing façades, in order to retain light, and the space around existing trees, to allow them to breathe. This resulted in maps that, before even considering planning regulations, gave a qualitative definition to the zones where construction was possible and wouldn't obstruct anything. That didn't mean that construction should take place in those spaces, but it gave an indication of what was possible. Then further series of criteria were added to refine the actual potential for density. Architecture is very complex, and fundamentally, urban planning is a simplification. This is why it is important to overlay elements without making a design, to allow all the traces and layers to appear—initially without any hierarchy other than the existing environment, which is a fixed element. That requires a thorough understanding of the sites and a close involvement. But it worked well with the students!

TM: We also realized that when you use the existing environment as a base, there is actually more freedom to design. We wouldn't necessarily design housing within a factory in the same way we would for a new build.

AL: We have often observed how transformation creates unique solutions, with atypical typologies that would never be accepted in a new building. It's also a way of improving quality, of making architecture evolve. The non-standard housing we create in transformation projects illustrates the importance of this kind of innovation, and it helps to demonstrate that there is no reason you couldn't do it in a new building.

TM: The notion of density that you have introduced is also interesting because it doesn't require a set amount of square meters for offices and for housing...

AL: Yes, absolutely. It is very important that the sites determine the level of density and that later we combine this with a needs analysis or an assessment of the objectives determined by other criteria. Afterwards we can see how the functions and density can be redefined based on this. Though the potential of the site is still a priority.

FG: This is completely counter to the way planning usually occurs.

AL: Yes, this is not how a masterplan works, which instead establishes everything that must occur, right to the end, at which point architecture gives shape to what the masterplan contains, in accordance with its rules and definitions. We take the opposite view. Today it should be architecture that drives planning.

FD: I liked it when we said we should be increasing density 100%... Except that 100% doesn't mean 100% concrete blocks up fifteen floors, it means 100% density taking into account what is already there. When I said that, I didn't know what would happen. It's not a question of "we can put a bit here and a bit there"; it was 100%, so we got answers and approach-based methodologies that were invented, I think, with things that were not fully developed but were certainly outside the systems we are familiar with. There was no design program, no guide...

FG: But there was the existing environment...

FD: The existing environment and the rules of the game—not theoretical, but social, cultural, spatial, etc. I don't know if it was as visible as all that, but it's about taking care of the individual and the group at the same time. So often we replaced things from the inside. We tried, we did what we could, but it's wonderful, it's an incredible capacity for work. We always got more than we imagined, we were astonished—the students were the ones asking us questions, they unsettled us... And then there were some ugly things that we would never have done. It's not a criticism, but you do question yourself, you say "well, yeah, that's the logical conclusion, a methodology," and you drop the question of judgment. I think that's beneficial too.

FG: It is obvious that you have opened up possibilities, without necessarily having an idea of what the end result was going to be. It was total experimentation and questioning, without too much restriction. Some students set off in a direction you would never have taken, for ten thousand different reasons that you are able to predict, but you check yourself and you say, "let's see..."

FD: Yes, because that's how life goes—you're on a path and then you veer slightly to the right. I really like the idea of an escape path. If there is a tiny hole in a pipe, the water that comes out this hole will be much more beautiful than the rest that comes out the end of the pipe. You have to make sure that there is a possible escape path. We were able to do this because the program was on the whole year. Knowledge from the first semester was available for the second. The thing about the work that the students do, is that they're often a little lost. You really have the feeling that this inventory work could be useful for the Ville de Renens, or for someone else. The students are not just trying to get good marks, they're also working to create material that could be available to a wider audience. They are part of a collective effort and it gives them a sense of recognition for their work. It's hard to develop this.

TM: The dual aspect of the studio, which is both open to possibilities and also has a down-to-earth perspective due to the existing environment, was also present in the references we required from the students; with both ways of living and construction modes and their structural significance.

AL: You have to refer to real situations, to observe them, understand them, and create a series of related references. This is what allows the essential qualities of a project to be defined. These references are fragments that help develop and establish the relationship between intention and design. I have noticed that the students often draw their housing plans quite mechanically and so the plans don't express the intentions of the values that are stated and used as a basis. It is so important to make an effort to observe, understand, and relate things to the design.

FG: It is absolutely fundamental to begin by analyzing what exists; these references allow us to understand that architecture is something that must first be thought about. Even construction, which is not purely technical, must be thought about first and then depicted.

AL: Technical matters and construction have a direct connection with space and use. An open construction, made with pillars, creates a free space, while repeated load-bearing walls create restrictions. It's not the same thing. Through this topic, we were able to talk quite specifically about a number of broad issues: construction, economy, or issues of resources and the environment.

FG: In the positive sense of the word, talking about construction without focusing on technical details, talking about the economy without doing calculations...

AL: Or talking about heating and the environment by using relatively simple principles.

FG: And yes, it's a way of making students understand that you can deal with issues concerning the environment, construction, economy, and space through the design, of course.

AL: Of course.

FG: And it makes these ideas understandable more quickly, rather than doing classes based on abstract notions that are entirely correct but difficult to integrate into a design project. We can see this in the fourth year, where the students find it difficult to connect a particular construction aspect with the ecology classes they have had. They find it difficult to include this aspect in the project, while the approach that is based on what exists, on touching and seeing things, does enable them to integrate it into the project process.

AL: These topics are dealt with in a much too technical manner, or from the point of view of very specific and exclusive knowledge that is very difficult for students to grasp—it all may seem exceedingly complex. The students are frightened by these subjects, when actually, they are most often based on commonsense principles and are related to design. For example, economy and financial aspects, which seem so specialized and inaccessible, do not actually mean knowing the price of each material and carrying out complex estimations. On the scale of the project, it's more about understanding what contributes to the cost of construction, such as complexity, the use of many different materials, and the difficulty in implementation. All this is better understood from a commonsense point of view. And then you have to keep the quantities and measurements in mind. Thinking about these issues is entirely connected to the project. And this does not devalue the construction. On the contrary. If you think about how you can do the same thing more simply, how to optimize things, you immediately touch on issues of budget, environment, and construction. This refocuses things on the essential elements and also creates the conditions for doing more and better.

It's a mix of intuition, pragmatism, knowledge, comparative analyses... and generally, if we do this, we are far better equipped to understand and tackle the issues before we start making calculations.

TM: It was possible to cover all these themes, as Frédéric has said, thanks to the decision to extend the topic over two semesters, with the inventory, references, and exercises in the first and the design projects in the second.

FG: What was particularly good about it, is that it wasn't compulsory. You decided to continue in this vein—you saw there was potential, and the students kept coming back, which isn't often the case. Personally, I don't like the rhythm imposed by the semesters. It's like a "one-shot" that ends up as a collection of projects.

FD: It's like a competition...

FG: Yes, that's right, and it's quite superficial. The right idea might be there, but we know it doesn't necessarily work like that. And as you say, some students need to go over a certain topic again. They have different work rhythms, and they learn to use inventories developed by others. This notion of collective work is extremely important. This runs counter to what generally happens in schools—in Switzerland but I think in France too.

FD: That's exactly how it is in France. With Anne and Jean-Philippe, we did a study for the CUB (Communauté urbaine de Bordeaux), where the aim was to find 50,000 housing units. There was a huge amount of data from many sources, and yet we realized that the data we had been given wasn't providing us with the information we needed. We found a guy who was in an office at the CUB, who knew so much, and yet he hadn't been asked to share what he knew. No one had thought to access this knowledge. The studio worked kind of like this—reusing material from others and finding out what had been done before I came by, before I arrived. The world hasn't just been created. And we also have to think about how our society is organized. Competitions in France are the same. Everyone wants to reinvent the wheel— because elections are coming up, because of this, because of that... But the issue of housing in Paris remains the same—no one can afford to buy an accomodation. Anyway, it's also a question of solving societal issues, and those things, that point of view, can only be done by students. The problem is that they end up crushed by these situations, there's no room for them. Their CVs are full of studios and offices.

FG: Schools are also responsible for the creation of these CVs, and they also create frustration. It's quite irresponsible to foster these illusions, to do design projects that give the totally wrong idea of what the students will do later in their careers. This focus on the existing environment (aside from the fact that it makes students realize that they can design a project anywhere) allows them to notice things and somehow frees them to question their role. It changes the way they see things.

FD: Perhaps the only negative, or rather, frustrating aspect for me is that we forced them to try and make the results of their thinking process equal, and once again we find ourselves back within a system that says we all need to produce the same thing that will be assessed and marked. You can see that in arriving at that end point, some have skipped a step in the thought process. Sometimes not achieving something is also an answer.

FG: It's also very important not to have preconceived ideas. The idea that buildings are not good or bad can sometimes unsettle students. You can't be rigid, you have to learn to understand why, and in which situation. In the third year we always have some students who are wary and who are not convinced by the quality of the buildings we are studying, but who gradually come to discover them, understand them, and love them.

FD: Yes, exactly!

FG: That is important, as are teachers' personalities and the ways they develop their teaching plans.

FD: I like what I don't like...

FG: I'm increasingly suspicious of my own preconceived ideas, that's for sure. We have also worked on some wonderful buildings, which is not easy either, but what is great about the students is that you don't have to hold back, you can do things that step outside of our current framework. When we worked on Le Corbusier's Unités d'habitation, the students put forward some really great typological transformations.

FD: And then there's the issue of judging heritage buildings: either they are considered to be heritage and they can't be touched or it's not heritage and so you can do whatever you want. Working on the Unités d'habitation with the knowledge of how they had been built and the awareness that great care had to be taken, but as part of this care, being able to bring together several Unités without upsetting the history of the work, to improve the whole, that was a delicate and careful exercise. We could say that everything is "heritage," and that's the end of it. But then, how do we determine the value of all these different forms of heritage?

FG: This often comes up in the studio. We work on buildings that have certain qualities but that are too recent, and so are not listed as such at an architectural level. It's interesting to see how some students try hard to assess something and others don't try at all—they're not sure of themselves, they panic a little, but actually it's exactly the same exercise—you have to learn how to understand, give yourself the means to do something, take a stance with regard to this, and develop a design that fits within the architectural value (in its wider sense) that you attributed to it.

AL: I think that actually we should start by broaching complex situations straightaway, to understand how they are made up. This would open our minds and develop a sense of critical thinking.

Students don't allow themselves to criticize. This is a shame because criticism can be constructive. It forces you to build and express an opinion, develop an argument. This is a major topic in architecture schools—what are the basics—and I think that today, the basics for an architecture student are to develop an intelligence and ability to observe and interpret, and develop a position—before learning more applied means or knowledge.

FG: Yes, I'm not sure that having a memorable teacher in the first year is a way of arousing the student's curiosity, which can often be rather polymorphous. Architecture is such a vast subject—we shouldn't think that all the students will end up designing buildings, that would be a shame actually, architecture is much greater than that.

AL: I have found in Zurich in past years that this is changing—there is much greater diversity in the teaching approach, and students' requirements are changing quickly too regarding their expectations around the job of an architect and how they see it.

FG: Perhaps it is also because there are people who teach with a different style, and that could be what triggers students' curiosity and opens their minds.

AL: Society is also evolving. The younger generations are worried about more fundamental questions such as the climate, the importance of conserving our resources. There is a lot of work to be done in order to find the right solutions. There are fundamental changes that need to happen. But often the response to these questions is to rely on tried and tested approaches and established solutions: this is the right way to do something, this doesn't work, you should build like this and not like that...

FG: Yes, it often seems as if these are ways of not thinking about the project and the responsibilities we have—there are procedures, you use biobased materials and all will be well... but that is not at all how it works.

AL: Yes, the answers to these huge problems cannot be reduced to simply using such-and-such a material and demonizing others. Today we have a tendency to make categorical decisions on whether something is good or bad. We are repeatedly asked why we are still using concrete, that it is not an environmentally friendly product, or polycarbonate, which is made from fossil-fuel based chemicals and has a high carbon footprint. These are misplaced and quite simplistic judgments. If we calculate the amount of CO_2 in materials on a transformation project such as the Grand Parc in Bordeaux, compared to its life span and what can be done with it, it is relatively small. And manufacturers today are really investing in clean technology.

FG: I think the responsibility does lie in some cases with teachers and how they explain these things.

AL: These issues should be treated with much more subtlety, intelligence, and responsibility, and not be weighed up in a simplistic equation about whether something is "good" or not.

TM: And there are often short-cuts and simplifications. With recycled concrete, for example, engineers often have to increase the proportion of cement in a mixture to compensate for the lack of manufacturer's guarantees or normative flaws. The result may be worse in terms of ecology, but the client can boast that it is "recycled."

AL: There is a lot of PR involved, and moralizing, but also, appreciation and judgment are based on estimations and this shows a lack of rigor. It is a shame that the students are caught up in these vague descriptions. We must demonstrate more judgment, through rigor and knowledge.

Today, the issue of reusing materials has become a new virtuous business model that must be followed. Reusing constructional elements from demolished sites has become compulsory and a criterion for good governance in new constructions, and without it, projects wouldn't reach the required standards. But if we were truly in an environmental and resource-saving mode, we should instead be asking ourselves why there is so much material to be reused? If this material is still good for construction, why was it dumped? If we could use what already exists in a better way, we wouldn't need to demolish and we would extend the life span of the existing environment. I believe that reuse has become an argument to justify demolition and a market that prevents us from developing a true cost-saving mindset. Reuse reduces our carbon footprint, but it isn't rigorous because the demolition that created these elements or material is never taken into account when making the calculations.

A better approach would be to use materials sparingly, to use as little as possible, without any preconceived ideas about the material. Building in wood without any optimization, with additives, without truly checking the origin of the wood, is not necessarily any better than a highly optimized concrete structure that will have a long lifespan and an ability to be transformed over time. What is needed is a case-by-case approach.

FG: I was discussing this with a friend, Jean-Pierre Cêtre, who has been an engineer for a long time, and he believes we are going to return to the construction details of the 1970s. It was done for budget reasons, pure and simple, and we are going to need to do it for budget reasons that extend to the question of ecology. Fundamentally, although people thought the future would be in monolithic, thick structures, things probably won't actually develop in that direction...

AL: It would be a good thing if we went back to a more inventive form of engineering based on more pragmatism, craft, and calculation, as well as a more realistic approach.

TM: One of the obstacles to this approach is that the time and fees necessary to optimize structures are often greater than the savings made in the cost of materials. But maybe this will change again...

FG: In any case, for the training of students I believe it is so important to have studios where things are more open, more considered, and on a larger scale. Architecture can be broken down into many different professions and it would be helpful to dissect a little more how we see these roles.

AL: To a certain degree, the survival of our profession also depends on this. We need to highlight its capacity and ability to deal with complexity and to find simple solutions for facilitating everyday life. It's a way of stepping outside the framework within which architects are often placed: building walls or making pretty pictures.

TM: The role of the architect is shifting towards the existing environment; this has been taking place for a while now.

AL: Yes, we need to work with what is already there. We need to think differently, look at things differently, and outline new approaches when designing projects. It's exciting, because you need to be inventive but humble too. It also means focusing much more on people and on improving quality of life. Working with what already exists and transforming it is now avant-garde. This is what I tell students when they become frustrated with projects in an existing environment, because they feel as if they cannot express their creativity. But this is changing.

FG: I appreciated how at the beginning of the semester you introduced the studio with the phrase "nothing is to be demolished." Now it is becoming a bit fashionable, but at the time it wasn't—well, not at the Polytechnic anyway. I can imagine how that must have caught the students' attention.

FD: "Never demolish," which comes from Jean-Philippe's writing in the *Plus* study, is one of his most often quoted phrases. When you say that, you're sometimes accused of being a total fascist, but once you've gotten past that you say ok, but if we're just going to demolish a little, what do we demolish? Creating this rule, even if you demolish afterwards, prevents you from demolishing before knowing what you are working on, unless you have thorough knowledge of a situation. This is the only instance in which you can. You must list everything that works before you list the things that don't.

FG: Demolition is not the first action, it only occurs after all of the knowledge has been gathered. It is an action that may occur after, if the project improves the overall situation. This is what we try to teach—the end result must be better than the current situation.

FD: We have to focus on improvement—whether for people or spaces, for anything actually. That's all we need to do.

1 Map showing years of building construction, history, inventory extract
2 Noise, road, and transport register, inventory extract
3 Parking, road, and transport map, inventory extract
4 Survey and vegetation summary, inventory extract
5 Afiro, building redesign, services, inventory extract
6 Bosch, Maillefer and Sapal factory, services, inventory extract

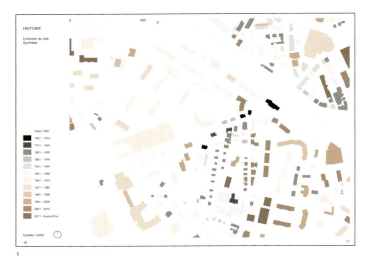

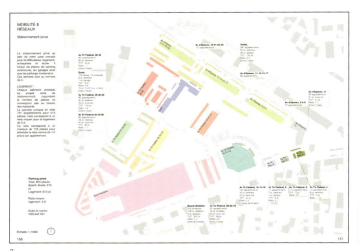

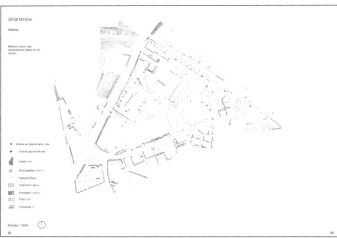

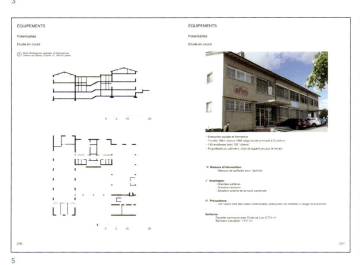

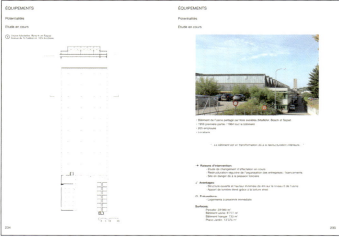

TEACHING THE PRESERVATION   260

7 General plan, housing, inventory extract
8 Avenue du Tir-Fédéral 16, housing, inventory extract
9 Avenue du Tir-Fédéral 39, housing, inventory extract
10 Avenue d'Epenex 10, housing, inventory extract
11 Alexandra Road Estate, reference repertory extract
12 Prefabricated concrete slabs, reference repertory extract

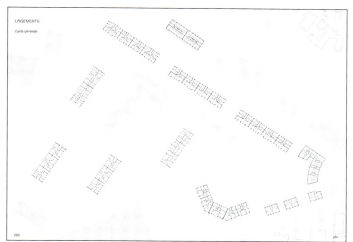

7

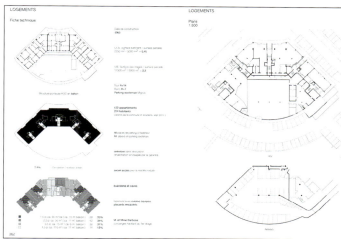

8

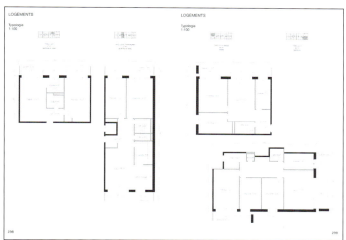

9

10

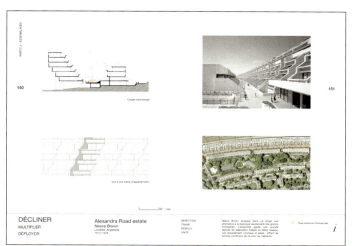

11

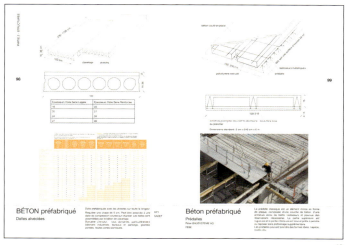

12

PROJECT TEACHING IN THE "PRESERVATION" ORIENTATION

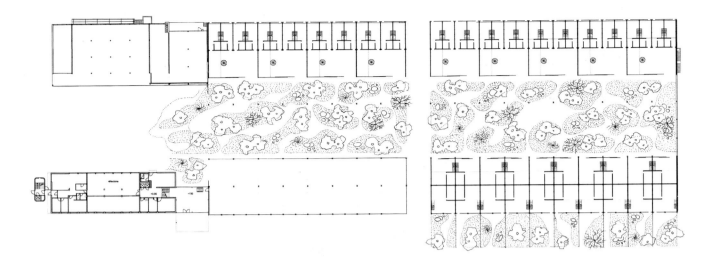

13

14

TEACHING THE PRESERVATION 262

13 Exercise inserting housing into the factory with a collective garden in the center and private gardens around the exterior
14 Exercise densifying the site, floor plan
15, 16, 17, 18, 19, 20 Exercise densifying the site, ground-floor garden plan, floor plan, images

17

15

18

19

16

20

263 PROJECT TEACHING IN THE "PRESERVATION" ORIENTATION

LINAZASORO & SÁNCHEZ

Fall 2018

Fuencarral—Global rehabilitation
José Luis Romany architect, 1956–1959

Professor: José Ignacio Linazasoro
Teaching assistants: Eduardo Blanes, Thierry Manasseh

Reviewers: Martin Boesch, Franz Graf

Visits: Madrid

Spring 2019

Munich—Rehabilitation of St. Bonifaz church
Hans Döllgast architect, 1946–1967

Professor: José Ignacio Linazasoro
Teaching assistants: Eduardo Blanes, Thierry Manasseh

Reviewers: Vitangelo Ardito, Franz Graf
Professor: Vitangelo Ardito

Visits: Munich

HOUSING AND THE SACRED

JOSÉ IGNACIO LINAZASORO
Linazasoro & Sánchez, Madrid

1

Working within the existing built environment has become a required aspect of contemporary projects. Architectural and urban projects no longer involve the simple expansion of cities or construction of buildings *ex novo*. As a consequence, historical centers have been abandoned and peripheries with no urban qualities have been created.

However, a much more important task now awaits us: working in the existing built environment to transform old and modern buildings.

The architecture of the twentieth century has produced masterpieces, certainly, but also many buildings of poor quality, or whose construction techniques cause problems today. It is necessary, on the one hand, to intervene on these twentieth-century buildings in order to adapt them to new requirements and new uses, and on the other hand, to intervene on the organization of the urban fabric of city centers and their periphery. This work consists of adding new architectural "layers" and very often adding new public spaces as well, primarily in suburban areas.

As a consequence, architecture schools must provide their students with the appropriate tools, tools that will allow them to intervene on the existing buildings and urban fabric, a practice which was until now reserved for a very small number of specialists.

Luckily the students themselves are showing increasing interest in this issue, in particular at the EPFL. This is surely thanks to Professor Franz Graf, who has developed this teaching program and ongoing research at the TSAM, alongside several architects invited to the EPFL as professors over the past few years.

In my career trajectory as an architect, I have often worked on projects carried out on existing built environments. From the very beginning of my career, I believed that architecture should be harmoniously integrated into its site, whether it was a new building or the transformation of an existing one. I have also had the opportunity to work on public spaces and have participated in the reorganization of several historical centers, such as the parvis of the cathedral in Reims.

2

Such experience acquired throughout my architectural practice has led me to intense reflection about these issues and today allows me to clearly state a few fundamental principles concerning projects in the existing built environment. This is what I tried to convey to students in the studio I led at the EPFL in the Fall 2018 and Spring 2019 semesters.

To begin with, one needs to start from a position of respect. Such a position must be accompanied, I think, by a deep knowledge of the history of architecture and construction, knowledge acquired through the work of an architect and not that of historians.

Ignorance of history and a lack of understanding of the architecture of buildings in which new layers are to be added are, I think, the cause of most unfortunate interventions. For many years, the existence of a true relationship between history and design has been forgotten, with history being considered as an independent subject and design as a totally capricious act, without any relation to culture whatsoever.

The second principle means having a forward-looking mindset and not simply remaining attached to analysis with the hope of deducing an answer.

I think that, contrary to what one might imagine, knowledge cannot exist without the presence of a creative mind. Some might believe that intervening in the existing built environment is the work of specialists who are the only people with sufficient knowledge of history and who are suspicious of all creative abilities; that they would indulge in analysis to find the answers. I believe, however, that this practice must go beyond analysis, and must include a creative act.

I think that a design project in the existing built environment must reflect the spirit of the time: a nineteenth-century intervention project is very different from a contemporary one.

A principle of harmony must be sought between the existing and the new, between the old and the contemporary, in order to find a unity between the two. For me, contrasting relationships are too easy and too dangerous. The search for harmony, while more difficult, is also more satisfying.

Musician Igor Stravinsky wrote about this question, and his thoughts can also be applied to architecture. Looking for harmony means reconstructing a new unity between "old and modern," between what exists and new layers. We must understand that there are two complementary fragments, each seeing its reflection in the other. If we analyze them in a detailed fashion, we recognize in architecture and in the urban fabrics of many towns of all these different time periods, an ensemble of successive layers, which endlessly renew the architectural and urban heritage. The beauty of this architecture is not as a sum of "pure" objects but is rather found in the harmony of the whole.

3

Within the framework of my teaching at the EPFL, accompanied by Eduardo Blanes and Thierry Manasseh, I tried to give the students tools that can be used to carry out this sort of design project.

I first insisted on the importance of understanding the site. To accomplish this, we made two study trips to visit the site for each project. The first was to Madrid, where we surveyed a late 1950s neighborhood before developing the first studio project. The goal was to introduce new public spaces and improve the different types of housing.

The intervention on some of the complexes built during the second half of the twentieth century was a very important and indispensable task. The neighborhood we chose showed great architectural quality, despite its current state. It was designed in the spirit of new Swedish complexes of the time, but with the economic means that Spain possessed at that moment. The work was, then, through the project, to renovate the housing while improving comfort by adapting to current requirements.

The complex was designed in the rationalist architectural style, forming isolated blocks with no real connection to the public space. We suggested that the students intervene on the existing empty areas between the buildings to create public spaces, connected to the strong topography of the site.

We took advantage of the trip to Madrid to also visit several buildings that I had designed, which have a close link to the existing built environment, such as the cultural center at Escuelas Pías or the church in Valdemaqueda. These two projects are on very different scales. The Escuelas Pías form a complex including a ruin that has been transformed into a library, thanks to the addition of a new layer to cover and adapt it. It also includes a contemporary building in keeping with the old: the organization of a square and an underground parking lot. The church in Valdemaqueda, on the other hand, is a smaller project which involved the addition of an apse to a Gothic church. Through this project, I was trying to create a religious space using constructional expression.

During our second trip, to Munich this time, we visited works by Hans Döllgast, in particular the Alte Pinakothek and the St. Bonifaz church, with the goal of adding to the latter a new library that would be attached to the partially reconstructed church.

Hans Döllgast's body of work is a crucial reference for projects in the existing built environment. He took part in the reconstruction of the city of Munich after the bombings of the Second World War, with projects on many monuments, including the Alte Pinakothek, various cemeteries, as well as the St. Bonifaz church. In all of his projects, Döllgast knew just how to interpret existing architecture, while adding significant transformations to adapt the buildings to new uses or to improve existing uses.

St. Bonifaz church was largely destroyed during the bombings, and only a fragment of the front section and the naves remained standing. Döllgast did not suggest rebuilding the destroyed naves and radiating chapel but transformed the front portion of the ancient basilica into a central-plan church. He also reinforced the columns by embedding them into new brick walls and replaced the missing wall decorations with plaster, allowing the materiality of the walls to be seen.

In the space of the old demolished nave, Döllgast created an archeological garden among the ruins.

In the 1960s, the monks asked the architect to extend the monastery into this garden section. He developed different propositions, but none was ever accepted. A concrete building with no relation to the existing buildings was later built.

After the students had analyzed the original building, the one reconstructed by Döllgast, and several of his unbuilt designs, we asked them to design a library on the site of the old archeological garden. The design needed to be adapted to the site by replacing the current concrete building and establishing a connection in scale and materiality with the church.

4

The students built models of the church to deepen their knowledge of the existing buildings before adding any new layers.

I think that in order to study what exists, historical analysis is insufficient. One also needs a knowledge of the spatial and construction qualities of the buildings. As such, models add a great deal of important information. The varying conditions of the church and the unbuilt designs were represented in similar fashions and on the same scale, which made it possible to evaluate and appreciate the spatial qualities of each proposition.

We tried, as much as possible, to analyze each construction system through models of construction sections.

The students worked in groups of two or three, in such a way as to allow for teamwork while also guaranteeing individual creativity. Teamwork is important, especially in the analysis phase, while individual expression must (I think) be favored in the design itself.

The complexity of an architect's work today requires experience in working as a team. This is why I think that the ideal group size for a student project is either two or three people: in order to stimulate debate without favoring individualism and without falling into a sort of "assembled" work.

All of the projects contained carefully done representations, using different colors to clearly distinguish what was kept, what was demolished, and what was added. The same color system was used by all the students.

Representation is fundamental in this kind of project, first of all for explaining but also to ensure that the degree of intervention can be measured and to allow comparisons between the different projects.

5

Over the course of the studio, we invited lecturers and architects specialized in this discipline for intermediary and final reviews, notably Franz Graf and Martin Boesch, as well as Vitangelo Ardito who also gave a lecture on his work.

Professor Graf directs the TSAM at the EPFL where he has taught for many years. His research and knowledge of modern architecture from constructive techniques are internationally known.

Martin Boesch has taught the "Riuso" project at Mendrisio for several years. He has developed many projects in the existing built environment that show his sensitivity and knowledge.

Vitangelo Ardito teaches construction at the Politecnico de Bari. His teaching is characterized by the use of models through which the links between architecture and construction are taught to the students. He carries out research on architects at the margins of modernity, such as Paul Schmitthenner and Hans Döllgast.

Finally, we published two books: the first, a compilation of student projects, permits an appreciation of their homogeneity as to the respect of stated fundamental principles and their differences as to the solutions found; the second, titled *Hans Döllgast and the Preservation Project*, draws the parallel between the German architect's work and the work developed at the EPFL.

These publications, created by Eduardo Blanes and Thierry Manasseh, were accompanied by an exhibition organized with the help of David Hoffert and Alexandre Tiarri, students from the studio. This exhibition showed Döllgast's projects at St. Bonifaz church through the work of the students' survey, drawings, models, and designs.

1

2

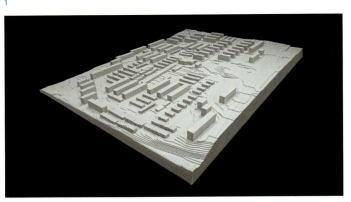
3

6

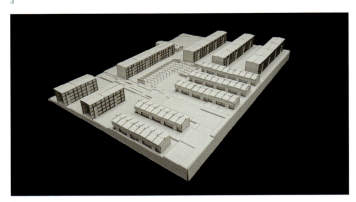
4

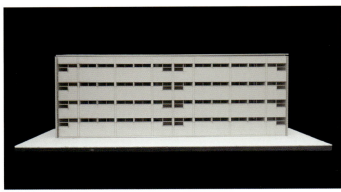
7

5

1 Fuencarral, adjoining houses in the foreground and multi-family dwellings in the background, 2018
2 Fuencarral, one of the three abandoned covered market halls, 2018
3 The Fuencarral complex, model
4 Fragment of the complex with the two kinds of dwellings organized around a market, model
5 Row houses with private gardens, model
6, 7 Multi-family dwellings, north and south façades, model
8 Redevelopment of a covered market into collective spaces for the residents and a festival hall
9 Regeneration of public spaces with the addition of businesses taking advantage of the sloped terrain, the addition of private gardens connected to the dwellings, renovation and transformation of existing dwellings

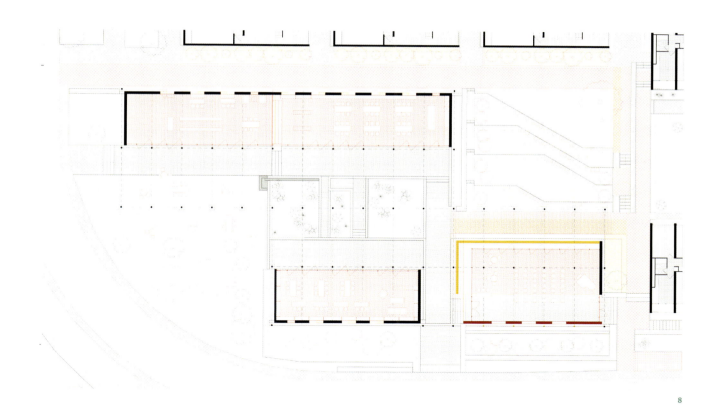

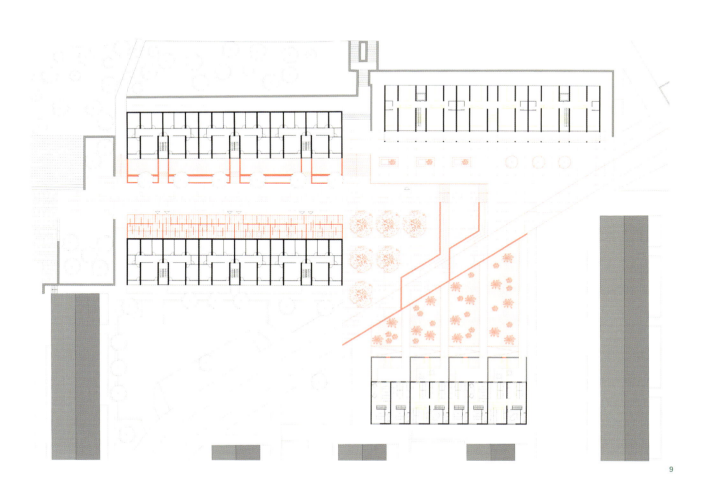

271　PROJECT TEACHING IN THE "PRESERVATION" ORIENTATION

10

11

12

TEACHING THE PRESERVATION 272

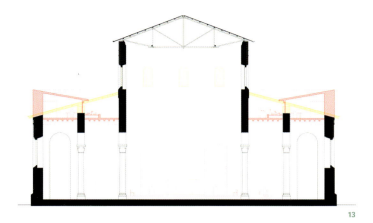

10 Redevelopment and extension of the San Lorenzo church in Valdemaqueda, José Ignacio Linazasoro, architect
11 St. Bonifaz church by Ziebland constructed in 1835–1847, rehabilitated in 1945 by Hans Döllgast
12 Exhibition *Hans Döllgast and the Preservation Project*, presenting the architect's different projects for St. Bonifaz church as well as the work from the studio students, EPFL, 2019
13 Rehabilitation project of the church and extension to include a library, by inverting the roof direction in keeping with Hans Döllgast's approach for this church and other projects
14 Rehabilitation project of the church and extension to include a library, by prolonging the typology and the character of the building in a contemporary fashion

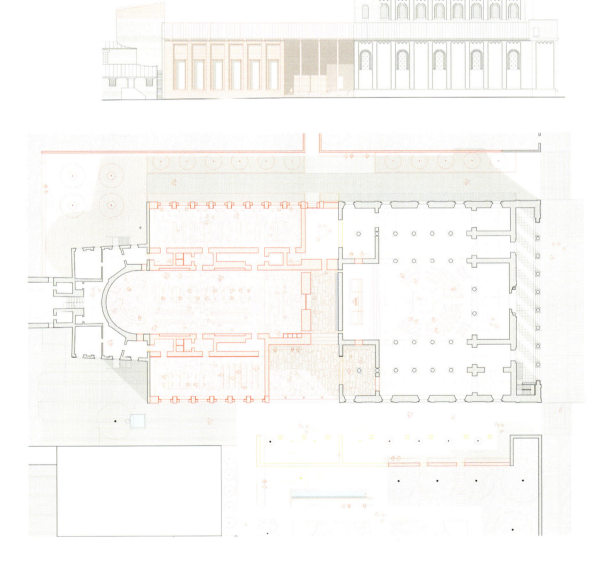

273 PROJECT TEACHING IN THE "PRESERVATION" ORIENTATION

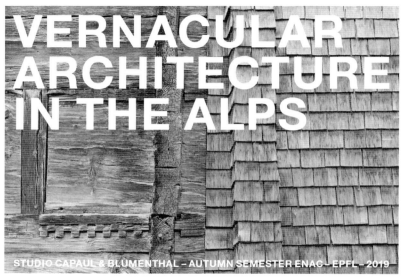

CAPAUL & BLUMENTHAL

Fall 2019

Vernacular architecture in the Alps
Regeneration of a parcel of land in the center of Lumbrein

Professors: Ramun Capaul and Gordian Blumenthal
Teaching assistants: Thierry Manasseh, Arabella Masson

Reviewers: Jürg Conzett, Franz Graf, Martin Steinmann

Visits: Grisons
Guide: Lezza Dosch

Spring 2020

The (abandoned) hotel in the Alps
Rehabilitation of the Tenigerbad Hotel in the Val Sumvitg

Professors: Ramun Capaul and Gordian Blumenthal
Teaching assistants: Thierry Manasseh, Arabella Masson

Reviewers: Christopher Bardt, Franz Graf,
Katarina Lundeberg, Catherine Gay
Lecturers: Satyajitt Chatterjee, Catherine Gay,
Jon Mathieu, Leo Tuor

Visits: Grisons
Guide: Marc Tomaschett, owner of the Hotel Tenigerbad

WORKING ON HERITAGE SITES IN ALPINE REGION

RAMUN CAPAUL
GORDIAN BLUMENTHAL
Capaul & Blumenthal Architekten, Ilanz/Glion

With its impressive mountain slopes and remote valleys, the alpine region is home to a largely preserved vernacular architecture that has emerged from agricultural practices. Yet at the same time, historical transportation routes from north to south and the development of alpine tourism have long brought outside influences and ensured exchange (including architectural exchange) with other cultures.

Vernacular architecture demonstrates the direct relationship between human needs, local conditions, and the built works that result from this—from temporary utilitarian constructions to buildings that have survived for centuries while adapting to the constant changes that have occurred in a regional context. The appearance of new types, such as sacred buildings, stately homes, hotels, or infrastructure works, instead emerges from profound social transformations that often go beyond local events and have a universal character. Their relationship to the place is thus not consubstantial nor immediately obvious. And their impact on the features of the settlements and the sociocultural context takes on even greater importance.

Although over generations certain traits belonging to vernacular architecture seem to have lost their *raison d'être*, we believe that sound elements for the design of current buildings can nevertheless be found within them.

For many decades there was a virtually unlimited supply of construction materials, but the growing requirements for the preservation of resources and sustainability have meant that choosing local materials and production procedures that need little transformation of raw materials is increasingly important. In order to ensure technically and economically viable processes going from raw material to completed work, and in order for these processes to ultimately contribute to high-quality built heritage, traditional artisanal knowledge is just as important as the benefits gained from technology.

Depending on the material chosen and how built forms are arranged, buildings, squares, streets, and gardens create spaces with a unique character. Identifying the architectural phenomena that result from multidisciplinary processes involving several factors and actors is an important basis for preserving and developing the qualities of the existing built environment.

During our two teaching semesters at the EPFL, we focused on the built heritage of mountain regions, and through our selection of two different building types and sites, we looked at various themes within vernacular architecture and preservation. The fall semester centered on a disused agricultural building in the historic village center of Lumbrein, and the spring semester looked at the Tenigerbad hotel complex in the Val Sumvitg, which has been abandoned for almost fifty years. In both cases the aim was to reflect on how the structure could be converted and thus revitalize the local area.

Vernacular architecture in the Alps

For many centuries, the limited availability of materials determined construction methods in alpine villages. Different types of buildings were continually being developed, modified, and refined. The industrialization and individualization of our society caused a break with the traditional built culture, and today, vernacular architecture is no longer a priority. However, it has the potential to enhance the local context and respond to current global architectural issues. The Grisons village of Lumbrein will provide the opportunity to understand how an alpine village and its architecture evolves. The various relationships between topography, road networks, public spaces, and buildings will be analyzed, as will housing typologies and the uses attributed to them. The aim is to produce, in the middle of the village, an architecture that is both contemporary and respectful of the built heritage, by drawing on knowledge gathered about the local culture and construction. (Extract from the studio presentation document, Fall semester 2019)

In order to reflect on issues of vernacular architecture within the built environment, we chose the Grisons village of Lumbrein, a typical example of how villages in the Val Lumnezia have evolved over time.

The built fabric consists of a compact accumulation of habitations, stables, and gardens that line a network of clearly defined public roads. The uniform orientation of the buildings results from the convergence of the direction of the slope and the constraints in terms of service roads.

Public spaces in Lumbrein can be seen on the one hand in sections of the main streets, along which several dwellings are lined up, thus protecting the stables at the back; and on the other hand in the fact that in some well-demarcated sections of the village, several habitations form a group of a public nature, oriented in such a way that they surround a common, unbuilt space. Another expression of public space is in the decoration of back façades overlooking a small street.

Built types and forms

In the center of the village, the historic built fabric mainly comprises houses with stacked and exposed wooden beams and log barn-stables. As the name suggests, construction using stacked wooden beams is a traditional solid-construction technique that involves stacking beams or logs that slot together at the corners.

The dominant type is a house divided along the roof ridge and comprising a transverse corridor, thus forming two dwellings. In the eighteenth century, most of these houses were built in their classic form, before undergoing many modifications in the nineteenth and early twentieth centuries. In Lumbrein, historic stone constructions are atypical. The oldest are the two medieval towers that were used as dwellings. The sacred buildings date from the Baroque period. In the early twentieth century, some public buildings, such as the school, were built in stone. From the middle of the twentieth century, the arrival of industrial materials meant that construction in stacked wooden beams, which for many centuries had characterized the region, came to a halt. Since then, most new buildings have been constructed with mixed building techniques.

Structural transformations

The structural changes that have affected mountain regions have been accompanied by a demographic exodus to urban centers. Today, the population of Lumbrein has stabilized with around 400 habitants. As a direct result of economic and social transformations, most new constructions—mainly primary and secondary residences—have been built on the periphery of the village. After the referendum on secondary residences and the restrictions it imposed in terms of building zones, and the revised law on land planning, construction activity once again shifted towards the center of the village, where historic houses and former farm buildings were transformed into vacation homes.

As the percentage of secondary residences rose to more than 50% in all the villages in the Val Lumnezia, the question arose of the balance between primary residences, secondary residences, and public buildings.

Project topic

At the edge of the square located to the west of the church and the main road is a disused farm building belonging to the parish. It holds an important position because it marks the separation between the unbuilt space next to the church and the garden it borders to the east.

The aim of the semester was to develop an idea to preserve the urban qualities of the place and infuse it with new life, whether by converting the building, which has fallen into disuse, or by replacing it with a new construction. In order to determine which new function would suit the space, students had to identify the various needs and interests present in the village and the valley, while making sure that the planned new content would be compatible with the structure of the stable. If this latter requirement could not be adhered to, a new construction would have to be proposed.

During the design of the new building, students had to consider what they had learned from the analysis of the site and explore issues concerning the building's situation in relation to the topography, the street, and the square. In addition, they had to consider the vernacular character of the architecture, not only from a historical perspective but also as the seed from which they would develop the project.

An abandoned hotel in the Alps

The aim of this semester is to develop a scenario for the future of the Tenigerbad. The history of the Tenigerbad and Waldhaus buildings, and their remote location in the middle of a fascinating natural landscape is the basis for the development of this project. Students will have to identify the architectural potential of the historic buildings in terms of cultural heritage and put forward suggestions for how to revitalize it. Some parts of the complex could be demolished or replaced, and new functions could be introduced to create synergies with the existing buildings. Studying the evolution of tourism will influence how students develop the project, as will their consideration of the relationship between the resort and the landscape, and its importance for the inhabitants of the region. (Extract from the studio presentation document, Spring semester 2020)

1 "And finally, note that the reanimation process upsets one of the cardinal axioms of modern architecture: the container precedes the content, function follows 'form.' The observation of the qualitative compatibility therefore implies prior research on an appropriate need for an existing building; in sum, it consists of finding the hand to fit the glove," André Corboz, "Bâtiments anciens et fonctions actuelles: esquisse d'une approche de la 'réanimation'," *Das Werk*, no. 11 (1975): 992–994.

Tenigerbad

To understand the genealogy of the hotel complex at Tenigerbad in the Val Sumvitg, information collected on the original hot springs was just as important as the history of the discovery of the Alps and the development of early tourism infrastructure. By way of an introduction to the Spring semester, historian Jon Mathieu presented the historical aspects in a lecture entitled "Rush to the Alps: The Age of Mountain Glory." During the study trip, we were able to visit several historic and recent hotels in the Grisons. Like Hotel Schatzalp in Davos or Hotel Waldhaus in Flims, the Tenigerbad hotel had traversed several different eras and had been marked by a change in requirements in terms of tourism. Unlike the above-mentioned hotels, however, Tenigerbad is in an isolated valley, far from a center with specific tourism infrastructure. The last extension carried out on the hotel was to mark the beginning of its decline. Despite several attempts to breathe new life into it, the hotel has been disused for almost fifty years.

Revitalization

The aim of the semester was to develop a plan to bring the hotel back to life—which would inevitably raise questions about its relationship with the surrounding landscape. Although these "rural hot springs" of the sixteenth century were a fundamental part of the landscape, which was dotted with small agricultural buildings, and were part of the social life of the valley's inhabitants, the current hotel complex today appears, due to its size and derelict state, to be out of date and disconnected from the location. Furthermore, a prolonged vacancy generally results in an insidious decline in the symbiosis between the physical substance of a building and its original function.

The issue of revitalization did not only bring up the question of size and the architectural quality of the buildings, its use as a hotel was also called into question. It was thus necessary to match the new "content" to the existing "container," in order to find the correct "hand to fit the glove," to use the metaphor so dear to André Corboz.[1]

The survey of the different parts of the complex was an important basis for evaluating the existing buildings and exploring their potential to determine the project strategy. This survey, which the students carried out in groups, included information about the history of the various buildings as well about their typology, construction, materialization, and their condition.

Built in different eras, the buildings were assessed in light of their specific architectural qualities and their importance to the overall complex. In the design projects there were therefore differentiated levels of intervention, ranging from the demolition of some groups of buildings to the construction of new structures within the complex, as well as renovation projects. Some projects suggested demolishing the structures from the hotel's most recent expansion, in order to reestablish the original spatial qualities of the Waldhaus park. Other projects sought to rehabilitate, through large-scale interventions, the most recent buildings that imitated alpine architecture, while yet others counted on the restoration of surface coverings and the preservation of traces left by time to give new life to the space.

1

2

3

4

5

8

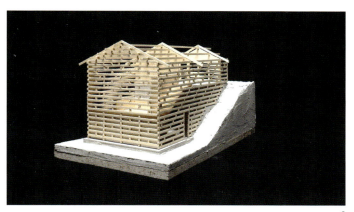

6

9

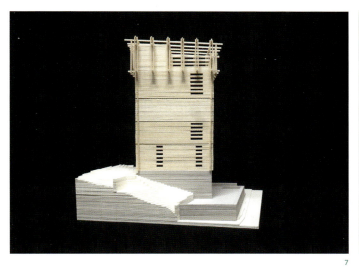

7

10

1 The village of Lumbrein in the Val Lumnezia
2 One of the two medieval towers in the village
3 Project site, a stable and barn located on a plot in the center of the village, next to the church and directly connected to the main road
4 Typical dwelling for two families, with in this case the façade overlooking one of the village's public spaces rather than towards the slope and view
5 Village center, model

6 Reconstruction of the building in a similar template that would have an excavated cellar for maturing cheese and a cheese-making factory in the upper part
7 Construction of a third (public) tower in the village, designed to house the archives of the Val Lumnezia
8 Sculpture required from students at the beginning of the semester to represent their feelings about the site and the project
9 Addition of a communal bread oven, using the same principle that existed in another part of the village, with the rehabilitation of the barn as a shared space
10 Rehabilitation of the stables to house a "werkhof" for inhabitants or visitors to use

11

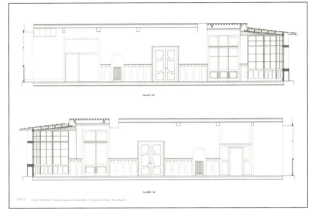
12

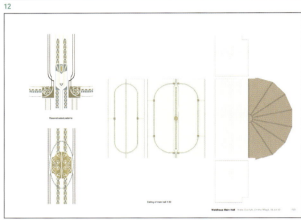
13

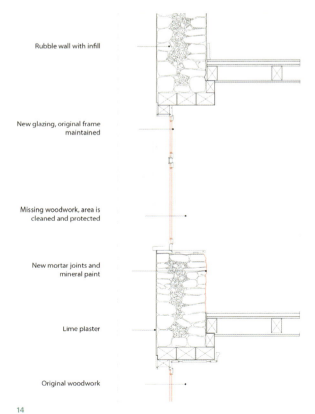

Rubble wall with infill

New glazing, original frame maintained

Missing woodwork, area is cleaned and protected

New mortar joints and mineral paint

Lime plaster

Original woodwork

14

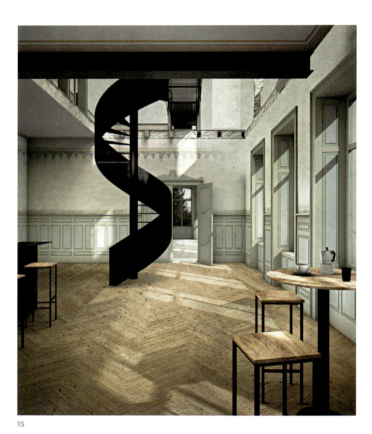
15

TEACHING THE PRESERVATION   282

16

17

18

19

20

21

11 The Tenigerbad hotel and its later additions to the back, model
12, 13 Central hall at the Waldhaus, interior elevations with wood joinery, ceilings, and decorative paintings, extract from the "Raumbuch"
14, 15 Rehabilitation of the Waldhaus as an artist's residence, by conserving and taking advantage of alterations to the building, which would modify its typology, such as the space created by the collapse of some floor levels, image and construction section

16, 17 Rehabilitation of the Tenigerbad complex as studios and artist's residence, with various renovation, reconstruction, and rehabilitation interventions depending on the building, images
18, 19 Rehabilitation of the Waldhaus as a writer's retreat, with demolition of annexes and rehabilitation of the grounds, images
20, 21 Rehabilitation of the complex as a university complex for research on the environment, with transformation, renovation, and reconstruction of the annexes, images

Beznau
Dessiner les paysages d'après

EPFL_ENAC | semestre d'automne 2020
Professeure invitée Martina Voser | Assistante Coralie Berchtold

Mitholz
Dessiner les paysages d'après

EPFL_ENAC | semestre de printemps 2021
Professeure invitée Martina Voser | Assistante Coralie Berchtold

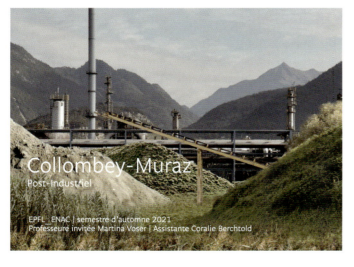

Collombey-Muraz
Post-Industriel

EPFL_ENAC | semestre d'automne 2021
Professeure invitée Martina Voser | Assistante Coralie Berchtold

Engiadin Ota
Scénarios Paysagers

EPFL_ENAC | semestre de printemps 2022
Professeure invitée Martina Voser | Assistante Coralie Berchtold

VOSER

Fall 2020

Beznau
Depths of field

Professor: Martina Voser
Teaching assistant: Coralie Berchtold

Reviewers: Isabelle Duner, Reto Pfenninger, Dieter Dietz, Jürg Frey, Franz Graf, Christophe Girot, Daniel Jauslin

Visits: Beznau

Spring 2021

Mitholz
Drawing the later landscapes

Professor: Martina Voser
Teaching assistant: Coralie Berchtold

Reviewers: Isabelle Duner, Reto Pfenninger, Dieter Dietz, Jürg Frey, Franz Graf, Carola Anton, Christophe Girot, Daniel Jauslin, Sibylle André, Simon Bailly, Peter Wullschleger, Beat Kälin, Martin Trachsel

Visits: Mitholz

Fall 2021

Post-industrial
Collombey-Muraz

Professor: Martina Voser
Teaching assistant: Coralie Berchtold

Reviewers: Reto Pfenninger, Dieter Dietz, Franz Graf, Catherine Gay Menzel, Alexandros Fotakis, Ute Schneider, Philippe Coignet

Visits: Collombey-Muraz and Attisholz

Spring 2022

Engiadin'Ota
Landscape scenarios

Professor: Martina Voser
Teaching assistant: Coralie Berchtold

Reviewers: Reto Pfenninger, Dieter Dietz, Franz Graf, Alexandros Fotakis, Nicola Braghieri, Sofia Prifti, Marco Rampini, Yann Junod

Visits: Haute-Engadine and Attisholz

CULTIVATING THE LANDSCAPE

INTERVIEW WITH MARTINA VOSER (mavo Landschaften, Zurich)

This interview is the product of a conversation between Martina Voser, Franz Graf, and Thierry Manasseh, April 29, 2022.

Franz Graf (FG): The idea behind this conversation is to understand how your work, at a project design level, deals with the notion of preservation. For us, it has always been obvious and extremely important, but it deserves to be explained clearly.

Martina Voser (MV): I agree with you that it's very important, especially in the Swiss context, where our national identity, economy, and marketing all rely in large part on issues of landscape. We have a very rich cultural landscape of which only the classical landscapes, the "historic" or "natural" ones, are sometimes protected and therefore preserved. The privilege of working with students is that we've been able to look more deeply into the question of the impacts on Swiss cultural landscapes caused by climate change and the evolution of society.

I prefer the German term *Denkmalpflege* when speaking of preservation. It contains the word *Pflege*, or "care." Taking care of something doesn't necessarily mean safeguarding or keeping, despite what the French word for preservation—*sauvegarder*—might imply. In fact, taking care includes the idea of change. There is never a status quo in landscape and the question of care is intrinsically linked to the fact that it is constantly in transformation.

During these two years of teaching at the EPFL, we chose to work on different landscapes that were very typically Swiss: Beznau, Mitholz, Collombey-Muraz, and the Haute-Engadine. We wanted to have a fair amount of diversity between plains and alpine regions. What all the sites had in common was that they will face major changes in the next few decades: the closing of the Beznau nuclear power plant, which also raises the question of the relationship between energy transition and Swiss landscape; the risks involved in evacuating the village of Mitholz where the Swiss army had previously stocked several tons of explosives in a cliff that is no longer accessible; the ground decontamination during the dismantling of the refinery at Collombey-Muraz; or even the management of water and the melting of permafrost in the dry alpine region of the Haute-Engadine, which is increasingly concerned by cuts in water supply and forest fires.

We then asked ourselves: how will these changes impact the cultural landscape? What must be conserved or renewed and what will Switzerland's identity look like in the future?

Our approach seemed to me very similar to your studio's approach: trying to understand how to give new life to buildings or landscapes, while seeking to discover the spirit of the place and defining its values. Our questions are similar, even if the scale is very different [laughs]. Another major difference is the question of vocabulary, since their training forces students not only into new scales, but also requires them to become familiar with and develop a language for speaking about and describing their projects.

FG: I think the scale you deal with is fantastic, as is your commitment to the issue of landscape. The values and methods are familiar—the view, the respect, the analysis—but the dimensions, which go far beyond what we study in the studio, seem to me indispensable to the training of young architects.

MV: One of the challenges in our teaching is understanding just how much we should explain to them and how much they can explore themselves. In our studio, we have decided to follow an iterative method, between intuition and precision, between reading and writing. At the beginning of the semester, an initial spatial hypothesis is formulated—in an image or a drawing—and then, there is a good deal of back and forth between developing and analyzing. This iteration aims to help them to let go and to not become paralyzed when faced with the imposing scale of our research sites and the complexity of the issues. Often when faced with a beautiful work of architecture or a magnificent landscape, we freeze and stare in sheer fascination and passive contemplation. Encouraging the students to maintain an active gaze and draw up a proposition for developing the work, from the very first day, helps to reduce their fear.

And then, group analyses, which are not at all the same as those done in pairs, pique their curiosity and their desire to understand the site, and above all reassure them as to their intuitions. They allow the students to exchange their knowledge, which helps the group dynamic and the collective intelligence. We work with several layers of reading, and this way of breaking these down in order to better understand them—through their structures as well as through their systems—is similar to your approach in the studio. We work with geology, water, vegetation, infrastructure, and building, among other things.

FG: It's true that it is very close to what we do and it's also a question of viewpoint: how do we look at things? What you bring is a much broader view, very different from that of architects, and one that we really need. We really enjoy having you at our reviews because you question the architectural object more broadly in its context.

MV: It's a whole package. Doing a semester on landscape architecture allows for diving into the systems and dynamics—an object influences the systems and vice versa. Sometimes architects construct without ensuring that this exchange takes place. When working with landscapes, this is impossible since everything is connected—the ground, the water, the plants, the people—and we can't separate them. This is a good thing for architects to learn, isn't it?

Thierry Manasseh (TM): Yes, it's essential. Overspecialization means that we break the project into diverse specialties. We see clearly that the good projects are those where there is close collaboration from the very beginning—we see a continuity between the building and the landscape. For this reason, it seems important to me to make students aware of the vocabulary and the issues, so that they have the tools to speak with specialists in their future projects.

You have already taught architects in several different schools—USI, ETHZ, and EPFL—have you also taught any landscape architecture programs? And if so, do you teach them differently?

MV: I have only taught architects, which is surprising [laughs]. If I were invited to teach in a landscape architecture program, I would offer a workshop on the themes of spatiality, structures of space, and of conceptual thought.

I was trained as an architect and so I learned that to design projects you need to collaborate with many specialists. For our "WolkenWerk" project, I was lucky enough to work with an excellent biologist, with whom we were able to engage in a rich exchange of ideas. I had ideas on spatial structures, layers, depths, scenography with, of course, habitats already in mind, and he knew how to express these concepts with the help of different combinations of plants. The structural aspect that we learn in architecture is indispensable. I feel as if the education of landscape architects in Switzerland is today more focused on ecology than it is on the design of spaces.

Another tool of the architect that I use daily, and that I encourage my students to apply to landscape projects, is the use of types. Our work is by its very nature so hybrid that typologies can help us clarify, simplify, and explain our thoughts. This brings us back to the need for a precise and specific language and vocabulary. There is a lot to learn from architecture and its training for landscapes.

FG: This is why it is so useful to create links between the professions and expertise at the university level, in order to allow for a maximum of exchange and ease of communication.

MV: Absolutely. Especially in the complex and intense world in which we live. Things move and change continually and it's even more important to find a balance between knowledge of "empty" and "full" spaces. The issues of today cannot always be solved by architectural objects (the "fulls"). The "empties" and the "fulls" must receive the same care, must be placed at an equal level, and interact as much as possible.

The university is the ideal place for such exchange: learning the keys to reading, a little vocabulary, developing a certain sensitivity and a different way of looking at things. When I was studying at the ETH in Zurich, we had a history of urbanism class, but even though it was interesting, it focused on volumes (the "fulls"). Christope Girot teaches a class on the history of landscape in Zurich, at the bachelor's level, which lays the foundations, but I think that really it is by working on projects that the notions are best assimilated.

FG: Our students were lucky enough to visit your project in Attisholz, and I was struck by the ideas they developed afterwards. This semester we are working on the Vidy wastewater treatment plant, where the total demolition of certain tanks is not very far away. As we learned about your project, we realized that we can look at things differently: we can appreciate them, analyze them, we can even make something else, and this is terrific. Even if in the framework of architecture we are just beginning to understand the importance of working on existing structures, it seems to me that in a landscape context this is even more fundamental. I wonder about the fact that in the program at EPFL, this aspect seems to be absent. And it's true that we have common visions—between preservation and your work on the territory—in that it's an approach, a viewpoint, a way of doing, which have comparable methods.

MV: What impresses me with your work and your classes is that you don't concentrate only on buildings that obviously need to be preserved. You must above all explain the value of the places you choose. In Switzerland, we always feel like we have so many landscapes and that it isn't necessary to preserve them all. But if we look at the Mitteland, it's completely gone, we have destroyed it on a grand scale. The Mendrisiotto is the best example. They had this vision of a paradise on the top of a mountain, but the valley has been completely built up. It's because they didn't begin taking care early enough. In this same way we have lost many buildings because it wasn't obvious that they needed to be taken care of. What I love about this aspect of preservation, is the respect and love for the objects. I always approach a site with respect, and only then do I look at whether something needs to be changed and how to do so. But one first needs to be able to read the space and that's why it seems important to me to teach it.

FG: We feel like we are spoilsports here [laughs]. We're talking about something we share, a respected thing, which most people agree on in principle. Yet, in reality, it's destruction that usually wins.

MV: In Switzerland, the development of the profession of landscape architects began with gardeners, those who took care of the *Umgebung* (that which surrounds). To change this perception of the profession (which is still a reality), I am convinced that we must explain it at university, at a time when we can still ask questions. This is where there is a real opportunity in teaching landscape to architects.

FG: But you, how did you come to this world of landscape?

MV: It wasn't done consciously, more by curiosity; it was a process, just like those we find in the landscape, and that's where I found the best place to develop my interests [laughs]. Looking back, my student work was already very focused on the exterior. Landscapes seemed freer to me, and there was no need to choose which school we wanted to belong to, as was the case in architecture at the time.

FG: You come from Grisons. How has that impacted your vision of nature and landscape?

MV: What's interesting is that in the mountain regions there is still this mentality that the landscape is abundant and that there is no need to make any special efforts to take care of it. People don't see any use for landscape architects. The project we are working on at the moment in Bondo is innovative in this respect. Usually landscape architects are not called upon for infrastructure projects of this kind.

But what has perhaps influenced me the most, since childhood, is notions of scale and transformation in a landscape. These issues are the subject of current research in our studios.

Drawings and representation are difficult on these two levels: how can we do an architectural drawing on a very large scale with the spatial qualities of the project? It's not an easy task, and often during the first part of the semester, the architectural drawings are not very impressive. The students must also differentiate between an architectural drawing and a map. The latter is not necessarily spatial but can show systems or primary structures. The second difficulty is that of representing the transformations, the procedures, the dynamics. The different landscape spaces change constantly.

To encourage and to downplay their apprehension about scale, we begin the exercises as early as possible. This semester, beginning in the second week, the pairs were asked to produce a map of the entire Haute-Engadine with a design proposition. It's a difficult exercise, but one that was successful.

Working with the landscape means learning to let go, to not get lost in the details; it isn't possible to control everything. You need to decide what you want to control, direct, or leave alone.

With our WolkenWerk project, the clients asked me questions about the project development, and I had to answer honestly that I didn't know everything [laughs]. As I am working with the canton's forestry strategy, I can't say precisely which trees need to be removed, those are things that will be decided as we go, we can't plan everything. But we learn to work with strategies and that's why it is indispensable to have a spatial vision.

FG: Teaching helps to transport the students into a universe that they don't yet know, and in your case it's exactly that: to be confronted with a whole valley and to propose a design project.

MV: *The panic room* [laughs]! Out of all the projects, those that begin with uncertainty, the unknown, are often the best because those are the projects that lead to innovations. When you are in your comfort zone, you rarely ask yourself the right questions. Our studios ask very open questions and students must take clear stances. There is no one right answer and never two identical projects. It's always very moving to see the students present their projects at the end of the semester, knowing where they started. It's a huge progression and I think they are very brave.

TM: The advantage of landscape and of the large scale is that it is more difficult to start with an image or a simple reference to be applied. We have to start with knowledge gained from the analysis of the site and also rely on our intuition. The projects are thus well-founded and specific. Once this methodology has been learned, it can be applied to architecture too.

MV: At the end of my studies, the international style—not at all contextual and specific—was very popular. In landscape, we must consider the context, to understand where the space begins and ends, not to mention climate.

Today, landscape is quite fashionable. People take us very seriously when we speak of the value of a tree, which was not at all the case at the beginning of my career. That's great but there is still a risk that we'll talk only about biodiversity and ecology and not enough about space. It's important to develop this culture. I worry about the lack of historical and cultural understanding. There is too little debate on these issues. For example, we speak a great deal about the impact of climate change on cities, but very little about its effect on the landscape. Teaching offers the ideal platform for these discussions.

FG: I agree completely. There is a cultural vacuum. We are focusing much more on factual questions. How do you explain the lack of interest in these issues in architecture schools?

MV: In my practice, we are constantly faced with questions of renovating buildings, which are not only technical but also cultural questions. It's obvious and a very serious political issue. The challenges are similar for landscape, and yet less developed. There is a gap between what society asks for and what we can offer.

As for Swiss landscape, there are very few people who speak and who take a position. This could give the impression that there is only one viewpoint. But it shouldn't be forgotten that the profession is still quite young. In the past, the landscape was taken care of by farmers and engineers—today we have to train those who will be involved with the land in the future so that they have a real sensitivity to the challenges inherent in landscape.

PROJECT TEACHING IN THE "PRESERVATION" ORIENTATION

1 Construction of the Beznau power plant in 1967
2-4 The structure of the nuclear power plant, an important legacy of Switzerland's nuclear industry, is made accessible and transformed into a recreational landscape. The existing elements are carefully studied and specifically reworked in order for the new spatial structure of the island to permit a large variety of uses in the future

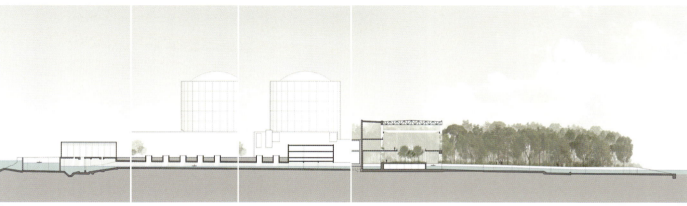

TEACHING THE PRESERVATION 292

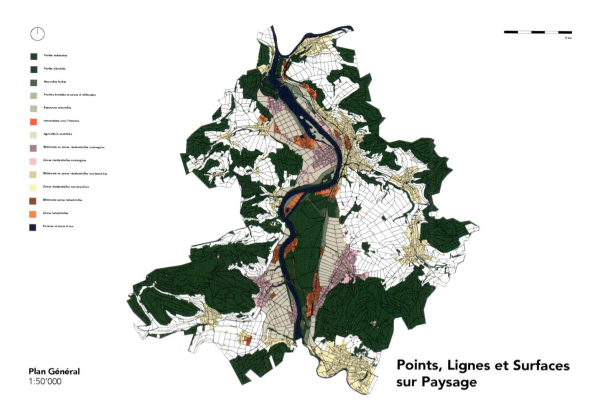

Plan Général
1:50'000

Points, Lignes et Surfaces sur Paysage

5

Industries

5-8 In order to protect and supply the biggest underground waterway in Switzerland, a new landscaped structure is put into place. Special drainage systems retain, clean, and filter the meteoric water. The new natural elements are integrated into the structures of habitat, industry, and agriculture, and confer a strong identity to the valley

Coupe
Canaux d'infiltration dans les rues
1:50

Activités Humaines

6

Industries

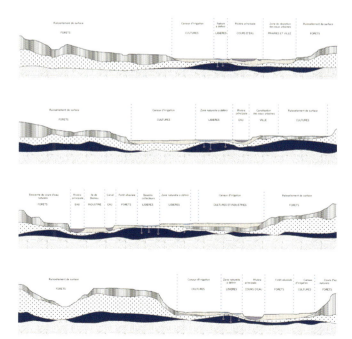

Coupe
Noues entre bâtiments industriels
1:50

Activités Humaines

7

Coupes Profondeur des Nappes
Géologie des sols

8

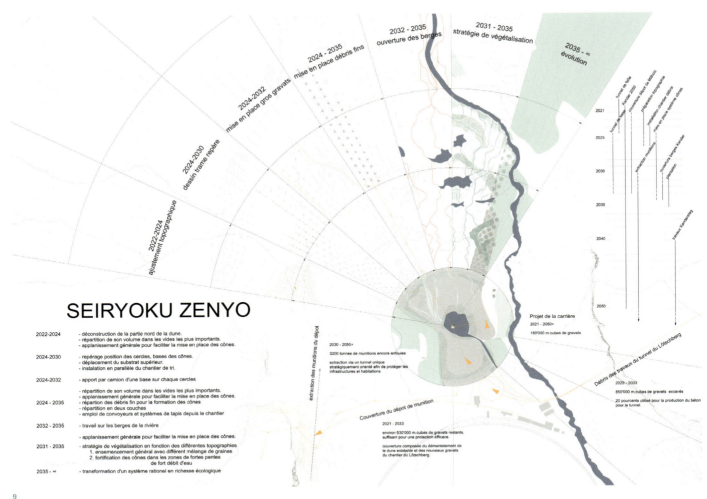

9

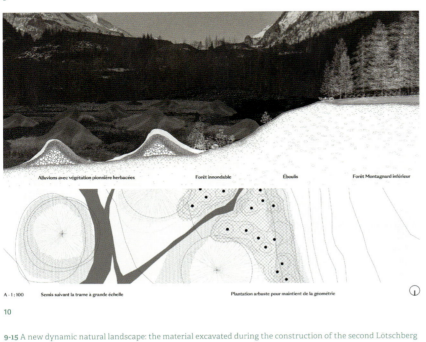

10

9-15 A new dynamic natural landscape: the material excavated during the construction of the second Lötschberg tunnel is carefully arranged to create new and diverse habitats that can develop by means of erosion and succession

11

TEACHING THE PRESERVATION   294

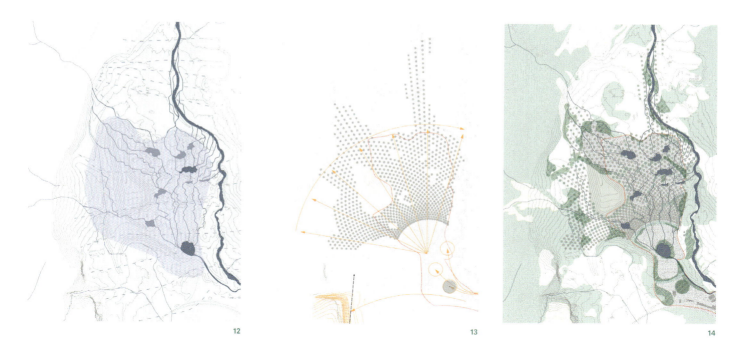

12 13 14

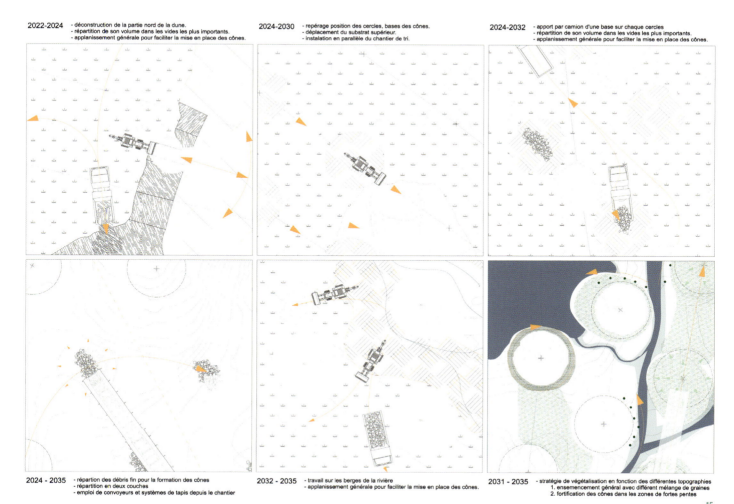

295 PROJECT TEACHING IN THE "PRESERVATION" ORIENTATION

16

17

16-22 Today, lacking in sufficient forested surfaces, the Chablais plain does not seem ready to meet the current climatic and environmental emergency. Faced with the use of renewable construction materials and with the idea of preserving its biodiversity, this fluvial region is seriously lacking forested areas. To respond to these multiple issues, the project proposes a new forest structure over the whole valley, based on three complementary interventions: the first seeks to reconnect and increase the alluvial forests, as well as connecting the forests to the mountain flanks; the second attempts to create productive high forests across the valley in order to meet the growing need for wood; the third introduces feeder plantations inside the towns in order to offer new food sources for the residents. With its long-term vision and plan for immediate action, the project will bring to life the current landscape and offer to its residents a new attractive and resilient plain

18   19   20   21

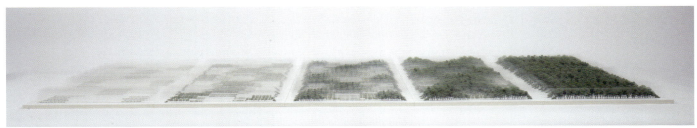

22

TEACHING THE PRESERVATION   296

23-27 An invisible problem is hidden in this largely industrialized valley: soil pollution. Contamination, along with questions of how to handle excavated earth, are the starting point for this project. The project proposes a method which, on the one hand, allows polluted sites to be treated via phytoremediation with the goal of improving the soil's biodiversity and, on the other hand, best employs the excavated material on a regional scale

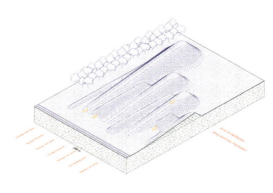

24

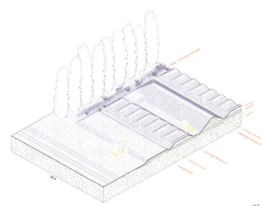

25

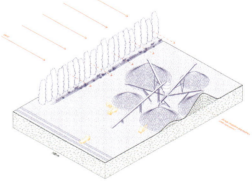

26

23

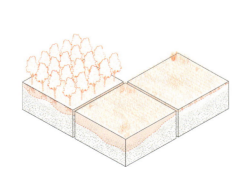

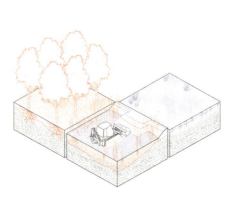

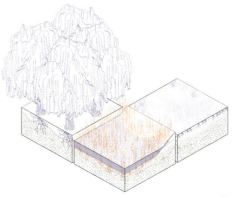

27

297 PROJECT TEACHING IN THE "PRESERVATION" ORIENTATION

FRANZ GRAF
THIERRY BUACHE

MASTER'S PRESERVATION PROJECT

The final step of architecture studies at the EPFL is the Master's Project (MP), which represents the synthesis of the academic curriculum and, in most cases, the transition to the professional world. This is where students put to good use the tools acquired during their studies and internships in order to develop a project they choose themselves. The first semester in this final academic year is devoted to the preparation of a theoretical dissertation and the second is for the development of an architectural project. With the help of a supervisory group including an academic director, a professor, an EPFL lecturer (and until 2017 a specialist), the students—alone or in pairs—first develop the theoretical element before beginning their design project. Forming part of the projects overseen by the TSAM Laboratory, these two semesters cover aspects that are intrinsically connected: theoretical research and a practical exercise as complementary concepts for the comprehensive development of a preservation project.

1 This is the number of master's projects that were supervised by the TSAM Laboratory from 2008 to 2022.

2 Interview with Stéphanie Morel, February 2, 2022
3 Interview with Julie Vulliet, February 2, 2022.

4 Interview with Fabian Roth, February 2, 2022.

Among the almost eighty master's projects supervised by the TSAM over the past fifteen years,[1] the twenty presented here portray various topics related to preservation. Through a series of interviews, these former students have looked back over their projects and the teaching of preservation from the vantage point of their professional and post-academic experience. What first emerged was a careful consideration of the definition of architectural preservation: the importance of resources, both material and cultural. From buildings recognized as important structures to a more diffuse or "ordinary" heritage, the built environment should first be observed in order to uncover its particular architectural values.

> *We always try to look for what makes a building special, what are the qualities or elements that should be preserved in order to highlight them in the design project."[2]*

The identification of the existing qualities of a building or site is directly related to its observation and analysis. In practice, this knowledge is developed through a survey of the existing environment. From construction details to the overall plan, observations and drawings allow for the identification of architectural and landscape intentions, the historical aspects of the construction as a means of revealing the qualities of an architecture.

> *From this teaching, we also learned how to get to know a building. In the beginning, we would look at a building several times without initially noticing any particular heritage value. It takes time to identify a building's qualities; it is not spontaneous. You have to be patient."[3]*

> *Learning how to perceive the existing environment through a careful survey is still very useful to us."[4]*

In a second phase, much of the discussion turned to what a design project looks like in a professional context. It would appear that there is generally a certain distinction between design projects developed in an academic milieu and those in the professional milieu. The time available, financial aspects, and restrictions related to the project management of a site seem to be the main differences. But the idea of the survey and the analysis of the existing environment, as well as its relation to the project, are important elements in the teaching of preservation. Understanding the existing environment as a vector for the project establishes an approach or a method that can be applied to preservation projects but also to projects related to new constructions.

5 Interview with Sophie Wobmann, February 2, 2022.
6 Interview with Charlotte Glatt, February 2, 2022.

7 Interview with Jérôme Wohlschlag, February 2, 2022.

" *I have retained this way of observing in my projects today, and it goes beyond preservation in a general sense, becoming part of the practice of reusing existing materials, in buildings and in public spaces. Through this teaching I can better appreciate issues of reuse."5*

" *This approach is very useful in the professional world. For transformation projects or projects occurring in the existing environment, it is normal today to carry out a survey and do historical research. It's not a big deal and we have all the tools we need to do it quickly."6*

Preservation does not only mean conserving what already exists at all costs; the analysis process allows for separating the structural parts to be retained from those that may be modified. This knowledge allows the potential of transformation, extension, or conversion to be revealed. It is an approach that guides the interventions of a contemporary project within an existing architectural style and enables a project's many possibilities to be defined.

" *The fact that we had analyzed the building in detail allowed us to intervene freely, sometimes quite substantially, but always with respect. This is not an approach that prevents construction; on the contrary, many diverse design projects can be created for the same object."7*

Primarily related to the preservation of twentieth-century built heritage, master's projects are designed to understand a building, a group of buildings, or an architectural site, with all its historical, material, and built determining factors, in order to develop intervention strategies adapted to the heritage value of the existing environment. The topics of the preservation projects are endless and involve multiple and varied subjects, which we have chosen to bring together here in three categories—one way among many others of reading them.

Heritage as resource

The idea of a resource in architecture is established generally as a physical or cultural asset that belongs to people or communities. Considering an architectural object or site as a resource allows for making it the main subject of a preservation project. The resource

Opening photo Model of the renovation project for the Bologna stadium, done as part of a master's project in 2022, 1:50 scale becomes the means of developing a project, which can be understood at once as the tool and as the framework.

In projects transforming old industrial sites (like the Chavalon power plant, the Zurich shunting station, or the Geneva wastewater treatment plant), we have observed that abandoned heritage sites can be highlighted through a preservation project and restored to their substance and use. The industrial history of these sites thus becomes a resource for the project, and the technical and spatial specificities of the architecture becomes a means to redefine uses. Other projects look at the resource principle in the reading of a type of intervention or a typological logic. After studying vertical extensions or the morphology of towers in a certain region, the extension projects of a block of residences in Servette and the renovation of the Maladière towers are based on a theoretical resource, that of the state of art of a piece of architectural heritage and its potential for development.

By considering these cultural notions of a "vernacular" architecture, a work of heritage can also be seen as a resource on a territorial scale. The project to rehabilitate neighborhood housing in Santiago, Chile, answers the needs of a community by basing itself on a construction representative of a specific culture. In the projects of the Weil am Rhein residential district or the extension of La Chevalière residence near Chambéry, the contemporary reinterpretation of a *Siedlung* from the 1930s and housing from the 1970s determine the preservation project. Conserving existing elements leads to the construction of new housing inspired by history and architecture, a sort of balance between old and new that allows for territorial continuity.

Monumental constructions

In the case of architectural objects whose heritage value is established and recognized, the preservation project addresses the crucial question of the effect that its quality has on an intervention, of what position to take. By addressing the contemporary needs of a piece of heritage, there are a multiplicity of possible interventions, which vary from imitation to contrast.

Whether speaking of nationally important objects—such as the industrial buildings by Mayer & Souter in Renens, the vestiges of the Expo 64 in the Vallée de la Jeunesse, Le Plaza in Geneva, the home-studio of André Wogenscky and Marta Pan in Saint-Rémy-lès-Chevreuse, and the Capuchin convent in Sion—or internationally relevant buildings such as the works of Le Corbusier in Saint-Dié and Ronchamp, any confrontation of high heritage-value architecture with a new use or new needs requires special attention. The additional difficulty is perhaps found in the interpretation of this value in order to intervene in an objective manner.

Again, the possibilities in preservation of monumental heritage are rich. They range from a mindset of preservation, which leads to the restoration of the work through its conservation and the annexed construction (at a certain distance) in the case of Ronchamp, to an approach employing minimal and detailed intervention in that of Saint-Dié. This type of architectural object requires considerable knowledge of the architect's work in order to be able to intervene in a balanced fashion without freezing a project in place in an overly anecdotal way. It's necessary to find a particularly subtle balance between what exists and what is new.

The value of the ordinary

Studying diffuse or so-called "ordinary" structures—common because of their number or their function—often results in the discovery of remarkable qualities. What we mean by ordinary is architecture that isn't visible, that blends in or merges into a context that is its own. The view taken—or rather the lack of a view—on ordinary heritage erases the special qualities of the architecture, and the preservation project allows for metamorphosizing the situation. The projects that endeavor to reveal these qualities make it possible to create a body of knowledge about buildings that would seem, for the most part, to be uninteresting. In the case of the vacation homes in Cap Camarat, the university campus in Neuchâtel, the nursing home in Kriens, or the school in Bergières, these preservation projects discern the potential for extending quality architecture in response to new needs and uses.

We see that the projects on works of architecture not believed to have any heritage value are also those that lead to the possibility of intervening in a more incisive fashion, but always with respect for the existing qualities. This has resulted in detailed and comprehensive interventions such as the extension of the CERN in Geneva, the Swiss Federal Agricultural Research Station in Changins, or the ski resort in Flaine.

In any event, these projects show that the preservation project makes it possible to meet current needs while conserving the existing heritage. It seems then to be a means of reconciling the cultural and material preservation of architecture. It's an obvious way to answer the challenges of sustainable development, as well as that of financial savings. Because while today it is clear that the reuse of a building is more efficient than the principle of demolition-reconstruction, academic projects—among other things—emphasize this paradigm.

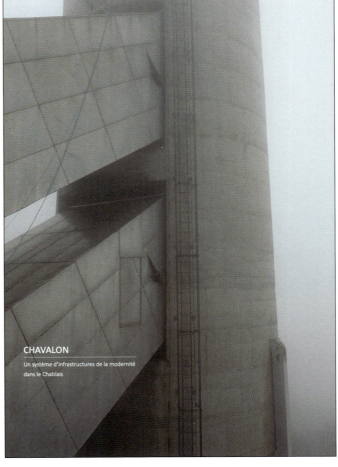

CHAVALON

Un système d'infrastructures de la modernité dans le Chablais

TEACHING THE PRESERVATION 304

1 Presentation text by Emanuelle Jaques, 2017.

CHAVALON OPENS TO THE PUBLIC: REHABILITATION OF A FORMER COAL-FIRED POWER PLANT, ITS GONDOLA LIFT, AND WORKER HOUSING, VOUVRY (VS)

2017

Student:
Emanuelle Jaques

Supervisory group:
Franz Graf, Paola Viganò, Stephan Rutishauser, Martin Boesch

Project title:
Chavalon: A system of modernist infrastructures in the Chablais

"The Chavalon coal-fired power plant, built at high altitude due to environmental concerns, overlooks the Rhône Valley and is visible within a twenty-kilometer radius, from Bex to Vevey. Built in 1965, it closed for good in 1999, after thirty-five years of service. Everyone knows this 'monstrosity.' It inspires contradictory feelings, part disgust and part fascination. Visible from afar, just like a lighthouse, it is one of the Chablais' most prominent structures. With its 75,000 m^2 surface area, the site has great potential. It comprises two platforms upon which the factory and cooling towers have been built, seventeen houses downhill of the plant, and a gondola infrastructure connecting it to the valley floor in only four minutes.

This redevelopment project involves initially making it an open space, accessible to the public and connected to transport networks. The idea is to create a site with interconnected functions: tourism, culture, spaces for working and creation, leisure. This superposing of functions ensures that it can be occupied across a day, week, month, and season. The first problem to solve was that of transport. The new gondola terminal, on the main platform, traces a north-south axis—a large pedestrian avenue that crosses the site along its length and is the very heart of the project. The issue was then to demonstrate that these industrial structures, at first glance without interest, in fact have real potential in terms of the diversity and quality of the spaces. Qualities that belonged to the existing structures, without having to carry out costly or complicated interventions."[1]

1 Site plan
2 1:10,000 scale model of the area
3 Section (machine and boiler room)
4 Interior view (machine room)
5 General plan of the power station buildings
6 Floor plans (machine and boiler rooms)
7 Plan and elevation of one cooling tower (vacation apartment variant)

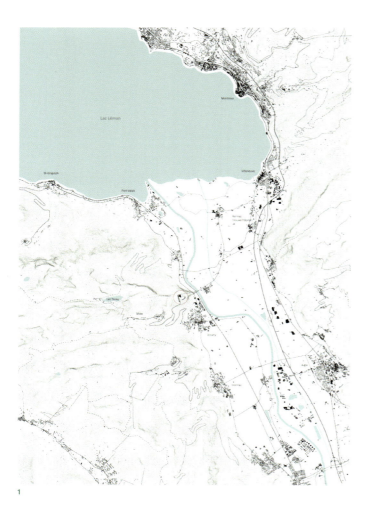

TEACHING THE PRESERVATION

4

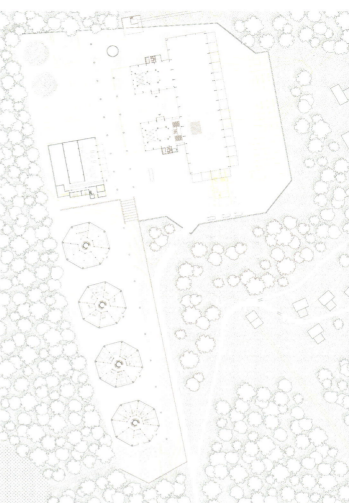

5

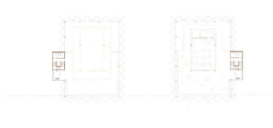

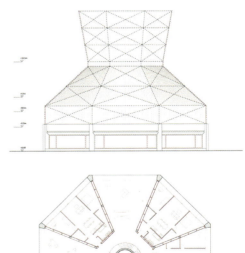

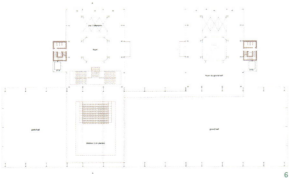

6

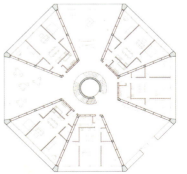

7

307 MASTER'S PRESERVATION PROJECT

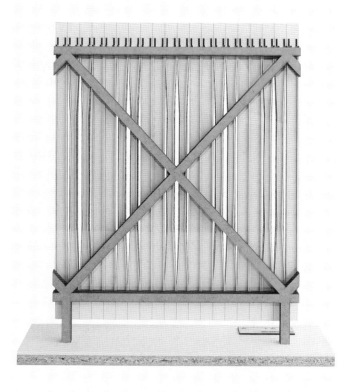

GÜTERBAHNHOF ZÜRICH

- ANALYSE ET RELEVÉ DE L'ANCIENNE GARE DE TRIAGE DE ZÜRICH -
- PROPOSITIONS DE REHABILITATION -

ENONCÉ THÉORIQUE

STÉPHANIE MOREL & FABIAN ROTH

DIRECTEUR PÉDAGOGIQUE // FRANZ GRAF
PROFESSEUR ÉNONCÉ THÉORIQUE // FRANZ GRAF
PROFESSEUR EPFL // AURELIO MUTTONI
MAITRE EPFL // MICHAEL WERNER WYSS
EXPERT EXTERNE // MARTIN BOESCH

2012 / 2013
EPFL

1 Introductory text by
Stéphanie Morel and
Fabian Roth, 2022.

REHABILITATION AND EXTENSION OF ZURICH'S OLD SHUNTING STATION INTO A CONVENTION CENTER

2013

Students:
Stéphanie Morel and Fabian Roth

Supervisory group:
Franz Graf, Aurelio Muttoni, Michael Wyss, Martin Boesch

Project title:
Güterbahnhof Zürich: Analysis and summary
of Zurich's old shunting station

"Situated in the heart of a rapidly developing neighborhood, Zurich's old shunting station was declassified and then demolished in 2021 to make room for the Zurich justice center and police station. The aim of our master's project was to find a new use for the building, enabling a densification of the site, as well as the preservation of the high-quality existing structure and spaces, no longer considered to be of worth. After carrying out historical research and a complete survey of the existing buildings, it was suggested that the Zurich Convention Center, which was looking for a new site at the time, could move into this space.

We therefore focused on the existing spaces that should be preserved, such as the interior courtyard, which was originally occupied by freight trains, as well as depots whose "saw teeth" indicate the building's original function. We sacrificed the administrative building, which could not accommodate the new project, and replaced it with a raised structure to house the large convention rooms. This freed up space on the ground-floor level for a public walkway, while simultaneously giving a new look to the complex. Finally, the addition of a hotel tower to the west of the plot balanced out the ensemble by densifying the site and allowing the depot spaces to be preserved, leaving them almost entirely in their original state."[1]

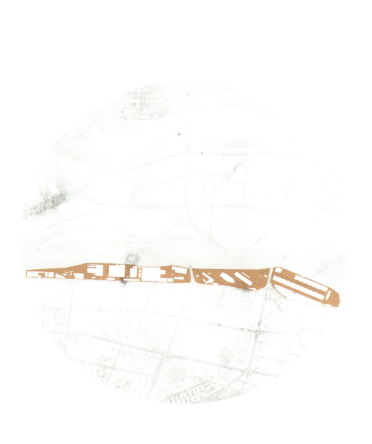

1

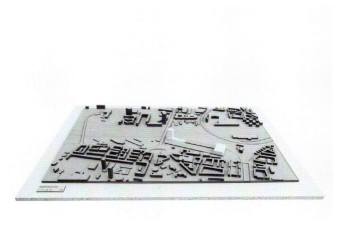

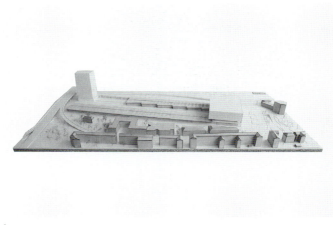

2

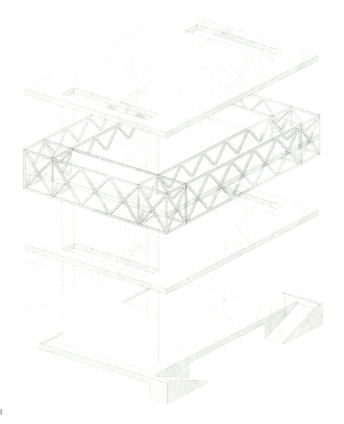

1 Site plan and future development zone
2 1:500 and 1:200 scale models
3 Structural axonometric drawing (primary structure: crossed wire mesh attached to the reinforced concrete core; secondary structure: metal lattice beam fixed to each cross of the primary mesh; tertiary structure: metal I-beam)
4 Transverse section of the depots and west façade of the center
5 1:100 scale model of the depots
6 Floor plan of the center
7 Detail section

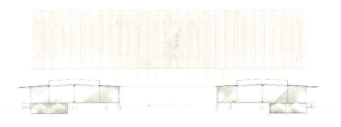

3

4

TEACHING THE PRESERVATION 310

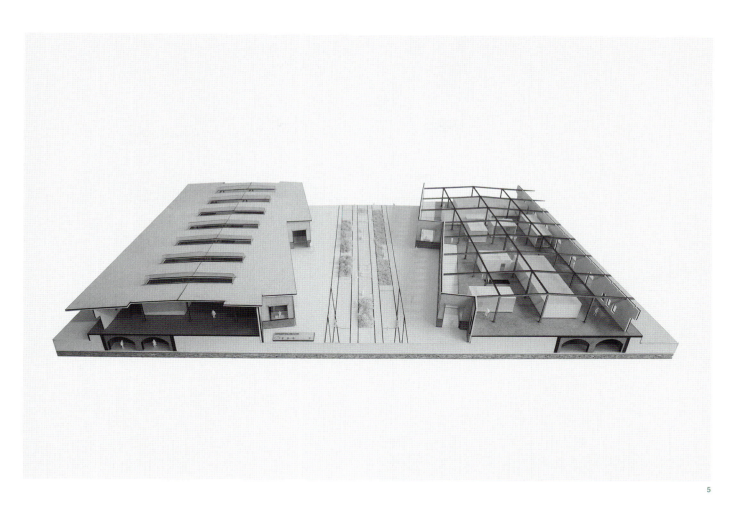

5

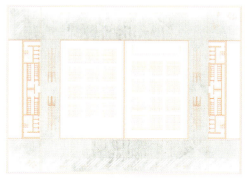

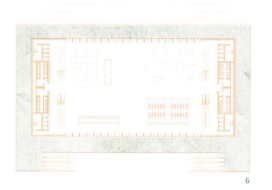

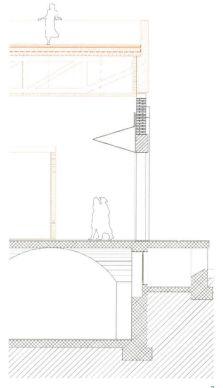

6
7

MASTER'S PRESERVATION PROJECT

Aïre III
**Sauvegarde d'un patrimoine industriel
La station d'épuration d'Aïre de Georges Brera**

Enoncé théorique de Master
EPFL - ENAC - SAR

TEACHING THE PRESERVATION 312

1 Introductory text by
Thierry Buache, 2017.

THE AÏRE WASTEWATER TREATMENT PLANT: A NEW SPACE FOR ARTISTIC CREATION AND DISTRIBUTION IN GENEVA

2017

Student:
Thierry Buache

Supervisory group:
Franz Graf, Christof Holliger, Yvan Delemontey, Béatrice Manzoni

Project title:
Aïre III—The preservation of an industrial heritage site:
Georges Brera's Aïre wastewater treatment plant

"Inaugurated in 1967 and having undergone many transformations in the intervening years, the Aïre wastewater treatment plant today comprises two abandoned buildings: the administrative building and the old sludge treatment plant, known as the 'Porteous.' In view of their preservation, this project puts forward a conversion strategy by way of an overall scenario of functions and uses, and a method for reusing the existing site based on the architectural, material, and historical analysis of the buildings.

Located in a bend in the Rhône River, the buildings' new cultural vocation is revealed via an architectural and landscape promenade along the river. The administrative building is converted into a space for artistic creation, with the former office spaces and laboratories housing studios for artists and craftspeople, while the 'Porteous' is transformed into an arts center, with these large former industrial areas becoming the ideal location for performances, exhibitions, and various installations. Through this function-based design, the historical connection between the two buildings is reestablished and their new use ensures their continuation. The project also uses this unique setting to showcase the banks of the Rhône River and provide a public space where the collaboration between various cultural and institutional actors, as well as inhabitants in the neighborhood, can bring this new cultural space to life."[1]

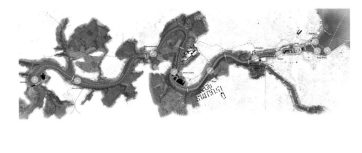

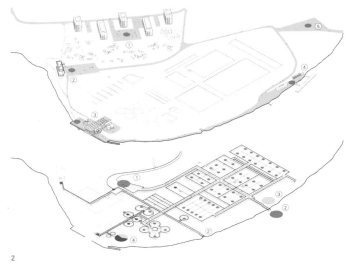

1 Aerial view of the Aïre peninsula and hydrographic plan of the Rhône in Geneva
2 Axonometric drawing of the project's technical and energy components (biogas)
3 Exploded axonometric drawing of the administrative building
4 Plan and section of the administrative building
5 Exploded axonometric drawing of the Porteous building
6 Construction section of the Porteous building
7 1:500 scale model of the banks of the Rhône River

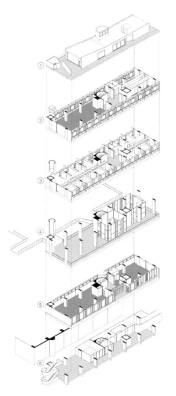

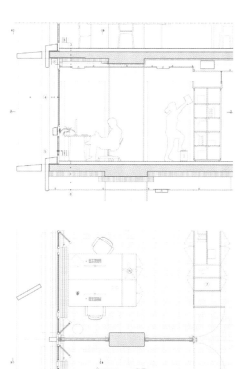

TEACHING THE PRESERVATION 314

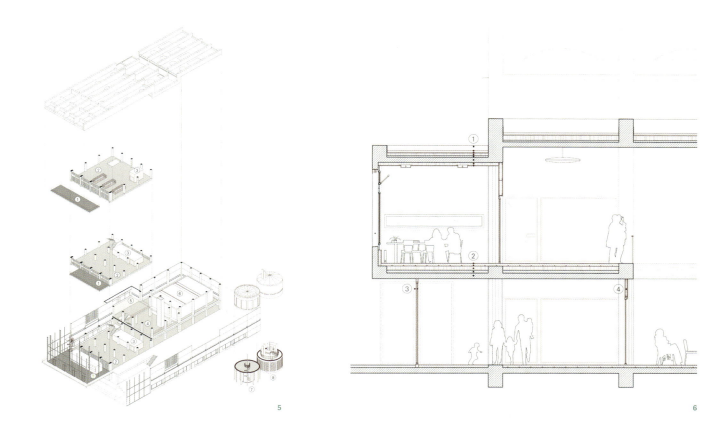

5

6

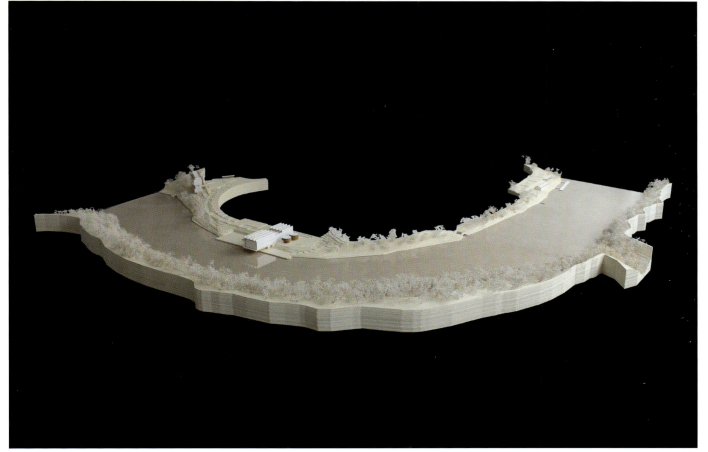

7

315 MASTER'S PRESERVATION PROJECT

1 Introductory text by
Delphine Dufour, 2022.

A HORIZONTAL CITY OF ROOFS: VERTICAL EXTENSION AND REHABILITATION OF A BLOCK IN GENEVA

2019

Student:
Delphine Dufour

Supervisory group:
Franz Graf, Thomas Keller, Yvan Delemontey

Project title:
Vertical extension study in Geneva, 2008–2018

"Since 2008, the city of Geneva has been promoting the densification of its neighborhoods to combat urban sprawl. This project falls within the city plan, as it proposes the rehabilitation and vertical extension of a 1950s block. It includes three buildings designed by the same architects and arranged around a courtyard. The idea here is to introduce a mix of functions and, as a social project, increase the number of apartments while respecting the intrinsic qualities of the existing buildings.

In line with the urban characteristics of the adjacent streets, the height of each building is increased with the addition of two to four storeys, plus a rooftop space. The new roof level creates a shared rooftop, which will provide the inhabitants with an inhabitable space they can make their own, thus compensating for the disturbance due to the works. In order to maximize the space available for everyone, the three rooftops are connected by stairs and a footbridge, creating a new horizontal city above the streets. Each roof has a different feel to it, thanks to the different styles and materials used. The top levels provide inhabitants with a quiet and secluded area in the heart of the city.

This vertical extension brings typological diversity to the housing, ranging from studios to often floor-through six-bedroom apartments. The existing apartments are retrofitted and refurbished, bringing an improvement in energy efficiency while retaining the existing heritage value of the façade. Finally, the ground-floor tenants will be relocated to the new upper storeys and the lower space will be occupied by a daycare center and shops to promote the functional diversity of the block."[1]

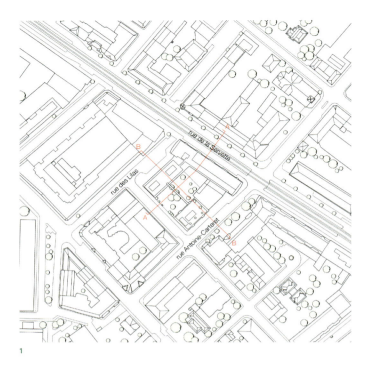

1

1 Situation plan for the block
2 Sections A-A and B-B
3 Plans: existing level and vertically extended level
4 View of the Rue Antoine-Carteret rooftop
5 View of the Rue des Lilas rooftop
6 Structural axonometric drawing (bottom) and new upper levels (top)
7 Construction section Rue de la Servette

2

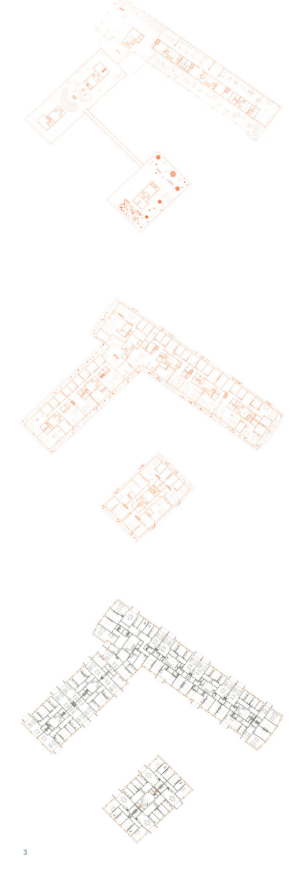

3

TEACHING THE PRESERVATION 318

4

5

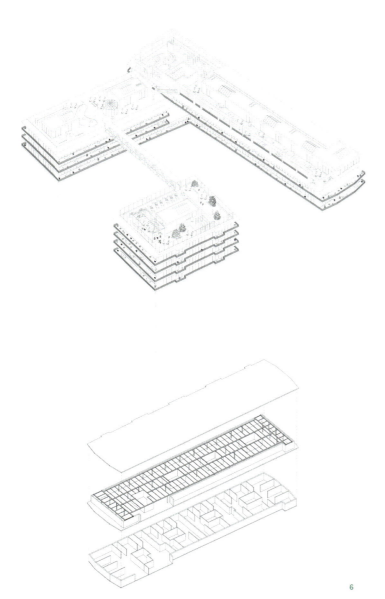

6

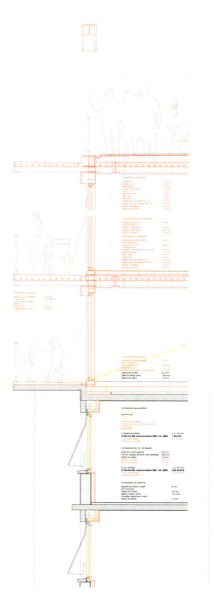

7

MASTER'S PRESERVATION PROJECT

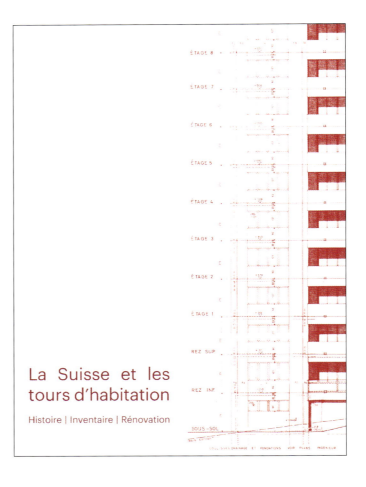

La Suisse et les tours d'habitation

Histoire | Inventaire | Rénovation

TEACHING THE PRESERVATION 320

1 Introductory text by
Sébastien Rouge, 2019.

GAINING HEIGHT:
RENOVATION OF THREE TOWERS
IN MALADIÈRE, LAUSANNE

2019

Student:
Sébastien Rouge

Supervisory group:
Franz Graf, Corentin Fivet, Stephan Rutishauser

Project title:
Switzerland and its housing towers: History, inventory, renovation

"Switzerland's housing towers are gradually reaching the end of their first cycle of life. Built for the most part during the post-war boom years, they now need to be renovated. After a study of the three towers in Maladière, three different yet interconnected scenarios have emerged that highlight the potential in renovating housing towers.

As these towers are listed in the national inventory, the first scenario primarily seeks to preserve their heritage value by opting for a restoration of the façades and a transformation of the apartments. The two other scenarios involve a process of densification. The second is effected through a vertical extension that continues in line with the existing built environment, conserving the rigor of the façades and the outline indicated by the plan, while the third breaks with the original architectural principles and follows a process of addition through extension and the addition of increased height.

In the three scenarios, the quality of life of the inhabitants is improved by adapting the apartments to today's styles of living, providing diverse types of housing—thus welcoming greater social diversity—and by including a wider range of activities. The renovation of the housing towers falls within current policies aiming to increase density in urban centers by adapting to the needs and demands of today's society. It contributes to a new and contemporary face of the city."[1]

1

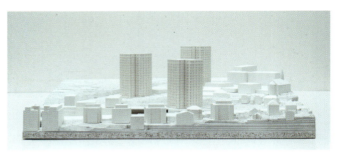

2

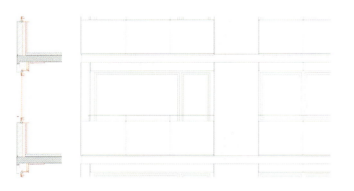

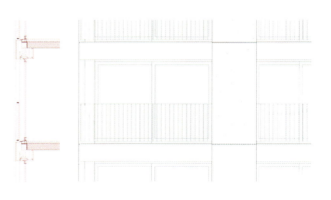

3

4

TEACHING THE PRESERVATION   322

1 Site plan for the Maladière towers
2 1:500 scale model of the project variants
3 Plan, section, and elevation of scenario 1, preservation
4 Plan, section, and elevation of scenario 2, vertical extension
5 Axonometric drawing of the towers, scenario 3, radical change
6 Plan for scenario 3
7 Detail plan and façade for scenario 3

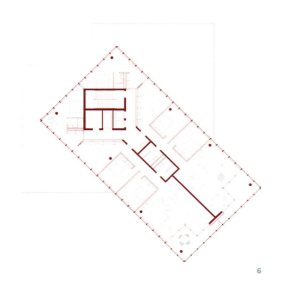

323 MASTER'S PRESERVATION PROJECT

LE LOGEMENT AU CHILI

DES POLITIQUES AUX RÉALISATIONS

Anna Neuhaus & Manon Kivell

1 Introductory text
by Manon Kivell and
Anna Neuhaus, 2022.

FROM TERRITORY TO HOUSING: THE REHABILITATION OF THE MARTA BRUNET NEIGHBORHOOD IN SANTIAGO, CHILE

2019

Students:
Manon Kivell and Anna Neuhaus

Supervisory group:
Franz Graf, Bruno Marchand, Stephan Rutishauser

Project title:
Housing in Chile: From policy to construction

"Housing in Chile is distinguished by the mass construction of neighborhoods comprising identical three-floor housing blocks, known as C blocks. These were designed during the dictatorship of General Pinochet (1973–1990) in order to meet the urgent need for housing. Today, these 133,000 housing blocks spread across the whole country pose major problems for a number of reasons: they no longer correspond to the needs of their inhabitants (they have a generic floor space of 42 m^2, no matter the size of the household), no thought was given to public spaces, and access is obstructed by the informal extensions built by the inhabitants. For this design project, the topic of preservation was not only focused on the built environment, but also on the social issues of conservation and improvement of these living spaces.

Drawing inspiration from a Chilean model *'perro, parrilla, patio'* (which could be translated as 'dog, barbecue, patio'), the design project for the Marta Brunet neighborhood in Santiago seeks to create public spaces and high-quality shared facilities, as well as typological variation that matches the needs of the inhabitants and can be applied to other areas in the country with C blocks. One-off extensions also modify the urban morphology by integrating patios that enable community activities and introduce different levels of privacy into the urban plan. Finally, the development of an extension in the form of a 'plug-in' into the façade provides the opportunity for a generic and cost-effective intervention, able to be quickly implemented on all C blocks throughout Chile."[1]

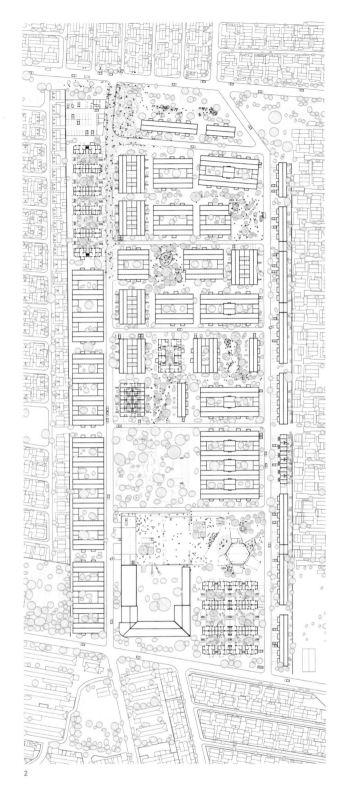

1 Map of Chile depicting the housing typology
2 Site plan for the Marta Brunet neighborhood
3 Photograph of models showing different housing typologies
4 Plan of individual single-bay houses (top) and plan of double-bay houses with patio (bottom)
5 Section (top) and axonometric drawing of extensions

TEACHING THE PRESERVATION   326

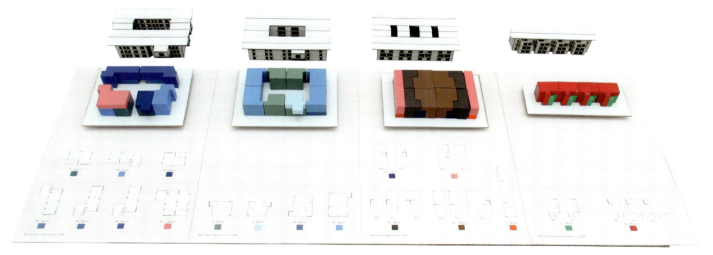

3

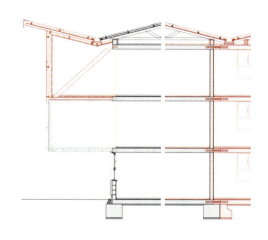

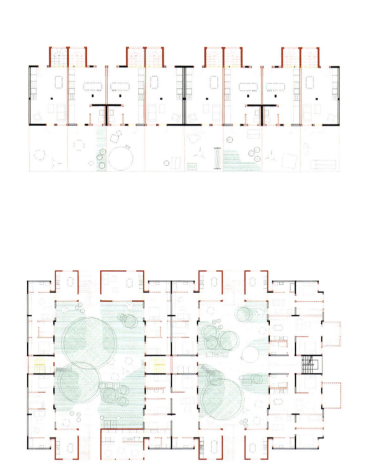

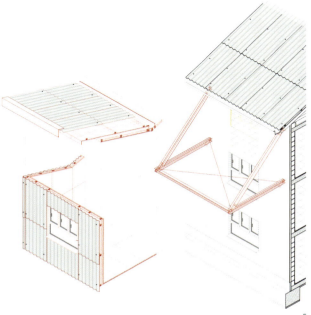

4 5

327   MASTER'S PRESERVATION PROJECT

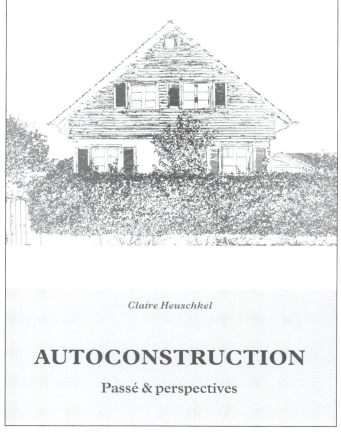

Claire Heuschkel

AUTOCONSTRUCTION

Passé & perspectives

1 Introductory text by
Claire Heuschkel, 2022.

REINTERPRETING SELF-CONSTRUCTION OF HOUSING IN WEIL AM RHEIN

2021

Student:
Claire Heuschkel

Supervisory group:
Franz Graf, Elena Cogato Lanza, Thierry Buache

Project title:
Self-construction: Past and perspectives

"My master's project deals with the issue of self-construction through the study of a *Siedlung* (meaning 'settlement') built in the 1930s in Weil am Rhein, Germany. It is a theoretical exploration focused on houses that at first glance appear quite ordinary. Their distinctive feature resides in the fact that they were self-constructed (by the residents themselves), due to a shortfall in or even non-existence of personal financial contributions. But over time these architectural creations, despite the modest means, have taken on real cultural and historical significance. Post-industrial community initiatives at self-construction have always been related to the economic, political, ideological, and technological context of their time.

My master's project, consistent with the theoretical approach, is not a 'traditional' preservation project. It involves the contemporary reinterpretation of the question of self-construction: on one hand through the concept of new housing on a huge piece of land that extends the existing Siedlung, and on the other by the integration of one of these houses into the new neighborhood and its transformation into a laboratory for self-construction."[1]

1 Site plan
2 Exterior view of the project for the housing neighborhood
3 Elevation of an existing house type (top) and section and elevation of a new construction (bottom)
4 Axonometric drawing of an existing house type (left) and a new construction (right)
5 Construction section of the new housing
6 Façade and material of the new housing
7 Plan of the new neighborhood and outdoor layout, axonometric drawing of moveable mediation elements

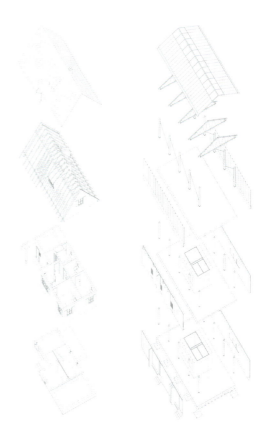

TEACHING THE PRESERVATION   330

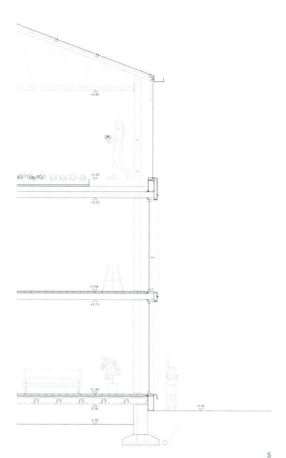

5

6

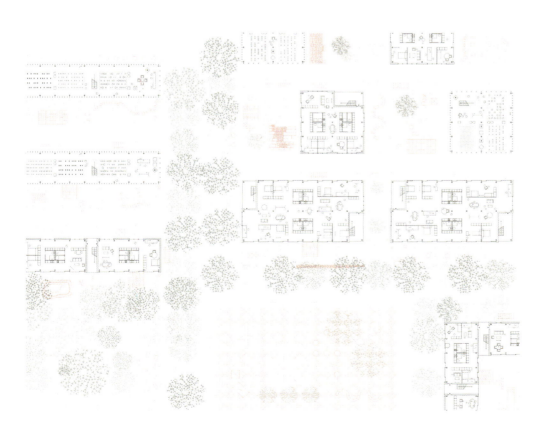

7

331   MASTER'S PRESERVATION PROJECT

La Chevalière

Etude et diagnostic d'un spécimen de l'habitat intermédiaire français des années 70.

Clément Perrier et Delphine Millet

Enoncé théorique de Master - Architecture
15 Janvier 2018

Ecole Polytechnique Fédérale de Lausanne
Directeur pédagogique: Prof. Franz Graf
Maître EPFL: Dr. Yvan Delemontey

1 Introductory text by Delphine Millet and Clément Perrier, 2018.

LA CHEVALIÈRE: PRESERVATION AND EXTENSION OF ONE EXAMPLE OF THE FRENCH "INTERMEDIARY HABITAT" OF THE 1970S

2018

Students:
Delphine Millet and Clément Perrier

Supervisory group:
Franz Graf, Jean-Louis Scartezzini, Yvan Delemontey

Project title:
La Chevalière: Study and diagnosis of one example of the French "intermediary habitat" of the 1970s

"Built in the 1970s in Bissy, near Chambéry, the La Chevalière residence provides an example of a new form of living: part individual, part community. For many, this construction is today seen as an early form of an eco-neighborhood. Therefore, this preservation and extension project seeks to update and deepen the body of research about the 'intermediary habitat.' The project begins with the design of grouped participatory housing, each unit with access to private outdoor spaces. The housing is designed as a flexible cell that allows future movement and is therefore sustainable.

Both the new construction and the preservation of the existing housing emphasize passive energy efficient solutions and parsimonious use of materials. The cells are grouped together in neighboring units around a common patio—a more community-centered space. Backstreets, accessible by small electric vehicles, outline a series of urban thresholds right up to the houses, connecting the biodiversity of the landscape plan to the Chartreuse mountain range. By preserving the existing farm buildings, the project is enhanced by community programs. The diverse functions within the residence are even more important given that this new neighborhood brings back to life the links between La Chevalière, Bissy's historical center, and its public services. It densifies the suburban fabric without causing a break in scale. From the house to the neighborhood, the residents can make the most of the balance offered by the sobriety of the chosen solutions."[1]

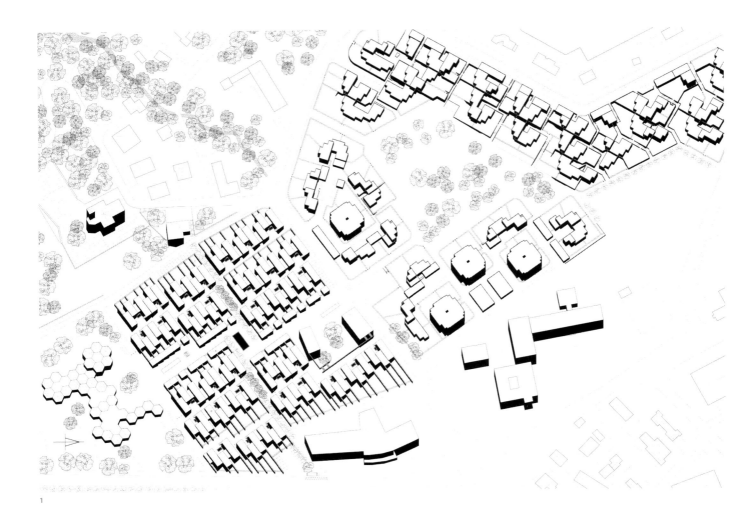

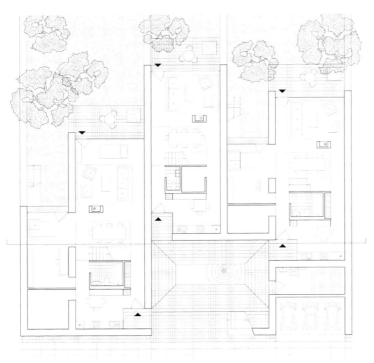

1 Site plan
2 Ground-floor plan of the extension
3 Section of the extension project
4 Perspective view of the courtyard in front of the new houses
5 Axonometric construction drawing
6 Plan of the existing houses in La Chevalière, now renovated
7 Detail section

4

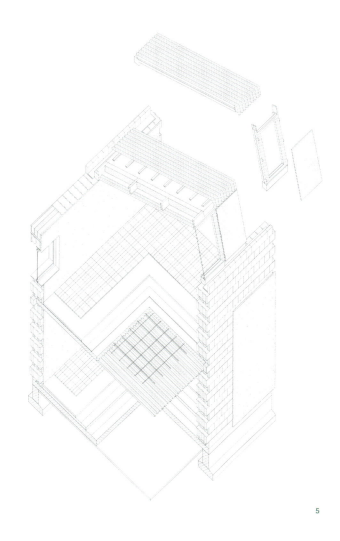

5

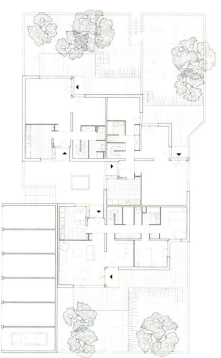

6

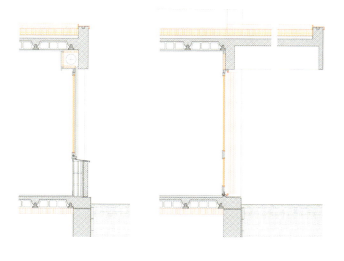

7

Le site industriel du Closel à Renens

De la mort d'un site à la naissance d'un lieu

Enoncé théorique

Lucien Favre

Directeur pédagogique - Franz Graf
Professeur Énoncé théorique - Franz Graf
Professeur EPFL - Eugen Brühwiler
Maître EPFL - Michael Werner Wyss
Expert externe - Martin Boesch

2014-2015
EPFL - ENAC - SAR

1 Introductory text by
Lucien Favre, 2022.

THE CLOSEL INDUSTRIAL SITE IN RENENS

2015

Student:
Lucien Favre

Supervisory group:
Franz Graf, Eugen Brühwiler, Michael Wyss, Martin Boesch

Project title:
The Closel industrial site in Renens

"Closel, an industrial site in Renens, was in 2015 a complex interweaving of buildings of various construction dates, various architectural values, various uses, and various states of conservation. In the 1960s, the industries present on the site had called on renowned architects such as Jean-Marc Lamunière and Frédéric Brugger. After these industries had all left the site, the first element of the master's project was to think about the use of the site in its built entirety, relative to a changing urban context.

Once the appropriate mix of uses had been decided on, the intervention principle was to respect the structuralist principles of the site rather than the buildings as distinct units. The work done on removing and adding elements from a structure designed from the beginning to evolve, coupled with a respect for the original heritage essence and the improvement of overall energy efficiency, enabled this industrial site to be reconciled with the city and its users."[1]

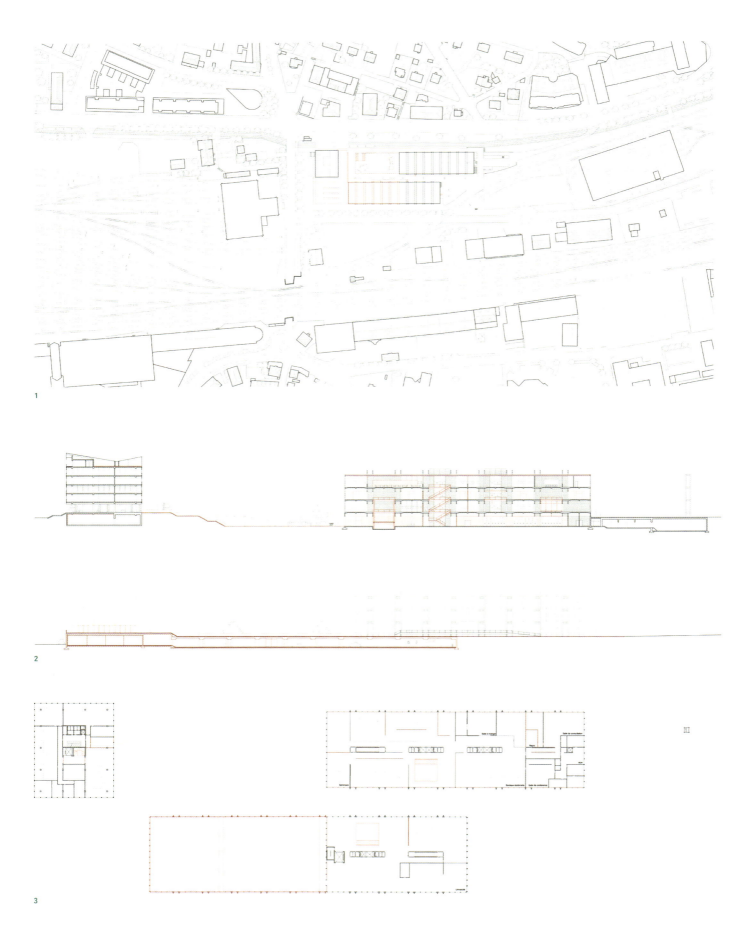

TEACHING THE PRESERVATION   338

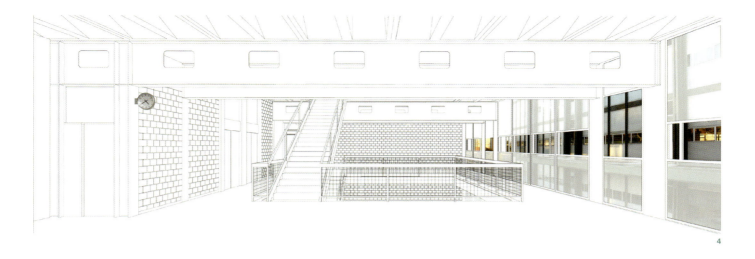

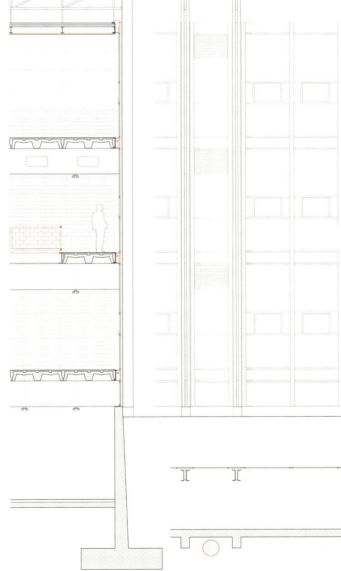

1 Site plan
2 Longitudinal sections of the north buildings (top) and the gallery (bottom)
3 Plan of the second level of the buildings
4 Perspective view from the south building
5 Perspective view from the north building (top) and from the gallery (bottom)
6 Construction section, elevation and plan

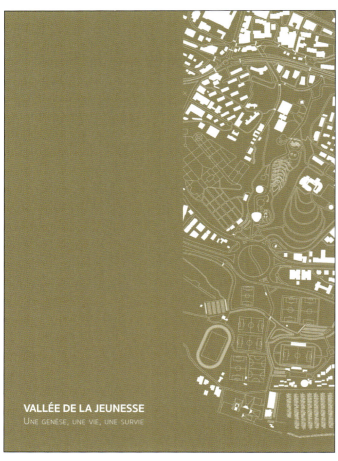

VALLÉE DE LA JEUNESSE
Une genèse, une vie, une survie

TEACHING THE PRESERVATION 340

1 Introductory text
by Darine Dadan and
Anouar M'Himdat, 2022.

ORGANICITY AND ATEMPORALITY: THE BUILT ENSEMBLE OF MICHEL MAGNIN AT THE EXPO 64. REHABILITATION OF THE EXPERIMENTAL HERITAGE IN THE VALLÉE DE LA JEUNESSE, LAUSANNE

2019

Students:
Darine Dandan and Anouar M'Himdat

Supervisory group:
Franz Graf, Bruno Marchand, Giulia Marino

Project title:
The Vallée de la Jeunesse: Genesis, life, survival.
A study on the potential of the Vallée de la Jeunesse
from the context of the Expo 64 to that of today

"Our master's project deals with the preservation of an important heritage site in Lausanne inherited from the Expo 64: the Nestlé kindergarten, an experimental building created by architect Michel Magnin and left forgotten in a park with much untapped urban potential.

The Nestlé kindergarten is a spectacular interweaving of three concrete elements (two concave and convex shells connected by a slanted footbridge) that link into and merge with the Vallée de la Jeunesse. The kindergarten is one of the few remaining traces from the Swiss National Exhibition held in 1964. Today it unfortunately no longer looks like it used to: it has undergone several interventions, some of which have distorted the original ensemble so brilliantly envisaged by Michel Magnin. Our project puts forward possibilities for the preservation of the building that are based on the architect's early studies, such as his vision of a space in which people can meander, the relationship with the light, or even the choice and use of raw materials.

As the object cannot be separated from its surroundings (the Vallée de la Jeunesse), the rehabilitation had to bring value through its context at an urban scale. This study enabled us to understand how the city of 'tomorrow' was viewed in the 1960s and allowed us to shed new light on the incredible diversity in the architecture of movement and landscape in service to the local community."[1]

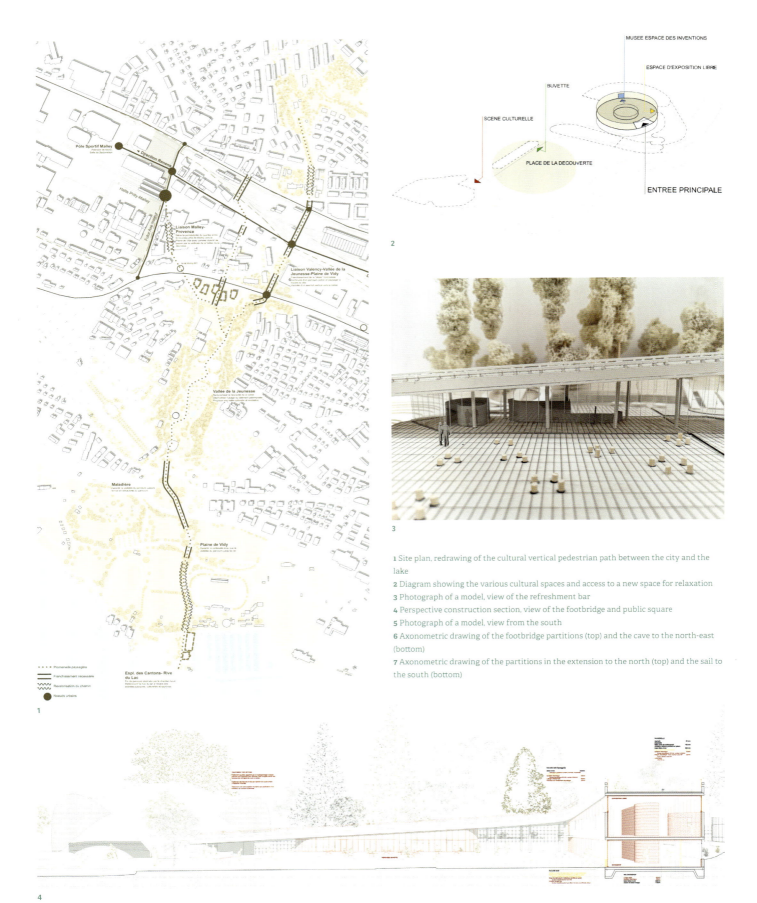

1 Site plan, redrawing of the cultural vertical pedestrian path between the city and the lake
2 Diagram showing the various cultural spaces and access to a new space for relaxation
3 Photograph of a model, view of the refreshment bar
4 Perspective construction section, view of the footbridge and public square
5 Photograph of a model, view from the south
6 Axonometric drawing of the footbridge partitions (top) and the cave to the north-east (bottom)
7 Axonometric drawing of the partitions in the extension to the north (top) and the sail to the south (bottom)

TEACHING THE PRESERVATION   342

5

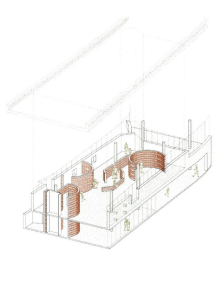

6 7

343   MASTER'S PRESERVATION PROJECT

Un avenir pour les salles de cinéma indépendantes

1 Introductory text by
Tchaya Bloesch and
Jennifer Huynh, 2022.

LE PLAZA: A NEW CINEMA NEIGHBORHOOD

2013

Students:
Tchaya Bloesch and Jennifer Huynh

Supervisory group:
Franz Graf, Yves Pedrazzini, Christian Bischoff, Martin Boesch

Project title:
The future of independent movie theaters

"The main subject of our master's project results from the closing of Le Plaza cinema in Geneva, whose main theater had been condemned despite several unsuccessful attempts at preservation. The theater had been listed and then unlisted. It had been closed for nine years when we began our study. Its remarkable architectural values, as well as its uncertain future, encouraged us to choose Le Plaza and focus our preservation project on this outstanding example of a modern heritage building.

The theater's location, in the heart of a neighborhood only five minutes from the train station, demonstrated the possibilities for reuse due to the number of surrounding activities. The space had the potential to make the area more attractive by combining shops, services, urban infrastructure, and cultural activities.

The theme of preservation was concrete, and it involved a major challenge, providing strong motivation for us to focus on this subject. The search for documents was not always easy, and despite several efforts, we were not able to visit the site."[1]

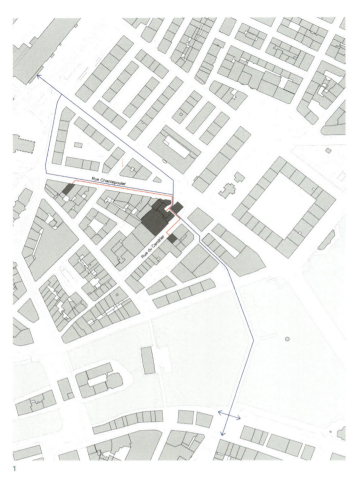

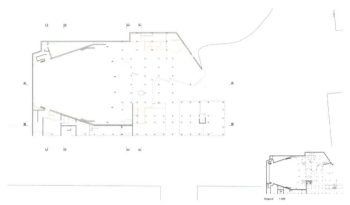
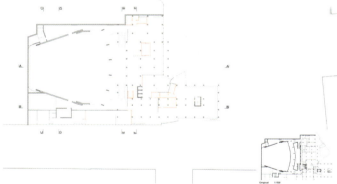

1 Site plan of Le Plaza
2 Model split down the center of the project design
3 Diagrams showing distribution of different uses and access
4 Plan of the basement level and lower and upper ground-floor levels
5 View above the ice cream stand
6 Project design sections
7 View from Rue Chantepoulet

TEACHING THE PRESERVATION 346

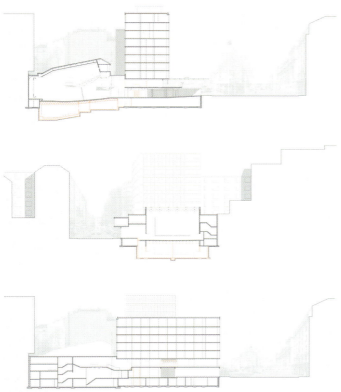

347 MASTER'S PRESERVATION PROJECT

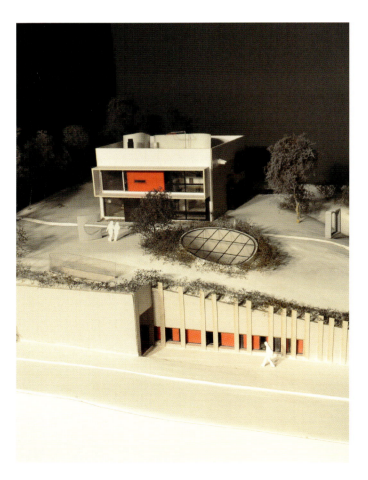
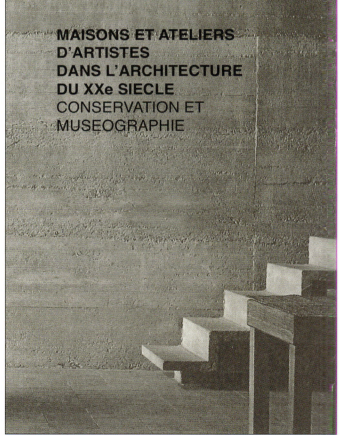

1 Introductory text by
Audrey Aulus, 2022.

ANDRÉ WOGENSCKY AND MARTA PAN'S HOUSE-STUDIO: CONSERVATION, MUSEOGRAPHY, AND EXTENSION (YVELINES, F)

2015

Student:
Audrey Aulus

Supervisory group:
Franz Graf, Elena Cogato Lanza, Giulia Marino, Dominique Amouroux

Project title:
Artists' houses and studios in twentieth-century architecture

"In 2011, a new future began to unfold for the House-Studio of André Wogenscky and Marta Pan. A manifesto for the combined oeuvres of architecture and sculpture, it became the headquarters for the foundation that would promote this rich legacy, listed as a French historic monument. Since then, the Institution has been thinking of the most appropriate museography for opening to the public, one that would be in complete harmony with André Wogenscky's words: 'Every house should be a shelter, a dwelling, and a temple.'

The conservation/restoration project was the first part of the study. It became clear that transforming this complex legacy into a museum would be the best way to maintain its integrity, without creating other functions that would necessitate substantial works. For the Foundation to function correctly and welcome guests, specific spaces are necessary, which resulted in an assessment of the possibilities for on-site extension. This extension would ensure that interventions on the house-studio would be minimized, while showcasing the couple's numerous works, stored in the house. This was made possible by the study of a detailed program established on the basis of several criteria defined in the project abstract.

In view of the essential relationship between the archives, the Foundation, the consultation process, and the museum extension, grouping all these elements on one site seemed logical. Out of a concern for integrating and respecting the views established between architecture, sculpture, and nature, the extension (the shape of which was based on a museum itinerary) extends into the slope of the garden, thus redefining the street façade and inviting passers-by to come and discover the space."[1]

1 Site plan for the house-studio
2 West elevation
3 Ground-floor plan
4 First-floor plan
5 View of the project design from the street
6 Intervention detail of the house-studio
7 Plan and section of the extension project

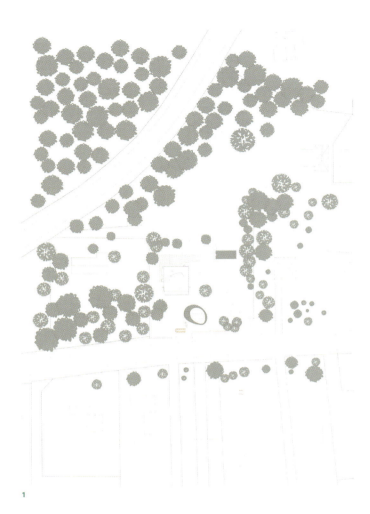

1

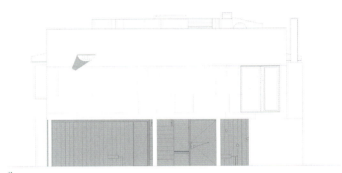

2

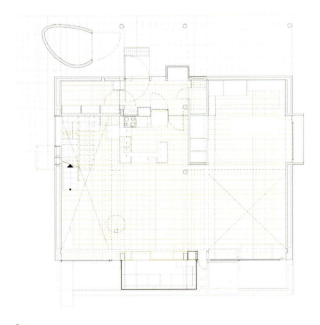

3

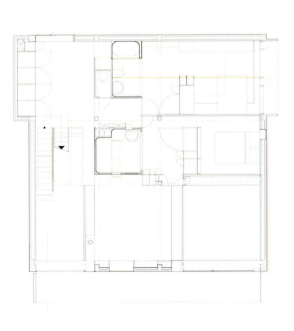

4

TEACHING THE PRESERVATION   350

5

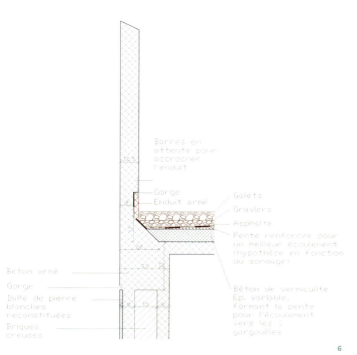

6

7

351 MASTER'S PRESERVATION PROJECT

Architecture conventuelle et modernité

Enoncé théorique de master
Ecole Polytechnique Fédérale de Lausanne
Clémentine Artru

1 Introductory text by
Clémentine Artru, 2022.

RESTORATION AND EXTENSION OF THE CAPUCHIN CONVENT, SION

2020

Student:
Clémentine Artru

Supervisory group:
Franz Graf, Bruno Marchand, Théo Bellmann

Project title:
Convent architecture and modernity

"The subject of my diploma is the restoration and extension of the Sion Capuchin convent, one of two modern architectural edifices of national importance in Valais. Its particularity is to have been built in 1631 before having undergone different restorations during the twentieth century, notably after the damage caused by the 1946 earthquake. My analysis focused on the work of architect Mirco Ravanne, who was commissioned between 1962 and 1968, to improve the 'valid' structures and enlarge them. In the 1980s, the Fondation Emera began renting the east wing and the renovation work harmed its legibility. One specific renovation intervention on the south wing, between 2014 and 2016 was carried out, on the other hand, with respect for the building's heritage value.

My research, based on archival documents, aimed at restoring the space under the pilotis of the east wing designed by Mirco Ravanne: the water feature and the cloister were thus rebuilt. One option for an entry to the Fondation Emera was to place it on the south side of the convent. A central space was given back to the refectory, today little used. This space is seen as a place for the residents of the convent to meet. The vegetable garden, on the south-east side, has also been redeveloped, with direct access to the Maison des Évolénards.

Finally, defining a more public entrance to the convent, a new wing offers exhibits concerning the history of the edifice and the artists who participated in the work of Mirco Ravanne. On the top floor, an art therapy workshop is directly connected to the living spaces of the Emera residents."[1]

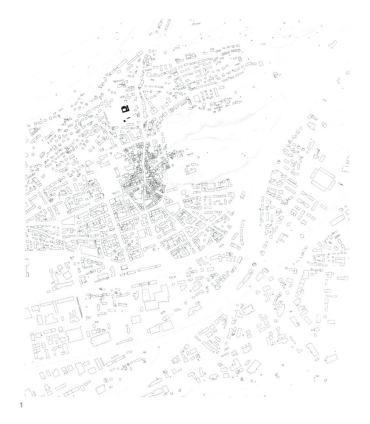

1 Site plan for the convent
2 Photograph of the existing convent
3 Plan of the whole convent site, including the Saint-François cemetery
4 Plan of the extension project, second floor
5 Section of the convent and the extension project
6 View from the new garden
7 Axonometric construction drawing of the extension
8 Axonometric drawing of the various uses

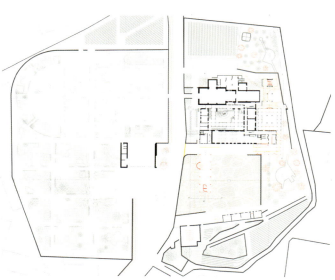
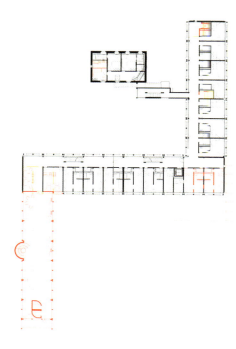

TEACHING THE PRESERVATION 354

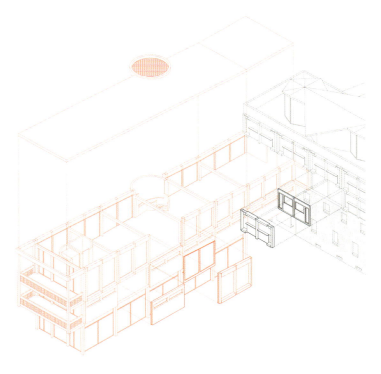

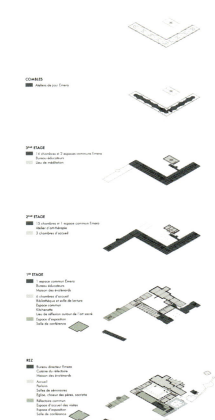

355 MASTER'S PRESERVATION PROJECT

1 Introductory text by Virginie Bally and Marie-Laure Allemann, 2022.

RONCHAMP, FROM THE CHAPEL TO THE VILLAGE: STRATEGIES FOR SITE ENHANCEMENT (F)

2017

Students:
Virginie Bally and Marie-Laure Allemann

Supervisory group:
Franz Graf, Eugen Brühwiler, Yvan Delemontey, Martin Boesch

Project title:
Ronchamp: From monument to site (1950–2016)

"Our master's level project focused on Le Corbusier's Notre-Dame du Haut chapel in Ronchamp, very recently classed as a UNESCO world heritage site. We began by studying the monument and its history, then its surroundings on several different scales in order to define the strengths and weaknesses of the monument and the site. Our work then suggested a global intervention strategy, which had as an objective to give back to the chapel and its surroundings its authenticity, to valorize the local heritage, and to revitalize the whole village in order to reinforce its attraction to tourists.

From treating fissures to urban planning and the rehabilitation of several key places, everything was designed to respect and satisfy—in a sustainable fashion—as many current challenges as possible: patrimonial, economic, social, and environmental. Our master's project deals with the invigoration of a historically important site, listed at ICOMOS (International Council on Monuments and Sites). The project showed us that preservation goes well beyond restoring a monument itself. Each edifice has its own history—a precise historical context during which it was built, but also a unique geographic site with which it interacts more or less well.

The preservation of a historic building sometimes also implies digging into the social, environmental, and economic context in which it is located. Beginning with the restoration of the chapel, we found ourselves creating a plan of action aimed at revitalizing the entire village of Ronchamp."[1]

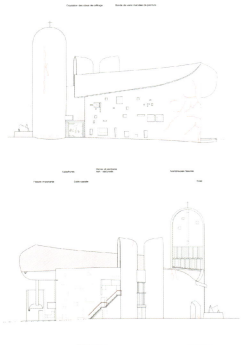

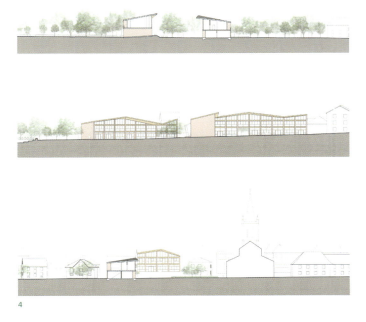

1 Site plan
2 Model of Ronchamp village
3 South (top) and north (bottom) façades of the Ronchamp chapel and restoration work
4 Sections of the village project
5 Perspective view of the church square
6 Plan of the ground floor of the new dwellings
7 Construction section of the transformed Sainte-Marie coal mine

TEACHING THE PRESERVATION   358

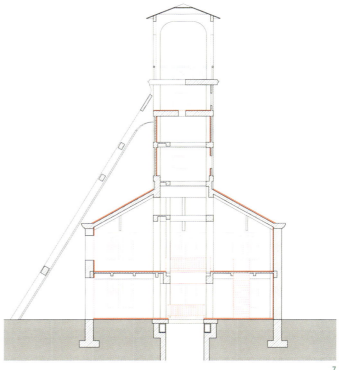

359 MASTER'S PRESERVATION PROJECT

**LA MANUFACTURE CLAUDE ET DUVAL
DE LE CORBUSIER À SAINT-DIÉ**

ÉTUDE ET PROJET DE SAUVEGARDE

THIERRY MANASSEH

1 Introductory text by
Thierry Manasseh, 2022.

A SCHOOL OF HAUTE COUTURE IN SAINT-DIÉ: CONSERVATION, CONVERSION, AND EXTENSION PROJECT OF THE CLAUDE & DUVAL FACTORY BY LE CORBUSIER, 1946–1951 (F)

2014

Student:
Thierry Manasseh

Supervisory group:
Franz Graf, Luca Ortelli, Yvan Delemontey, Bernard Bauchet

Project title:
Study of a work by Le Corbusier: The Claude & Duval factory

"First, the object of study: the Claude & Duval factory in Saint-Dié, built by Le Corbusier just after the war, where he applied for the first time a series of new architectural principles in his production. This is a little known building, but it is quite exceptional, as is the architect's attitude towards the existing built environment. The building took over the site of a partially demolished factory and is linked to its remaining parts. The rubble from the demolition was recovered and used to construct some of the new walls.

The second specificity results from the first. Given the quality of Le Corbusier's building, its state of conservation, the reorienting of its activity following the decline of the textile industry, as well as the presence of old factories, this project was the opportunity to experiment with the diversity of actions that the word "preservation" includes: gaining as exhaustive an understanding as possible of the existing built environment, its history, abandoned ideas and material reality; establishing a position with regard to the existing environment; conservation, restoration, renovation, reuse, extension, etc."[1]

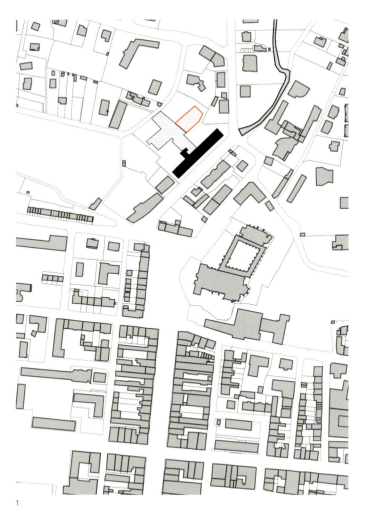
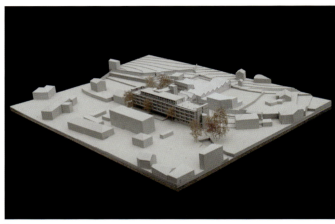

1 Site plan of Saint-Dié
2 Model of the project site and surroundings
3 Plan of the first floor
4 Plans of levels 3 and 4 and the southeast elevation
5 Model section of the intervention project
6 Transverse section (bottom) and roof detail (top)
7 Construction sections of the fixed partitions in the existing building (top), section and elevation of the façades of the extension (bottom)

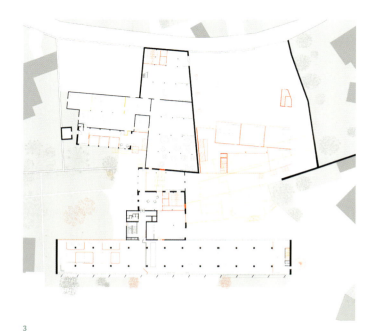
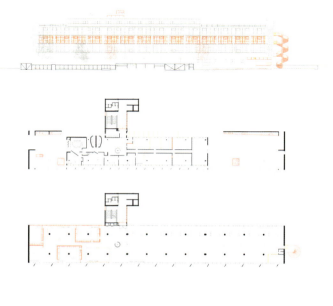

TEACHING THE PRESERVATION 362

5

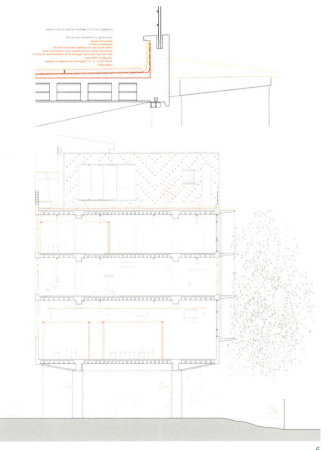

6

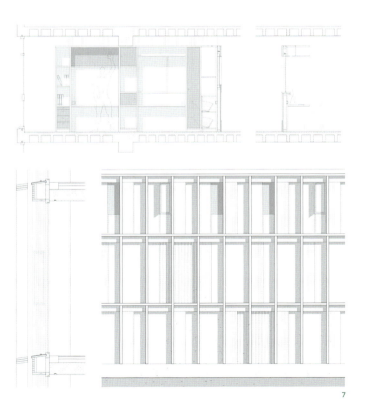

7

363 MASTER'S PRESERVATION PROJECT

Villégiature en Côte d'Azur

Le village de vacances *Le Merlier*
de l'Atelier de Montrouge, 1959-1965

Charlotte Glatt
Enoncé théorique de Master - Architecture

Professeur Franz Graf, Directeur pédagogique
Yvan Delemontey, Maître epfl
Laboratoire des Techniques et de la Sauvegarde de l'Architecture Moderne

Environnement Naturel Architectural et Construit
Ecole Polytechnique Fédérale de Lausanne

16 Janvier 2012

1 Introductory text by
Charlotte Glatt, 2022.

VACATION HOUSING ON THE CÔTE D'AZUR: PRESERVATION AND EXTENSION OF LE MERLIER VACATION VILLAGE— CAP CAMARAT, ATELIER DE MONTROUGE, 1959–1965 (F)

2012

Student:
Charlotte Glatt

Supervisory group:
Franz Graf, Patrick Mestelan, Yvan Delemontey, Philippe Gueissaz

Project title:
Vacation housing on the Côte d'Azur:
Le Merlier vacation village by the Atelier de Montrouge, 1959–1965

"In the twentieth century, in a climate of economic optimism, the emergence of a society of leisure led to new considerations; resort tourism proved to be a particularly propitious and innovative terrain for modern architecture. The Atelier de Montrouge (Jean Renaudie, Pierre Riboulet, Gérard Thurnauer, and Jean-Louis Véret) was commissioned in 1959 by Louis Arretche to plan a group of vacation homes on a plot of land with wild vegetation, plunging into the sea, at Cap Camarat on the Ramatuelle peninsula. Taking inspiration from Mediterranean villages, but in a resolutely modern language, the architects planned several groups of dwellings, like so many variations of combinatory assemblages. Only Le Merlier would see the light of day. It is considered today to be an important manifestation of the engaged and innovative practice of the ATM.

It is currently in good condition and is undeniably attractive, but it is nevertheless a question of ensuring its durability by carrying out some work necessary for its functional autonomy and by stimulating the interactions among residents. Defined strictly in terms of the site's reception potential, these additions are more in line with the original intent; the projected hotel accommodation extends the established distributional system. The reception, in contact with the village, links together the activities of organizations and public entities all the way to the seaside." [1]

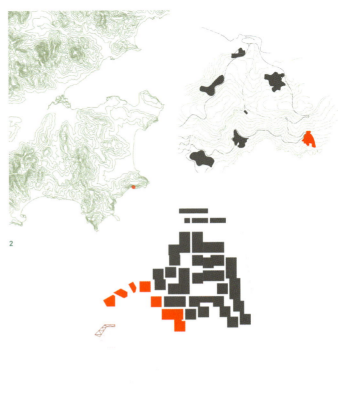

1 Ground plan
2 Ramatuelle peninsula and ATM's plan of the complex. 1959
3 Diagram showing the interventions
4 Transverse section of the depots and west façade of the center
5 Plan of common spaces (altitude +36m)
6 View from the side
7 Plan and section of the project
8 Sections of the dwellings

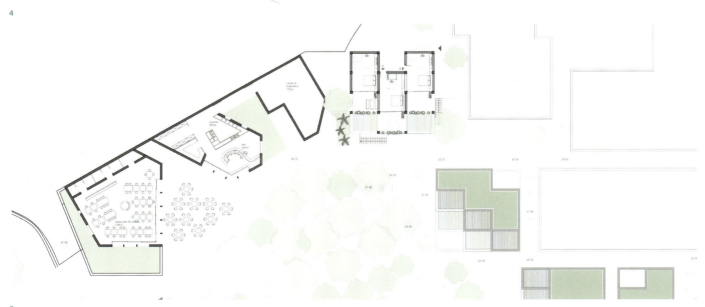

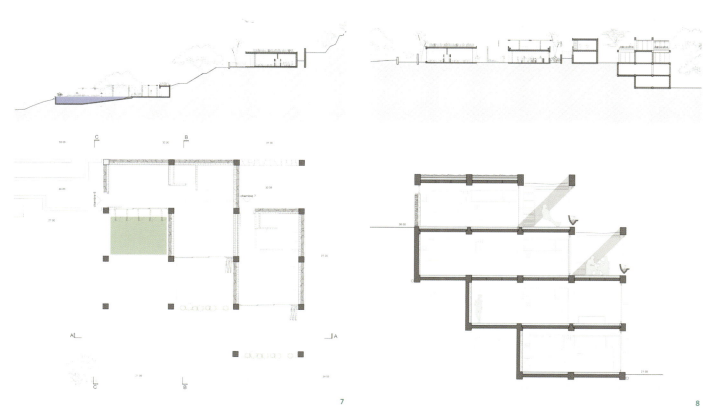

367 MASTER'S PRESERVATION PROJECT

Conservation du patrimoine bâti du XXe siècle et mise en conformité

Un journal d'observations entre théorie et rencontres

Marie Majeux

Directeur pédagogique : Franz Graf
Professeur : Luca Ortelli
Maître EPFL : Jean-Louis Scartezzini

Enoncé théorique
Master en Architecture
Ecole Polytechnique Fédérale de Lausanne

Lausanne, janvier 2020

1 Introductory text by
Marie Majeux, 2022.

AWAKENING OF A UNIVERSITY CAMPUS, NEUCHÂTEL: PRESERVATION, TRANSFORMATION, EXTENSION. GEORGES-JACQUES HAEFELI, 1966–1971

2020

Student:
Marie Majeux

Supervisory group:
Franz Graf, Luca Ortelli, Pietro Florio

Project title:
Conservation of twentieth-century built heritage and compliance:
A journal of observations from theory to encounters

"This master's project focused on the university campus in Neuchâtel, a complex designed by architect Georges-Jacques Haefeli in 1971, in the midst of a shortage of student housing in the city. The campus is suggestive of a large concrete sculpture with which Haefeli asserts his brutalist architecture. This complex is listed as "note 1" in the architectural census of the canton of Neuchâtel and is part of the city's modern heritage. It is made up of rooms for students, a restaurant and cafeteria, study spaces, classrooms, and a theater. The living spaces are designed in a permeable manner, and the architect sought to achieve a certain flexibility for their use.

Today, although the rooms are still inhabited, the campus seems to be asleep. Most of the living spaces are unused or rented to third parties. This master's project postulates that preserving this heritage must first include maintaining its original function and puts forward several interventions in order to reinforce the student presence on the site: the residence tower is improved from the point of view of user comfort, the three study rooms are transformed into exhibition spaces, and an extension is planned in the form of a public garden and new student housing. This work is based on a preliminary analysis of the building and on interviews with people who have known the campus at different moments in its history. It is meant to be completed by the different degrees of intervention proposed."[1]

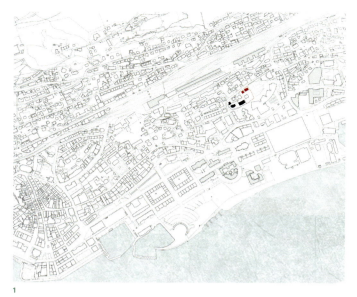

1
2

1 Site plan of the university campus
2 Perspective view of the terrace
3 General section
4 General plan of the campus
5 Section of the project showing the materials used
6 Plans of the transformations of the dwellings
7 Perspective construction section with improvement variants
8 General axonometric drawing

3

4

TEACHING THE PRESERVATION 370

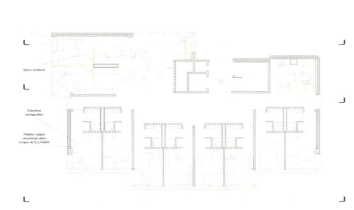

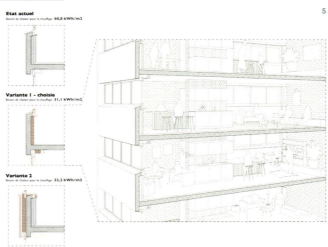

MASTER'S PRESERVATION PROJECT

STRUCTURES D'ACCUEIL POUR PERSONNES ÂGÉES
ADAPTATION AUX NORMES ET À L'ÉVOLUTION DES MOEURS

Enoncé théorique de master
Julie Vulliet · Sophie Wobmann
EPFL Architecture 2012-2013

Groupe de suivi
Le professeur Franz Graf, directeur pédagogique
Christian Bischoff, maître epfl
TSAM-Laboratoire des Techniques et
de la Sauvegarde de l'Architecture Moderne

Remerciements
Nous tenons à remercier Pierre Bonnet et la direction de l'EMS Résidence de la Rive,
André Salvisberg, Lothar Sidler et la commune de Kriens, Guido Hübscher, Gilles Pirat
ainsi que Fanny Wobmann-Richard et Etienne Piergiovanni.

1 Introductory text
by Julie Vulliet and
Sophie Wobmann, 2022.

REHABILITATION OF THE ALTERS- UND PFLEGEHEIM GROSSFELD (LU)

2013

Students:
Julie Vulliet and Sophie Wobmann

Supervisory group:
Franz Graf, Bruno Marchand, Christian Bischoff, Pierre Bonnet

Project title:
Facilities for the elderly:
Adaptation to standards and changing customs

"Numerous facilities for the elderly built during the modern period (1920–1970) reveal themselves—while still functioning—as ill-suited for current customs and needs. The architecture of these establishments has evolved and developed dramatically over past years, on the one hand to respond to a lack of available beds, but also to offer buildings that better correspond to today's ways of life and standards. The modern period is over, but its buildings still stand. They enrich our common heritage and are witnesses to a history that must be preserved.

This is the case for the Alters- und Pflegeheim Grossfeld built in Kriens between 1966 and 1968 by Lucerne architect Wlater Rüssli. The building has found itself at the heart of a debate over its future because it is slated for demolition. The transformations proposed by our rehabilitation project are an alternative to this radical decision. Beyond the adaptation to standards and the reduction of the building's energy footprint, the main objective of this project is to regenerate the building's status within the urban fabric, while improving its general functionality. The major challenge is to succeed in increasing the quality of life of both residents and staff, by seeking a balance between institution and domestic space."[1]

1 Site plan
2 Project model
3 Ground-floor plan
4 Plan of the second floor
5 Façade of the rehabilitation project
6 Axonometric construction drawing
7 Plan and section of the dwelling
8 Plan of the third floor
9 Sections of the project

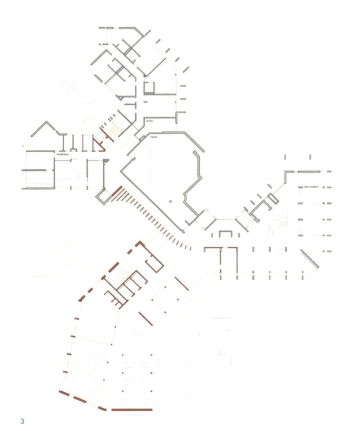
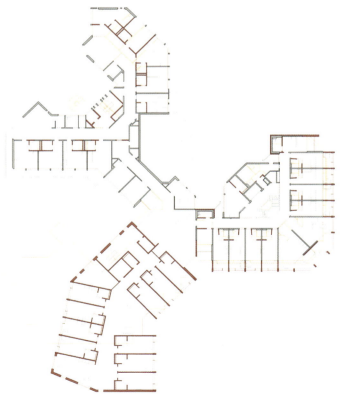

TEACHING THE PRESERVATION 374

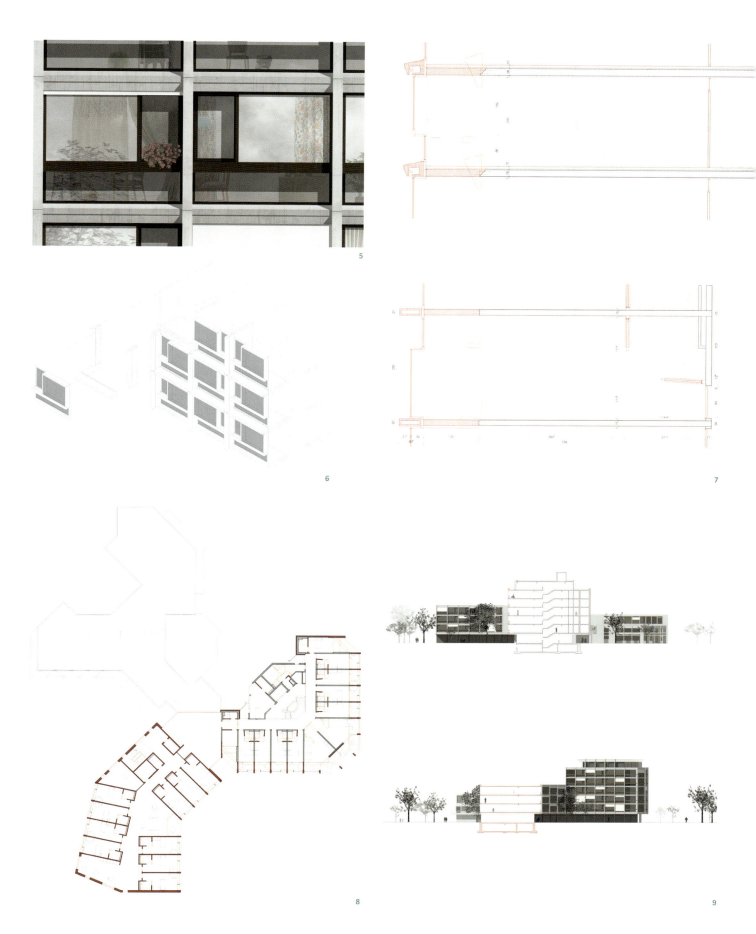

375 MASTER'S PRESERVATION PROJECT

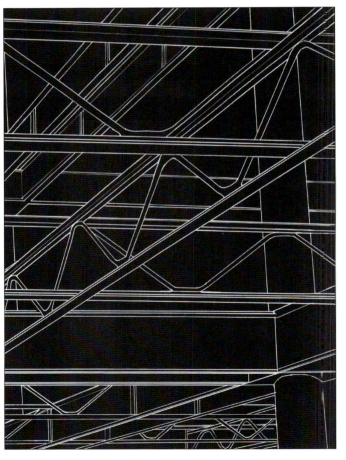

TEACHING THE PRESERVATION   376

1 Introductory text by
Matthieu Hoffmeyer, 2018.

PRESERVATION AND EXTENSION OF A CROCS SCHOOL: THE BERGIÈRES COMPLEX IN LAUSANNE (M. LÉVY, B. VOUGA, 1968–75)

2018

Student:
Matthieu Hoffmeyer

Supervisory group:
Franz Graf, Jean-Louis Scartezzini, Giulia Marino

Project title:
The CROCS system for schools
in the Canton of Vaud: Construction and relevance

"Inaugurated in 1975, the Bergières Middle School was built according to the industrialized construction process called the 'CROCS system.' Situated on a steeply sloped piece of land, the buildings are of high architectural quality and present an authentic character. The complex is also remarkable because of its state of conservation: it is one of the last examples of the emblematic CROCS schools, which marked school construction in French-speaking Switzerland but which have often been subjected to heavy transformations these last few years. Its material integrity—no building from the group has been modified—offers tremendous renovation potential. Because the project recommends the preservation of such an architectural object, integrating as it does the notions of user comfort and energy savings, the project proposes a strategy of restoration and respectful updating, founded on the architectural, material, and historical analysis of the CROCS program. The optimization of the technical network reduces consumption dramatically, while conserving the carefully refurbished existing envelopes. Because of the demographic growth and the addition of a public after-school care service, the question of extending the complex arises. The new buildings expand on the qualities of the existing ones with a contemporary architectural concept. On a site-wide scale, the pathways and exterior spaces are also redesigned."[1]

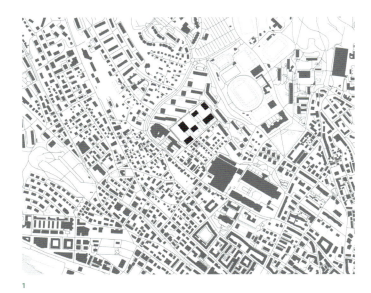

1 Site plan
2 Longitudinal section of the site
3 Plan of the building complex
4 Model of the site
5 Axonometric construction drawing of the CROCS system
6 Axonometric drawing of the extension project and the façade
7 Section and elevation of the preservation detail

TEACHING THE PRESERVATION   378

4

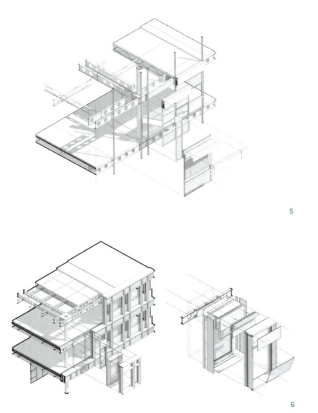

5

6

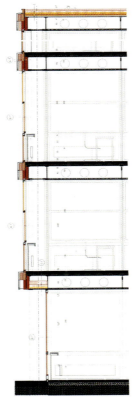

7

TEACHING THE PRESERVATION 380

1 Introductory text by
Jérôme Wohlschlag, 2022.

PRESERVATION AND EXTENSION OF THE "MAIN BUILDING COMPLEX" AT CERN (1954–1960)

2011

Student:
Jérôme Wohlschlag

Supervisory group:
Franz Graf, Luca Ortelli, Giulia Marino, Martin Boesch

Project title:
The main building complex at CERN in Geneva

"My diploma project had as a goal the preservation and extension of the 'main building complex' at CERN in Geneva, an initial construction phase that today is at the heart of a township that has been developing over the past sixty years as the site's experiments continue.

For the construction of their first research site, the founding members of CERN called on Rudolf Steiger—a major protagonist of modern Swiss architecture, whose work with Max Erst Haefeli and Werner Max Moser met with great renown—as well as his son Peter Steiger, and engineers Carl Hubacher, Hans Rudolf Fietz, and Hans Hauri. From 1954 to 1960, they designed a coherent ensemble with high technical requirements and an expressive architecture of exceptional quality.

It is therefore a question of restoring the integrity of the work and confirming the central role of the Main Building—the object of a preservation project respectful of the existing built environment—by reassigning it with its missing functions and by reconnecting it with adjoining public spaces. The project relies on the definition, across the site as a whole, of two distinct spaces: one with an institutional character, given structure by the main building complex, and the other with an industrial character, which developed in an unplanned way. The preservation of this ensemble presents an undeniable heritage interest and will allow CERN to reinforce its identity and reorganize a site that has developed until now with no clear overall vision."[1]

1 Site plan of the center
2 Plan of level 2
3 Longitudinal sections of the extension project
4 Axonometry of the interventions (top) and section of the extension project (bottom)
5 Aerial views of the main buildings of the center
6 Construction section of the preservation project

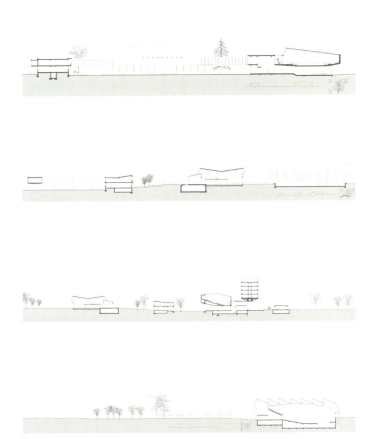

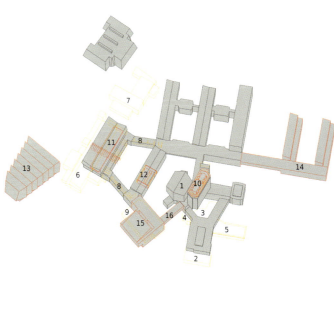

TEACHING THE PRESERVATION 382

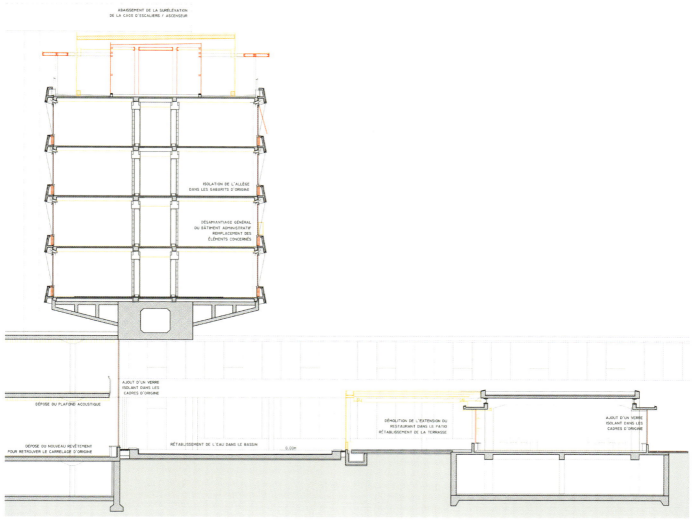

MASTER'S PRESERVATION PROJECT

Préfabrication esthétique

L'expérimentation architecturale des Wenger en Suisse

HISTOIRE | ANALYSE

HOFFERT David
TIARRI Alexandre

Énoncé théorique de Master en architecture
École Polytechnique Fédérale de Lausanne

Directeur pédagogique : GRAF Franz
Maître EPFL : DELEMONTEY Yvan

1 Introductory text
by David Hoffert and
Alexandre Tiarri, 2022.

THE IMPLEMENTATION OF AESTHETIC AND SUSTAINABLE PREFABRICATION: A NEW FORUM FOR THE PRESERVATION OF THE SFRA IN CHANGINS (NYON, VD)

2020

Students:
David Hoffert andAlexandre Tiarri

Supervisory group:
Franz Graf, Eugen Brühwiler, Yvan Delemontey

Project title:
Aesthetic prefabrication:
Architectural experimentation by the Wengers in Switzerland

"Through the preservation of the Swiss Federal Agricultural Research Station (SFRA) in Changins, built by Heidi and Peter Wenger in the 1970s, we wanted to respond to the conservation issues specific to the building studied, but also to question the techniques implemented today to meet the challenges of sustainability.

The preservation strategy takes the form of an extension of the Wengers' building, a Swiss icon of total prefabrication using concrete, allowing the site to be enriched with new functions and thus proposing a much larger complex. Between imitation and differentiation, this new language of extension, which aims at a significant coherence between form and material, is placed in the continuity of the original building. The architectural principles of the Wengers—infinite growth of the plan and synergy between structure and network—are maintained, but the existing structural shapes are reinterpreted. After a critical analysis of the original prefabricated system and its comparison with other constructions of the same time period, we proposed a new synergistic system capable of meeting the constructive challenges of our time, notably thanks to the use of innovative materials. The preservation of a remarkable work of the twentieth century in the service of constructive innovation: that was our project approach."[1]

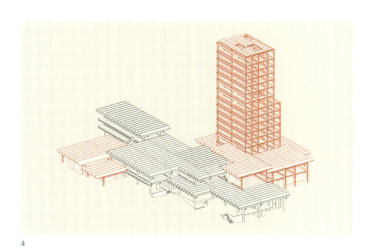

1 Site plan, town of Nyon
2 View of the work site phase
3 Interior view of the learning center
4 Axonometric drawing of the extension
5 General plan of the project, ground floor, and surroundings
6 Elevation of the extension project
7 Plan of levels 7, 8, and the roof terrace
8 Construction section
9 Axonometric drawing of the intervention between the existing and new (bottom), and section of the project (top)

TEACHING THE PRESERVATION 386

6

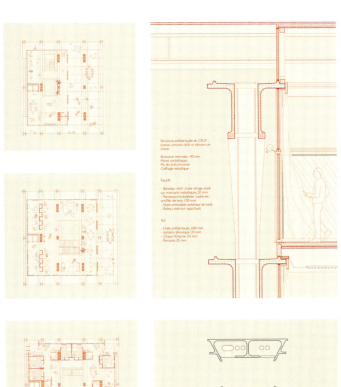

7

8

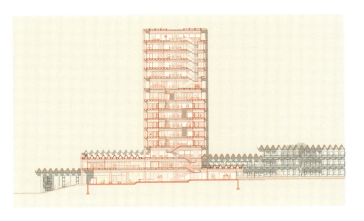

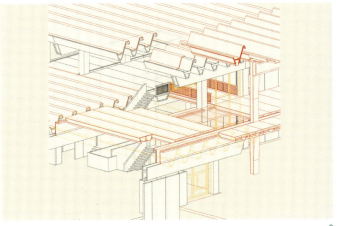

9

387   MASTER'S PRESERVATION PROJECT

TEACHING THE PRESERVATION   388

1 Introductory text by
Laetitia Bernasconi and
Joël Loutan, 2022.

REGENERATION OF A MOUNTAIN SITE: A CASE-STUDY ON FLAINE (HAUTE-SAVOIE, F)

2011

Students:
Laetitia Bernasconi and Joël Loutan

Supervisory group:
Franz Graf, Luca Ortelli, Yvan Delemontey, Martin Boesch

Project title:
The preservation of mountain architecture of the second post-war period:
Regeneration of a mountain site: a case-study on Flaine (Haute-Savoie, F)

"'Increasing heritage value' are the words that best describe the work we carried out over the course of our master's project. Indeed, it was with the aim of conserving the identity and revitalizing the winter sports resort of Flaine, in the Haute-Savoie in the French Alps, that we proposed a lasting solution that fits into the landscape and meets today's economic requirements: the regeneration and extension of the hotel 'Le Totem,' designed, like the rest of the resort, by architect Marcel Breuer.

This project includes the complete renovation of the hotel, which now offers spacious rooms and an interior design that references the original furniture, which was modern for its time. As for the extension, built in the shape of a base upon which a tower is erected, it provides new spaces such as the baths, conference rooms, and luxurious rooms that radiate outwards and open up to the entire landscape. Marrying the curves of the levels, this tower acts as a landmark and comprises six facets made of prefabricated concrete elements, a reinterpretation of the Sun and Shadow panels developed by the famous American architect. Through our thinking process, we have approached the theme of preservation on all scales and in all its aspects: from urbanization to the constructive detail of the panels, from the restoration of the material substance to the reinterpretation of the original elements. We have arrived in this way at an architectural proposition that is the opposite of the great real estate projects of our time, which are more financial products with the sole objective of profitability to the detriment of the preservation of landscapes and architectural quality."[1]

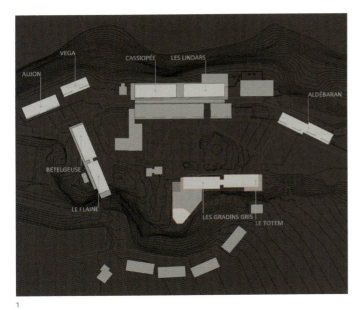

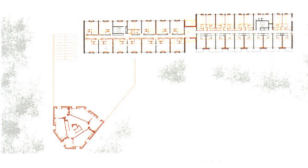

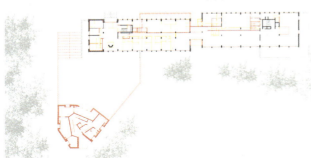

1 Site plan of the forum
2 Model of the site
3 Plan of the upper ground floor and the first floor
4 Section of the preservation project
5 General section of the existing buildings
6 Project model
7 Axonometric construction drawings
8 Construction section and elevation

TEACHING THE PRESERVATION   390

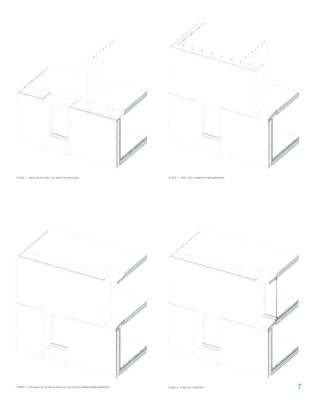

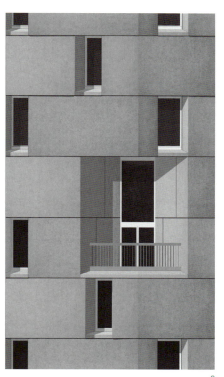

391 MASTER'S PRESERVATION PROJECT

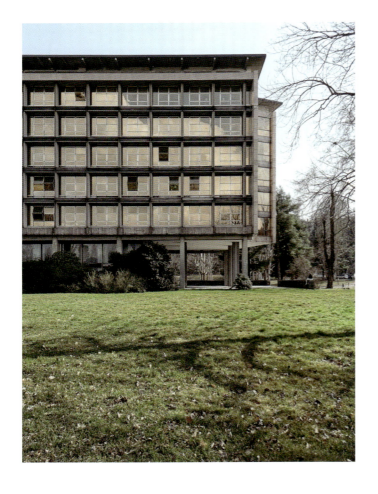

1 Introductory text by
Giuseppe Galbiati and
Fortunato Medici, 2022.

INTERVENTION METHODOLOGIES FOR INCREASING THE VALUE OF MODERN HERITAGE: APPLICATIONS TO THE OLIVETTI OFFICE BUILDING AND THE ICO PRODUCTION COMPLEX IN IVREA

2019–2020

Students:
Giuseppe Galbiati and Fortunato Medici

Supervisory group:
Franz Graf and Giulia Marino (EPFL),
Gabriele Masera and Manuela Grecchi (PoliMi)

"This master's project, the result of a collaboration between EPF Lausanne and the Politecnico di Milano, aims at the preservation of several buildings completed by the Olivetti company in Ivrea between 1940 and 1960 and today known as UNESCO world heritage sites: in particular, the first Olivetti office building, designed between 1959 and 1963 by architects Gian Antonio Bernasconi, Annibale Fiocchi, and Marcello Nizzoli, was the object of a thorough study.

Drawn from the exemplary preservation project and upgrading to current energy standards of Le Lignon housing complex in Geneva, the multi-criteria methodology developed by the TSAM Laboratory was used and adapted to the Italian case, in order to establish an intervention solution that was coherent with the existing built environment, according to UNESCO directives and in the perspective of the new planned usages.

The first objective was to retrace the history of the building from an architectural and technical point of view and understand the elements of value and the construction techniques used at the time. A thermal study allowed us to define the energy consumption of the complex in its current state and establish several intervention scenarios. Finally, thanks to a multi-criteria analysis and the adoption of an evaluation matrix, the optimal solution was identified.

This approach, which is presented as a project tool organized according to general guidelines, can be applied by analogy to other buildings in the UNESCO site. In conclusion, for the Olivetti administrative building, it is possible to reduce energy consumption by 55% compared to its current state, while maintaining its intrinsic characteristics. The guidelines for the administrative building can therefore be adapted to other buildings on the UNESCO site of Ivrea."[1]

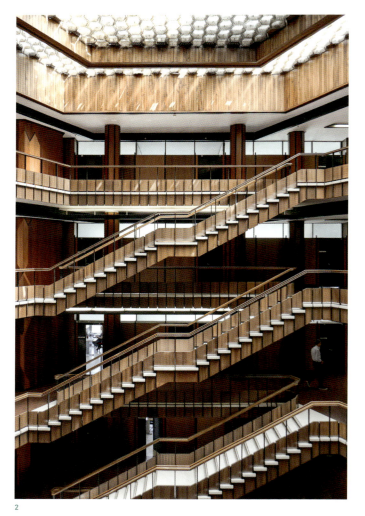

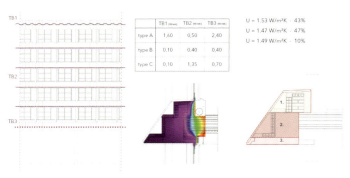

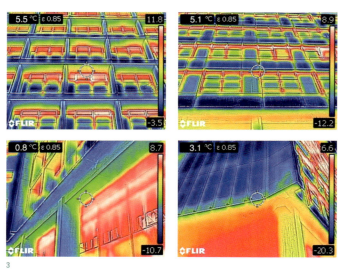

1 Site plan
2 Interior photograph showing staircases
3 Study of the thermal bridges
4 General collage of the project
5 Graph showing the thermal values
6 Proposition for improvement of the envelope with variants

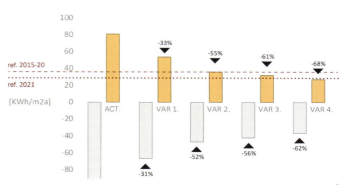

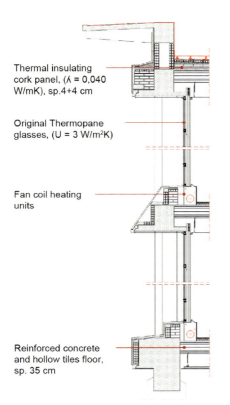

Current State

Thermal insulating cork panel, (λ = 0,040 W/mK), sp.4+4 cm

Original Thermopane glasses, (U = 3 W/m²K)

Fan coil heating units

Reinforced concrete and hollow tiles floor, sp. 35 cm

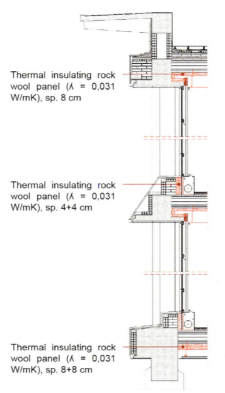

Variant 1
(internal insulation)

Thermal insulating rock wool panel (λ = 0,031 W/mK), sp. 8 cm

Thermal insulating rock wool panel (λ = 0,031 W/mK), sp. 4+4 cm

Thermal insulating rock wool panel (λ = 0,031 W/mK), sp. 8+8 cm

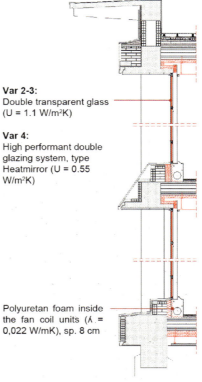

Variant 2-4
(internal insulation + glass replacement)

Var 2-3:
Double transparent glass (U = 1.1 W/m²K)

Var 4:
High performant double glazing system, type Heatmirror (U = 0.55 W/m²K)

Polyuretan foam inside the fan coil units (λ = 0,022 W/mK), sp. 8 cm

MASTER'S PRESERVATION PROJECT

1 Introductory text by
Giuseppe Galbiati, 2022

THE PRESERVATION OF BUILDINGS WITH SUSPENDED STRUCTURES AND LIGHT FACADES: AN INNOVATIVE METHODOLOGY FOR THE RETROFITTING OF MODERN HERITAGE (1960–1980)

2020–2023

Doctoral candidate:
Giuseppe Galbiati

Thesis co-supervisors:
Franz Graf and Giulia Marino

Supervisory group:
Elena Cogato Lanza, Bernard Deprez,
Aurelio Muttoni, and Denis Zastavni

"After my master's studies, an interest in the field of preservation of modern architecture guided my choices towards academic research through a co-tutored PhD set up between EPFL and UCLouvain. This research represented a deepening of the methodology of intervention developed by the TSAM Laboratory, but applied here to a fascinating and innovative construction type, sometimes forgotten by the history of architecture: buildings with suspended structures and light façades. The outcome of the results is expected to be twofold: on the one hand it allows for the rediscovery of history, architecture, and the constructive techniques of these unique edifices, and on the other hand, it allows its methodological soundness to be demonstrated. Indeed, by developing a method for intervening on buildings with strong constraints in terms of architectural and constructional qualities, it is possible to use the same approach, but simplified, for a more common built heritage.

This methodology allows the definition of an intervention strategy that is respectful of buildings with heritage value and that also addresses energy issues. For the practical application, three buildings in three different European countries were chosen: the former BP headquarters in Antwerp (Stynen, De Meyer, 1960–1963), the former Olivetti headquarters in Florence (Galardi, 1969–1971), as well as the administrative buildings on Place Chauderon in Lausanne (Willomet, Dumartheray, Prouvé, 1969–1974)."[1]

1 Former Olivetti headquarters in Florence
2 Axonometric drawing of the façade of the former Olivetti headquarters
3 Construction section of former Olivetti headquarters
4 Façade of the administrative building on Place Chauderon in Lausanne
5 Axonometric drawing of the envelope elements of the administrative building on Place Chauderon
6 Thermal analysis of the envelopes of the administrative building on Place Chauderon

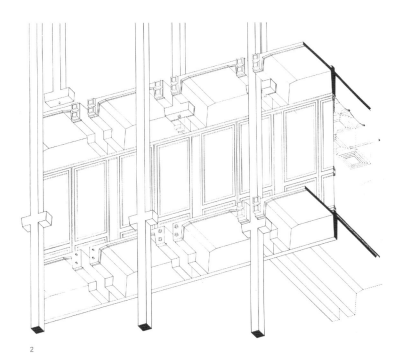

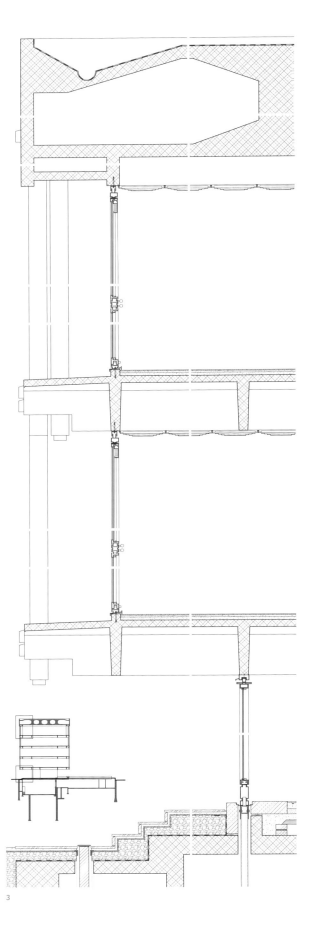

TEACHING THE PRESERVATION 398

4

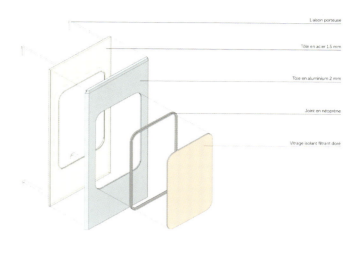

5

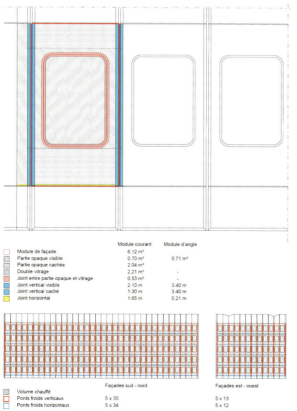

	Module courant	Module d'angle
Module de façade	6.12 m²	
Partie opaque visible	0.70 m²	0.71 m²
Partie opaque cachée	2.04 m²	-
Double vitrage	2.21 m²	-
Joint entre partie opaque et vitrage	0.53 m	-
Joint vertical visible	2.10 m	3.40 m
Joint vertical caché	1.30 m	3.40 m
Joint horizontal	1.65 m	0.21 m

	Façades sud - nord	Façades est - ouest
Volume chauffé		
Ponts froids verticaux	5 x 35	5 x 13
Ponts froids horizontaux	5 x 34	5 x 12

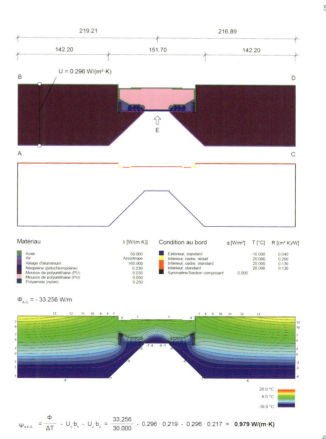

$$\Psi_{A-C} = \frac{\Phi}{\Delta T} - U_1 \cdot b_1 - U_2 \cdot b_2 = \frac{33.256}{30.000} - 0.296 \cdot 0.219 - 0.296 \cdot 0.217 = \mathbf{0.979 \ W/(m \cdot K)}$$

6

399   MASTER'S PRESERVATION PROJECT

FRANZ GRAF
GIULIA MARINO

BY WAY OF
AN EPILOGUE

HOW PRESERVATION CONTRIBUTES TO A CULTURE OF SOCIO-ECOLOGICAL TRANSITION: ELEVEN SHORT CONSIDERATIONS FOR TODAY

Preservation

Our first consideration deals with the question asked of all actors in the *"Baukultur"* (the building culture): whether the landscape, architectural heritage, and the existing built environment could converge to depict the rich diversity and complexity of our future habitat, and thus create the vision of a nascent culture driven by the socioecological transition. It's necessary, then, to rebuild, to try to imagine, and to remodel the architectural design process without endangering its potential for evolving towards a new kind of practice.

As regards the reutilization of architecture, we must be careful not to drown in the mainstream current that has developed over the past few years—the terms reuse, adaptive reuse, and revitalization have become omnipresent and at the same time devoid of meaning. Preservation is—and has been for a very long time—a structured and living practice. We must be precise and exacting, like the stance held by the Architectural Institute of ENAC-EPFL on the subject. We are clearly referring to the term "preservation" which identifies a process of critical thought encompassing the theory and the cultivated and responsible practice of work in the existing built environment, as it began to appear at the beginning of the twenty-first century, and which the activity of an association like Docomomo, occupied with the documentation and preservation of modern and contemporary architecture, and some pioneering work sites have clearly demonstrated. Preservation finds itself de facto and in its own right in the nascent culture of the socioecological transition, which founds its project on heritage—qualitative architecture in the largest sense—as a cultural and economic resource. Let us return to the writing of the founding historian-theoreticians of conservation and preservation, namely Aloïs Riegl and Cesare Brandi, but also in architectural styles such as those of the Smithsons, Alison and Peter, who recognize the "as found" (what is "already there") as a basis for design. While it is important to use the correct words and to make them explicit, it is also so that we don't systematically regress to a pseudo-Esperanto that simplifies complex notions and brings everything down to the lowest common denominator.

Approach(es)

A second consideration focuses on the attentive and close way of looking that preservation demands of us. "We all work on the existing built environment," a colleague said recently, although he tends to systematically destroy that built environment before beginning any project. Will there really be nothing new beneath the sun, in project practice? There is no destructive intervention or tabula rasa, no embalming or therapeutic relentlessness of what exists, nothing new unless it is the very close view we take of materiality and what it constructs and represents. This view encourages our awareness of the double project of conservation and the new, implacable and paradigmatic, which must build on its clearly oxymoronic character, but a subtle and intelligent oxymoron, like those composed by Gunnar Asplund or Hans Döllgast in their architectural work, but also those of Angelo Mangiarotti or Jean Prouvé in some of their creations. They continue today in some singular contemporary practices, such as the Weiterbauen or the Plus strategy.

This double oxymoron-project must be able to be read by the viewer, with due respect to theoretical and practical construction. Architecture, while drawing on its own physical structure, uses music, where one is at once composer and interpreter (Luigi Payreson, 1988), and literature, where one is at the same time writer and translator (Umberto Eco, 2003) but also detector and provocateur of "archi-texts" (Gerard Genette, 1979).

Method

A third consideration concerns our ability to see, view, analyze, and reflect on a detailed reading as a first and foundational act of project design. This reading is achieved through survey, drawing, close-up immersion, description, discovery, re-discovery, and re-cognition, giving us a new description of architecture and its materiality, another history of architecture created with the cognitive tools of architects.

This consideration must lead to our understanding of the built environment as primary text and unique document as well as the recognition that we use the marvelous tools at our disposal very poorly, such as digitalization as a tool to replace the existing. Such use is merely a kind of smoke and mirrors, a manipulation to avoid the materiality when the tool could just as well be used to deepen our understanding of the built environment and make it resonate, and not—as is sometimes the case—be used a pretext for demolition by arguing for a digital preservation of that which is so precarious.

Education

The educational potential of preservation in teaching and research has been put to good use for more than twenty or so years now. It calls on multiple social and scientific disciplines, the history of architecture and architects, the construction of architecture and its materiality, the theory of architecture and the project, the questioning that is simultaneously abstract and very concrete of all that surrounds us in the broadest sense, from the littlest spoon to the entire territory, in short, what cultivated and responsible architecture has always been about.

Let's note the complexity in profiling the figures of these new architects who juggle with history, the project, construction, drawing, the physical aspects of the building, and ecology. A complexity that we have already encountered and where the architect-historian, intellectual, and practitioner that we offered to train twenty years ago, is in fact and by his or her constitution an off-camera figure, a figure at the margins, nonexistent in the established university and professional categories. While it is unlikely that the transition will spring from too fixed a discipline, it is just as unlikely that it be imposed by positions that are too marginal.

Values

This fifth consideration is also about the importance of a qualitative evaluation of all architecture, not only the legendary giants such as Le Corbusier's Unités d'habitation or the Ronchamp chapel, Pier Luigi and Antonio Nervi's Palazzo del Lavoro, Marcel Breuer's Flaine resort, but also the architectural works of Heidi and Peter Wenger, Jean-Paul Darbellay, François Maurice, Otto Senn, Otto Glaus, Georges Brera, Paul Waltenspühl, Eduardo Vittoria, Rudolf and Peter Steiger, Jacob Zweifel, Heinrich Strickler, and many others. We need to re-read minor architectural works to give them the value they deserve and to avoid their demolition, be present during their adaptations, derive our strength from the wealth of the existing built environment and not on the normative performance to be achieved.

If we are to understand the distance between monumental heritage and ordinary buildings, or even diffuse architecture, we must not radicalize this difference, but relativize it, all the while identifying the qualities of the architectural work.

Palimpsest

We must definitively reconsider the structural character of the building as a palimpsest. This stratigraphy is impossible to separate from the building and its life. We had even outlined a way of looking at the history of architecture on the basis of its stratification, additions, and modifications, on its nature as a palimpsest, this well-established idea of André Corboz, the palimpsest of the inflexible Corboz, to whom the whole world refers—and he deserves it—and to whom we still look for intellectual inspiration, such as "revitalization," however vague and inefficient this principle is today.

Since the end of the 1960s, and not only in the academic world, the mental and practical inertia of demolition-reconstruction has established itself firmly in the world of construction—surely due to a poor understanding of the word "sustainable." Instead we should reactivate a targeted and correct intervention and return to the question of perpetual and systematic upkeep, which many people, from the humblest of professionals to the most highly regarded scientists, praise and whose benefits are being rediscovered.

Fragility

The absurdity of any indiscriminate pre-project destruction can be treated as a seventh consideration. How can it seem original to conserve what exists, when this strategy is simply correct, right, well thought out? Pierre Caye called his beautiful, recently published book *Durer* [To Last], which proposes "elements to transform the productive system."

It is necessary, before acting, to introduce a critical value judgment on the architectural quality after intervention. Will the architectural work be better? But let's define this "better" or at least redefine it systematically: is it urban and architectural quality, environmental and ecological, social and economic? Otherwise, it's better to refrain from intervening, to not degrade the existing work, and instead to redo the project with conscientiousness and determination. We also have to be lucid when it comes to alterations from a so-called improvement, energetic improvement, for example. Let us question the benefit of different layers of expanded polystyrene which accumulate during the second or third renovation of buildings, like those of Georges Candilis that we have closely studied, when the rather rudimentary load-bearing structure can no longer support them. How can it be said that the European-wide energy renovation of architecture in which we live, unavoidable and demanded loudly and clearly by a crushing majority, is a planned, systematic, and naive demolition of existing built works, if there isn't a qualitative project that accompanies what is today no more than a technical and disastrous gesture. Sergio Los said it as early as the 1960s, it is absurd to oppose—and to separate—the materiality of architecture and the technoscientific question, the immateriality of the project and the issue of culture.

Reproduction?

In this eighth consideration, we believe that the values of age and newness of a building, which exist in themselves, are to be relativized and should not be confronted, and that their historicity is rather difficult to go against. At a time when the preservation, conservation, or restoration of a mineral-based plaster, a wall from the Middle Ages, stained-glass windows, or Catalan arches is a common practice in the doctrine of preservation and is not difficult to carry out, we allow ourselves simultaneously to simply replace materials, such as the windows and frames of the twentieth century. They would be fragile and difficult to reproduce, and since they aren't called "old," they must meet norms that have become dizzyingly and exponentially stricter in recent years. The "old" is easier to restore, the new is easier to replace.

We see such absurdities daily: superb neon lighting from the 1950s is sacrificed for a banal LED reproduction for questions of energy efficiency, without any real energy calculations and without any real cultural framework against which to judge its quality or the loss that its disappearance signals. Why should something that was considered a masterpiece by international architecture critics seventy years ago become intolerable today? Why should the aluminum window frames that allowed, for example, thousands of students to take advantage of the park and the wooded areas in which their classrooms were situated, become unthinkable for the school comfort of today? At a time when we will probably and reasonably have to get used to living indoors with much lower temperatures in winter, can we really stigmatize them as unacceptable? Will the artistic value be replaced without any cultural loss by the use value? And who will be the judge of this?

Lassitude

The ninth consideration touches on the disinterest and lassitude that have become common among architects when carrying out preservation, a field that is demanding both intellectually and in practice. "Recycling" in a broad sense allows for more freedom, and we take great pleasure in discovering a little-known tradition: the Ronchamp chapel is built with stones from the pre-existing church, Giampiero Mina's Cinema-Teatro in Blenio reproduces the architecture of the Alps with wood left over from the construction of the Olivone dam, Gustav Peichl reused the windows of his own house during later additions to the building. In short, we must enlarge and water down the meaning of the terms *preservation*, *rehabilitation*, *renovation*, *restoration*, *conservation*, *restitution*, *transformation*, etc., and we must update them to modern tastes, simplify them, like the buildings themselves... It must be said that the trivialization of the exercise is well suited to the lowering of requirements by heritage authorities everywhere, probably provoked by the disinterest of public powers on a European scale. This recently nearly led to a permanent disfiguration of the absolute masterpiece of the Maison du Peuple de Clichy, Paris, avoided by a ministerial intervention at the very last minute, or the application of the 110% bonus rule in Italy, which is dangerous for a sensitive heritage site such as the Palazzo Ina au Corso Sempione 33, Milan, by Piero Bottoni, if it is not listed as quickly as possible.

Silence

Our tenth consideration concerns the benefits of silence and invisibility in the preservation project, which means that after four years of study and ten years of work, the 125,000 square meters of the facade of Le Lignon housing complex have conserved their original architectural qualities while half the energy consumption of this "energy sink," aside from the work site, has been cut without anyone noticing. The applied research that we have conducted at the TSAM is considered paradigmatic for the energy conservation of post-war buildings on the

European scale and beyond, a vast project that was meant to remain silent and invisible, thus allowing today's project architects and civil servants from various departments to take credit for it . . . It is built on a simple and effective methodology, based on a balance between energy, economy, and heritage, but which is nevertheless opposed by the managers of large housing complexes that could benefit from it, as they are more interested in maintaining a free hand over what they consider to be their sole property, without any external right of inspection. The issue of cost-saving will be fundamental in the global energy transition. Working at a large scale imposes contained costs, even in a country like Switzerland where well-off towns and businesses buy zero carbon certificates at unbelievable prices.

Baukultur?

A final consideration: we must also be conscious of the risk that no matter how valid the preoccupations with energy transition, sustainable development, and the materials that allow it, they may again provoke an erasure of the fundamentals of architecture, its spatial composition, and its materiality, as we saw in the 1960s, when sociology and political positions pilloried Le Corbusier, guilty of all possible urbanistic blunders, while Carlo Scarpa was quite simply banished from production. This was followed by postmodernists, digital deconstructivists, and now by advocates of the exclusive use of biobased materials, still outside the scope of the discipline, although these preoccupations would permanently modify the shape and materiality of architecture, and with it, the *Baukultur* as a whole.

SPEECH GIVEN BY JOSEPH ABRAM AT THE PRESENTATION OF THE INSIGNIA OF ARTS AND LETTERS TO FRANZ GRAF, AT THE 5TH RÉGION-ARCHITECTURE GRAND-EST CONFERENCE, ON NOVEMBER 29, 2019, AT THE REIMS CONGRESS CENTER

Ladies and Gentlemen,
Colleagues and friends,

It is an honor for me, as well as a pleasure, to speak today about the exemplary career of an architect who has devoted all his energy towards teaching and research. Franz Graf is a professor at the École polytechnique fédérale in Lausanne and the Accademia di Mendrisio. He is head of the Laboratory of Techniques and Preservation of Modern Architecture (TSAM). He has played a leading role in the renewal of restoration practices in modern architecture. As president of the Swiss section of Docomomo (Documentation and Conservation of the Modern Movement), he has helped raise the public's awareness of architecture.

Born in 1958 in Valencia, Spain, Franz Graf studied architecture at the École polytechnique fédérale in Lausanne. He worked for several agencies in Spain, France, and Switzerland, before opening his own architecture firm. Initially a lecturer in Geneva, and then for almost fifteen years in Mendrisio and Lausanne, he has carried out important research on modern construction systems and published numerous articles, in particular on Jean Prouvé, Luigi Moretti, and Angelo Mangiarotti. He headed a research program on the evolution of light façades from an energy efficiency, cost-saving, and heritage point of view, and, with Bruno Reichlin, he led a project developing the *Encyclopédie critique pour la restauration et la réutilisation de l'architecture du XXᵉ siècle*. Again with Bruno Reichlin, he was curator of the *Jean Prouvé, la poétique des objects techniques* exhibition, created by the Vitra Design Museum in 2005, which toured Europe and Japan. He was curator of the exhibition on the Institut Marchiondi by Italian architect Vittoriano Viganò, held in Mendrisio in 2008 and Milan in 2009. Since 2021 he has been a member of the expert committee for the restoration of the works of Le Corbusier.

I wish to underline the innovative character of the books edited by Franz Graf as part of the TSAM. I am thinking, in particular, of the work dedicated to those prolific constructors, the Honegger brothers, whose oeuvre of primarily residential work contributed to the creation of Geneva's modern identity. They are known in France for having participated, with Marcel Lods, in the creation of the Grandes Terres in Marly-le-Roi, one of the most remarkable post-war housing projects. Franz Graf brings all available resources to bear, from the practical inventory to speculation on architectural thought and on the mechanisms of technical rationality. He gives coherence to his large body of work through descriptive notices and essays combining biographical adventures, modern forms of housing, technical analyses, the relationship with artistic practices, heritage assessment, and the development of innovative preservation strategies. We must also cite his book devoted to Georges Addor, another key player in Swiss post-war architecture, whose production was perhaps, during his lifetime, the least recognized of any. Franz Graf firmly grounds his analysis in the concrete, bestowing on the built object a renewed epistemological status. He breathes fresh life into buildings judged by others to be dull and repetitive, probably due to the impeccable walls that envelope them. His exploration of the curtain walls produced during the intense construction activity of the 1960s reveals sophisticated techniques, as do his analyses of other characteristics of the built environment. In view of the materiality of buildings and the complex progression that comes after it, he employs an adaptable approach, transforming theoretical knowledge into a tool for intervention. The result is a more open-minded and rigorous concept of historical research, which enhances, in turn, the analyzed trajectories. The study he devoted to Le Lignon housing complex received an award from the Swiss Society of Engineers and Architects (SIA) for its pragmatic approach and for its respect of the cultural values exhibited by the existing environment. His works give an unbiased idea of the specificity of architectural objects, of their semantic wealth, and the heterogeneous values they convey. In today's world, those underlying requirements take on a decisive element. They form a kind of antidote to the indifference that physically threatens, in many places around the world, our post-war heritage.

Dear Franz, as I said at the beginning of this introduction, it is an honor for me, and a pleasure, to present you with the insignia of Arts and Letters, and more particularly here in this magnificent city of Reims, which is becoming ever more beautiful. Over the past fifty years, I have only been here about ten or so times—before my studies to see the cathedral, and then, during those studies and as a young researcher, to visit the masterpiece of engineering that is the Maigrot-Freyssinet Hall, and the glorious concrete building that is the Hôtel des Postes, by François Le Cœur, one of Anatole de Baudot's best students and also one of the few constructors to admire Perret. And on top of that, I am truly lucky to be presenting you with this award as part of the Région-Architecture framework, that wonderful invention by Lorenzo Diez, and in front of a crowd who knows, perhaps more than anyone, what architecture still has to accomplish to ensure its recognition by the wider public and by decision-makers. Dear Franz, through your dedication and passion, you are contributing enormously to this. Please accept my sincere congratulations.

Joseph Abram
Architect, professor emeritus at the École nationale supérieure
d'architecture de Nancy

LIST OF GUEST LECTURERS AT THE TSAM LABORATORY

Joseph ABRAM, Katia ACCOSSATO, Francesca ALBANI, Carmen ALONSO, Silvia ALONSO, Dominique AMOUROUX, Christophe AMSLER, Aymeric ANTOINE, Vitangelo ARDITO, Aurora ARMENTAL RUIZ, Mark ARNOLD, Francisco ARQUES, Clémentine ARTRU, Maria Chiara BARONE, Alessandra BASSI, Bernard BAUCHET, Hélène BAUCHET, Christian BAUD, Anja BEER, Gilles BEGUIN, Giorgio BELLO, Yves BELMONT, Tim BENTON, Laetitia BERNASCONI, Alain BERSET, Édith BIANCHI, Serge BINOTTO, Bernadette BLANCHON, Gordian BLUMENTHAL, Jacques BLUMER, Peter BÖCKLIN, Elisabeth BOESCH, Martin BOESCH, Alberto BOLOGNA, Patrizia BONIFAZIO, Pierre BONNET, Véronique BOONE, Jean-Jacques BORGEAUD, Daniel BOSSHARD, François BOTTON, Brian BRACE TAYLOR, Vincent BRADEL, Daniela BRAHM, Winfried BRENNE, Henri BRESLER, Tarramo BROENNIMANN, Jürg BRÜHLMANN, Eugen BRÜHWILER, Thierry BUACHE, Kilian BÜHLMANN, Jörg BÜRKLE, Thomas BURLON, Chloé BUTSCHER, Jean-François Cabestan, Chantal CALLAIS, Ivan CAMARGO, Ramun CAPAUL, David CAPELL, Maristella CASCIATO, Hana ČERVINKOVÁ, Jean-Pierre CÊTRE, François CHATILLON, Frère Marc CHAUVEAU, Paul CHEMETOV, Agnès CHEMETOV, Laurent CHENU, Jean-Marie CHEVRONNET, Cristiana CHIORINO, Emmanuel CHRISTE, Dominique CHUARD, Stefano CIURLO WALKER, Catherine CLARISSE, Elena COGATO LANZA, Catherine COLEY, Roberto CONTE, Jürg CONZETT, Benoît CORNU, Monica CORRADO, Martin CORS, Pierre-Alain CROSET, Kira CUSACK, Katharina DALCHER, Darine DANDAN, Carlotta DARÒ, Jacques-Louis DE CHAMBRIER, Florian DE POUS, Nicolas DE WUSTEMBERGER, Pascale DEJEAN, Nicolas Delachaux, Guillaume DELEMAZURE, Pauline DELESSERT, Jeanne DELLA CASA, Guy DESGRANDCHAMPS, Claudia DEVAUX, Aloïs DIETHELM, Gilles DOESSEGER, Gabriele DOLFF-BONEKÄMPER, Jean-Pierre DRESCO, Frédéric DRUOT, Jean-Marc DRUT, Marc DUBOIS, Pierre DUFOUR, Catherine DUMONT D'AYOT, Jean-Christophe DUNANT, Christian DUPRAZ, Pierre-Alain DUPRAZ, Rémi DUVAL, Katrin EBERHARD, Denis ELIET, Frank ESCHER, João Pedro FALCÃO DE CAMPOS, Laurent FAULON, Lucien FAVRE, Éric-J. FAVRE-BULLE, Arne FENTZLOFF, Marc FERAUGE, Corentin FIVET, Pierre FREY, Reto GADOLA, Patrice GAGLIARDI, Emmanuelle GALLO, Bénédicte GANDINI, Mauro GANDOLLA, Jordi GARCÈS, Pierre-Antoine GATIER, Françoise GAUTHIER, Matthieu GAUYE, Enrico GIACOPELLI, Dominique GILLIARD, Ludovic GILLON, Christian GILOT, Pasquale GIORDANO, Petra GOLDMANN, Michel GOUTAL, Carmel GRADOLI, Philippe GRANDVOINNET, Claudio GRECO, Roberta GRIGNOLO, Sylvia GRIÑO, Olivier GROSSNIKLAUS, Jacques GUBLER, Ravi GUNEWARDENA, Remo HALTER CASAGRANDE, Boris HAMZEIAN, Pia HANNEWALD, Thomas HASLER, Serge HAUTIER, Roland HEGNAUER, William HERAUD, Luis Francisco HERRERO, Sonja HILDEBRAND, Thomas HILDEBRAND, Adrian HOCHSTRASSER, David HOFFERT, Bärbel HÖGNER, Cédric HUMAIR, Christophe HUTIN, Roland IMHOF, Tullia IORI, Fulvio IRACE, Emanuelle JAQUES,

Martine JAQUET, Aline JEANDREVIN, Thierry JEANMONOD, François JOLLIET, Christophe JOLY, Didier JUILLERAT, Julia JULEN, Alexandre KABOK, Manon KIVELL, Richard KLEIN, Gilbert KNORR, Yvan KOLEČEK, Hans-Joachim KRAFT, Gerold KUNZ, Michel LABRECQUE, Anne LACATON, Gilles LAFAURIE, Massimo LAFFRANCHI, Jean-Yves LE BARON, Sébastien LAHONDÈS, Ruedi LATTMANN, Laurence LAVALETTE, Pierre LEBRUN, Laurent LEHMANN, Véronique LÉONARD, Alain LÉVEILLÉ, José Ignacio LINAZASORO, Ueli LINDT, Florence LIPSKY, Jean-Louis LODS, Joël LOUTAN, Jacques LUCAN, Markus LÜSCHER, Thomas LUSSI, Jean-François LYON-CAEN, Anouar M'HIMDAT, Stephan MÄDER, Thierry MANASSEH, Caroline MANIAQUE, Bruno MARCHAND, Christophe MARGUERON, Monika MARKGRAF, Vincent MAS DUBERC, Philippe MATHEZ, Dario MATTEONI, Claude Anne-Marie MATTER, Jessica MATTHEY-DE-L'ENDROIT, François MAURICE, Joan MAURIN, Radu MEDREA, Philippe MEIER, David MERZ, Christel MÉTRAILLER, Yvan MÉTTAUD, Philippe MEYLAN, Laura MILAN, Delphine MILLET, Maryline MONNIER, Gérard MONNIER, Delphine MOREL, Patrick MOSER, Reto MOSIMAN, René MOTRO, Rolf MÜHLETHALER, Sebastian MÜLLER, Aurelio MUTTONI, Hermann NÄGELE, Massimo NARDUZZO, Sabine NEMEC PIGUET, Joëlle NEUENCHWANDER FEIHL, Anna NEUHAUS, Markus NITSCHKE, Danielle NOISET, Michel NOISET, Erwin OBERWILLER, Sebastien OESCH, Asdis OLAFSDOTTIR, Valérie ORTLIEB, Sergio PACE, Rémi PAPILLAULT, Bernard PAULE, Danièle PAULY, Stefano PEREGO, Jan PERNEGER, Clément PERRIER, Carmen PERRIN, Yves PERRINJAQUET, Charles PICTET, Nathalie POCHON, Marike POLOCSAI, Fernando PORTÉ-AGEL, Maria PORTMAN, Uta POTGIESSER, Philippe POTIÉ, Benoît POUVREAU, Eduardo PRIETO, Françoise PROUVÉ, Élise QUANTIN, Margarida QUINTÃ, Gilles RAGOT, Marco RAMPINI, Ginette RAPALLI, Daniel REBMAN, Robert REBUTATO, Martin REICHERT, Bruno REICHLIN, Delphine REIST, Mathias REMMELE, Didier REPELLIN, Jacques REPIQUET, Ignacio REQUENA RUIZ, Sophie RICHELLE, Urs RINIKER, Antoinette ROBAIN, Marie ROCHER, Franz ROMERO, Hans ROTH, Flora RUCHAT-RONCATI, Stéphane RUDAZ, Antti RÜEGG, Arthur RÜEGG, Stephan RUTISHAUSER, Renato SALVI, Giulio SAMPAOLI, Manon SAMUEL, Marielle SAVOYAT, Jacques SBRIGLIO, Christoph SCHLÄPPI, Alexander SCHLATTER, Anton SCHLEISS, Silvio SCHMED, Sven SCHMID, Christiane SCHMÜCKLE-MOLLARD, Christoph SCHNEIDER, Beate SCHNITTER, Pascal SCHNYDRIG, Martin SCHREGENBERGER, Bernard SCHÜLE, Donato SEVERO, Roger SIMOND, Annette SPIRO, Laurent STALDER, Ernst STREBEL, Isa STÜRM, Anna SUTER, Jo TAILLIEU, Alain TAVÈS, Jean TERRIER, Patrick THURSTON, Alexandre TIARRI, Barbara TIRONE, Ana TOSTÕES, Nuno VALENTIM, Lucas VAN ZUIJLEN, France VANLAETHEM, Meritxell VAQUER, Pascal VARONE, Andreas VASS, Jean-Luc VEYRET, Annalisa VIATI, Jean-Jacques VIROT, Martine VITTU, Danièle VOLDMAN, Markus VON BERGEN, Martina VOSER, Damian WALLISER, Leentje WALLISER, Yves WEINAND, Matias WENZEL, Jérôme WOHLSCHLAG, Cristina WOODS, Ivan ZAKNIC, Maruša ZOREC, Cyril ZOZOR, Vivian ZUFFEREY.

IMAGE CREDITS

The numbers refer to pages in this book, the letters to the order of images on the page, from top to bottom and from left to right.

|| RECENT PHOTOGRAPHS || ARGE Lussi+Halter, Lucerne / photo Leonardo Finotti: 39a **|** Arrea Architecture, Ljubljana / photo Tadej Bolta: 39d **|** Mounir Ayoub: 184–185 **|** Javier Azurmendi: 272a **|** Boesch Architekten, Zurich: 38 **|** Eduardo Blanes: 270ab, 272b **|** Michel Bonvin: 39b **|** Pierre-Yves Brunaud: 222d **|** Lucien Caceres: 23b **|** Estudio Alberto Campo Baeza, Madrid / photo Javier Callejas: 33c **|** Enrico Cano: 20a **|** Capaul&Blumenthal Architekten, Ilanz / Glion: 280a-d **|** Paul Chemetov / © 2022, ProLitteris, Zurich: 39e **|** Yvan Delemontey: 57a, 57b, 62 (drawing) **|** Kevin Dolmaire: 41b **|** Filip Dujardin: 41a **|** Escher GuneWardena Architecture, Los Angeles (© Eames Foundation, Pacific Palisades): 242a **|** Frank Escher: 243gh **|** Douglas Friedman / Trunk: 242d **|** Alexandre Gameiro, Pier Luigi Surano: 298–299 **|** Rémy Gindroz: 43c **|** Gpkp, Wikicommons: 34a **|** Gzzz, Wikicommons: 44a **|** Alain Herzog / EPFL: 8–9, 58a, 110, 114ab, 118a-d, 138, 142, 146, 156, 162, 168, 172, 272c **|** Martin Linsi: 40b **|** Giulia Marino: 22c, 23c, 28b (© 2022, ProLitteris, Zurich), 30a, 37a, 37b, 42 (© FLC / 2022, ProLitteris, Zurich), 43b, 43d, 44b, 45b, 49d, 50b **|** Claudio Merlini: 22b (© 2022, ProLitteris, Zurich), 29b (© 2022, ProLitteris, Zurich), 29d, 415 **|** Grant Mudford: 242c **|** Studio Narduzzo, Treviso: 40a **|** Lucile Pierron: 16–17 **|** José Manuel Rodrigues: 232c **|** City of Zurich Planning Department / photo Juliet Haller: 39c **|** TSAM-EPFL: 20b **|** Joshua White / JWPictures.com: 242b **|** Wikicommons: 45a **|** Michael Wyss: 52–53, 56

|| PUBLIC ARCHIVES || Académie d'Architecture / Cité de l'architecture et du patrimoine / Archive of Contemporary Architecture, Marcel Lods (and Association Beaudouin et Lods) collection: 220a **|** Archives Architectures Genève, Paul Waltenspühl collection: cover IVa (Paul Waltenspühl), 46 (Louis Bacchetta), 47a, 232b **|** Archives of the Canton of Vaud, Chavannes-près-Renens, SB 52/B-4-4: 45c **|** Archives of Modern Construction / EPFL, Lausanne, AAA collection: 50a; Jean-Marc Lamunière collection: 49a; Alberto Sartoris collection: 23a **|** HEPIA Archives, Lullier: 25a **|** Archives of the International Museum of Horology, La Chaux-de-Fonds: 21e **|** Library of Geneva, Center for Iconography / © 2022, ProLitteris, Zurich: 22a (Boissonnas) **|** Centre Pompidou, Mnam-CCI, Bibliothèque Kandinsky, RMN-Grand Palais, Jean Prouvé collection: 29a (© 2022, ProLitteris, Zurich), 31a (© 2022, ProLitteris, Zurich) **|** DR: 232a **|** ETH Bibliothek-Bildarchiv, Zurich: 19b (Comet Photo AG, 1969), 292a (Comet Photo AG, 1967) **|** National Institute of Industrial Property (INPI), Paris / US patent 246626: 33a **|** MuCEM, Jean-Dominique Lajoux collection: 222a

|| PRIVATE ARCHIVES || Gabriele Basilico Archives, Milan: 398a **|** Les Forces Motrices Hongrin-Léman SA Archives: 26a **|** Archives historiques Aluminium Suisse, Zurich: 29c **|** Private archives: 18a **|** Alberto Galardi private archives: 398b **|** Gigi Ghò private archives: 35acd **|** Archives Saint-Gobain, Blois: 19a **|** Fondation Le Corbusier, Paris / © 2022, ProLitteris, Zurich: 28a (Albin Salaün) **|**Max Bill Georges Vantongerloo Foundation, Zumikon / © 2022, ProLitteris, Zurich: 43a **|** Frank Lloyd Wright Foundation, Scottsdale): 34b

|| EXCERPTS FROM PUBLICATIONS || Sarah Adamopoulos and José Luís Falcão de Vasconcellos, *Liceu de Camões 100 Anos 100 Testemunhos* (Lisbon: Quimera, 2009): 232d **|** Architekturforum Biel, Franz

Füeg et al., *Max Schlup Architekt architecte*, (Sulgen: Niggli, 2013): 18c | *AS Architecture suisse*, no. 2, June 1972: 49c (Germond); no. 48, October 1981: 33b | *L'Architettura, cronache e storia*, no. 9, January 1962: 30b | *Bauen+Wohnen*, no. 1, 1956: 18b | *Schweizerische Bauzeitung*, vol. 92, no. 19, 1928: 21b | *Techniques et Architecture*, no. 6, June 1966: 31b (© 2022, ProLitteris, Zurich); no. 292, April 1973: 32a || **TSAM-EPFL** || "**Theories and Techniques of the Preservation Project" (master's level class):** 21a/21c (Laurie Bandiera, Baptiste Berrut-Maréchaud, Federica Grande, 2016–2017), 21d/21f (Mélanie Baptista De Sousa, Alexandre Gameiro, Jonathan Kiener, 2021–2022), 24a (Marine Frey, Matthias Jammers, Marine Manche, 2021–2022), 24b (Cindy Grohe, Florence Nyffeler, Sophie Paladini, 2019–2020), 24c (Ismene Ehrler, Océane Martin, Juliette Vincent, 2020–2021), 26bc (Mathias Gommier, Sébastien Rouge, 2017–2018), 27a (Annie Kaeppeli, Léonore Nemec, Pauline Schroeter, 2013–2014), 27b (Andrea Baraggia, Francesca Rabbiosi, 2013–2014), 27c (Audrey Aulus, Éloïse Barry, Vincent Bourassa-Denis, 2013–2014), 27d (Aurélie Bichsel, Frédéric Bouvier, Marie Sagnières, 2013–2014), 48 (Alison Blank, Kilian Cossali, Chloé Schindler, 2020–2021) | **"Comfort by Design in Twentieth-Century Architecture" (master's level class):** 32b (Antoine Casile, Marie-Ange Farrell, Pablo Fillit, 2020–2021), 35b (Julien Heil, Quentin Paillat, Arno Wust, 2020-2021) | **ENAC Project "Strategies and Techniques for the Reuse of Twentieth-Century Architecture (master's level class)":** 25b (Émérence Declerq, Tiffanie Paré, 2020–2021), 47b Marie-Laure Allemann, Virginie Bally, Odile Keller, 2015–2016), 49b (Solène Tossa, Aliénor Zaffalon, 2015–2016), 51abc (Alessandro Di Renzo, Giuseppe Galbiati, Benedetta Leway, 2019–2020) | **Lecture series "Project, History, and Construction: New Perspectives on Recent Heritage":** 36a-f | **Preservation Project Studio (bachelor & master):** 54 (May Ackermann, Konstantinos Dell'Olivo, Lorraine Kerhli, Amandine Martin, Nhien Nguyen), 55 (Oria Abbas, Carlotta Boxebeld, Loïc Flury, Amélie Gaillet, Camille Nicolet, Julie Riondel, Manon Thévenaz, 58b (Claudio Meletta), 59/91a/93a (Christophe Neyroud), 60 (Marina Capelli, Eva Ponzo), 66/67ab (Michael Desaules), 67c (Marjolaine Obrist), 67d (Clément Vulliez), 67e/68b (Chris Christen), 67f, 68a (Estelle Lepine), 69a (Telma Gonçalves), 69b (Annina Inäbnit), 70 (Delphine Quach), 71a (Laetitia Bernasconi), 71b (Inès Méttraux), 71c (Aline Villet), 71d/72a (Jérôme Wohlschlag), 71e (Théo Bellmann), 71f, 72bc (Christine Jalbert Laramée, Inès Méttraux, Aline Villet), 73 (Joël Loutan), 74 (Pierre Blanchet, Nathalie Pochon), 75a (Bertrand Batoz), 75b (Élodie Laurent), 75c (Claudio Meletta), 75d (Nathalie Pochon), 75e (Martin Risch), 75f, 76a (Andrea Pellacani), 76b (Manuel Potterat), 77 (Mathieu Hefti), 78 (Emma Bilham, Chloé Coninckx, Anna Küenzi), 79a (Jérôme Tacchini), 79b (Emma Bilham), 79c (Nikolaos Sofras), 79d (Pierre Le François des Courtis), 79e (Chloé Coninckx), 79f, 80 (Mikael Monteserin), 81a (Marie Cherix), 81b (Malaïca Cimenti), 82 (Anne-Fanny Cotting), 83a (Axel Ferret), 83b (Elena Broncano), 83c (Jennifer Huynh), 83d (Timothée Gauvin), 83e/85ab (Lorraine Kehrli), 83f, 84 (Lila Held), 86 (Noémie Wesolowski), 87a (Tchaya Bloesch), 87b (Cyril Lemray), 87c (Claire Maillet), 87d (Nicolas Pierret), 87e (Andreas Schmid), 87f, 88/91c (Adrian Meredith), 89a (Julie Vulliet), 89b (Sophie Wobmann), 90 (Jean-Denys Vesco), 91b (Stéphanie Morel), 91d (Lenart Harbich), 91e (Olivier Pellerin), 91f, 92a (Danny Te Kloese), 92b (Korab Ramadani), 93b (Didier Lambert), 94 (Samuel Barthoux), 95a (Hélène Fernet), 95b (Bruna Gomes Magalhães), 95c (Guillaume Hernach), 95d/99a (Thierry Manasseh), 95e (Aliénor Zaffalon), 95f, 96a (Christelle Brot), 96b (Line Frossard), 97 (Maurice Debons), 98 (Clemens Schagerl), 99b (Antoine Doms), 99c/100a (Stéphane Hasler), 99d (Catherine Seiler), 99e (Alexandre Jöhl), 99f, 100b (Tiphanie Paroz), 101 (Thierry Manasseh, Ngoc Quyen Nguyen), 102 (Flavien Burri, Nicolas Olivier), 103a (Lisa Balmer), 103b/104b (Pierre Chevremont), 103c (Annie Kappeli), 103d (Elezaj Lirëza), 103e (Zhongqu Lin), 103f, 104a (Lisa Balmer), 105ab (Lisa Guiraud, Zhongqu Lin), 106 (Roman Tschudin), 107a (Angélique Morand), 107b (Meret Hodel), 107c (Antoine Ducry), 107d (Camille

Mansuelle), 107e/109 (Héloïse Sierro), 107f, 108 (Adrien L'Hoste), 111a (Cyril Dériaz), 111b (Caroline Charvet), 111c (Floriane De Jong), 111d (Emanuelle Jaques), 111e (Tina Straubhaar), 111f, 112 (Thierry Buache, Cyril Dériaz, Lionel Durand, Grégoire Henrioud, Sara Theodori, Marie-Pascale Wellinger), 113a (Malik Boukhechina), 113b (Johan Cosandey), 115a (Laetitia Berger, Marc Olivier Seydoux), 115b (Chantal Blanc, Cyrielle Froidevaux), 115c (Luc Carpinelli, Arnaud Scheurer), 115d (Thibault Menny, Alexandre Rychner), 115e (Éloïse Barry, Vincent Bourassa), 115f, 116 (Marina Capelli), 117a (Marie-Laure Allemann), 117b (Stéphane de Weck), 119a (Nicolas Choquard, Michaël Beaud), 119b (Marie Gillioz, Mélanie Lacroix), 119c (Sebastian Kannewischer, Laurie Bandiera, Olivier Schmitt), 119d (Pedro Reyes, Aloïs Rosenfeld), 119e (Manuela Schöneneberger, Charles Legrand), 119f, 120-121(Anaïs Jaquier, Clément Perrier, Loïc Preitner, Pedro Reyes, Aloïs Rosenfeld), 122 (Amos Pirotta, Jonathan Maddalena, Lucie Morand, Camille Guntern, Sarah Marchini), 123a (Vincent Dorfmann, David Hoffert), 123b (Hugo Bonvin, Cynthia Coucet), 123c (Ludovic Fleichner, Ivo Raffi), 123d (Sofia Ferrari, Alexandre Tiarri), 123e (Camille Guntern, Lucie Morand), 123f, 124/126/128/130/132 (Victoire Courtaux, Sophie Marcolini, Charlotte Ganty, Maureen Soupe, Hugo Bonvin, Cynthia Coucet), 125ab/127ab/129ab/131ab/133ab (Vincent Dorfmann, Évariste Exposito, Sofia Ferrari, Anthony Genton, David Hoffert, Alexandre Tiarri), 125c/127c/129c/131c/133c (François Angel, Laura Ardizzone, Lorraine Gence, Sophie Heini, Manon Kivell, Loïc Kritzinger, Nora Molari, Anna Neuhaus), 134/136a (Tania Coutherez, Sophie Guilleux, Vincent Hauser, Anouar M'Himdat, Morgane Vuilleret), 135a/139e (Clara Ansselin, Anne Sermet), 135b (Clara Brun, Valentine De Giuli, Caroline Reich), 135c (Morgane Hoffstetter), 135d (Anouar H'Himdat, Charles Duwig), 135e (Sophie Guilleux, Morgane Wuilleret), 135f, 136b (Hanna Elatifi, Cindy Grohe, Alexia Kaas, Coline Pernet, Cécile Zaugg), 137a (Clara Ansselin, Charles Duwig, Alexandra Fuchs, Morgane Hofstetter, Anne Sermet), 137b (Laura Raggi), 139a (Vincent Hauser), 139b (Tania Coutherez, Anouar H'Himdat), 139c (Nordine Mahmoudi, Tobias Richterich), 139d (Benjamin Irion), 139f, 140ab (Clara Brun, Paola Falconi, Vincent Hauser, Morgane Hofstetter, Alexia Kaas, Laura Raggi), 141abc (Hanna Elatifi, Cindy Grohe, Coline Pernet, Cécile Zaugg), 143a (Micky Gerardi), 143b/147a (Noémie Ali, Claire Heusckel), 143c (Matthieu Gauye, Nicolas John), 143d (Maxim Andrist, Marco Lucas), 143e (Amandine Mathieu, Mathilde Thiriot), 143f, 144ab (Maxim Andrist, Candice Blanc, Romain D'Incau, Marianne Ghorayeb, Gégory Kramer, José Reyes), 145 (Rita Haodiche, Kevin Rodriguez, Mathilde Thiriot, Salomé Stoffel, Amélie Poirel), 147b (Maxim Andrist, Salomé Stoffel), 147c (Candice Blanc, Romain D'Incau), 147d (Rita Haodiche, Kevin Rodriguez), 147e (José Reyes, Jennifer Tribolet), 147f, 148 (Candice Blanc, Romain D'Incau, Marianne Ghorayeb, Mathilde Thiriot), 149ab (Noémie Ali, Claire Heuschkel, Amélie Poirel, Amandine Mathieu, Salomé Stoffel, Grégory Kramer), 150 (Alice Biber, Alexandre Gameiro, Tamara Lobo), 151a (Mathias Schopfer, Emmanuel Stump), 151b (Anna McCuan, Cathrin Schapfl), 151c (Alexandre Gameiro, Pier Luigi Surano), 151d (Garance Berger, Mathilde Linder), 151e (Delphine Klumpp, Mai Yamasaki), 151f, 152 (Mathilde Linder), 153a (Alexandre Gameiro, Mathias Schopfer, Emmanuel Stump, Pier Luigi Surano), 153b (Garance Berger), 154 (Leonne-Zoé Vögelin), 155a (Alice Biber), 155b (Sarah Hahusseau), 157a (Kastriot Dragusha, Mathieu Stutz), 157b (Oria Abbas, Loïc Flury), 157c (Amélie Gaillet, Camille Nicolet), 157d (Alberto Johnsson, Melinda Papi), 157e (Laura Périat, Christine Shehata), 157f, 158 (Amélie Gaillet, Camille Nicolet, Julie Riondel, Caroline Saint-Hilaire, Manon Thévenaz), 159a (Carlotta Boxebeld), 159b (Kastriot Dragusha, Lionel Scherz, Mathieu Stutz), 160-161 (group work), 163a (Élodie Michel, Silvio Gonçalves), 163b (Ella Bacchetta), 163c (Joana Dias Pinto, Leon Economidis), 163d (Lucas Rodriguez, Yann Schwaller), 163e (Anouk Chalaron, Elina Leuba), 163f, 164ab (Nora Bugmann, Anouk Chalaron, Joana Dias Pinto, Silvio Gonçalves), 165a/couverture IVb

(Samuel Dafflon, Camille Rieux, Lucas Rodriguez, Lise Sarda, Yann Schwaller), 165b (Malak Abdelhady, Florian Baeriswyl, Ella Bacchetta), 166 (Lucas Rodriguez), 167ab (Malak Abdelhady, Ella Bacchetta, Zoé Bahy, Joana Dias Pinto, Valmira Haziri, Elina Leuba, Élodie Michel), 169a (Mélanie Bauer, Basil Ferrand), 169b (Robin Gugger, Léa Guillotin), 169c (Louis Meier, Claire Montégudet), 169d (Marie-Ange Farell, Julien Heil), 169e (Antonio Pagano, Antoine Ricard), 169f, 170 (Liam Banctel, Mélanie Bauer, Albane Grimond, Antoine Ricard), 171ab (Célia Feole, Claire Hennel, Fidan Ibrahimi, Remo Panarese), 173a (Robin Gugger, Pacific N'Kiambi), 173b (François Born, Loïc Rey), 173c (Théo Gaspar, Eleni-Aline Rizou), 173d (Karen Schuller, Paul Savary), 173e (Marco Landert, Sidney Wirth), 173f, 174 (Elia Bianchi, Chiara Pezzetta, Driss Veyry), 175a (Théo Gaspar, Claire Hennel, Flavia Mizel, Loïc Rey), 175b (Robin Gugger, Fidan Ibrahimi, Khalil Mokaddem)

|| MASTER'S PRESERVATION ORIENTATION STUDIOS || **Hubmann & Vass Studio:** 190ab, 196ab (Chen Jianfeng), 196cdef (Bruna Gomes Magalhães), 197a-c (Rui Agnelo), 198a-c (Lawrence Breitling, Sébastien Guidi), 198d-g (Saeko Terada), 199a-c (Louis Jucker, Régis Widmer) **| Bosshard & Vaquer Studio:** 200ab, 208a (Lucien Favre, Yvan Mattenberger, Régis Widmer), 208b/209c (Annika Hansen, Jennifer Monnet, Claire Rosat), 208c (Arnaud Paquier, Clara Rubin), 208d/209b/211c (group work), 209a (Alice Chénais, Roland Freymond, Gaspard Garcier), 210a (Annika Hansen), 210b (Laetitia Bich), 210c (Virginie Ganz, Cécile Klaus), 210d-h (Peter Nic, Mélanie Rouge, Béatrix Woringer), 211ab/211d-g (Aurélie Dupuis, Kaori Pedrazzoli, Marion Vuachet) **| Eliet & Lehmann Studio:** 212ab, 220b (group work), 220c (Florim Asani), 220d (Nathalie Grobéty), 220e (Jérémie Jobin), 220f (Chantal Blanc), 221a (Chantal Blanc, Nathalie Grobéty), 221b (Fanny Vuagniaux), 221c/223d-f (Antoine Girardon, Jérémie Jobin), 222b (Jérémie Jobin, Rafaël Schneiter), 222c (Nicolas Chatelan, Lisa Robillard, Katia Sottas Kacou), 223a-c (Roxane Doyen) **| Falcão de Campos Studio:** 224ab, 233a (Thierry Buache, Adrien Dauvillier, Sara Teodori, Marie Weillinger), 233b (Coralie Comte, Dominik Kreutzer, Élise Lecat, Loïc Marconato et Cléa Petitpierre), 233c (Niels Fantini, Cédric Gil, Micael Henriques, Louise Nicolas, Juliette Vautey, Antoine Vauthey), 233de (Arthur Blanc, Camille Brachet, Sarah Clénin, Camille Dupont, Benjamin Gmür, Evelyne Lorenzi, and Ardian Syla), 233f/233h (Anne-Sophie Blunier, Marina Capelli, Mathilde Loiseau, Eva Ponzo, Marta Salvat, Axelle Vandenbroucke), 233g (Florim Asani, Arthur Blanc, Thierry Buache, Sarah Clénin, Elise Coudray, Aline Cousot, Eleonora Forato, Loïc Marconato, Evelyne Lorenzi, Ardian Syla), 234b (Louise Nicolas, Juliette Vautey), 234c (Marie-Laure Allemann, Virginie Bally), 234d (Benjamin Gmür, Thomas Revel), 235a (Élise Coudray, Aline Cousot) **| Escher & GuneWardena Studio:** 236ab, 243a (Louis Desplanques, Sébastien Fasel), 243b (Marie Gillioz), 243c (Oscar Persson), 243d (Nicolò Rimoldi), 243e (Alessandra Bassi, Louise Gueissaz), 243f (Damien Gisler), 244ab (Amaya Cogordan-Gillet), 244c-f/245ef (Sébastien Fasel), 245ab (Nina Haftka), 245cd (Louis Desplanques), 245gh (Louise Gueissaz) **| Lacaton & Druot Studio:** 246, 260a (Sofia Iglesias Vicinay, Sarah Marchini, Sébastien Rouge, Mara Rutigliani, Wendy Tokuoka, Jean-Loup Tscheulin), 260bc (Charlotte Ganty, Manon Kivell, Anna Neuhaus, Maureen Soupe, Juan Carlos Villanueva), 260d (Ian Bichelmeier, Delphine Dufour, Elsa Gaugue, Mélanie Lacroix), 260ef (Corentin Badoux, Tobias Cebulla, Darine Dandan, Anouar M'Himdat, Lucie Vogl), 261a-d (Louis d'Aubigné, Sara Davin Omar, Mathieu Hofer, Nina Kleber, Théophile Legrain, Tristan Wicht), 261ef (group work), 262a (Tobias Cebulla, Louis d'Aubigné, Sara Davin Omar, Delphine Dufour, Elsa Gaugue, Nina Kleber), 262b (Mégane Krebs, Anouar M'Himdat, Sarah Marchini, Sébastien Rouge, Jean-Loup Tscheulin), 263a-f (Darine Dandan, Delphine Dufour, Charlotte Ganty, Manon Kivell, Anna Neuhaus, Maureen Soupe) **| Linazasoro & Sánchez Studio:** 264ab, 270c (Francesca Bianchi, Christophe Dindault, Florence Nyffeler, Hugo Pachoud, Jérémy Prongué, Ziyad Ryser), 270d (Émilie Beytrison, Lothaire Creppy,

Cynthia Da Silva, Marie Menninger, Meril Sabo, Letizia Vanelli), 270e-g (Marine Chapatte, Laurie Charron-Lozeau, Marine Gerard, Pierre Girard, David Hoffert, Sophie Paladini, Alexandre Tiarri), 271a/273a (Laurie Charron-Lozeau, Marine Gerard, Sophie Paladini), 271b (Cindy Grohe, Zoé Salomon), 273b (David Hoffert, Alexandre Tiarri, Nina Mosca) | Capaul & Blumenthal Studio: 274ab, 281a (group work), 281b (Laura Sacher), 281c (Nina Burri), 281de (Coline Boyer), 281f (Franz Bohnacker), 282a (Erik Hellström, Adam Söderblom, Kristina Ehrling), 282bc (Niels Galitch, Émilie Wägli), 282de (Quentin Huegi, Florian Millius), 283ab (Justine Estoppey, Niels Galitch, Émilie Wägli), 283cd (Lisa Virgillito), 283ef (Erik Hellström, Adam Söderblom) | Atelier Voser Studio: 284a-d, 292b-d (Alexandre Gameiro, Pier Luigi Surano), 293a-d (Emérence Declercq, Simon Wüst), 294a-c/295a-d (Antoine Iweins, Simon Wüst), 296a-f (Marco Landert, Sidney Wirth), 297a-e (Karen Schuler, Arno Wüst)

|| MASTER'S PROJECTS || Emanuelle Jaques: 304ab, 306a-c, 307a-d | Stéphanie Morel, Fabian Roth: 308ab, 310a-d, 311a-c | Thierry Buache: 312ab, 314a-d, 315a-c | Delphine Dufour: 316ab, 318a-c, 319a-d | Sébastien Rouge: 320ab, 322a-d, 323a-c | Manon Kivell, Anna Neuhaus: 324ab, 326a-b, 327a-c | Claire Heuschkel: 328ab, 330a-d, 331a-c | Delphine Millet, Clément Perrier: 332ab, 334a-c, 335a-d | Lucien Favre: 336ab, 338a-c, 339a-c | Darine Dandan, Anouar M'Himdat: 340ab, 342a-d, 343a-c | Tchaya Bloesch, Jennifer Huynh: 344ab, 346a-d, 347a-c | Audrey Aulus: 348ab, 350a-d, 351a-c | Clémentine Artru: 352ab, 354a-e, 355a-c | Marie-Laure Allemann, Virginie Bally: 356ab, 358a-d, 359a-c | Thierry Manasseh: cover I, 360ab, 362a-d, 363a-c | Charlotte Glatt: 364ab, 366a-e, 367a-c | Marie Majeux: 368ab, 370a-d, 371a-d | Julie Vulliet, Sophie Wobmann: 372ab, 374a-d, 375a-e | Matthieu Hoffmeyer: 376ab, 378a-c, 379a-d | Jérôme Wohlschlag: 380ab, 382a-d, 379ab | David Hoffert, Alexandre Tiarri: 384ab, 386a-e, 387a-d | Laetitia Bernasconi, Joël Loutan: 388ab, 390a-e, 391a-c | Giuseppe Galbiati, Fortunato Medici: 392ab, 394a-c, 395a-c | Giuseppe Galbiati: 396, 398c, 399a-c | Claudio Merlini, 415

The authors have contacted the rightful owners of each work to the best of their knowledge. If any errors or omissions are found, they would be grateful if the persons concerned would inform them.

"Common Center" of the Swiss Federal Agricultural Research Station of Changins, Heidi & Peter Wenger architects, Nyon, 1969–1975, status 2020